The Dynamic
World of Ukiyo-e

I0727962

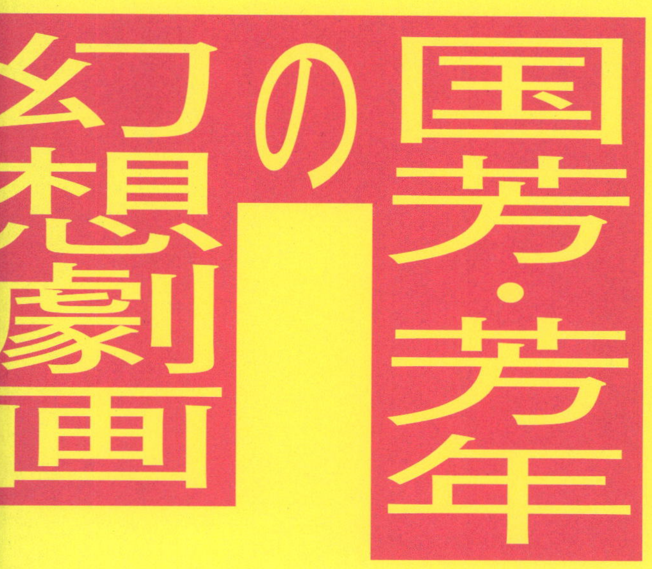
幻想劇画の国芳・芳年

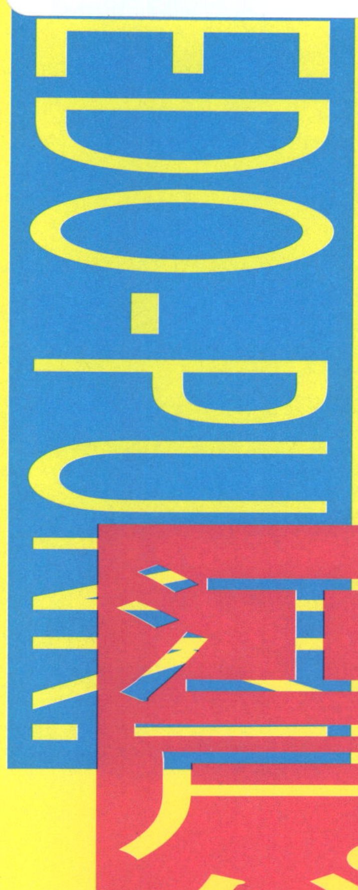
EDO-PUNK!
江戸パンク！

by Kuniyoshi,
Yoshitoshi & Others

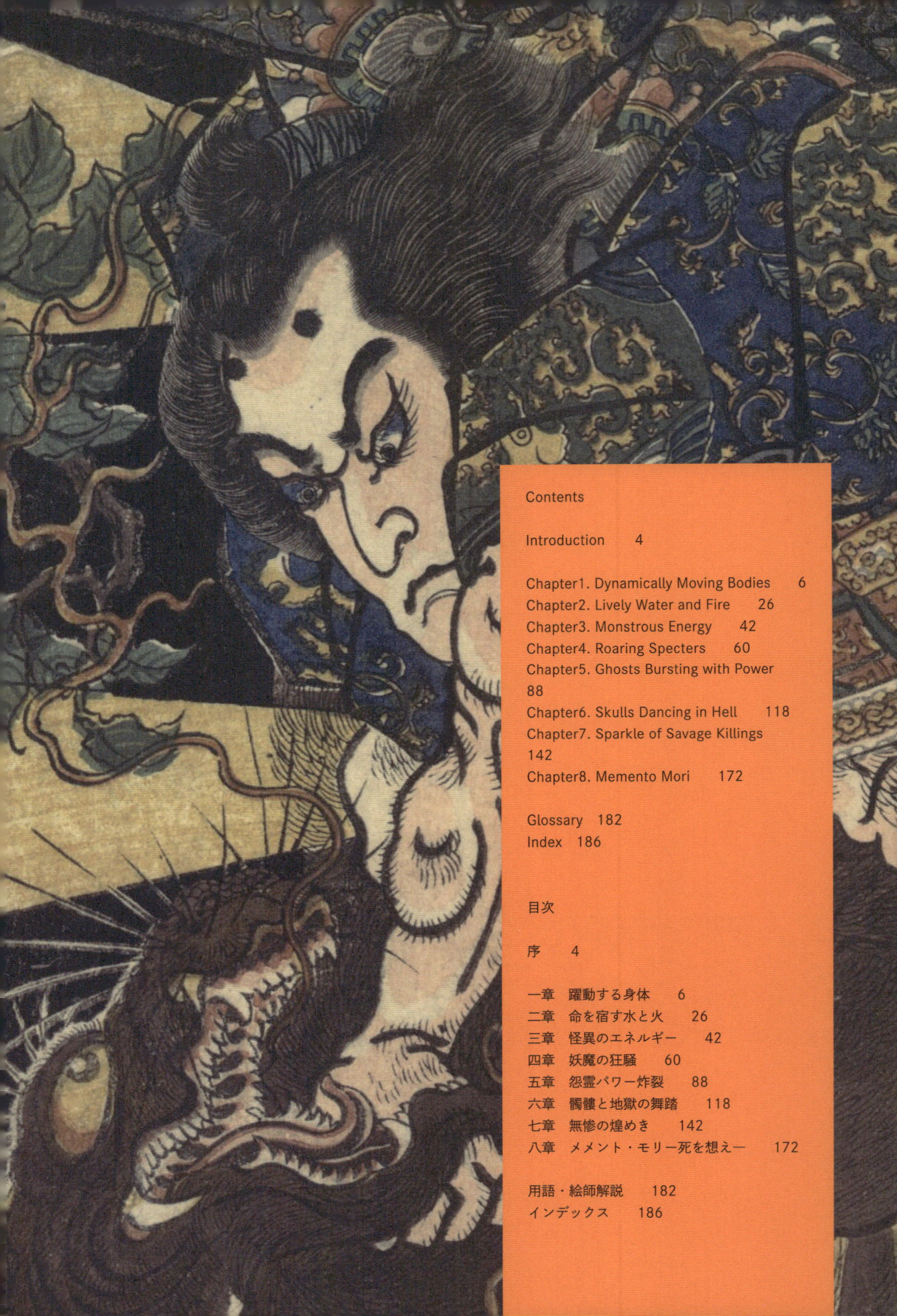

Contents

Introduction 4

目次

序 4

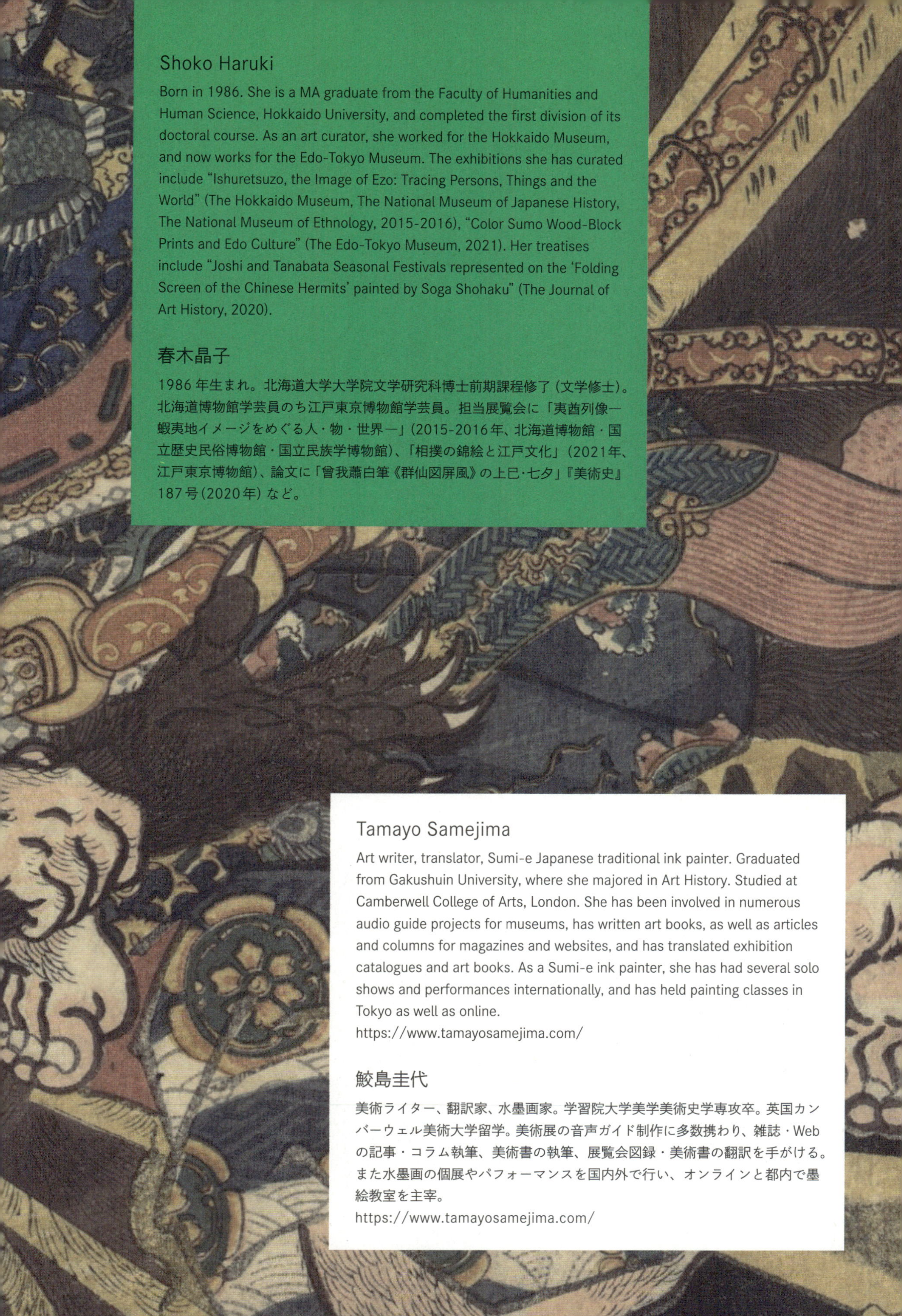

Shoko Haruki

Born in 1986. She is a MA graduate from the Faculty of Humanities and Human Science, Hokkaido University, and completed the first division of its doctoral course. As an art curator, she worked for the Hokkaido Museum, and now works for the Edo-Tokyo Museum. The exhibitions she has curated include "Ishuretsuzo, the Image of Ezo: Tracing Persons, Things and the World" (The Hokkaido Museum, The National Museum of Japanese History, The National Museum of Ethnology, 2015-2016), "Color Sumo Wood-Block Prints and Edo Culture" (The Edo-Tokyo Museum, 2021). Her treatises include "Joshi and Tanabata Seasonal Festivals represented on the 'Folding Screen of the Chinese Hermits' painted by Soga Shohaku" (The Journal of Art History, 2020).

春木晶子

1986年生まれ。北海道大学大学院文学研究科博士前期課程修了（文学修士）。北海道博物館学芸員のち江戸東京博物館学芸員。担当展覧会に「夷酋列像─蝦夷地イメージをめぐる人・物・世界─」（2015-2016年、北海道博物館・国立歴史民俗博物館・国立民族学博物館）、「相撲の錦絵と江戸文化」（2021年、江戸東京博物館）、論文に「曾我蕭白筆《群仙図屏風》の上巳・七夕」『美術史』187号（2020年）など。

Tamayo Samejima

Art writer, translator, Sumi-e Japanese traditional ink painter. Graduated from Gakushuin University, where she majored in Art History. Studied at Camberwell College of Arts, London. She has been involved in numerous audio guide projects for museums, has written art books, as well as articles and columns for magazines and websites, and has translated exhibition catalogues and art books. As a Sumi-e ink painter, she has had several solo shows and performances internationally, and has held painting classes in Tokyo as well as online.
https://www.tamayosamejima.com/

鮫島圭代

美術ライター、翻訳家、水墨画家。学習院大学美学美術史学専攻卒。英国カンバーウェル美術大学留学。美術展の音声ガイド制作に多数携わり、雑誌・Webの記事・コラム執筆、美術書の執筆、展覧会図録・美術書の翻訳を手がける。また水墨画の個展やパフォーマンスを国内外で行い、オンラインと都内で墨絵教室を主宰。
https://www.tamayosamejima.com/

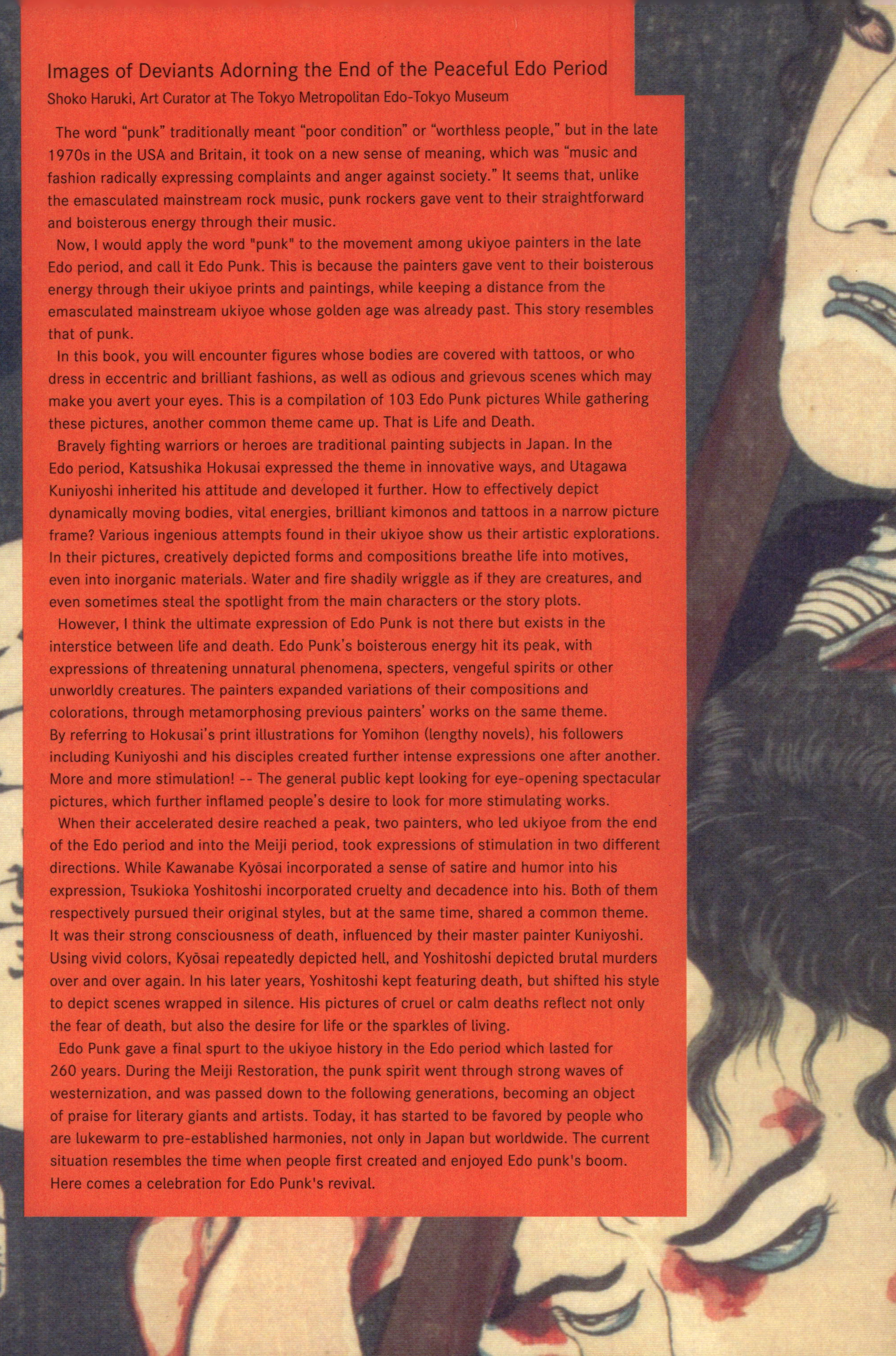

Images of Deviants Adorning the End of the Peaceful Edo Period

Shoko Haruki, Art Curator at The Tokyo Metropolitan Edo-Tokyo Museum

The word "punk" traditionally meant "poor condition" or "worthless people," but in the late 1970s in the USA and Britain, it took on a new sense of meaning, which was "music and fashion radically expressing complaints and anger against society." It seems that, unlike the emasculated mainstream rock music, punk rockers gave vent to their straightforward and boisterous energy through their music.

Now, I would apply the word "punk" to the movement among ukiyoe painters in the late Edo period, and call it Edo Punk. This is because the painters gave vent to their boisterous energy through their ukiyoe prints and paintings, while keeping a distance from the emasculated mainstream ukiyoe whose golden age was already past. This story resembles that of punk.

In this book, you will encounter figures whose bodies are covered with tattoos, or who dress in eccentric and brilliant fashions, as well as odious and grievous scenes which may make you avert your eyes. This is a compilation of 103 Edo Punk pictures While gathering these pictures, another common theme came up. That is Life and Death.

Bravely fighting warriors or heroes are traditional painting subjects in Japan. In the Edo period, Katsushika Hokusai expressed the theme in innovative ways, and Utagawa Kuniyoshi inherited his attitude and developed it further. How to effectively depict dynamically moving bodies, vital energies, brilliant kimonos and tattoos in a narrow picture frame? Various ingenious attempts found in their ukiyoe show us their artistic explorations. In their pictures, creatively depicted forms and compositions breathe life into motives, even into inorganic materials. Water and fire shadily wriggle as if they are creatures, and even sometimes steal the spotlight from the main characters or the story plots.

However, I think the ultimate expression of Edo Punk is not there but exists in the interstice between life and death. Edo Punk's boisterous energy hit its peak, with expressions of threatening unnatural phenomena, specters, vengeful spirits or other unworldly creatures. The painters expanded variations of their compositions and colorations, through metamorphosing previous painters' works on the same theme. By referring to Hokusai's print illustrations for Yomihon (lengthy novels), his followers including Kuniyoshi and his disciples created further intense expressions one after another. More and more stimulation! -- The general public kept looking for eye-opening spectacular pictures, which further inflamed people's desire to look for more stimulating works.

When their accelerated desire reached a peak, two painters, who led ukiyoe from the end of the Edo period and into the Meiji period, took expressions of stimulation in two different directions. While Kawanabe Kyōsai incorporated a sense of satire and humor into his expression, Tsukioka Yoshitoshi incorporated cruelty and decadence into his. Both of them respectively pursued their original styles, but at the same time, shared a common theme. It was their strong consciousness of death, influenced by their master painter Kuniyoshi. Using vivid colors, Kyōsai repeatedly depicted hell, and Yoshitoshi depicted brutal murders over and over again. In his later years, Yoshitoshi kept featuring death, but shifted his style to depict scenes wrapped in silence. His pictures of cruel or calm deaths reflect not only the fear of death, but also the desire for life or the sparkles of living.

Edo Punk gave a final spurt to the ukiyoe history in the Edo period which lasted for 260 years. During the Meiji Restoration, the punk spirit went through strong waves of westernization, and was passed down to the following generations, becoming an object of praise for literary giants and artists. Today, it has started to be favored by people who are lukewarm to pre-established harmonies, not only in Japan but worldwide. The current situation resembles the time when people first created and enjoyed Edo punk's boom. Here comes a celebration for Edo Punk's revival.

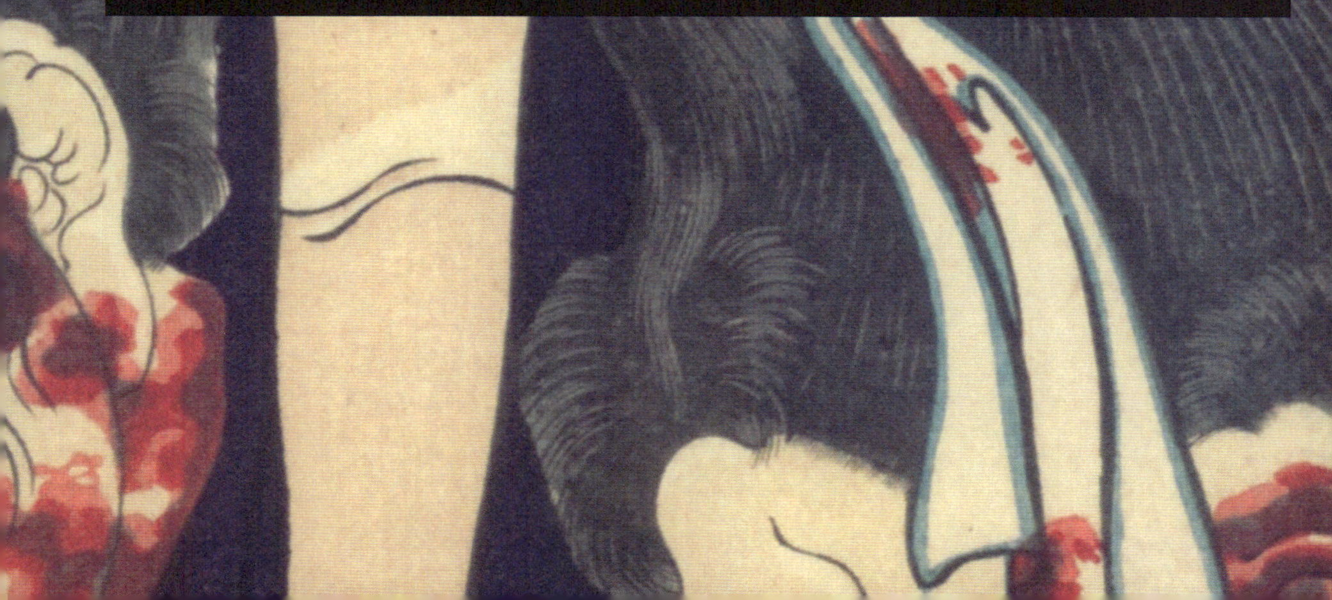

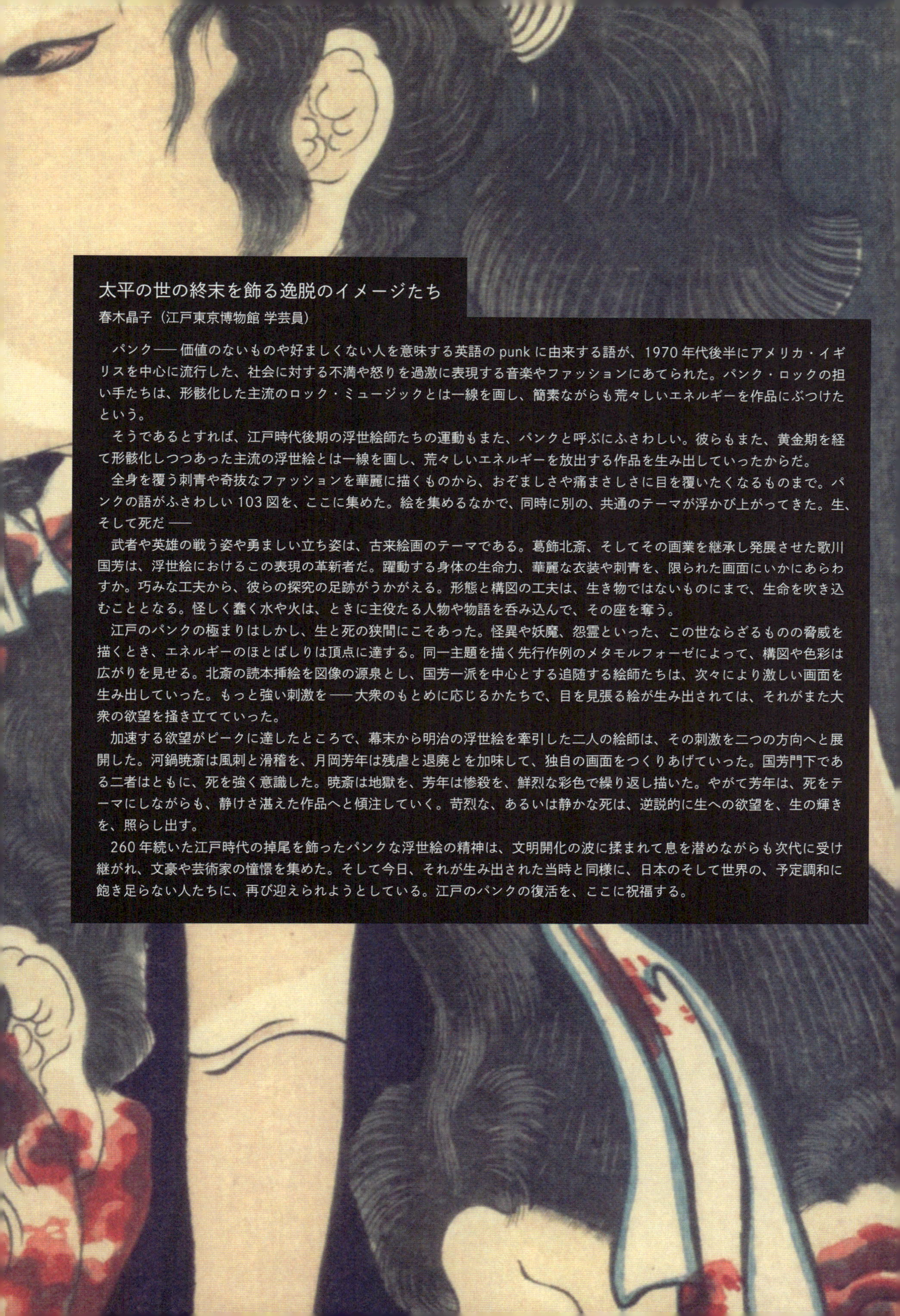

太平の世の終末を飾る逸脱のイメージたち

春木晶子（江戸東京博物館 学芸員）

　パンク──価値のないものや好ましくない人を意味する英語の punk に由来する語が、1970 年代後半にアメリカ・イギリスを中心に流行した、社会に対する不満や怒りを過激に表現する音楽やファッションにあてられた。パンク・ロックの担い手たちは、形骸化した主流のロック・ミュージックとは一線を画し、簡素ながらも荒々しいエネルギーを作品にぶつけたという。

　そうであるとすれば、江戸時代後期の浮世絵師たちの運動もまた、パンクと呼ぶにふさわしい。彼らもまた、黄金期を経て形骸化しつつあった主流の浮世絵とは一線を画し、荒々しいエネルギーを放出する作品を生み出していったからだ。

　全身を覆う刺青や奇抜なファッションを華麗に描くものから、おぞましさや痛ましさに目を覆いたくなるものまで。パンクの語がふさわしい 103 図を、ここに集めた。絵を集めるなかで、同時に別の、共通のテーマが浮かび上がってきた。生、そして死だ──

　武者や英雄の戦う姿や勇ましい立ち姿は、古来絵画のテーマである。葛飾北斎、そしてその画業を継承し発展させた歌川国芳は、浮世絵におけるこの表現の革新者だ。躍動する身体の生命力、華麗な衣装や刺青を、限られた画面にいかにあらわすか。巧みな工夫から、彼らの探究の足跡がうかがえる。形態と構図の工夫は、生き物ではないものにまで、生命を吹き込むこととなる。怪しく蠢く水や火は、ときに主役たる人物や物語を呑み込んで、その座を奪う。

　江戸のパンクの極まりはしかし、生と死の狭間にこそあった。怪異や妖魔、怨霊といった、この世ならざるものの脅威を描くとき、エネルギーのほとばしりは頂点に達する。同一主題を描く先行作例のメタモルフォーゼによって、構図や色彩は広がりを見せる。北斎の読本挿絵を図像の源泉とし、国芳一派を中心とする追随する絵師たちは、次々により激しい画面を生み出していった。もっと強い刺激を──大衆のもとめに応じるかたちで、目を見張る絵が生み出されては、それがまた大衆の欲望を掻き立てていった。

　加速する欲望がピークに達したところで、幕末から明治の浮世絵を牽引した二人の絵師は、その刺激を二つの方向へと展開した。河鍋暁斎は風刺と滑稽を、月岡芳年は残虐と退廃とを加味して、独自の画面をつくりあげていった。国芳門下である二者はともに、死を強く意識した。暁斎は地獄を、芳年は惨殺を、鮮烈な彩色で繰り返し描いた。やがて芳年は、死をテーマにしながらも、静けさ湛えた作品へと傾注していく。苛烈な、あるいは静かな死は、逆説的に生への欲望を、生の輝きを、照らし出す。

　260 年続いた江戸時代の掉尾を飾ったパンクな浮世絵の精神は、文明開化の波に揉まれて息を潜めながらも次代に受け継がれ、文豪や芸術家の憧憬を集めた。そして今日、それが生み出された当時と同様に、日本のそして世界の、予定調和に飽き足らない人たちに、再び迎えられようとしている。江戸のパンクの復活を、ここに祝福する。

躍動する

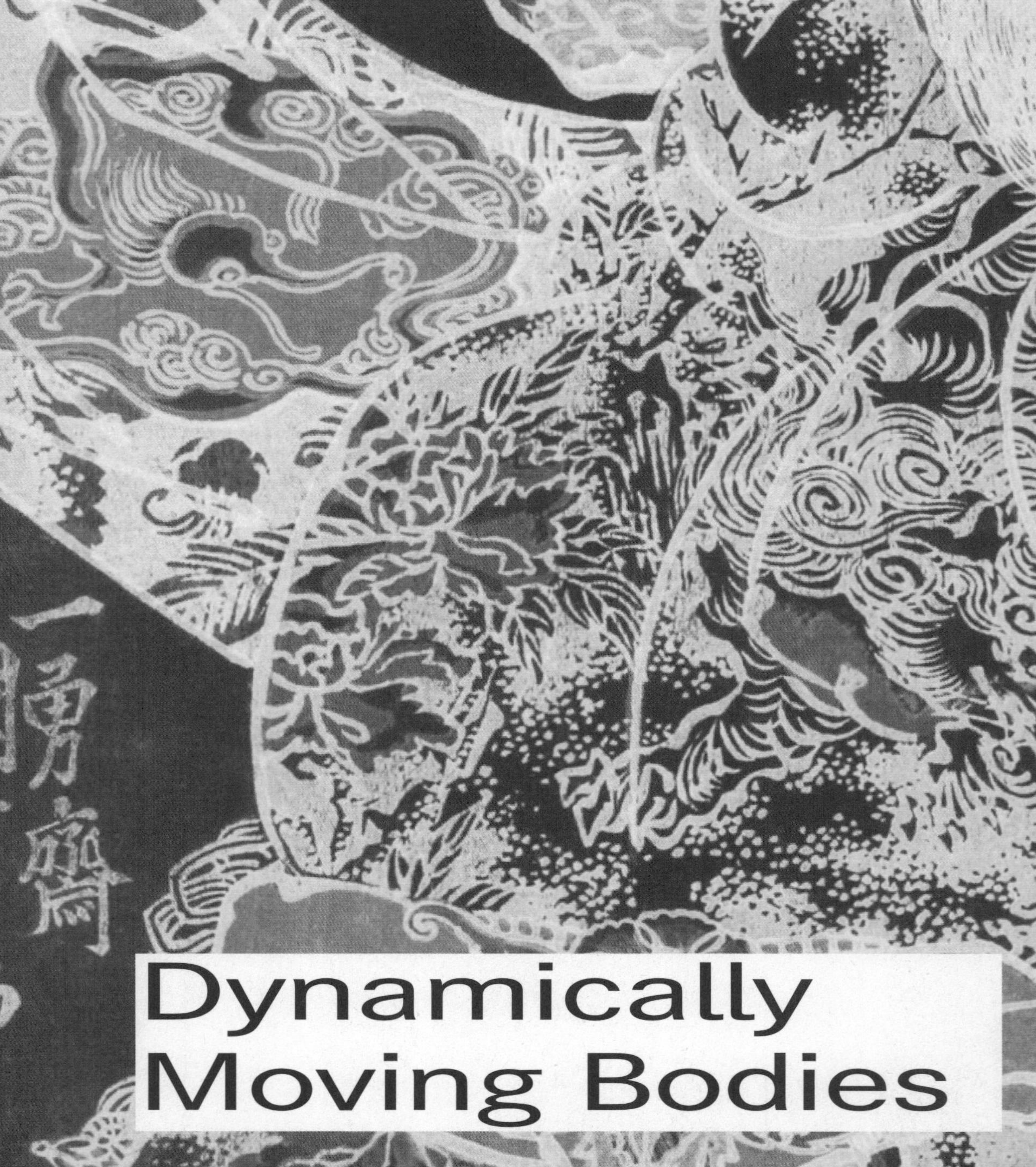

戦う姿や、勇ましい立ち姿。日本や中国の歴史上・伝説上の武者や豪傑を勇壮に描く浮世絵の「武者絵」は、江戸時代後期に目覚ましい発展を遂げる。その先駆者たる北斎や国芳は、破格の迫力で見る者を圧倒する作品を生み出した。スピードや勢い、パワーを存分に伝える武者絵の数々は、それが静止画であることを時に忘れさせる。たくましい身体をどのように画面におさめ、速さや強さをどのように表現したのだろうか。

Dynamically Moving Bodies

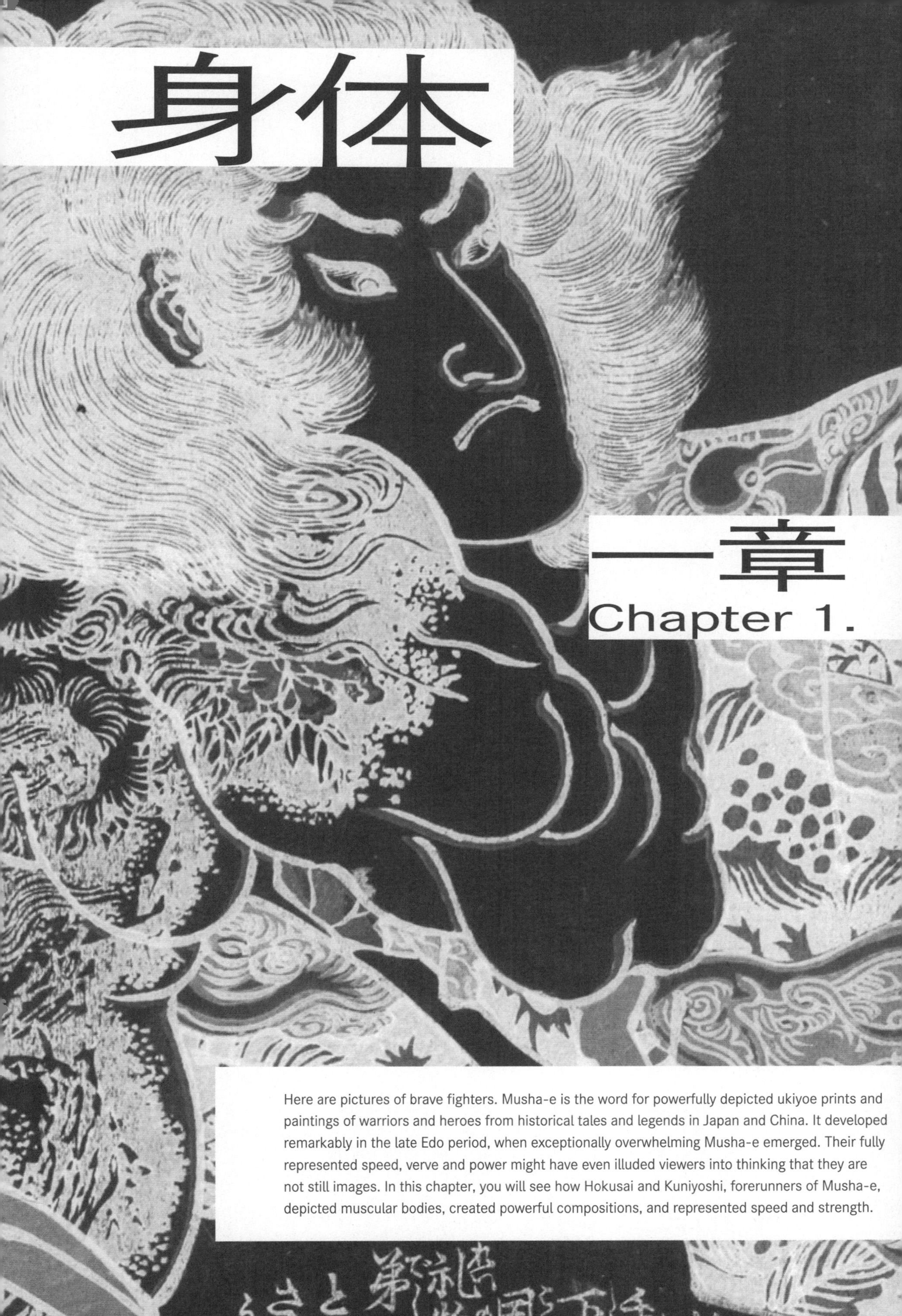

身体
一章
Chapter 1.
Here are pictures of brave fighters. Musha-e is the word for powerfully depicted ukiyoe prints and paintings of warriors and heroes from historical tales and legends in Japan and China. It developed remarkably in the late Edo period, when exceptionally overwhelming Musha-e emerged. Their fully represented speed, verve and power might have even illuded viewers into thinking that they are not still images. In this chapter, you will see how Hokusai and Kuniyoshi, forerunners of Musha-e, depicted muscular bodies, created powerful compositions, and represented speed and strength.

Kusunoki-tamonmaru Masashige and Yaono-be'ttō Tsunehisa / Katsushika Hokusai

Edo period, 19th century / Tokyo National Museum

The war chronicle "Taihei-ki" talks about the battles that happened from the end of the Kamakura period (c.1185-1333) to the Nanbokucho period (c.1336-1392). It was widely read in the Edo period and the story was adapted for literature, theatrical plays and other art forms. "Taihei-ki" depicts the real-life samurai Kusunoki Masashige as a smart warrior who fights successfully with unique battle plans. The character became a hero with a mass popularity. The picture shows Masashige in his youth, before the episodes written in "Taihei-ki." The pattern of his kimono resembles Kikusui-mon (pattern of floating flowers on a stream), which is the family crest of the Kusunoki clan. At the age of 12, Masashige may have already started going to battle against the Yao-no-be'ttō clan who had been an opponent of the Kusunoki clan. Here, Masashige lifts a stone basin in order to hit the bearded warrior. The warrior has a powerfully built body and wears an incredibly flashy kimono with Bishamon-kikkō pattern, which was developed from the pattern on the armor of Bishamonten (Vaisravana, a guardian god of Buddhism). He raises his big toe up and almost draws a sword. Such a pose traditionally symbolizes the strength of warriors and can also be found in kabuki theater plays.

Image: TNM Image Archives

楠多門丸正重 八尾の別当常久 ／ 葛飾北斎

江戸時代・19 世紀 ／ 東京国立博物館蔵

鎌倉時代末から南北朝時代にかけての動乱の歴史を伝える『太平記』は、江戸時代に盛んに読まれ、文学や演劇へと多彩に広まった。『太平記』に颯爽と登場し、常識破りな戦術で活躍する楠木（楠）正成は、大衆のヒーローとなる。本図が描くのは『太平記』に登場する以前の若かりし正成。衣服には楠木氏の家紋「菊水紋」を思わせる文様があしらわれる。楠木氏と敵対していた八尾の別当一族との戦いに、正成は 12 歳から出陣していたという。正成は石造りの手水鉢を持ち上げ、ど派手な毘沙門亀甲文の衣服から筋骨隆々とした四肢を伸ばす鬚面の武者に挑む。刀を抜かんとする武者が足の親指を立てる所作は、歌舞伎でも武者の力強さを伝える表現だ。

Musha-e by Katsusika Hokusai

These prints are from the only existing series of Musha-e (ukiyoe prints and paintings of warriors) by Katsushika Hokusai. Each scene shows two warriors overlapping one another and waging a battle, which fills the entire frame. The strikingly vivid colors and flashy patterns stand out against the navy backgrounds.
The signature " 為一 (I'itsu)" is the one that Hokusai used after the age of 61. He also signed the appellation during his seventies when he created "Thirty-six views of Mount Fuji." When he created this series, Hokusai reached his artistic maturity. The well-conceived compositions and punchy depictions are striking to the eyes and people never get tired of looking at them.

北斎の武者絵

葛飾北斎による、現存する唯一の武者絵のシリーズ 5 図を紹介する。いずれも、重なり合う二人の武者が、画面いっぱいに戦いを繰り広げる様を描く。濃紺の背景に、甲冑や装束の鮮烈な彩色や派手な模様が映える。画面に記される「為一」は、北斎が 61 歳以降に使用した画号すなわちアーティストネームで、《冨嶽三十六景》を手がけた 70 代のときにも名乗っていたもの。北斎の円熟期の作品だけに、巧みに練られた構図で、インパクトがあるうえに見飽きることがない。

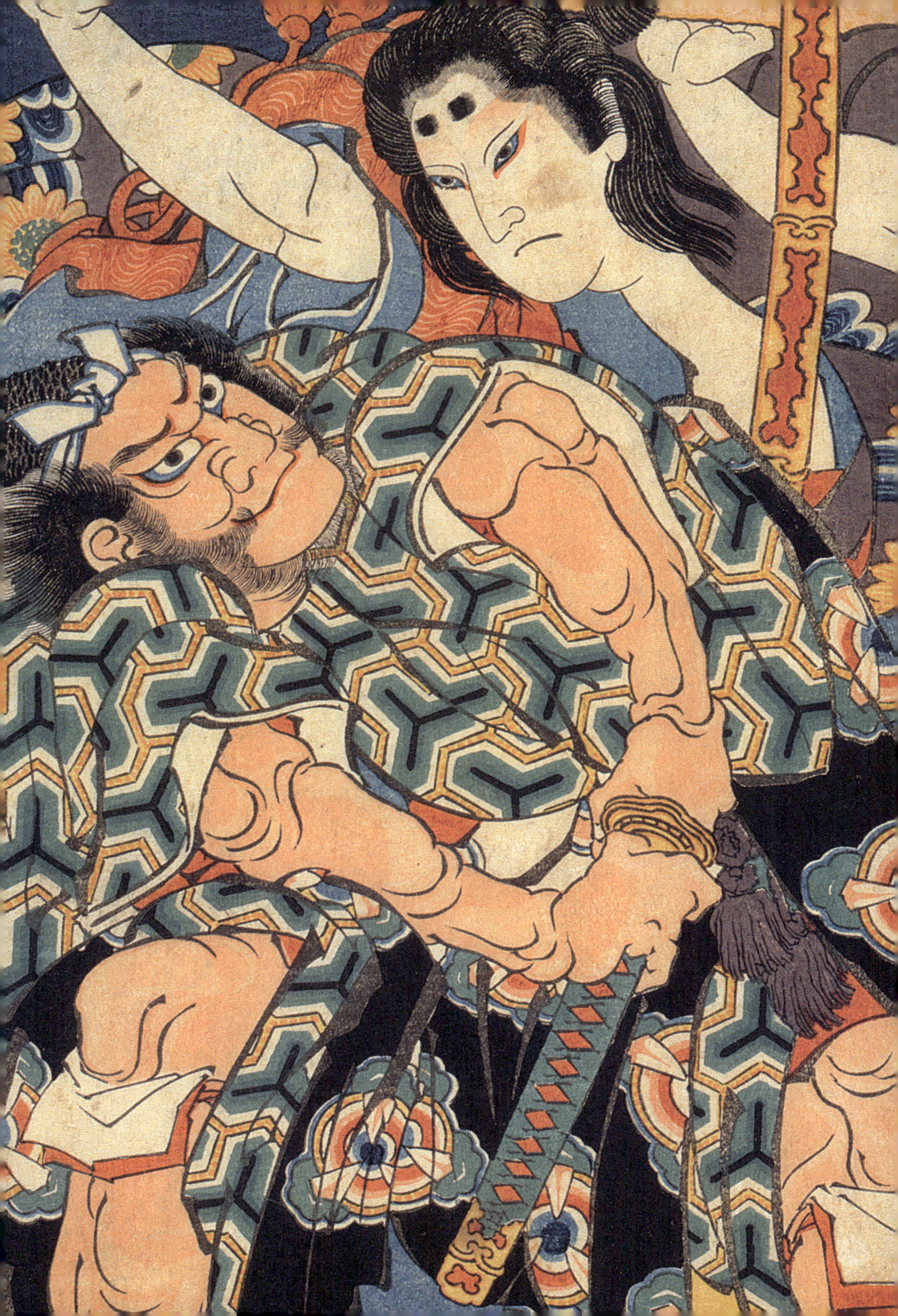

Kamakura-no Gongoro Kagemasa and Torinoumi Yasaburō Yasunori / Katsushika Hokusai

Edo period, 19th century / Tokyo National Museum

This picture depicts an episode from Gosannen no Eki (the Later Three Years' War) in the Heian period (794-c.1185). The two warriors are Kamakura Kagemasa, who was just 16 years old, and Torinoumi Yasaburō. Yasaburō shot Kagemasa's right eye with an arrow. With the arrow remaining in his eye, Kagemasa chased Yasaburō and shot him back with the same arrow in order to triumph against him. In this picture, Kagemasa holds a bow in his right hand, jumps on top of Yasaburō and points to his right eye. It is as if he intends to shoot the arrow back into Yasaburō's right eye. Hokusai made use of the whole frame by placing the warriors' arms, legs and swords reaching towards the four corners of the picture.

鎌倉の権五郎景政 鳥の海弥三郎保則 ／ 葛飾北斎

江戸時代・19 世紀 ／ 東京国立博物館蔵

平安時代、「後三年の役」に弱冠 16 歳で出陣した鎌倉景政と、鳥海弥三郎との戦いを描く。景政は弥三郎に右眼を射られるが、眼に矢がささったまま弥三郎を追いかけて、その矢を射返し勝利をおさめたという。本図で景政は、右手でその弓を握り、弥三郎に乗りかかってその右眼を指さしている。この矢を今からお前の右眼に突き返すぞ、と言わんばかりだ。四隅にのびるように手足や太刀を配置し、画面を最大限に利用している。

Image: TNM Image Archives

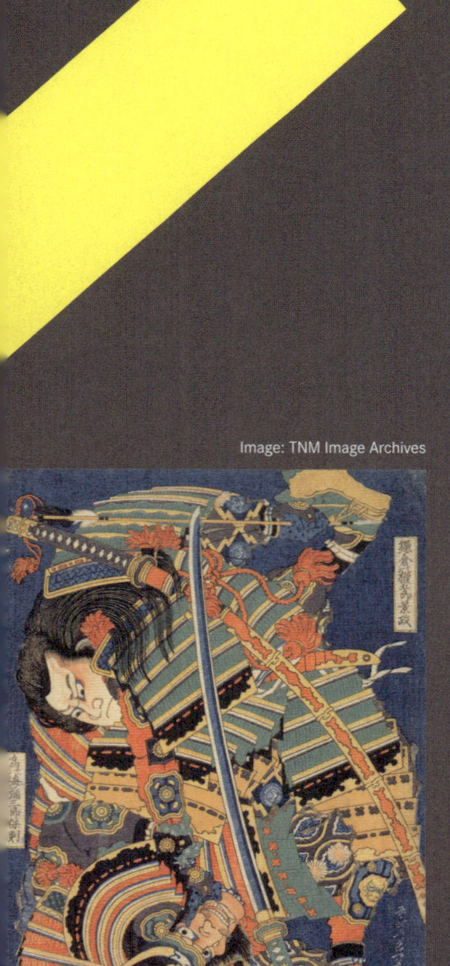

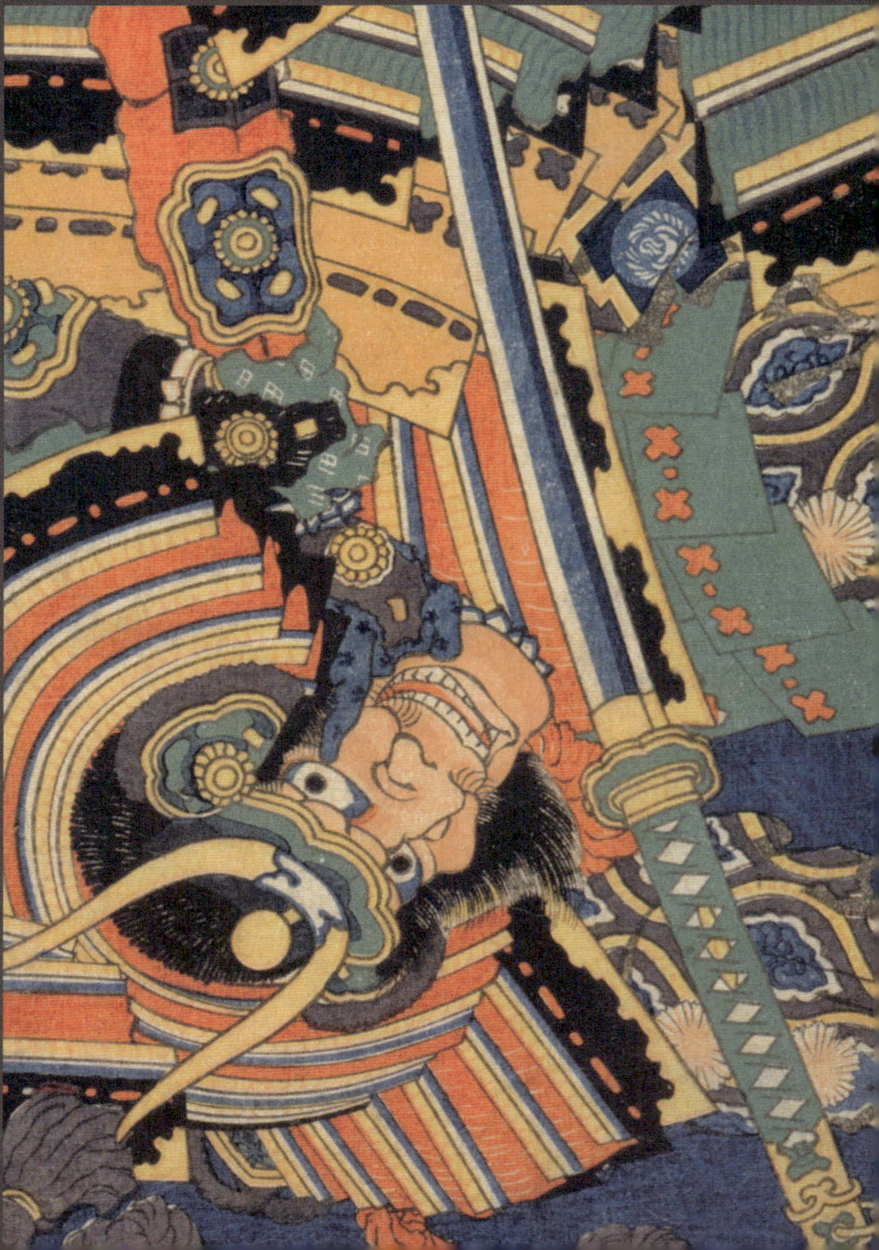

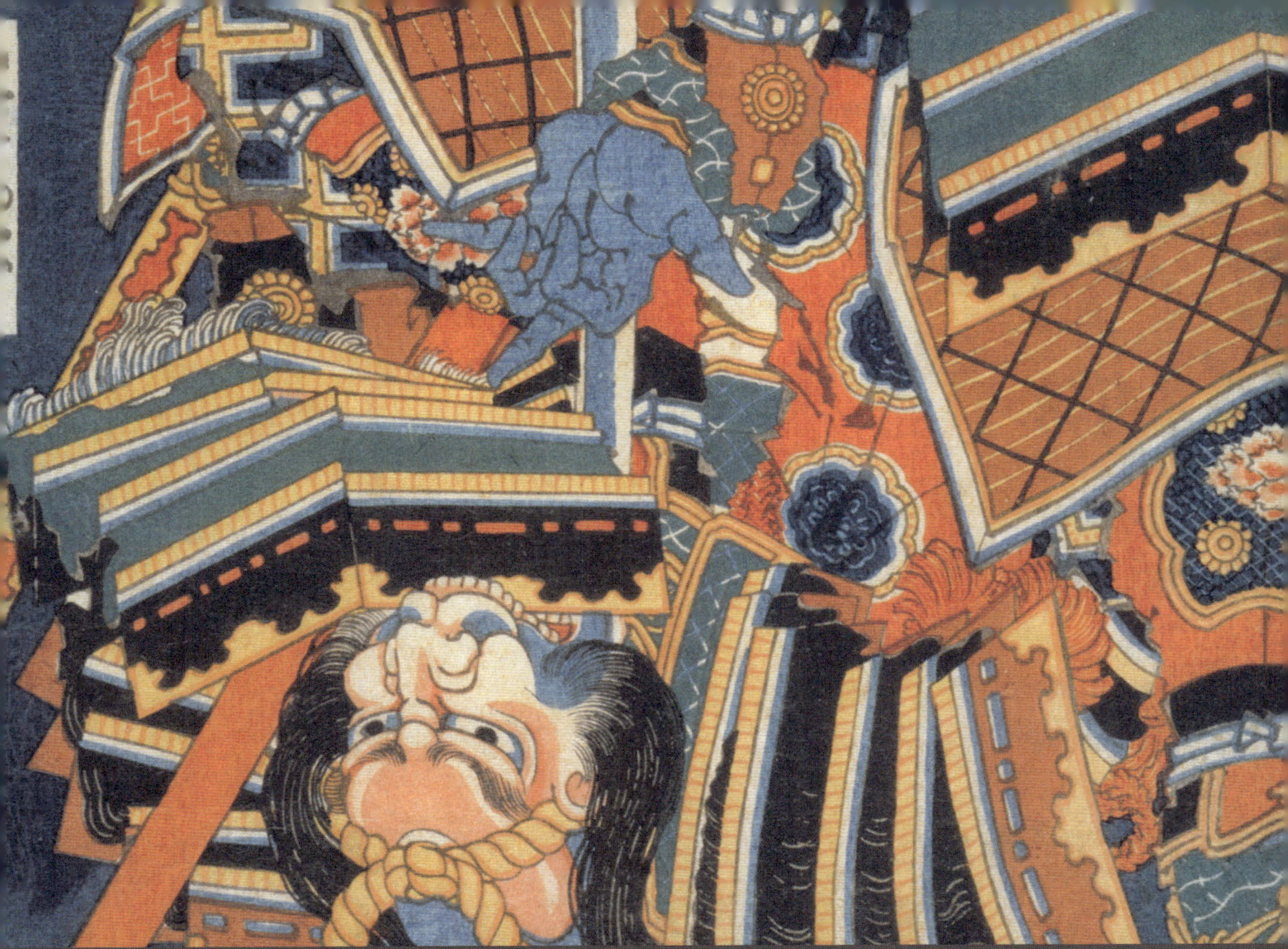

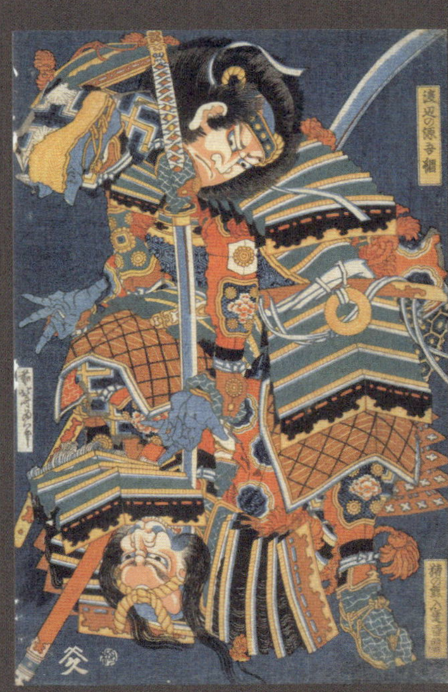

Image: TNM Image Archives

Watanabe-no Gengo Tsuna and Inokuma Nyūdō Raiun / Katsushika Hokusai

Edo period, 19th century / Tokyo National Museum

Watanabe-no Tsuna was a warrior in the Heian period and one of the four retainers of the warlord Minamoto-no them. There are many legends about them such as vanquishing the ogre Shuten Dōji in Mount Ôe and defeating another ogre at Rashō-mon Gate. This picture depicts another legend of his, which is about Yorimitsu and his four retainers eliminating a spider monster called Tsuchigumo. After being put to sleep by Tsuchigumo, Yorimitsu's life is threatened by Inokuma Nyūdō Raiun. This scene depicts the next moment where Watanabe-no Tsuna plunges a blade into Inokuma's throat. Opening his mouth and showing his teeth, Inokuma's hairs hang down from his upturned head. The hairs resemble demon's horns.

渡辺の源吾綱 猪の熊入道雷雲 ／ 葛飾北斎

江戸時代・19 世紀 ／ 東京国立博物館蔵

平安時代の武士・渡辺綱は、源頼光の配下で、四天王と呼ばれた忠臣の一人。大江山の酒呑童子退治や、羅生門の鬼退治などの伝説がある。本図は、頼光と四天王による土蜘蛛退治にまつわる物語を題材にしたもの。頼光の命を狙う猪の熊入道雷雲が、その寝込みを襲おうとしたところを、渡辺綱が返り討ちにする。喉元を突き刺されのけぞる猪の熊、その髪は逆さに垂れ下がり、鬼の角のようになっている。

Ōtomo-no Matori and Ōtomo-no Sukune Kanemichi / Katsushika Hokusai

Edo period, 19th century / Tokyo National Museum

The theme of this picture is derived from the Jōruri puppet play "Ōtomo-no Matori." The story is about Takamura Masamichi and his son Kanemichi trying to defeat Ōtomo-no Matori of the Kyushu Tandai (a local commissioner in Kyushu region), who raised a rebellion. In the end, Matori realized his own destiny and killed himself in order to offer his own severed head to Kanemichi. In this picture, Matori touches his forehead. The pose might express the moment of his realization. The opponent Kanemichi watches for a chance to attack with a sickle in his hand. Matori wears a kimono with a checkered pattern, and his upper body is depicted in a large circular form.

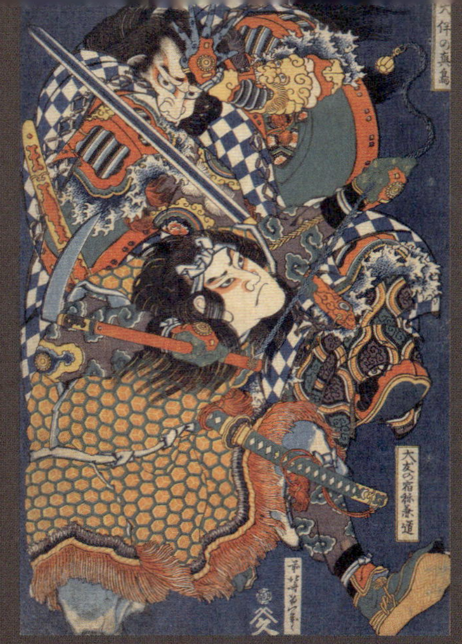

Image: TNM Image Archives

大伴の真鳥 大友の宿祢兼道 ／ 葛飾北斎

江戸時代・19 世紀 ／ 東京国立博物館蔵

浄瑠璃の演目「大友真鳥」を題材にする。九州探題大友真鳥の謀反を高村正道・兼道父子が打倒せんとするもので、最後には己の運命を悟った真鳥が自分の首を兼道に与える。本図で額に手を当てる真鳥の仕草は、悟りの瞬間を描いたものだろうか。対する兼道は鎌を構えて隙をうかがっている。方形の市松模様に身を包む真鳥の上半身は、全体で大きな円をつくるように構成されている。

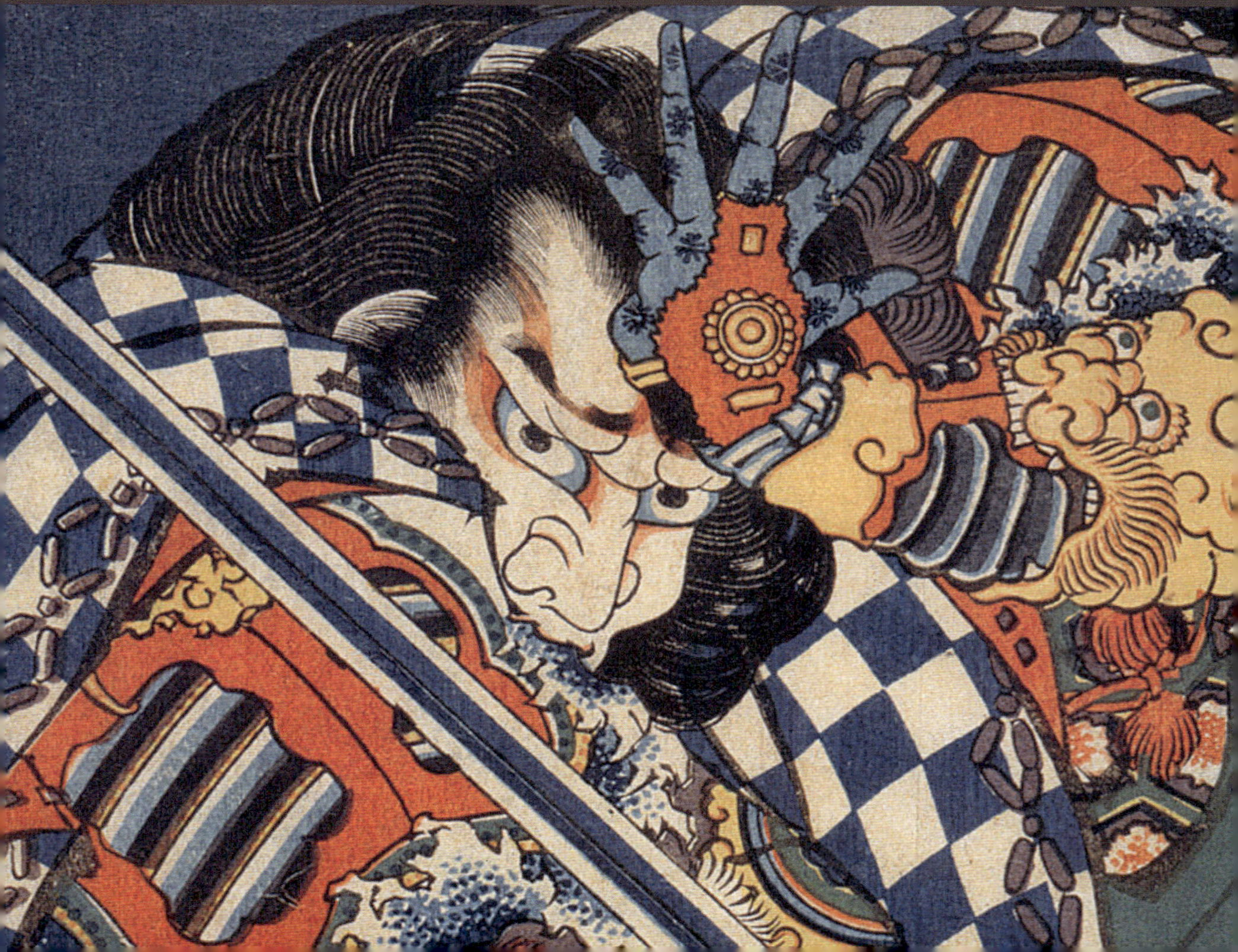

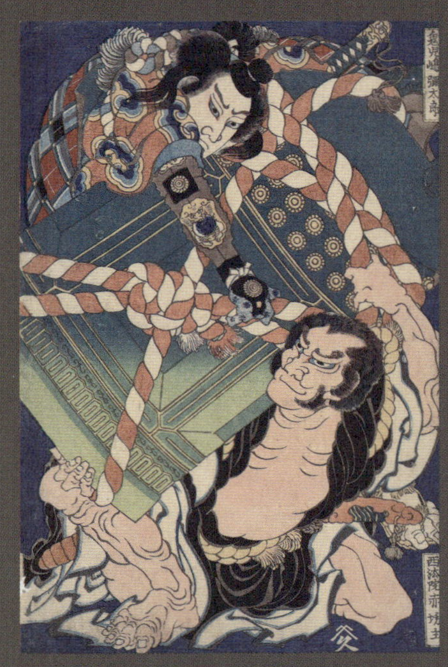

Oni-kojima Yatarō and Saihōin Akabōzu /
Katsushika Hokusai

Edo period, 19th century / Nagata collection, Shimane Art Museum

Kojima Yatarō was a retainer of Uesugi Kenshin, a famous warlord in Echigo Province. Because of his tremendous bravery, Yatarō was called Oni-kojima or Demon Kojima. The picture depicts the legend of Yatarō defeating the specter Akabōzu. Akabōzu committed a great number of wrongful acts, and one of them was the theft of a hanging bell from Rinsen-ji Temple. Uesugi Kenshin had an attachment to the temple, because he was entrusted there during his childhood. So, he ordered Yatarō, the bravest man in his force, to kill the specter. Yatarō defeated Akabōzu after a fierce battle and recaptured the bell. This picture depicts a scene of their fighting over the bell, and Akabōzu wears a weirdly relaxed smile.

鬼児嶋弥太郎 西法院赤坊主 ／ 葛飾北斎

江戸時代・19世紀 ／ 島根県立美術館（永田コレクション）蔵

越後の戦国武将・上杉謙信の家臣・小島弥太郎は、その剛勇ぶりから「鬼小島」と称された。本図は弥太郎が妖怪「赤坊主」を退治した伝説を描くもの。林泉寺の釣鐘を奪い、数々の悪行を行っていた赤坊主。幼少時に林泉寺に預けられた上杉謙信は、自軍で最も勇猛な弥太郎に退治を命じたという。弥太郎は死闘の末に赤坊主を倒し鐘を奪い返したというが、本図では余裕の笑みを浮かべる赤坊主と鐘を奪い合っている様子だ。

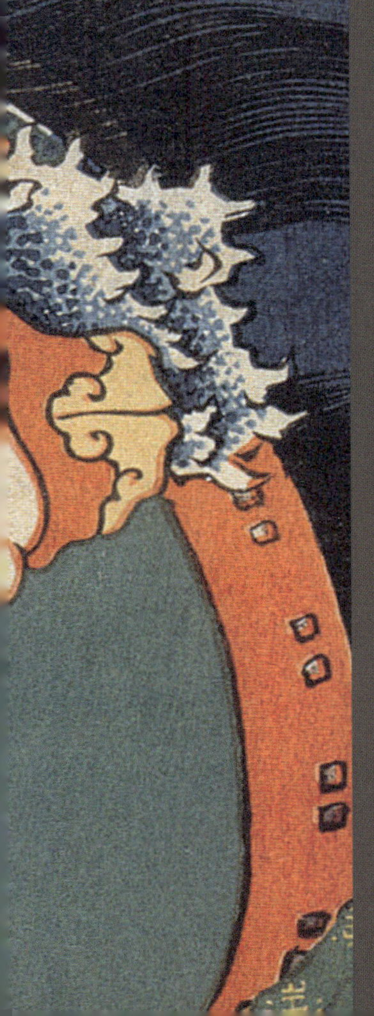

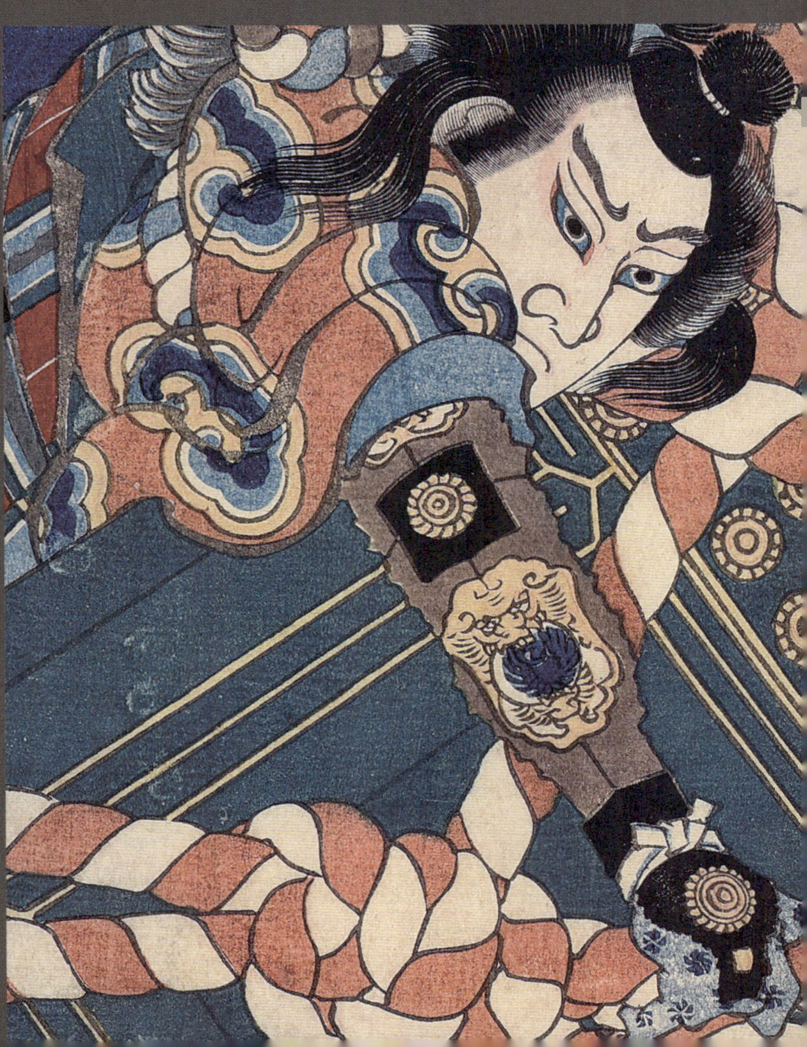

Kumonryū Shishin from "The 108 Heroes of the Popular Suikoden" / Utagawa Kuniyoshi

c.1827 / Photo : amana

Kumonryū Shishin first appears among the 108 heroes in the novel. As his name Kumonryū, meaning "tattoos of nine dragons," suggests, he has nine blue dragons tattooed on his shoulders, arms and chest, thus all over his body. He first appears in the story as a beautiful young man in his late teens, who is from a wealthy farm family and excellent in the military arts. The character gained popularity among people in Edo, current Tokyo. Among the 74 pictures of the series, there are three pictures featuring Shishin. This is the earliest example of these three and depicts dragon tattoos in indigo blue all over his body, except for his hands and feet. With the great success of the series, a tattoo boom might have happened among people in Edo.

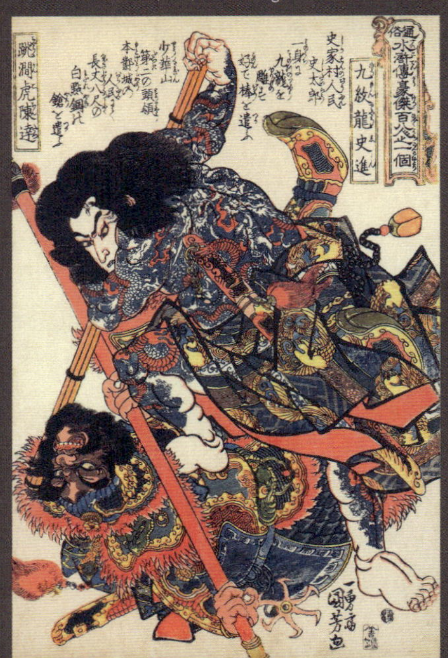

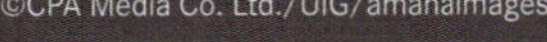

通俗水滸伝豪傑百八人之一個 九紋龍史進 / 歌川国芳

文政 10 年（1827）頃 ／ 提供：アマナ

全身に九つの青龍の刺青が彫られていたため、九紋龍のあだ名を持つ史進。豪農の家に生まれながらも武芸に秀でた美青年で、登場時は 20 歳前だった。江戸の人々に人気を得た史進は、74 図が確認される本シリーズのなかで重複して 3 図もつくられた。なかでも初期に出版された本作は、手足の先を除く全身に藍色の龍の刺青が表現されている。本シリーズのヒットは、江戸に彫物（刺青）ブームを巻き起こしたという。

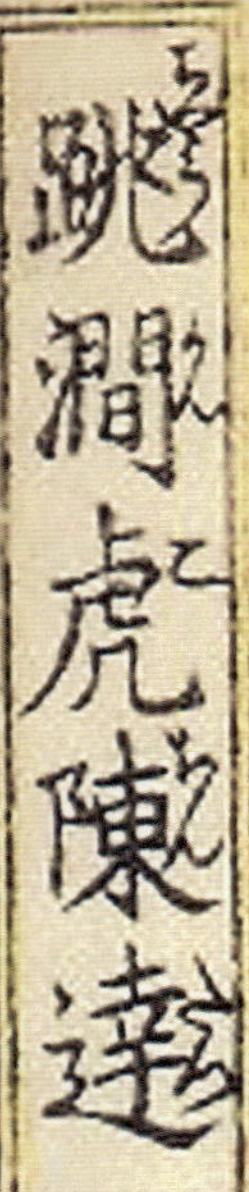

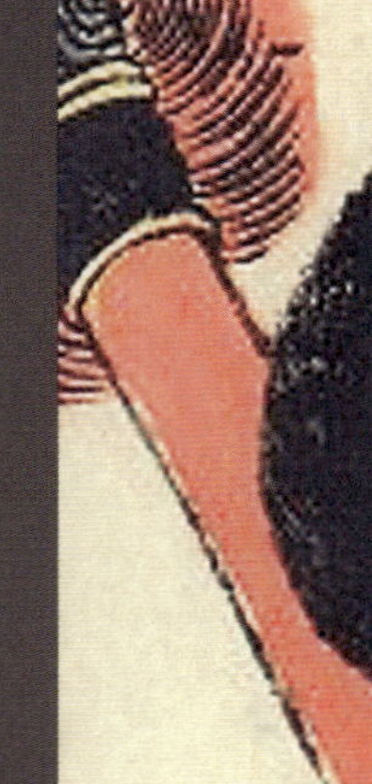

"Suikoden" (The Water Margin) by Utagawa Kuniyoshi

A well-known Chinese novel "Suikoden" (The Water Margin) became popular in Japan during the Edo period. The story is about 108 heroic figures who stray and are isolated from the world. Each of them fights in a great number of battles, until they finally gather at a natural fortress called Ryōzanpaku at the foot of Mount Liang. They then set out to defeat unscrupulous bureaucrats and save their country. Utagawa Kuniyoshi depicts the bold and ambitious men in this series of ukiyo prints. The series was sequentially published from around 1827, taking 10 years to complete. Currently, there are 74 different pictures which have been found and identified as part of the series. Kuniyoshi's depiction of exotic and powerful heroes quickly won him popularity. He gained fame as a painter and was widely called Kuniyoshi of Musha-e (ukiyo prints and paintings of warriors).

国芳の《水滸伝》

江戸時代には日本でも広まっていた中国の小説『水滸伝』は、108 人の豪傑が幾多の戦いを繰り広げながら梁山泊と呼ばれる自然の要塞に集結し、悪徳官吏を打倒し国を救うことを目指すようになる物語。歌川国芳がその豪傑たちを描いて大ヒットした本シリーズは、文政 10 年（1827）頃からおよそ 10 年かけて順次出版され、74 図が確認されている。迫力満点の異国の豪傑たちの姿はたちまち評判を得て、世間に「武者絵の国芳」の名を轟かせた。

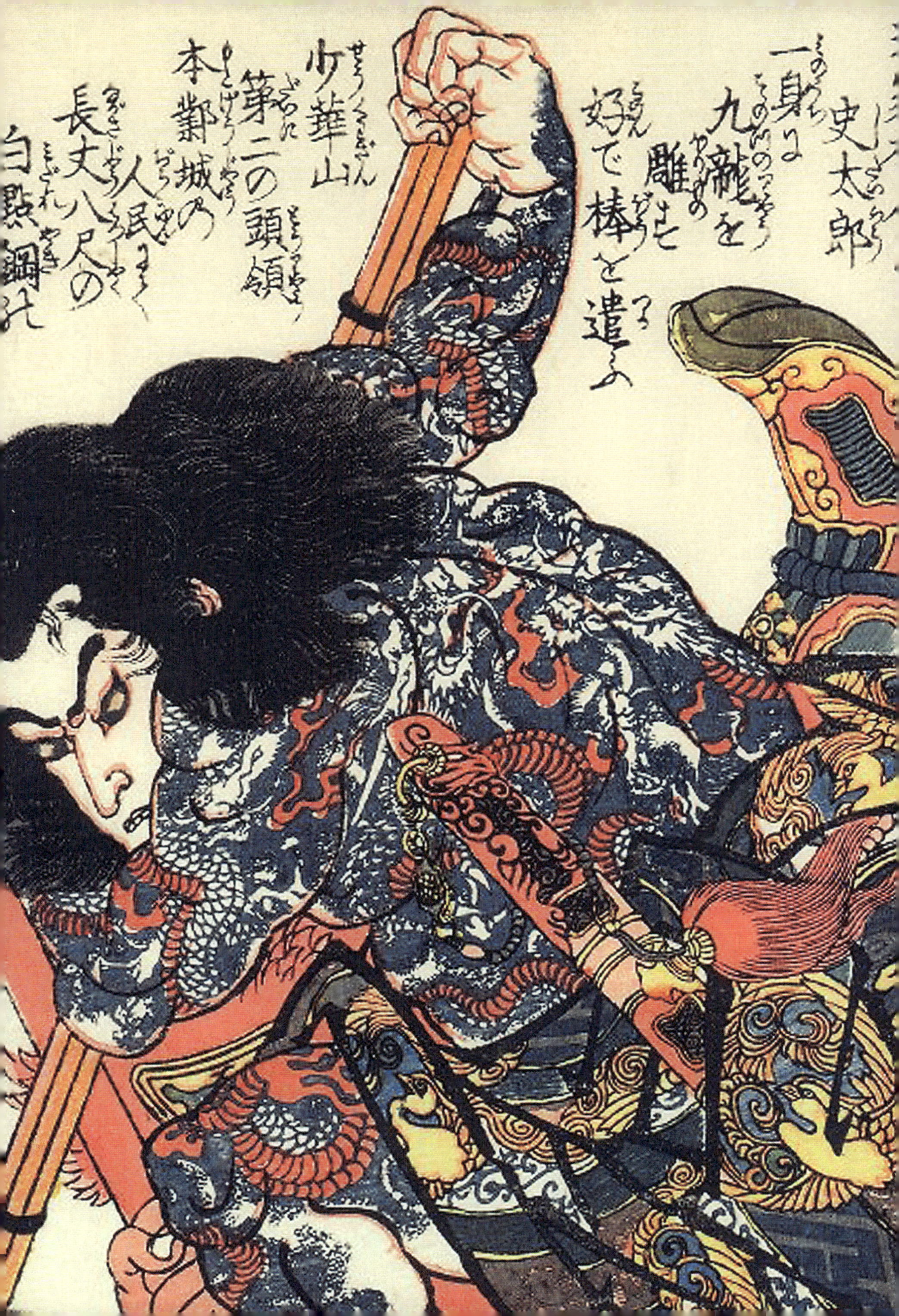
史太郎
一身より
九紋龍を
雕るゝ
好で棒を遣ふの
少華山
第二の頭領
本邽城の
人民
長丈八尺の
白點鋼れ

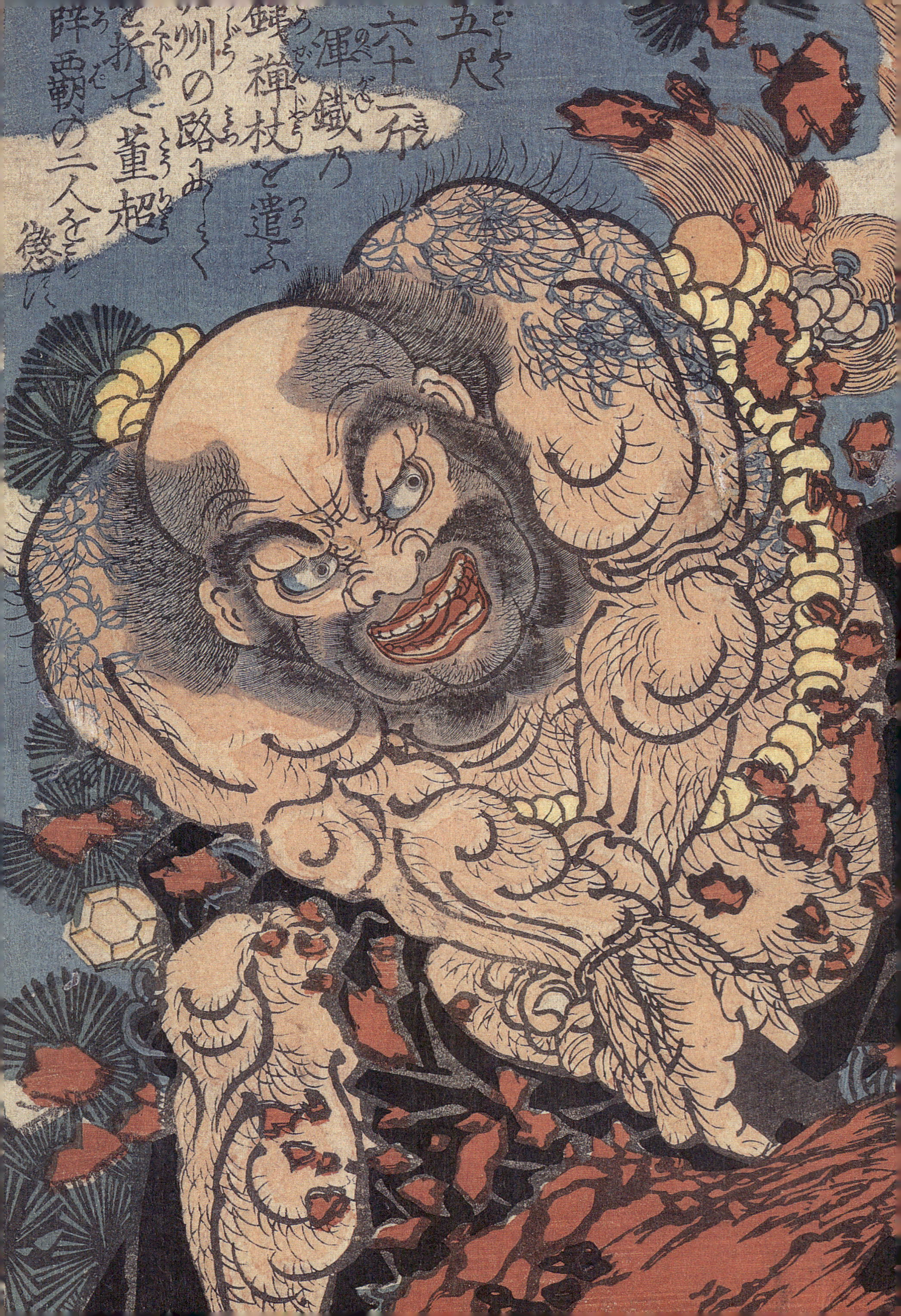

五尺
六十一斤の
渾鐵乃
蜿禪杖を遣ふ
州の路みしく
折で董超
瞱覇の二人を
懲し

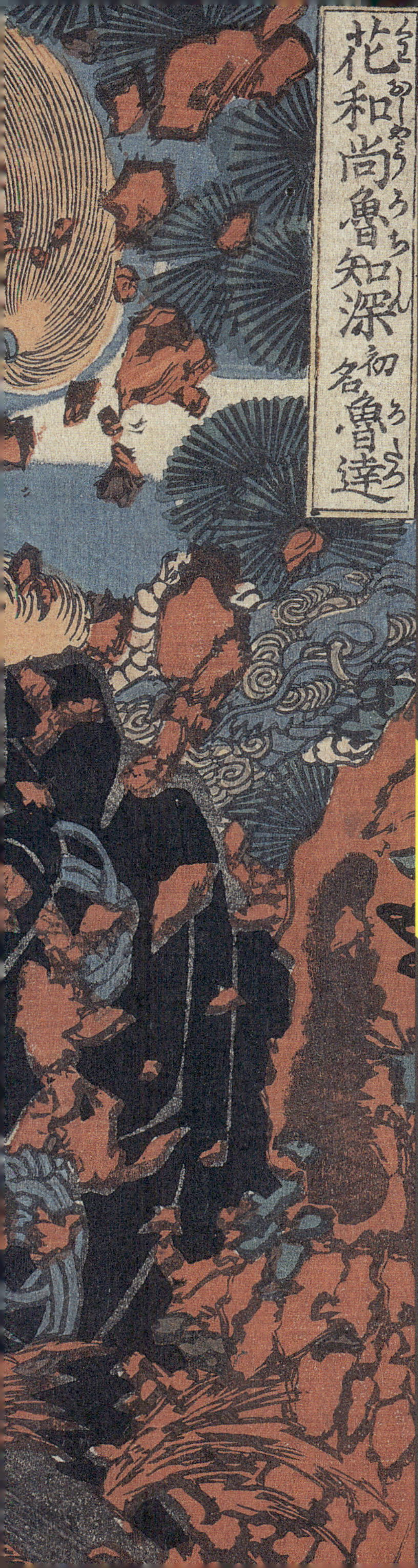

Kaoshō Rochishin Shomei Rotatsu from "The 108 Heroes of the Popular Suikoden" / Utagawa Kuniyoshi

1827 / Hagi Uragami Museum

In the story, Kaoshō Rotatsu beats an unscrupulous rich man who caused a father and a daughter to suffer. Then, he becomes a fugitive. In order to escape, he enters the priesthood and receives a Buddhist name Chishin. With his chivalrous spirit, he repeatedly tries to save others which results in him getting into troubles. Eventually, he joins the heroes' gathering at Ryōzanpaku. His name Kaoshō（花和尚）consists of the Kanji characters "flower（花）" and "priest（和尚）." In the Chinese language, the character 花 also represents "tattoo," thus his name means "priest with tattoos." In this picture, he has flowers tattooed on his shoulders and sides. It depicts the scene of Rotatsu intimidating a convoy official by splitting a pine tree, in order to save his associate Rin Chu who has been falsely accused. Rotatsu stabs a ritual Buddhist metal stick, which weights 37.2kg, into the pine tree. The broken tree pieces are scattered. To draw this picture, Kuniyoshi might have referred to Hokusai's illustrations in the book "New Suiko-gaden." The dynamic depiction has a tremendous impact, and viewers can almost hear Rotatsu's roar and the noise of the breaking pine tree.

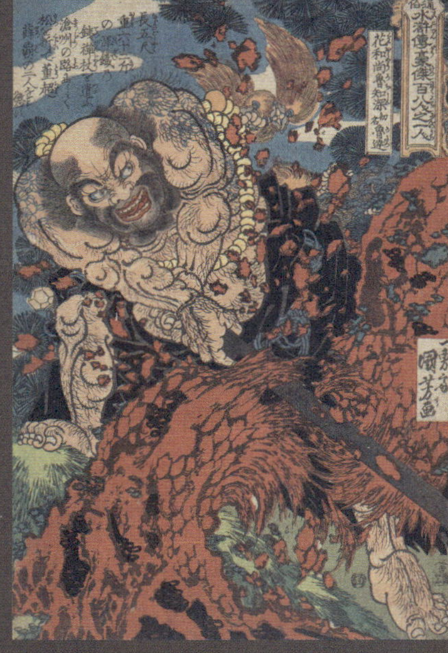

通俗水滸伝豪傑百八人之一人　花和尚魯知深初名魯達 / 歌川国芳

文政 10 年（1827）頃 ／ 山口県立萩美術館・浦上記念館蔵

中国語で「花」は刺青を指し、「花和尚」という通称は刺青坊主といった意味。本図の魯知深の肩や脇にも、花の刺青がある。人を助けてはトラブルに巻き込まれる魯知深。本図は濡れ衣を着せられた仲間を助けるため、松の木を叩き折って護送の役人を威嚇する場面。重さ 62 斤（37.2kg）の鉄禅杖（僧が携帯する錫杖）が松の幹にめり込み、折れゆく松の破片が飛び散る。怒号や崩れる松の音が聞こえてくるような、傑出した迫力の一枚。

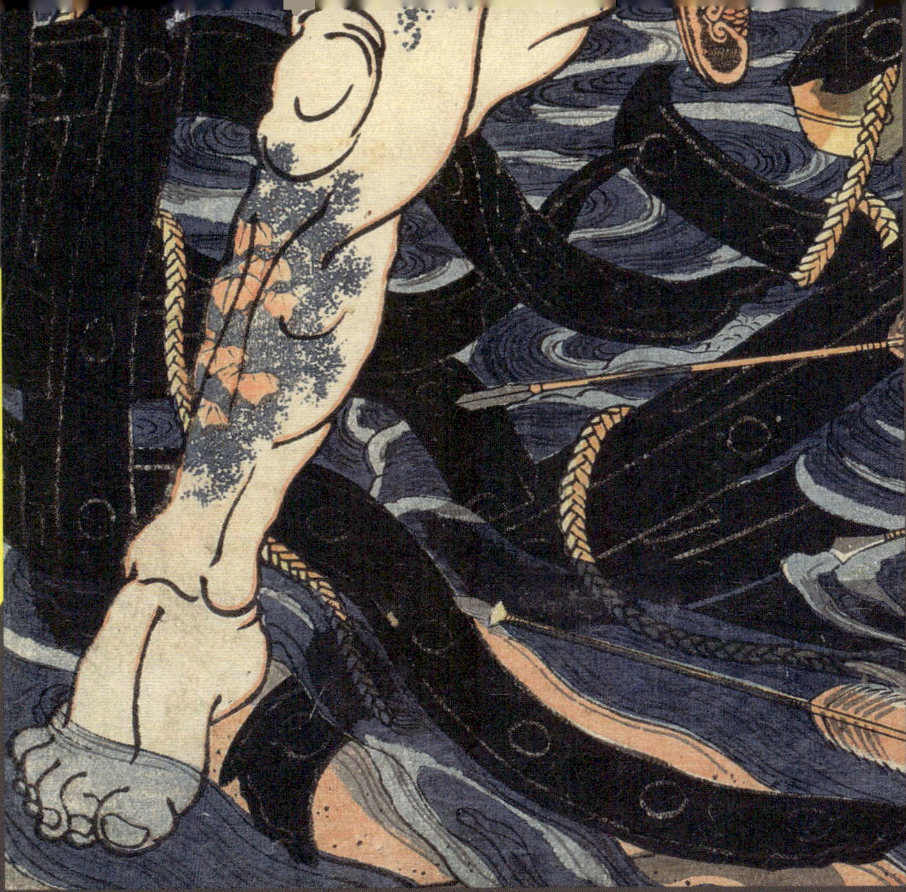

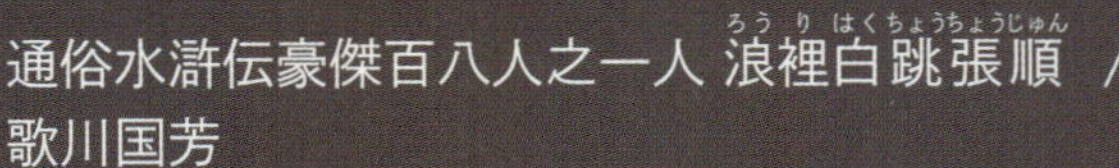

Rōri Hakuchō Chōjun from
"The 108 Heroes of the Popular Suikoden" /
Utagawa Kuniyoshi

c.1828 - 1829 / Tokyo National Museum

In the story, Rōri Hakuchō Chōjun runs a fish wholesaler in Jiangzhou
Province, and is such a good swimmer that he is able to spend seven days
and nights in water. Becoming a member of the heroes at Ryōzanpaku, he
plays an important role as the head of the marine force. Rōri Hakuchō is
Chōjun's nickname and it means that he can swim freely and invincibly, like
a dace fish swimming through waves. After suggesting to his associates that
they swim across a river to creep into a castle in Hangzhou Province, where
their enemies lock themselves in, Chōjun gets into the castle by himself.
This picture depicts that scene. In the original story, he fails to break a
water gate. But the text in the lower right of this picture reads that he
succeeded in breaking it. With a backdrop of iron bars which he broke and
under a shower of enemy's arrows, Chōjun would soon die in the battle. His
red loincloth and navy tattoo stand out against his skin, which is described
as being even whiter than snow in the story.

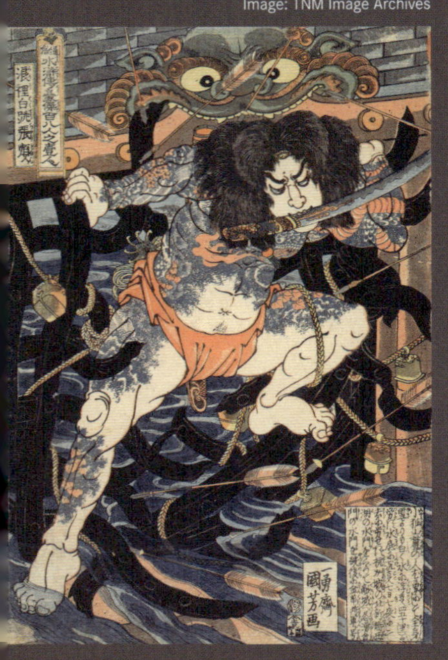

通俗水滸伝豪傑百八人之一人 浪裡白跳張順 /
歌川国芳

文政 11年（1828）- 文政 12年（1829）頃 / 東京国立博物館蔵

張順は水練（泳ぎ）の達人で、梁山泊では水軍の頭領となり活躍した。本図
は川を泳いで敵の城内に単身乗り込む場面。原作では水門を破れずに戦死す
るが、本図の説明では水門を突破したとされている。破壊した鉄格子を背に、
降り注ぐ敵の矢のなか死を迎えようとする張順。雪よりも白いというその肌
に、赤い褌と刺青の藍が映える。

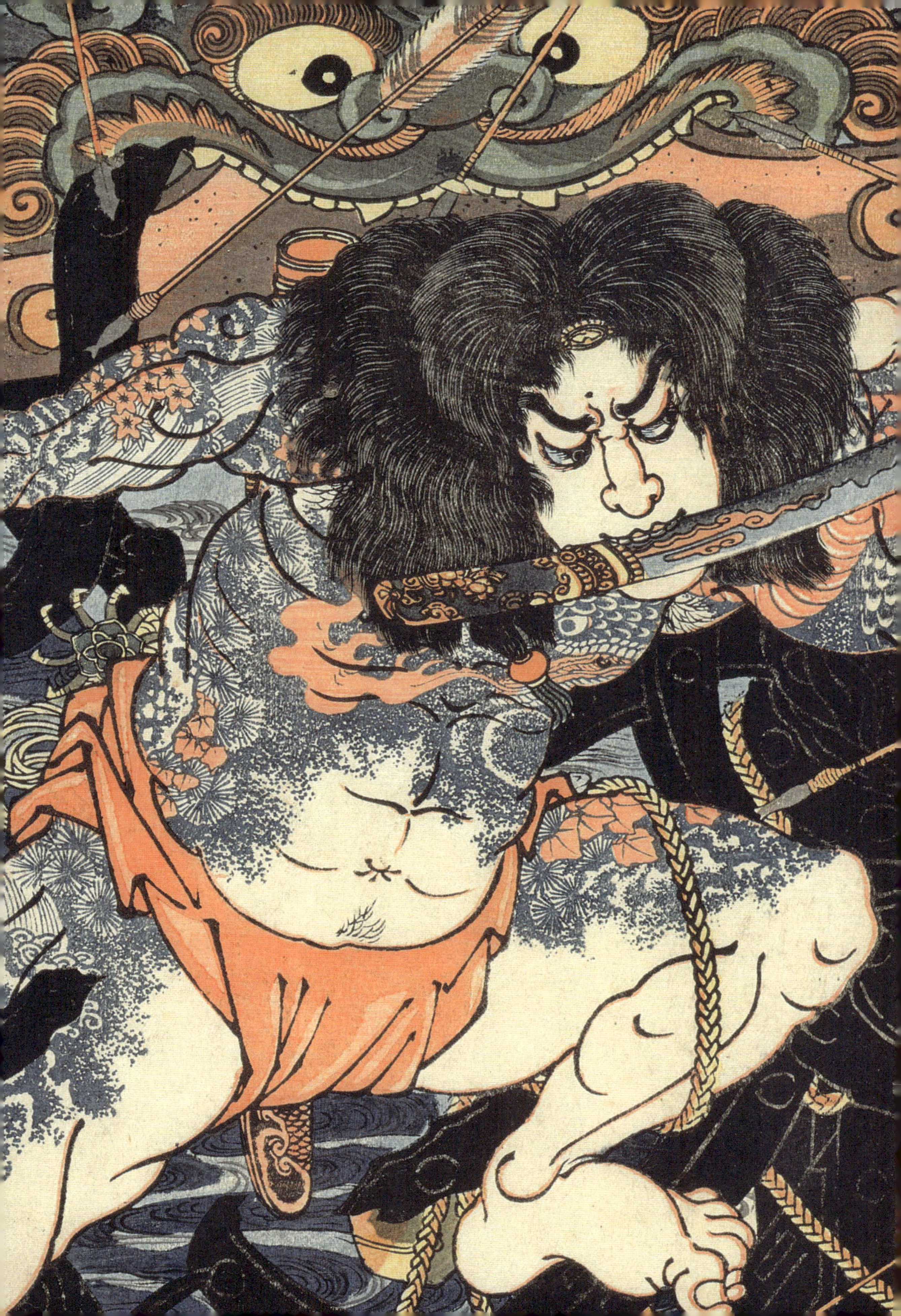

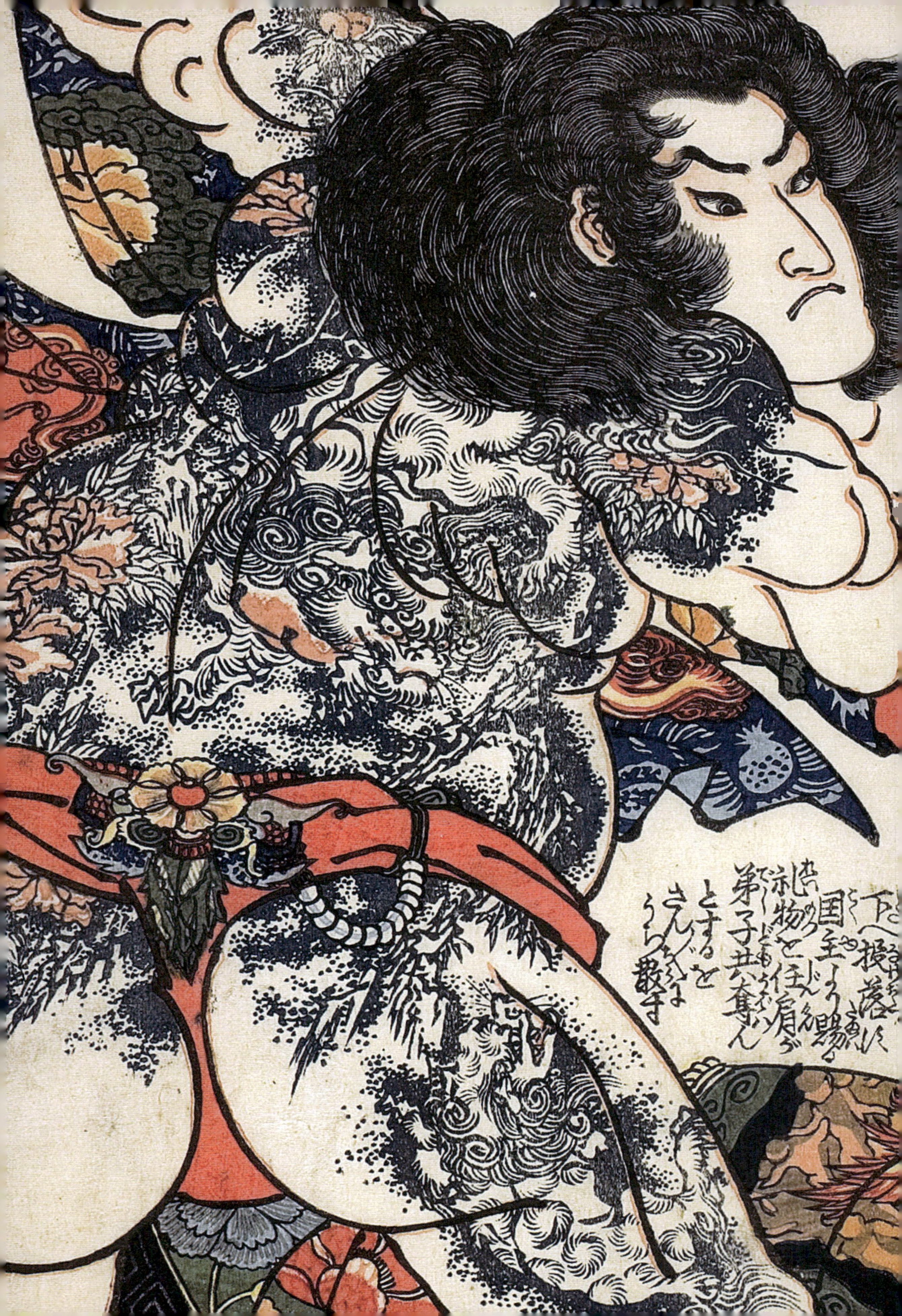

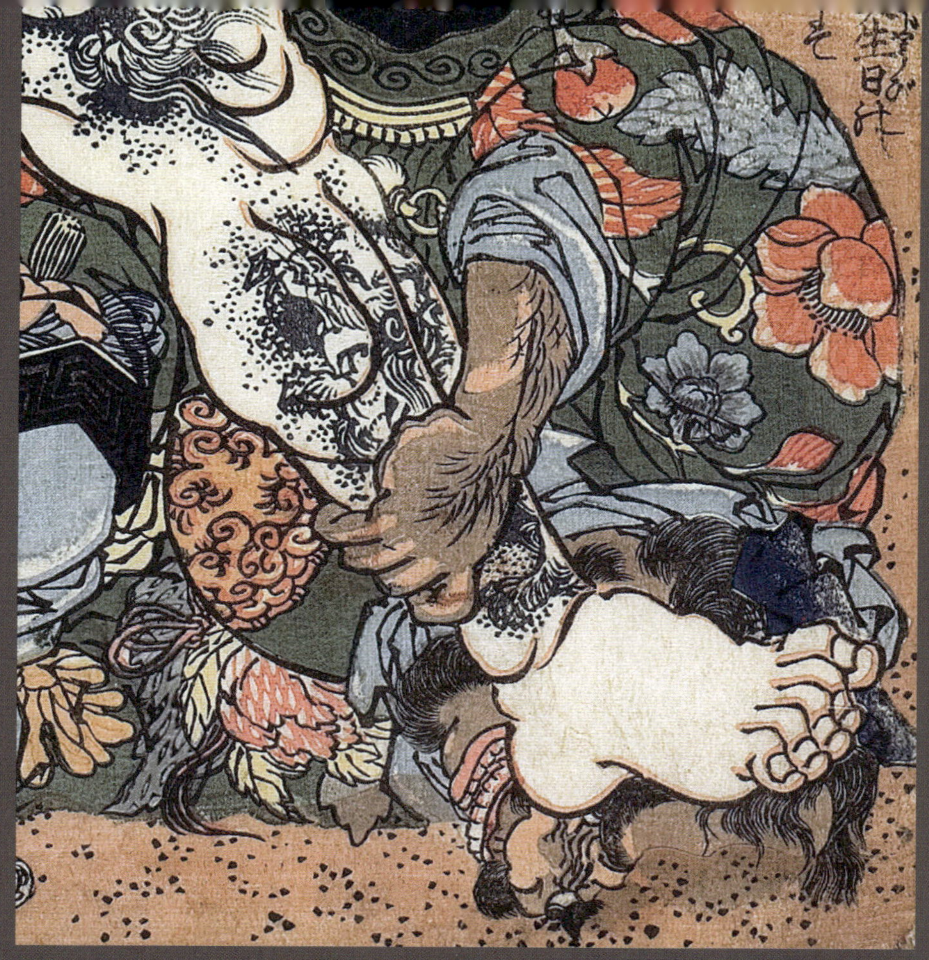

Rōshi Ensei from "The 108 Heroes of the Popular Suikoden" / Utagawa Kuniyoshi

1828 - 1833 / The Art Institute of Chicago

Ensei from Beijing is regarded as the most beautiful male character in the novel "Suikoden." In order to tattoo on his beautiful white skin, Ensei's master Gyokukirin Ro Shungi orders a highly skilled tattooist. The picture depicts his tattoo as a traditional pattern of peony and Karajishi, or a Chinese imaginary sacred lion. The Karajishi tattoo covers his back, hips and thighs. Only the blowing fires around the Karajishi and peony flowers are drawn in red. This tattoo design has been held in high regard among the series. In fact, many of the pictures in the series depict characters having their backs turned, which allows viewers to easily make out the tattoo designs. The series might also have worked as a sample book of tattoo designs in the Edo period.

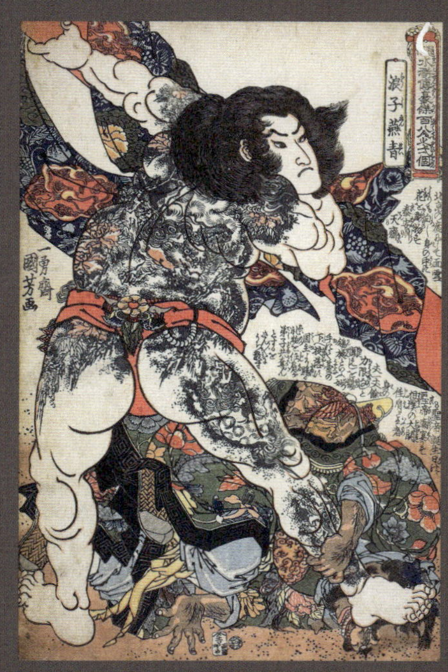

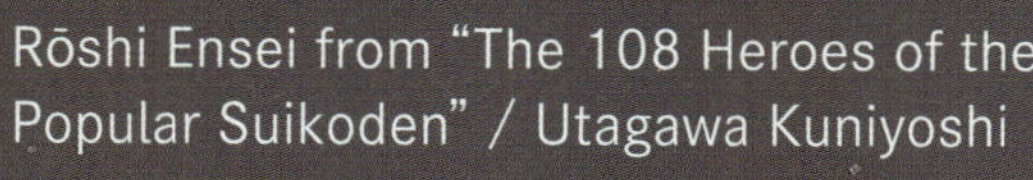

通俗水滸伝豪傑百八人之一個　浪子燕青 /
歌川国芳

文政 11 年（1828）- 天保 4 年（1833）頃 / シカゴ美術館蔵

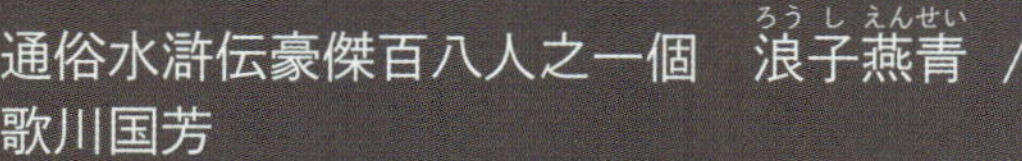

『水滸伝』きっての美男子とされる燕青。その白い肌の美しさ故に、主人の玉麒麟盧俊義は腕のある彫師に刺青を彫らせたという。背中を向け、牡丹に唐獅子の図柄を、わかりやすく示している。背面を向けたポーズが多いのは、本シリーズが刺青の見本帳、スタイルブックのような役割を果たしたためだろう。

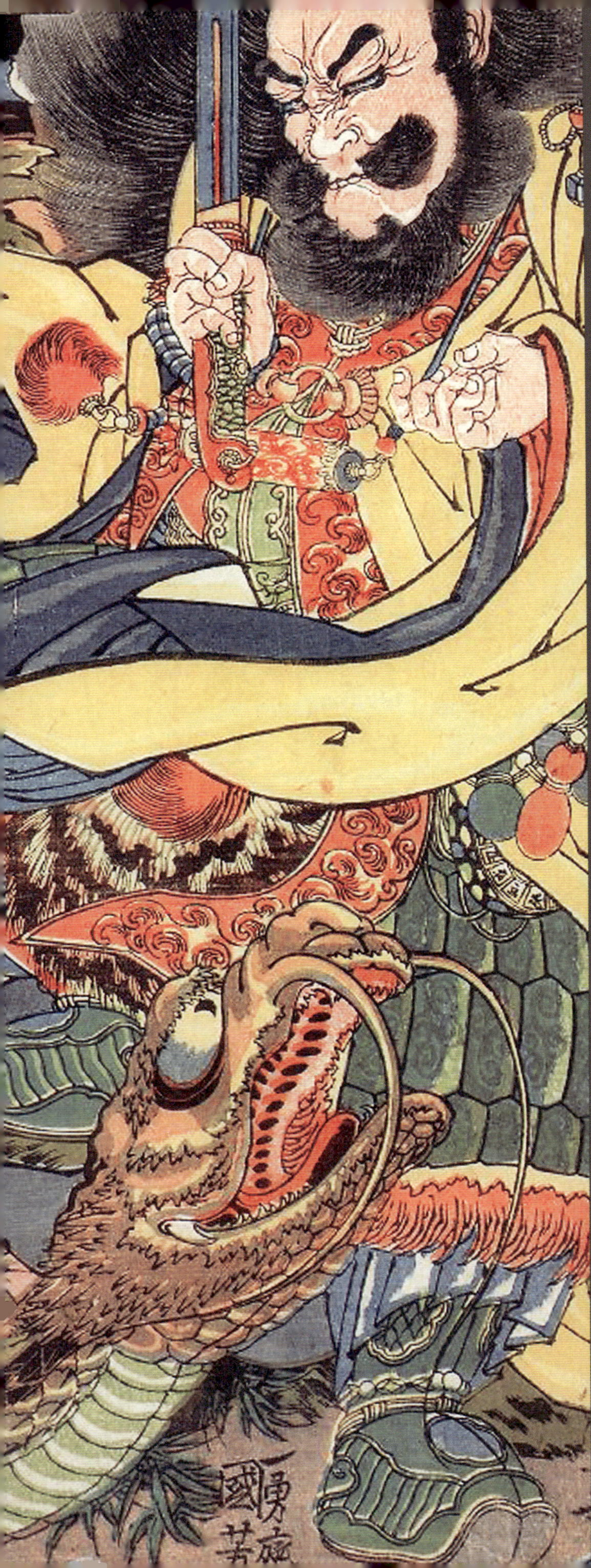

Nyūunryū Kōson Shō from "The 108 Heroes of the Popular Suikoden" / Utagawa Kuniyoshi

c.1828 - 1833 / Photo : amana

In the story, Kōson Shō is a Taoist under training and becomes a military strategist for the group of heroes gathered at Ryōzanpaku. By using Taoist methodologies, he gets his associates out of danger time after time. His clothes fluttering in the wind, the waves swelling, the clouds slashing the darkness. These unusual phenomena might be caused by a specter, who was summoned by Kōson Shō's methodology. He chews his bottom lip and rolls his eyes back. There are many wrinkles between his eyebrows and on the outer corners of his eyes. He quietly stands still, but his facial expression and the shape of his tensed fingers represent the strain he is under while using the Taoist methodologies.

通俗水滸伝豪傑百八人之一個 入雲龍 公孫勝 / 歌川国芳

文政 11 年（1828）- 天保 4 年（1833）頃 / 提供：アマナ

梁山泊の軍師を務めた公孫勝は、修行中の道士で、その道術でたびたび梁山泊軍の危機を救う。風になびく衣服や、巻き起こる波、漆黒の闇を切り裂く雲。異常な状況は、公孫勝の道術によって召喚された龍が引き起こしているようだ。下唇を噛み、白目を剥いた顔には、眉間や目尻に幾重にも皺が寄っている。静的な立ち姿でありながら、顔面の表情や力をこめた手先のかたちで、道術のために力む公孫勝の緊張が伝わってくる。

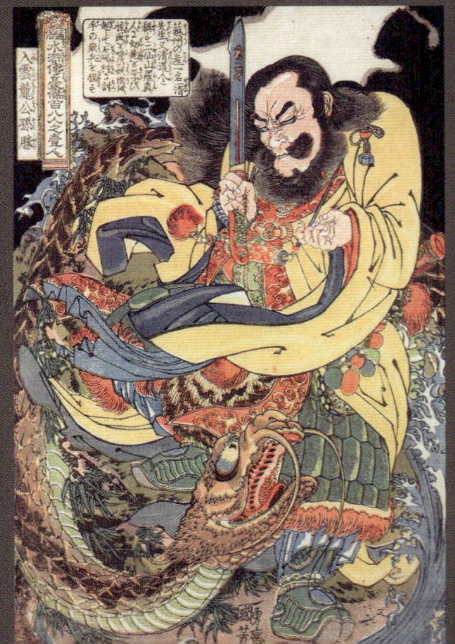

Iwanuma Kichirokurō Nobusato from "The 800 Heroes of the Japanese Suikoden" / Utagawa Kuniyoshi

c.1830 - 1835 / Hagi Uragami Museum

The text in this picture reads that a man named Iwanuma Kichirokurō Nobusato killed three giant newt monsters at an old pond in Sado Province. A similar episode to this is found in a book "Shokoku Kidan Hokuyūki" published in 1797, which is about a powerful man defeating six newts. In this picture, the black and red giant newts vividly stand out against the backdrop of the blue sky and river, as well as the green trees and rocks. The combination of the three giant newts creates a circular form around the man. This composition makes for a strong impact.

本朝水滸伝剛勇八百人一個 岩沼吉六郎信里 ／ 歌川国芳

天保元年（1830）- 天保 6 年（1835）頃 ／
山口県立萩美術館・浦上記念館蔵

図中の解説によれば岩沼吉六郎信里なる人物は、「佐渡国の古沼において大守宮の化しを三ツ迄たいじするといふ」。これと似た話に、佐渡の強者が 6 匹のイモリを退治したという話が勢州山人『諸国奇談 北遊記』（1797 年刊）にある。空や川の青、木々や岩の緑に、黒と赤の鮮烈な彩色で強烈に浮かび上がる 3 匹のイモリ。大小異なるそれらを巧みに組み合わせ、人物の周囲に円を描くように配置し、印象の強い画面をつくっている。

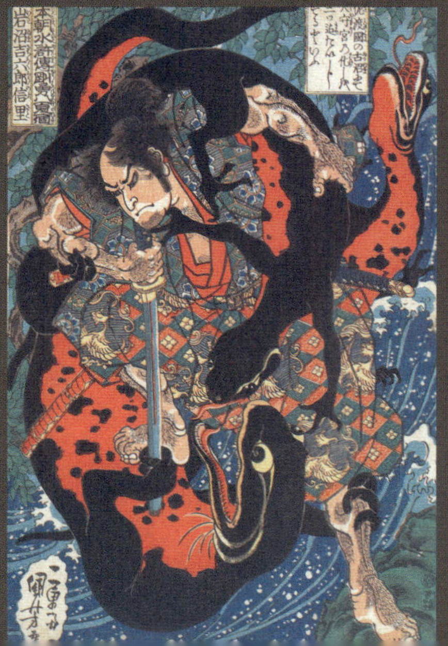

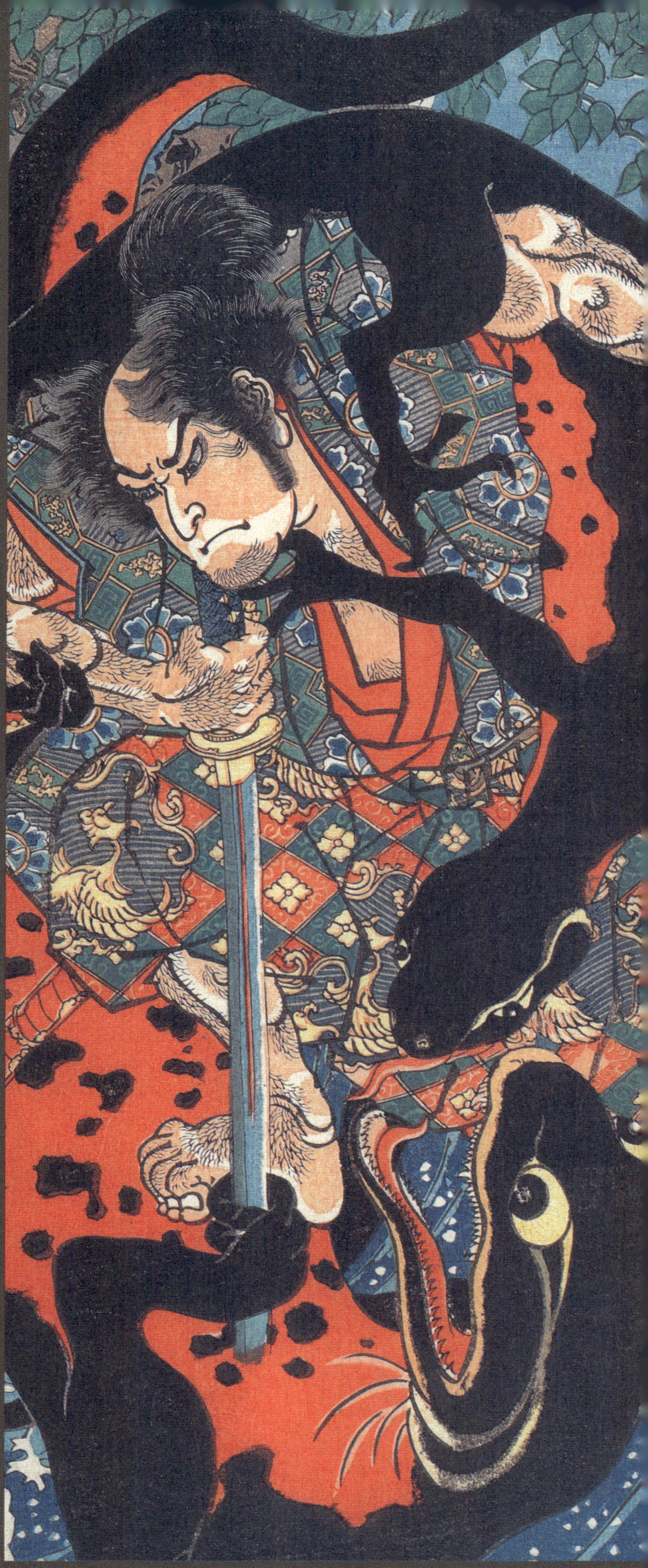

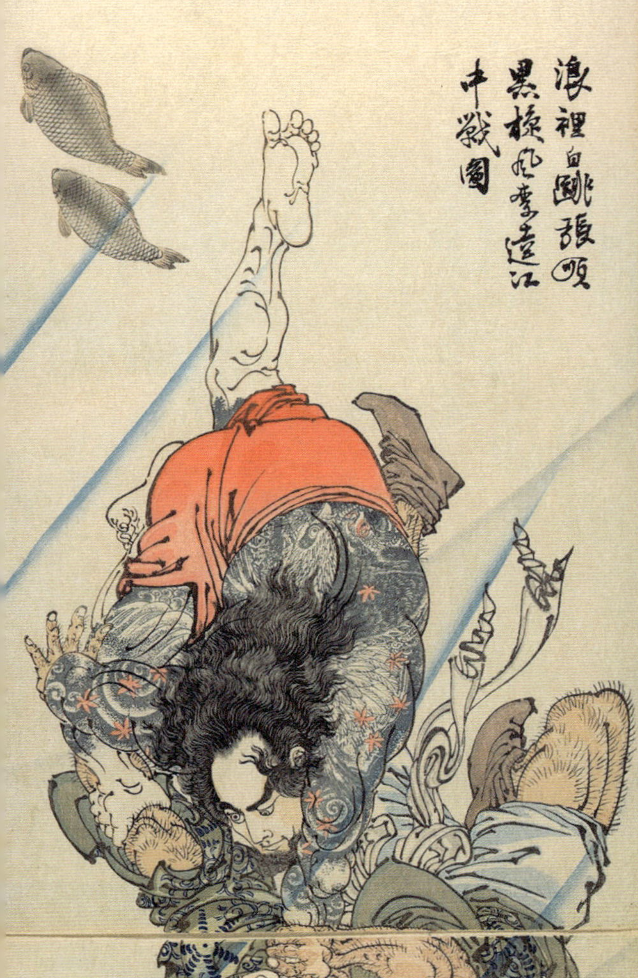

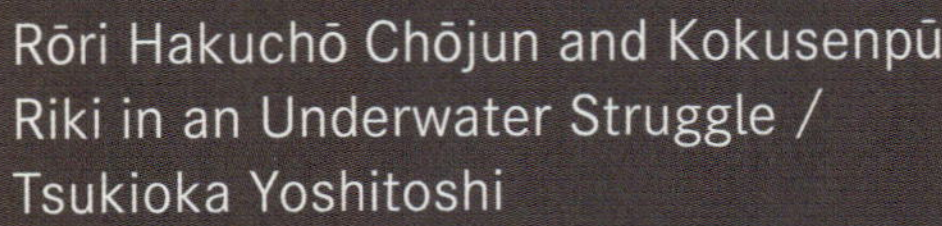

Rōri Hakuchō Chōjun and Kokusenpū Riki in an Underwater Struggle / Tsukioka Yoshitoshi

1887 / The Art Institute of Chicago

The faded blue lines illustrate that this picture takes place under water. The fish which are swimming towards the upper part of the vertically long frame represent that the two men are under deep water. It is a scene from "Suikoden," where Chōjun (P.18) fights with Riki and drags him into the water, since Chōjun is very good at swimming.Riki tries to fight back but rolls his eyes back in this picture, despite the fact that he is a member of the 108 heroes of "Suikoden," a large man, and extraordinary strong if he fights on land. Rōri Hakuchō is the nickname of Chōjun and means "white splash in waves." Riki's nickname Kokusenpū means "black whirlwind." Because of his agility, superhuman strength and dark skin, Riki is also called "Tetsugyū," meaning "black bull." Yoshitoshi might have referred to a picture by Kuniyoshi which features another character from "Suikoden," since it has a similar composition to this picture.

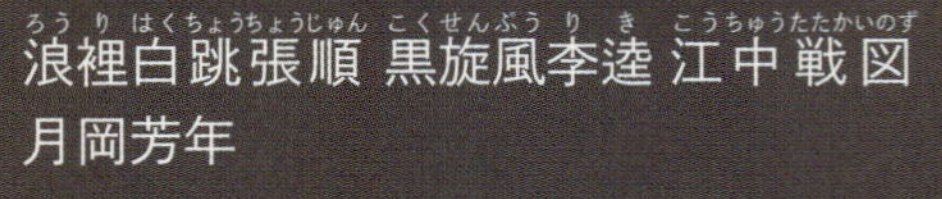

浪裡白跳張順 黒旋風李逵 江中戦図 / 月岡芳年

明治20年（1887）／ シカゴ美術館蔵

ぼかしを用いた青い筋は、そこが水中であることをあらわす。二枚の紙を繋げた縦長の画面の上方で、さらに上に向かって泳ぐ魚は、取っ組み合う二人が深い水の底にいることを示す。月岡芳年が得意の縦長画面に描くのは、『水滸伝』の豪傑、張順（P.18）と李逵の喧嘩。本図で抵抗虚しく白目を剥く李逵は、地上では怪力の大男である。浪裡白跳張順に対し、李逵のあだ名は黒旋風。素早い怪力の色黒であったためで、鉄牛とも呼ばれた。

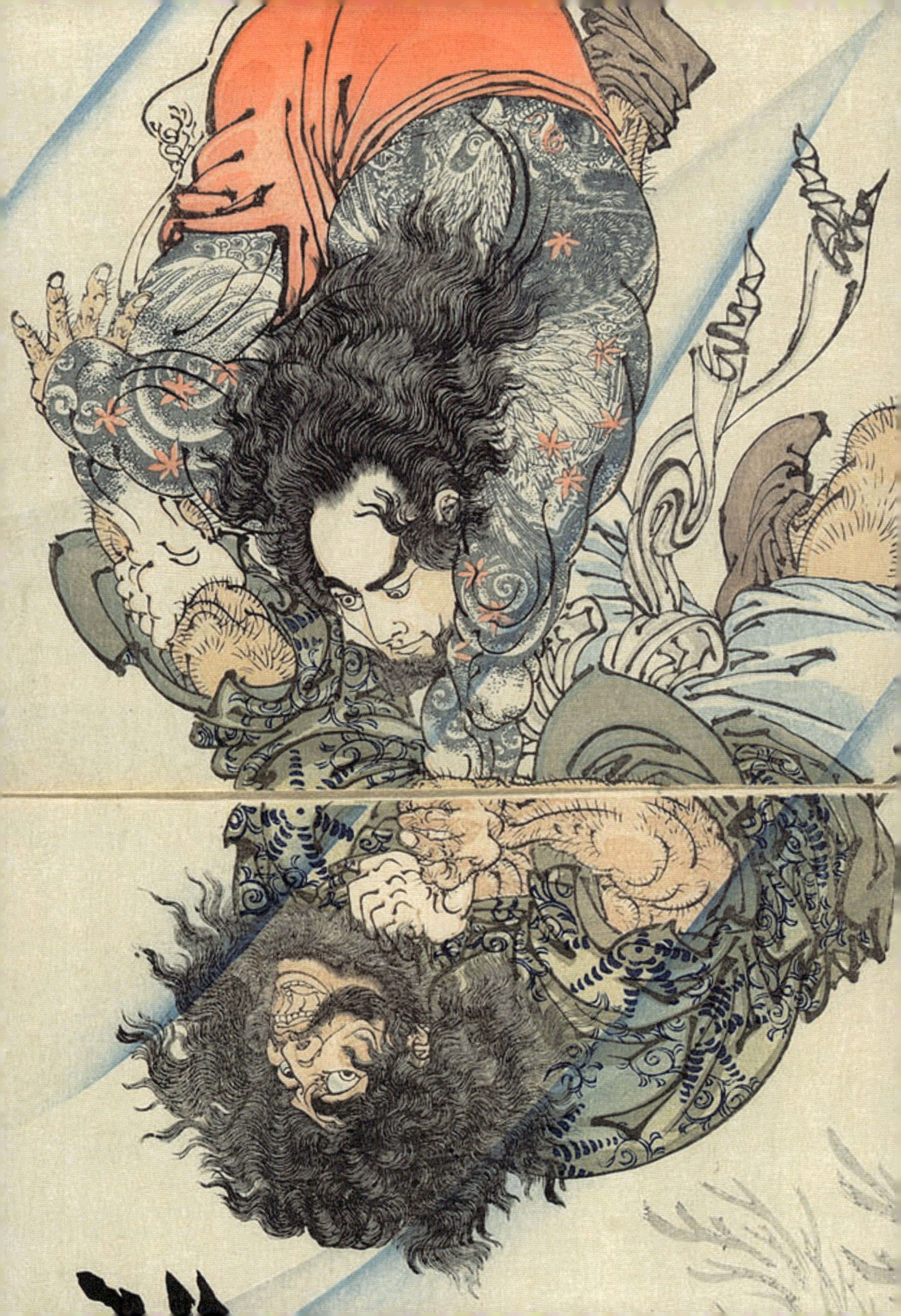

Lively Water and Fire

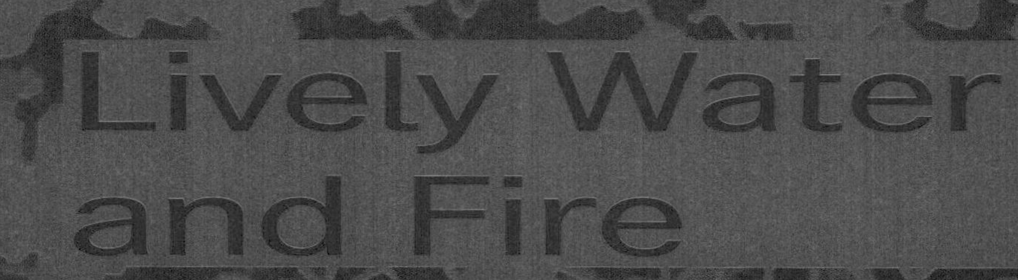

Here are pictures of water and fire which shadily wriggle as if they are creatures. They effectively color and support lively figures and dramatic stories, and even become main motives at times. Especially, pictures by Hokusai, who pursued water expressions, became great inspirational sources and widely influenced painters in the following generations. You would not believe your eyes to see those spectacular views created by masters of water and fire.

命を宿す
水と火

二章
Chapter 2.

まるで生きているかのように、怪しく蠢く水や火。それらは、ともに描かれる人物や物語をドラマチックに演出し、ときには主役の座を奪う。とりわけ水の表現を極めんとした北斎の足跡は、後世の絵師たちにとって、尽きせぬインスピレーションの源泉となった。水と火を制した絵師たちによる壮観な光景に、目を見張る。

Kirifuri Waterfall at Kurokami Mountain in Shimotsuke, from the series A Tour of the Waterfalls in Various Provinces / Katsushika Hokusai

c.1833 / The Sumida Hokusai Museum

Kirifuri Waterfall is regarded as one of the three most famous waterfalls in Japan. The name Kirifuri, meaning "falling mist," represents the water hitting against rocks and splashing mists. Water windingly runs down through gaps between the rugged and jagged rocks, like growing tree roots. Many parts of the picture are left in white to represent the water turning into a fine spray. The strange form of falling water is like an unknown creature, and the colors of navy and white create a vivid contrast. Among the series, this picture particularly makes a lasting impression on viewers. A similar depiction of a waterfall can be found in the Wano Country Arc from the famous Japanese manga "One Piece" by Oda Eiichirō.

諸国瀧廻り 下野黒髪山きりふりの滝 / 葛飾北斎

天保 4 年（1833）頃 ／ すみだ北斎美術館蔵

日光三名瀑のひとつ、段になった岩にあたって霧を噴き上げて落ちるところから「霧降の滝」と名づけられた滝だ。ごつごつとした尖った岩の隙間を、根を伸ばすように、うねりながら流れ落ちる水。白い部分を多くつくり、霧状になって流れる水をあらわしている。生けるが如きその奇怪な形に加えて、濃紺と輝くような白との強烈なコントラストに目を奪われる。本シリーズの中でも、とりわけ忘れられない印象をのこす一枚。尾田栄一郎による漫画『ONE PIECE』（910 話）の「ワノ」国にもこれとよく似た滝が登場する。

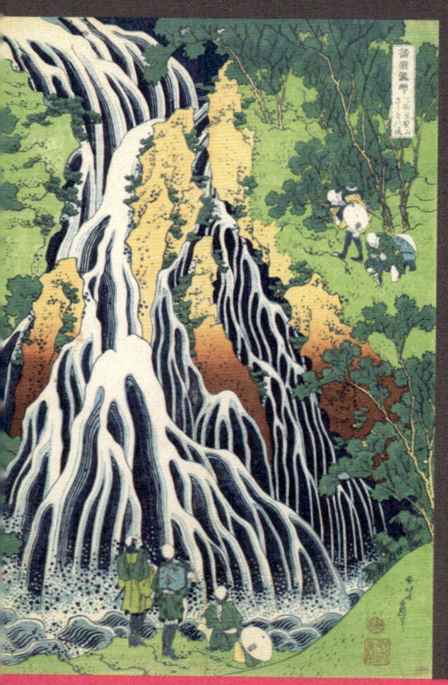

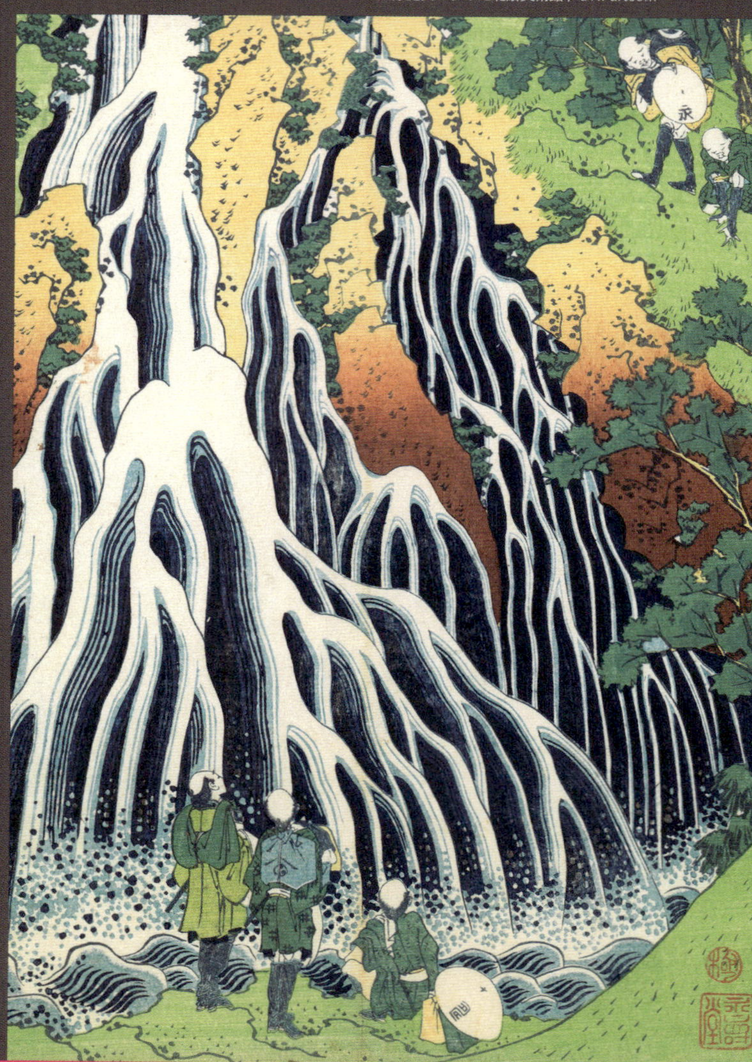

A Tour of the Waterfalls in Various Provinces

Having long perused his skills in depicting water, Hokusai finally mastered wave depictions in his print series "Thirty-six views of Mount Fuji," and then started improving his skills in order to draw waterfalls. This is part of a series of eight prints, each of which features a famous waterfall across Japan. The waterfalls were regarded as sacred and had been worshiped. The expression of falling water differs from picture to picture.

《諸国瀧廻り》

水の表現を追求した北斎は、《冨嶽三十六景》で「波」を極めたのち、「滝」に挑む。人々の信仰の対象となっていた各地の名瀑を題材とした 8 枚揃いのシリーズ。流れ落ちる水の表情が描き分けられている。

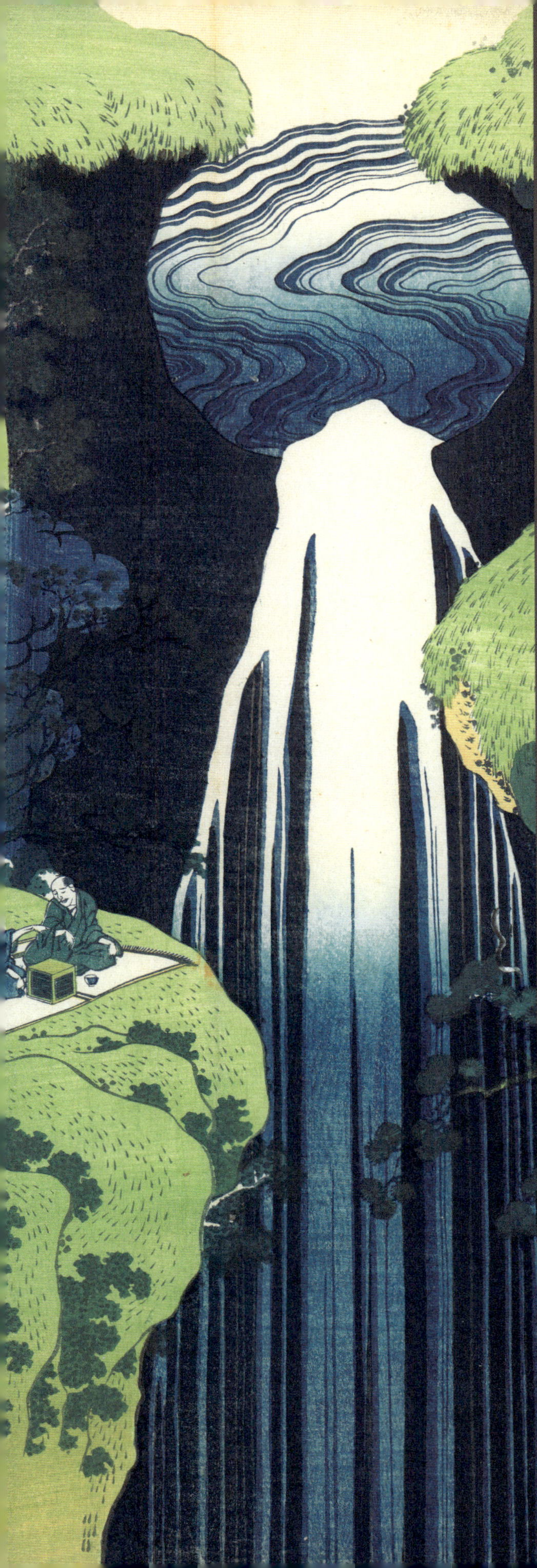

Amida Falls in the Far Reaches of the Kisokaidō Road, from the series A Tour of the Waterfalls in Various Provinces/ Katsushika Hokusai

c.1833 / The Sumida Hokusai Museum

Hokusai eagerly studied Chinese and Western paintings. We can see how much he learned about precise portrayals of subjects, the one-point perspective and other techniques, in his several realistic paintings. With such skills, Hokusai kept developing and hit his stride in creating his unique expression, which has never been able to be expressed in photography. The top of the waterfall is drawn in a hollowed circular form, in order to show viewers the water stream above, which cannot be seen from the bottom in reality. The stream has a form resembling a Japanese traditional pattern of water. The picture sophisticatedly expresses the sudden change of the stream on the top of the waterfall, and creates a contrast between the upper stream and the falling water. It is said that Amida Falls was named after a legend, which is about a trainee monk who witnessed Amitabha Buddha at a cave nearby. The picture spectacularly expresses this sacred tale.

諸国瀧廻り 木曽路ノ奥阿彌陀ヶ瀧 ／ 葛飾北斎

天保 4 年（1833）頃 ／ すみだ北斎美術館蔵

「阿弥陀ヶ滝」の名は、付近の洞窟で修行中の僧が阿弥陀仏の姿を目にしたことに由来する。神秘的なエピソードに恰好の、幻想的な光景が広がる。滝口を真ん丸にくり抜き、見えるはずのない落下前のたゆたう水を、文様のように描く。流れの変化で、相貌を一変させる水の、その瞬間を巧みに表現している。北斎は、中国や西洋の絵を学び、対象を克明に写す技術や、一点透視の遠近法を摂取した。写実的な絵を描く技術を持ちながら、写真では決してあらわすことのできない独自の世界を現出させる、北斎の真骨頂が発揮された一枚。

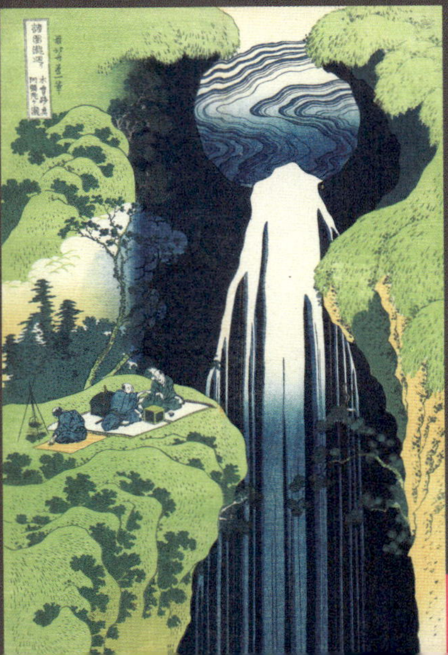

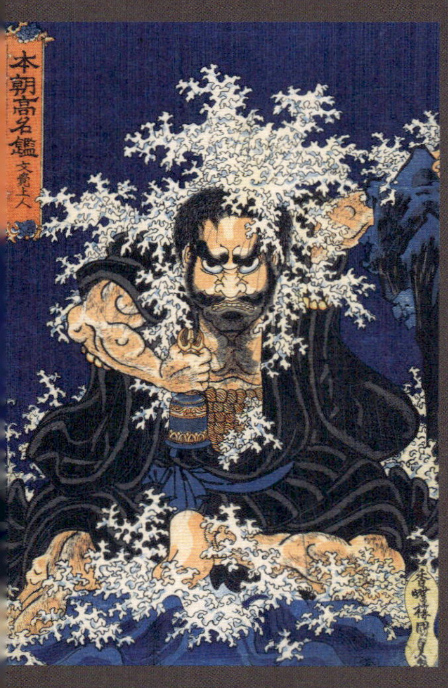

Priest Mongaku,
from the series A Mirror of Famous People of Japan / Utagawa Kunisada

c.1839 - 1840 /
Art Research Center, Ritsumeikan University

The picture depicts a waterfall with straight fine lines in the background, and flying spray which bounces around Mongaku. The expression of splashing water is unique and looks syrupy and sticky. The depiction of Mongaku raising his eyebrows, clenching his teeth and tightly clasping a rock represents the extreme water pressure.

本朝高名鑑 文覚上人 / 歌川国貞

天保 10 - 11 年（1839-40）頃 /
立命館大学 ARC 所蔵（arcUP4432）

背景の細かな直線と、跳ね返って飛び散る水により、滝を表現する。散り散りになった水のほとばしりの、まとわりつくような表現が独特だ。太い眉を吊り上げ、歯を食いしばり、がっしりと岩を掴む文覚の様子から、水圧の激しさがうかがえる。

Priest Mongaku

Priest Mongaku was a warrior called Endo Moritō before becoming a priest. Moritō wholeheartedly gave his heart to the stunning beauty Kesa, who was the wife of his friend, whom Moritō planned to kill. Moritō crept into their sleeping room to cut off his head, but actually ended up killing Kesa, who sacrificed herself for her husband. After accidentally killing someone he loved, Moritō had a deep regret and became a priest called Mongaku. Legend tells that, after Buddhist training, he suggested to a military commander Minamoto-no Yoritomo that he raise a rebel army. With his many legends, Mongaku became popular, featured in various literatures and theater plays in later periods. The most widely depicted legend among them was his Buddhist training in a waterfall at Mount Nachi, Kumano Province. After having been in the waterfall for several days, Mongaku died, but came back to life with help from attendants of Fudō Myōō, a Buddhist deity. Many painters have tried to depict the intense training scene, in order to capture the personality of Mongaku who survived through enormous tragedies.

文覚上人

文覚上人は、元は遠藤盛遠という武士だった。『平家物語』によれば、盛遠は友人の妻に恋するあまり友人を殺そうとし、誤って恋するその妻を殺してしまう。深く後悔し仏門に入り、修行ののち、源頼朝に挙兵を勧めたという。伝説に彩られ、文学や演劇にたびたび登場する文覚。錦絵では、熊野の那智山での滝の場面が頻繁に描かれた。数日にわたり滝に打たれ続けて息絶えた文覚は、不動明王の使いに助けられ、蘇生する。壮絶な人生に見合う激しい滝行の光景を、絵師たちはさまざまに工夫した。

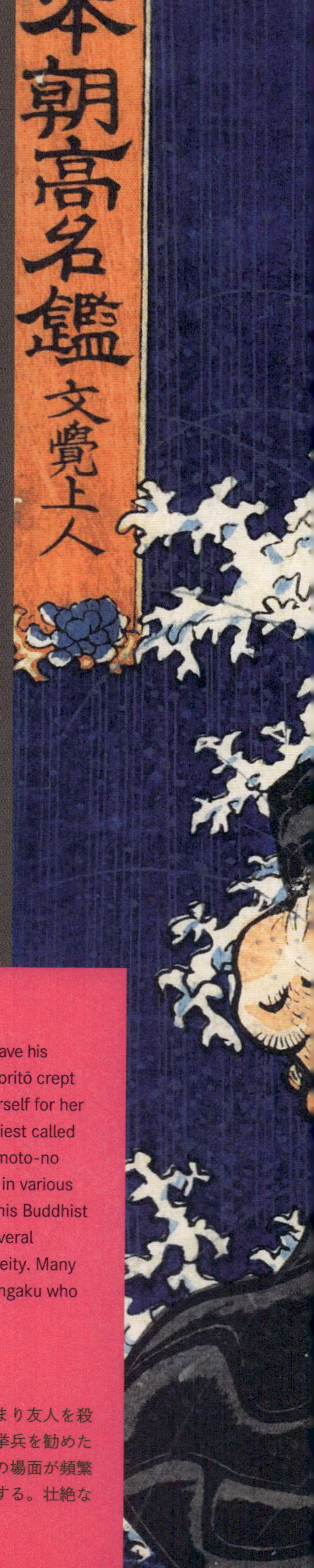

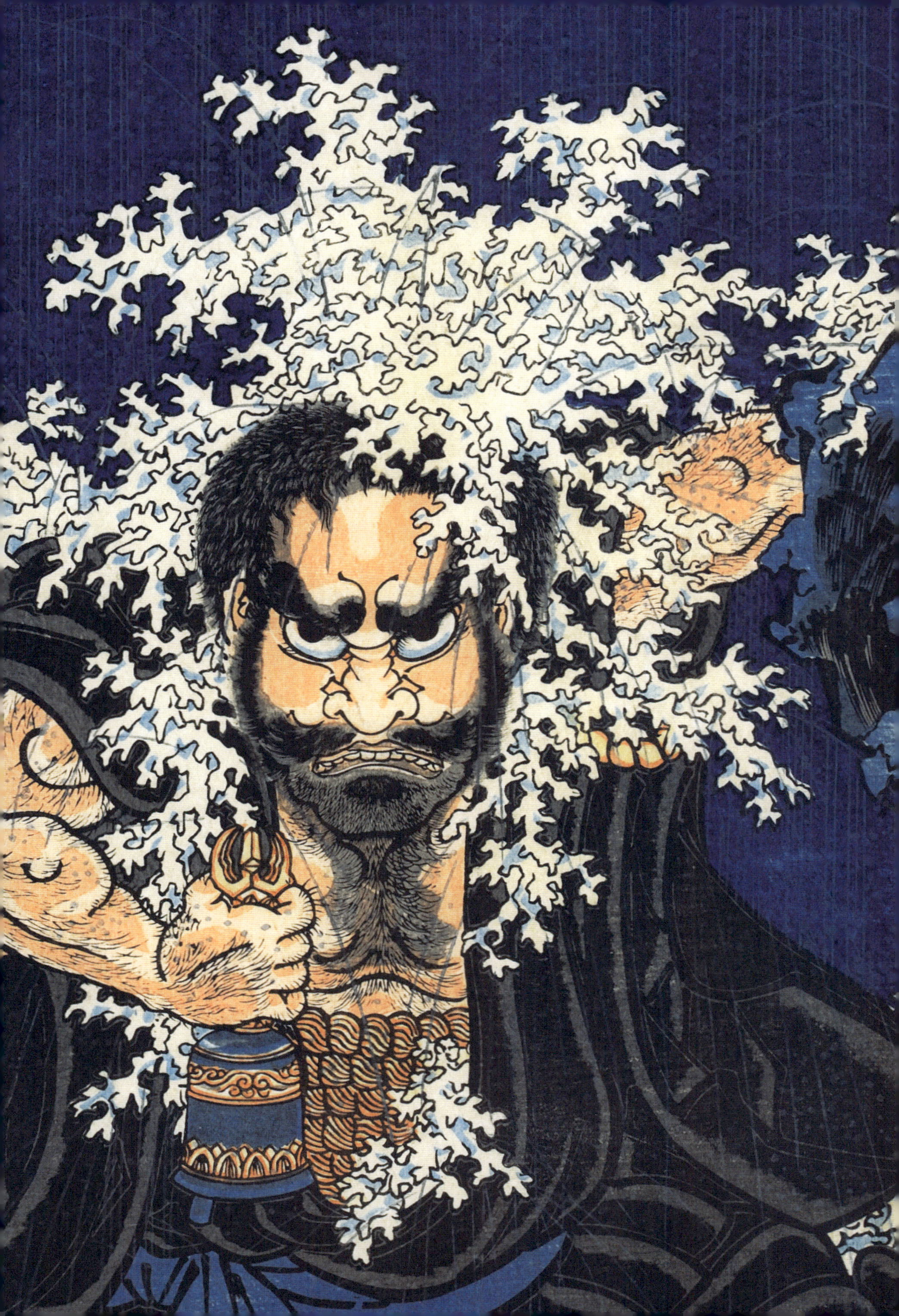

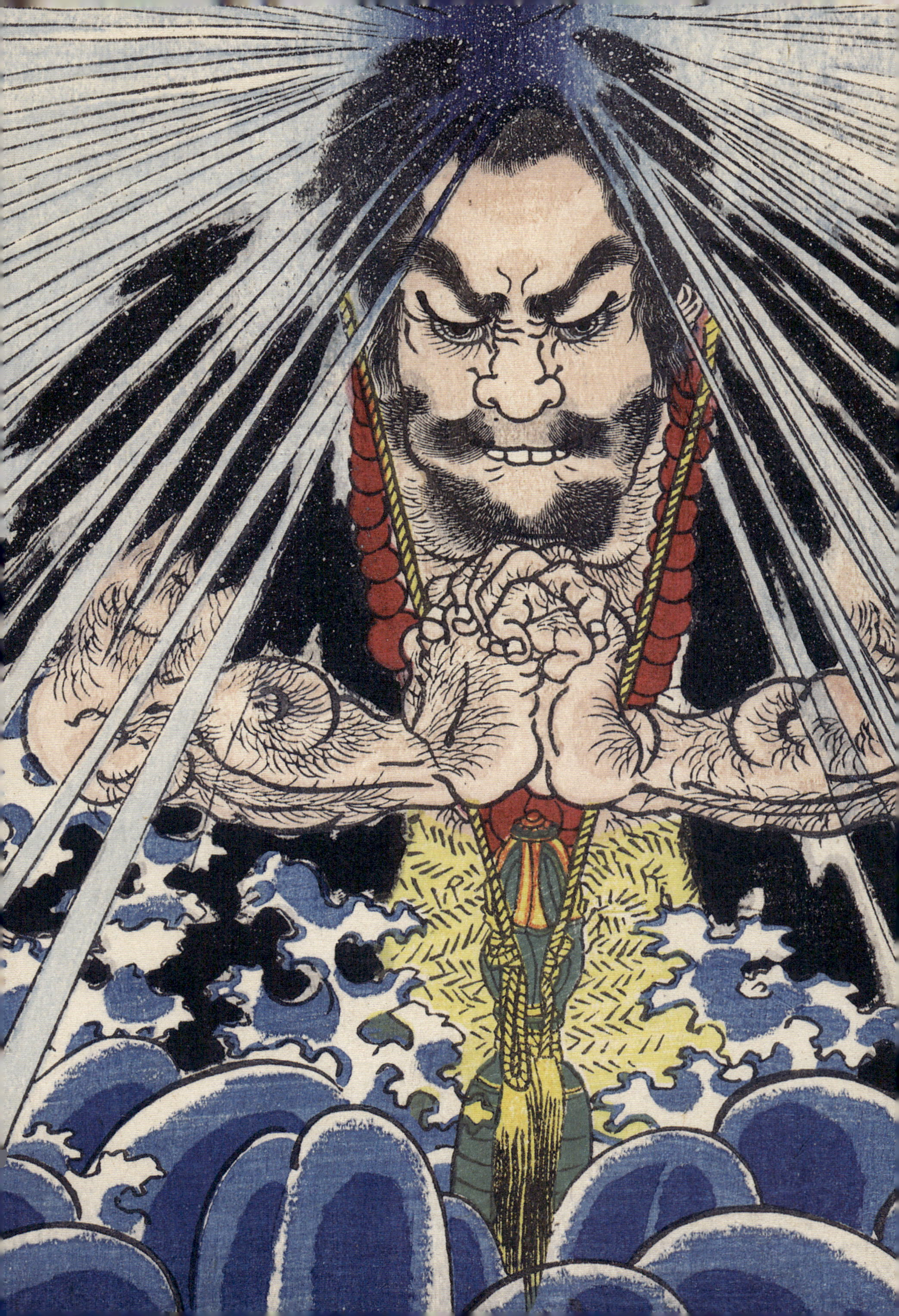

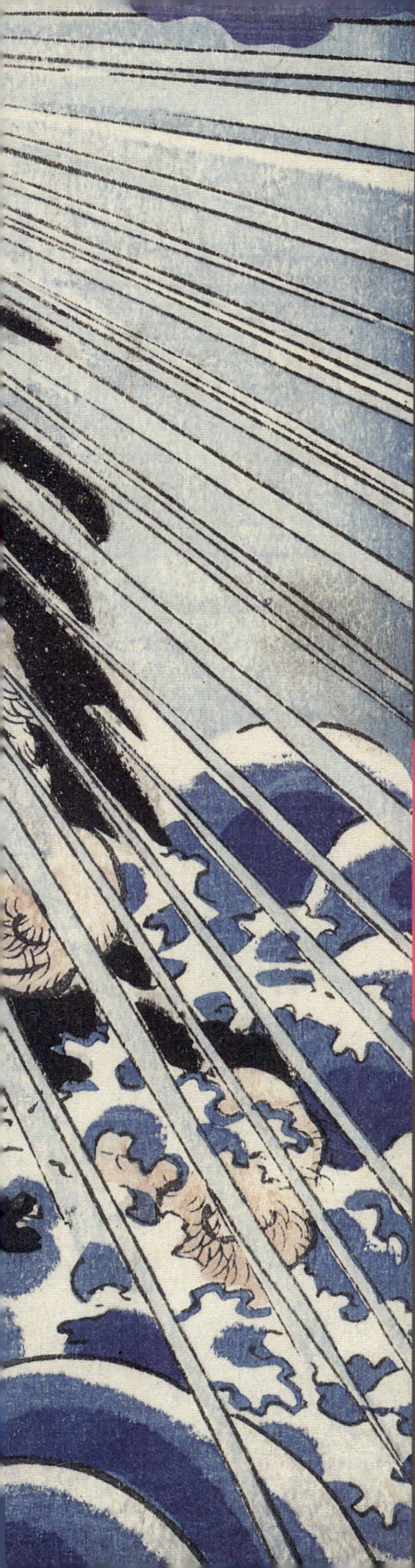

Priest Mongaku, Senbu,
from the series Kuniyoshi's Analogies for the Six Conditions of Nature /
Utagawa Kuniyoshi

1860 / British Museum

Mongaku puts his soul into his Buddhist training in the waterfall, under the gazes of Kongara-dōji and Seitaka-dōji, two attendants of Fudō Myōō, a Buddhist deity.The falling water bounces off his head and radially splatters.Clenching his teeth and clasping his hands together, he seems to be trying hard while undergoing his training.The upright vertical lines of the falling water, the fine straight lines of the splash, the choppy water around his waist, and the swell in the waterfall basin.Such a variety of water expressions can be found in this picture.

六様性国芳自慢 先負 文覚上人 ／ 歌川国芳

万延元年（1860） ／ 大英博物館蔵

不動明王の使い、金伽羅と勢多迦、二人の童子が見守る中、一心不乱に滝行に打ち込む文覚。頭頂部に落下した水が、放射状に飛び散っていく。やはり歯を食いしばりながら、固く両手を握り、必死に耐えている様子だ。垂直線と藍色の濃淡であらわされる落下する水、細かい直線となって飛び散る水、腰元で細かく波立つ滝壺で盛り上がる水。一枚の中に多彩な水の表現が凝縮されている。

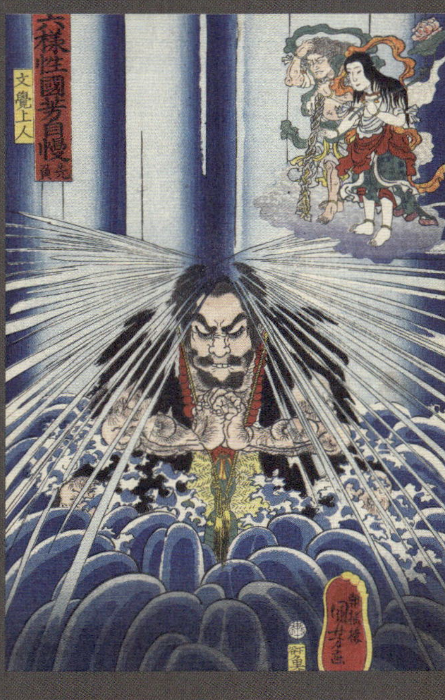

Priest Mongaku, from the series A Brief History of Japan in Pictures / Yamazaki Toshinobu

1879 / Art Research Center, Ritsumeikan University

Among a variety of pictures which feature Mongaku's training in the waterfall, this picture depicts him in the most invisible way. The main motif of this picture is no longer him, but the strong water stream which falls down, swells and almost swallows Mongaku. Only Mongaku's face and hands can be seen. We can also find standard motifs of his, raised eyebrows, clenched teeth and tightly clasped hands.

日本略史図 文覚上人 / 山崎年信

万延元年 (1860) /
立命館大学 ARC 所蔵 （arcUP5978）

この画題を描く数多の作品のなかで、文覚の姿がもっとも見えにくい一枚。落下して盛り上がり文覚を呑み込む水流が、主役の座を奪っている。顔と両手だけをわずかに見せる文覚は、相変わらず眉を吊り上げ歯を食いしばり、両手を固く握り合わせている。

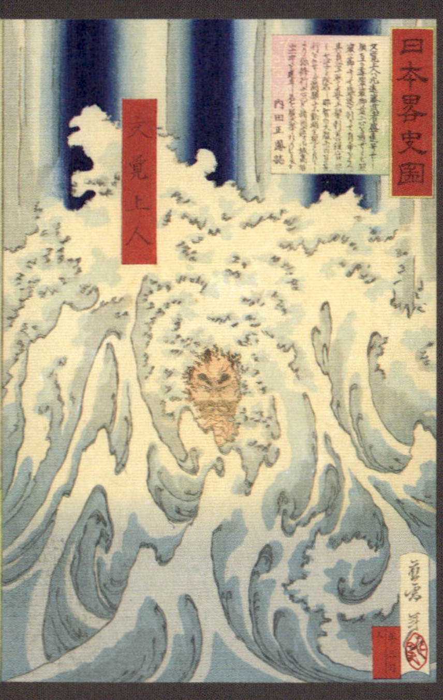

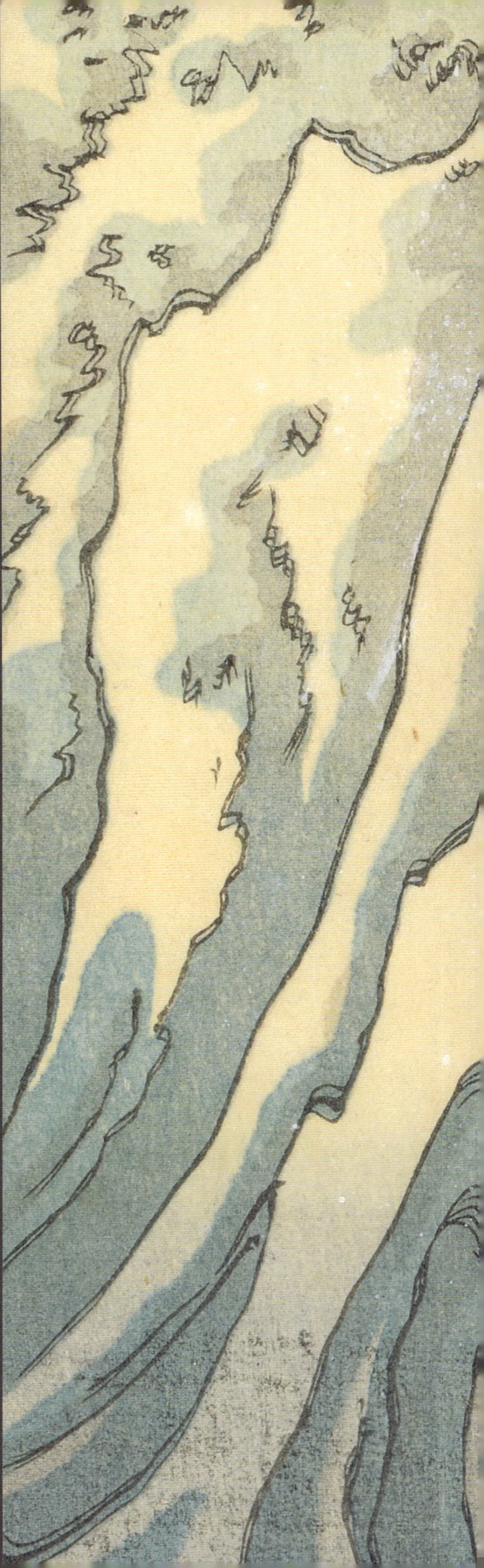

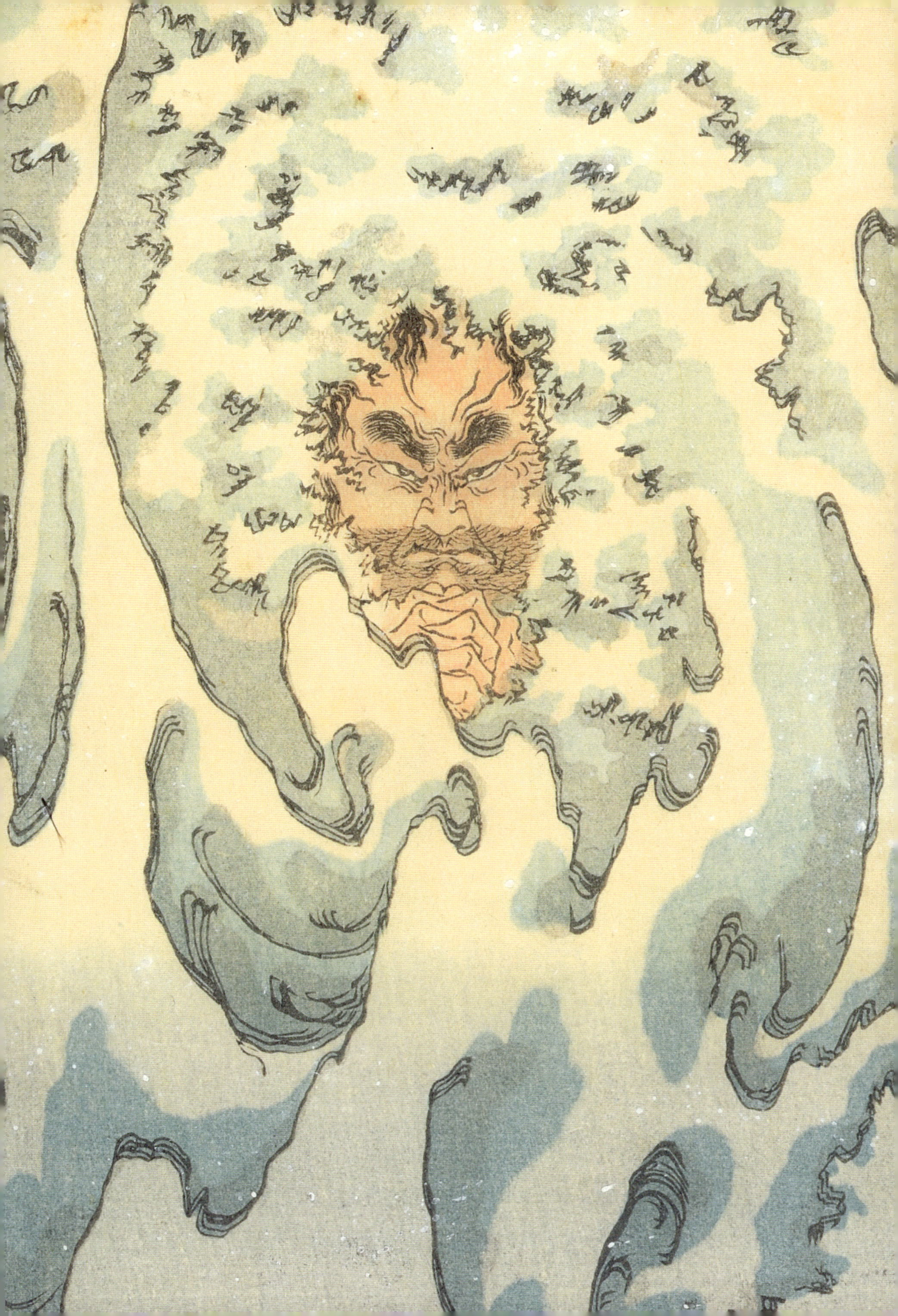

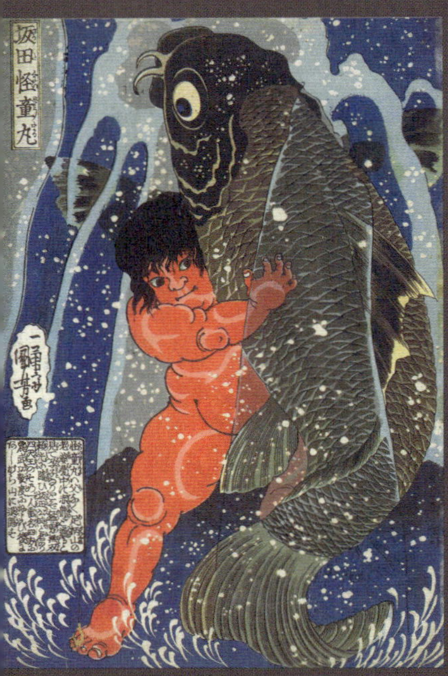

Sakata Kaidōmaru / Utagawa Kuniyoshi

c.1836 / Tokyo Metropolitan Library

Nowadays, Kaidōmaru is well-known by another name, Kintarō. The legend tells that he was extraordinarily strong and could even wrestle a bear to the ground since he was a child. Later, he became an attendant of a military commander Minamoto-no Yorimitsu and started calling himself Sakata Kintoki. He fought successfully defeating ogres and winning other battles. In this picture, he effortlessly brings up a huge carp which is larger than him. Both Kintarō and carp symbolize boys' healthy growth. Kintarō because he flourished and succeeded in life, and carp because they are believed to ascend waterfalls and transform into dragons. The contrast between his red skin and the splashing navy water, and the vigorously flipping tail of the carp create a vibrant impression. The translucent depiction of water makes viewers feel moisture and vital energy.

坂田怪童丸　/　歌川国芳

天保 7 年（1836）頃 /
東京都立中央図書館蔵

今日では金太郎の名でよく知られる怪童丸は、熊をも投げ倒す怪力で、のちに源頼光に仕えて坂田金時と名乗り鬼退治などで活躍する。本図では自身よりも大きな鯉をやすやすと持ち上げている。出世して活躍する金太郎も、滝を登り龍になるという鯉も、男児の健やかな成長をあらわす象徴。金太郎の赤い肌と水の藍の対比、弾ける水しぶき、尾を跳ね上げる鯉の勢いなどが、活力溢れる画面をつくっている。透き通るような水の表現も、潤いや生命力に溢れている。

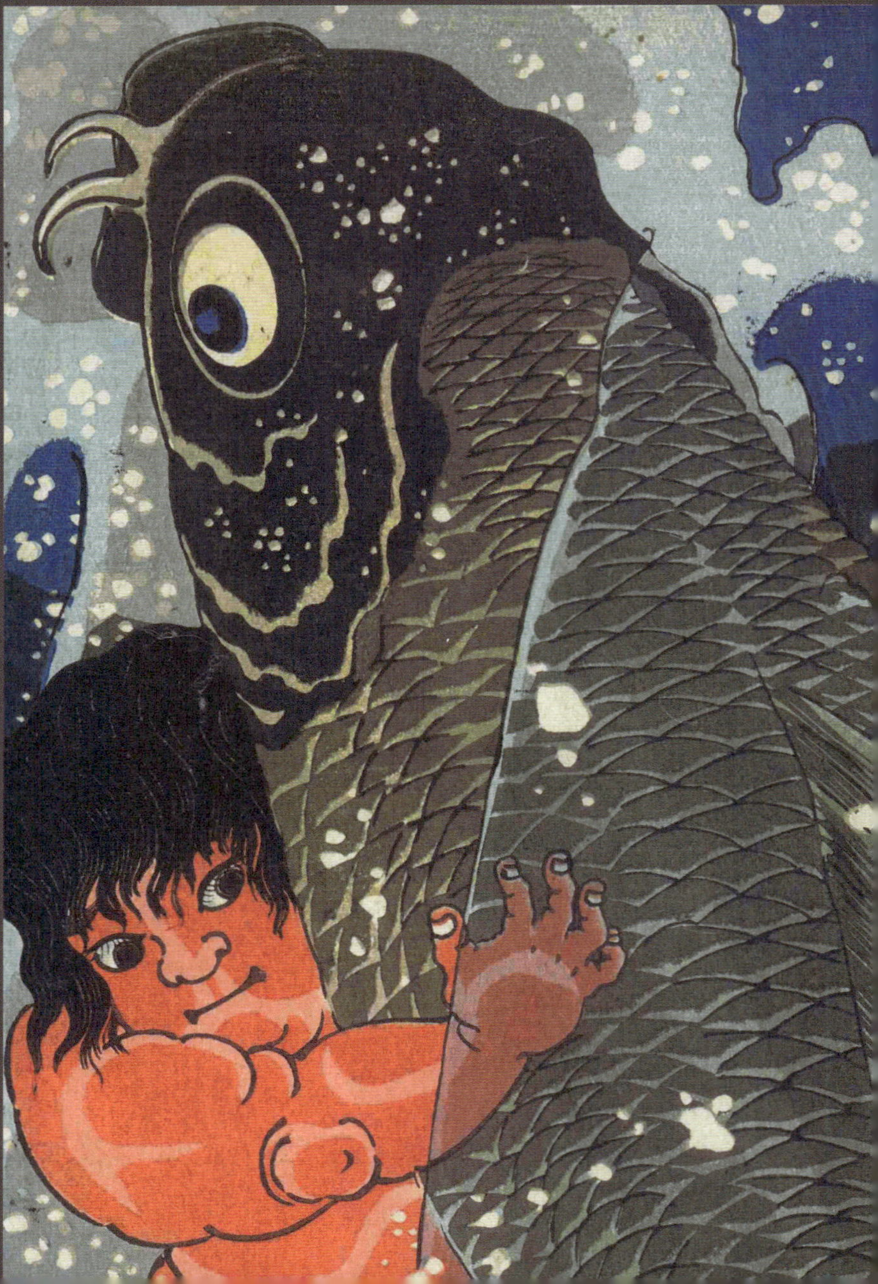

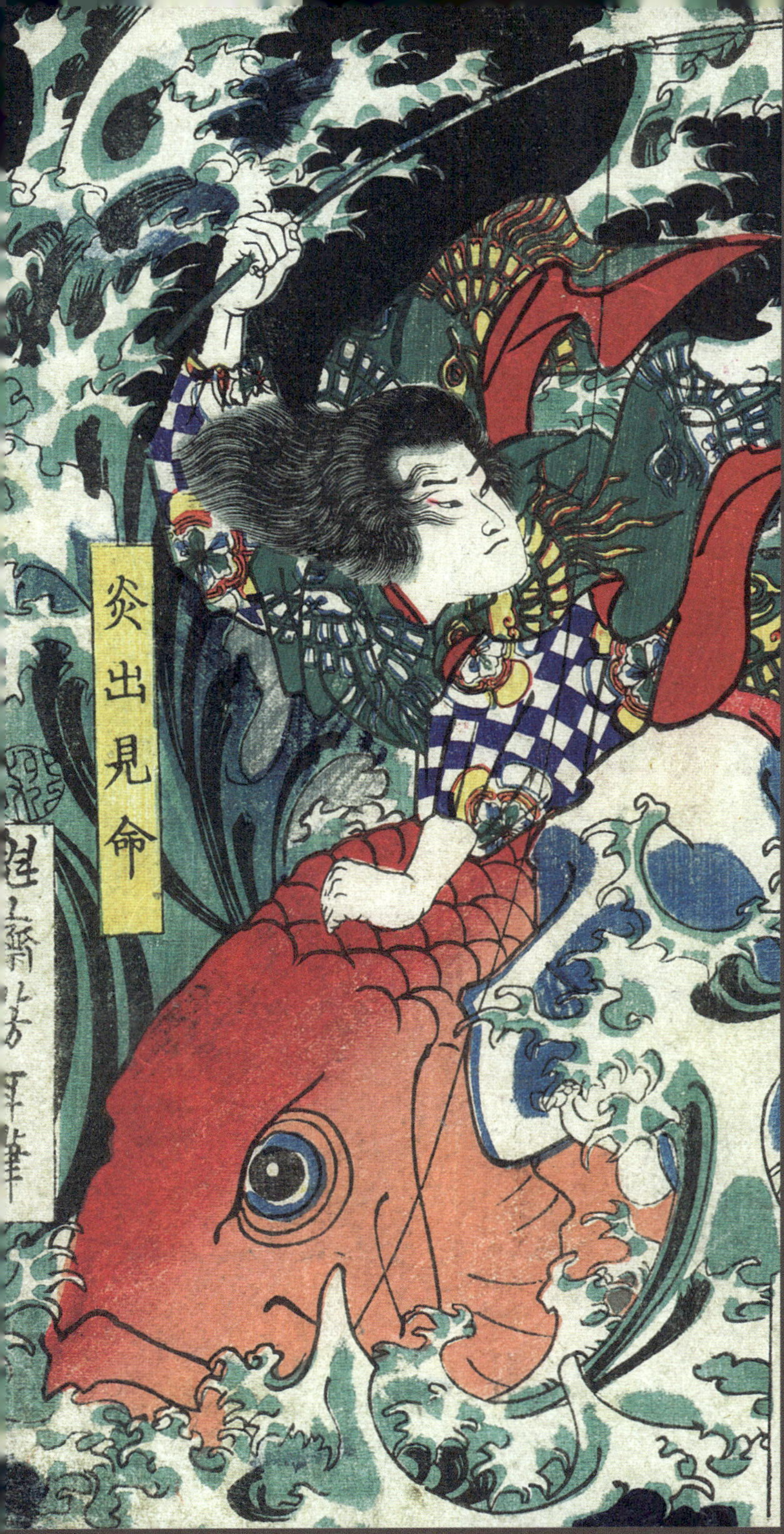

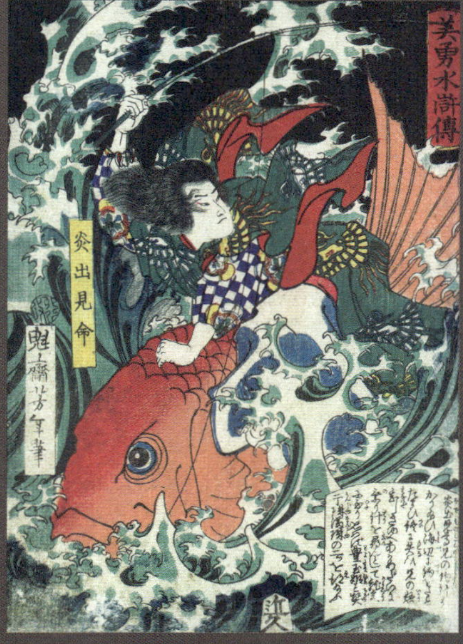

Hodemi-no Mikoto, from the series Beauty and Bravery in Suiko-den / Tsukioka Yoshitoshi

1867 / Photo : Aflo

Tsukioka Yoshitoshi depicted 50 pictures for this series, each of them expresses an old Japanese tale. This is the first picture in the series and features a story of Umisachi Yamasachi in Japanese mythology. Here, Hodemi-no Mikoto is on the way to the palace of the Dragon King under the sea. The story is about two brother gods, Hoderi-no Mikoto (widely known as Umisachi-hiko) who is good at fishing in the sea and Hodemi-no Mikoto (Yamasachi-hiko) who is good at hunting in mountains. One day, the brothers exchanged their livelihoods and their tools. Hodemi-no Mikoto lost his elder brother's fishhook, and drew his anger. Later, Hodemi-no Mikoto rode a sea bream to visit the palace under the sea and married Toyotama-hime, a daughter of the Dragon King. His flapping kimono sleeves effectively represent the powerful speed of the swimming sea bream. The strange image of the swelling water and his fishing pole create a large circular form, dramatically representing the story.

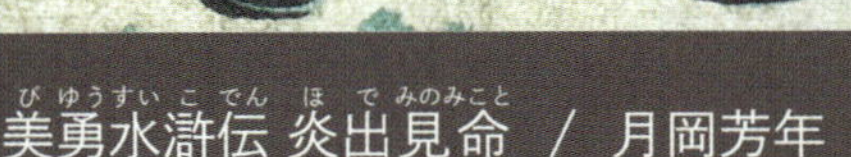

美勇水滸伝 炎出見命 ／ 月岡芳年

慶応3年（1867） ／ 提供：アフロ

月岡芳年が、日本の物語に取材して、50図を描いたうちの一図。シリーズの一番目に位置づけられる本図は、記紀神話の海幸山幸に基づき、竜宮へ向かう炎出見命（山幸彦）を描く。火照命（海幸彦）と炎出見命は兄弟で、それぞれ海での漁、山での猟を得意としていた。ある時兄弟がそれぞれの道具と生業を交換して出かけたところ、炎出見命は兄の釣り針を失くしてしまう。兄の怒りを買った炎出見命は、「あかめだい」に乗って龍宮を訪れ、豊玉姫と結ばれる。翻える衣から、勢いよく泳ぐ鯛のスピードが伝わる。奇怪に立ち上がる波と、炎出見命の持つ竿とが大きな円をつくり、物語を劇的に表現している。

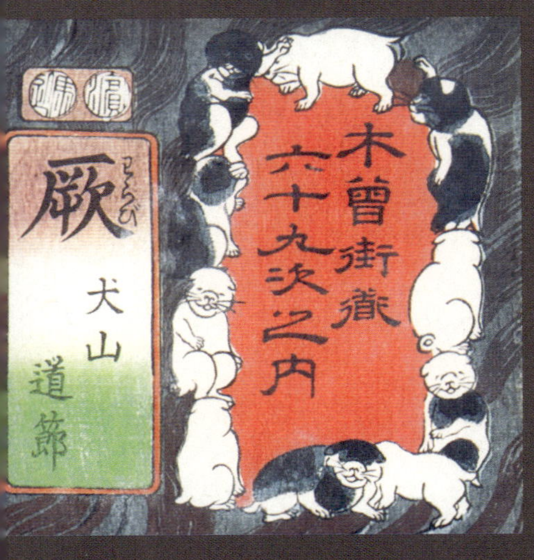

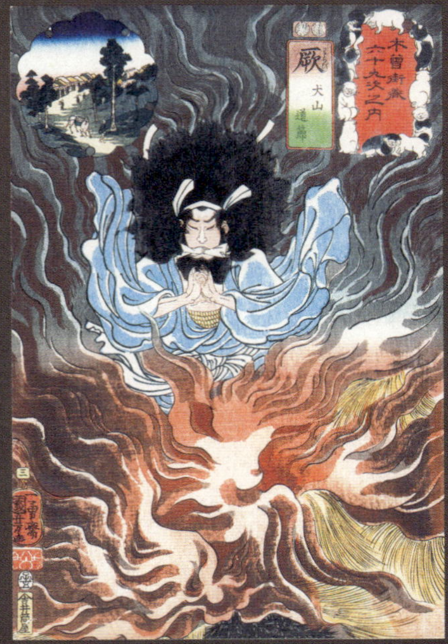

Inuyama Dōsetsu, Warabi, from the series The 69 Stations of the Kiso-kaidō Road / Utagawa Kuniyoshi

1852 / Hiroshige Museum of Art, Ena

This series consists of 71 pictures, each of them features a different town. But what Kuniyoshi depicted here was not usual landscapes, but famous scenes from Kabuki theaters or legends which he thought of, in association with the towns' names. The subjects of the pictures tell us that he was full of wit and made many plays on words. As for this picture, with the town's name being Warabi, he associated the phrase "fire of straw," "wara no hi" in Japanese. He depicted the warrior Inuyama Dōsetsu from the novel "Nansō Satomi Ha'kkenden," who is one of the eight warriors featured there and who is good at using fire in ninja martial arts. In the upper right corner of this picture, the title "The 69 Stations of the Kiso-kaidō Road" is written and surrounded by puppies. The blazing red fire rises upward and transforms into black smoke.

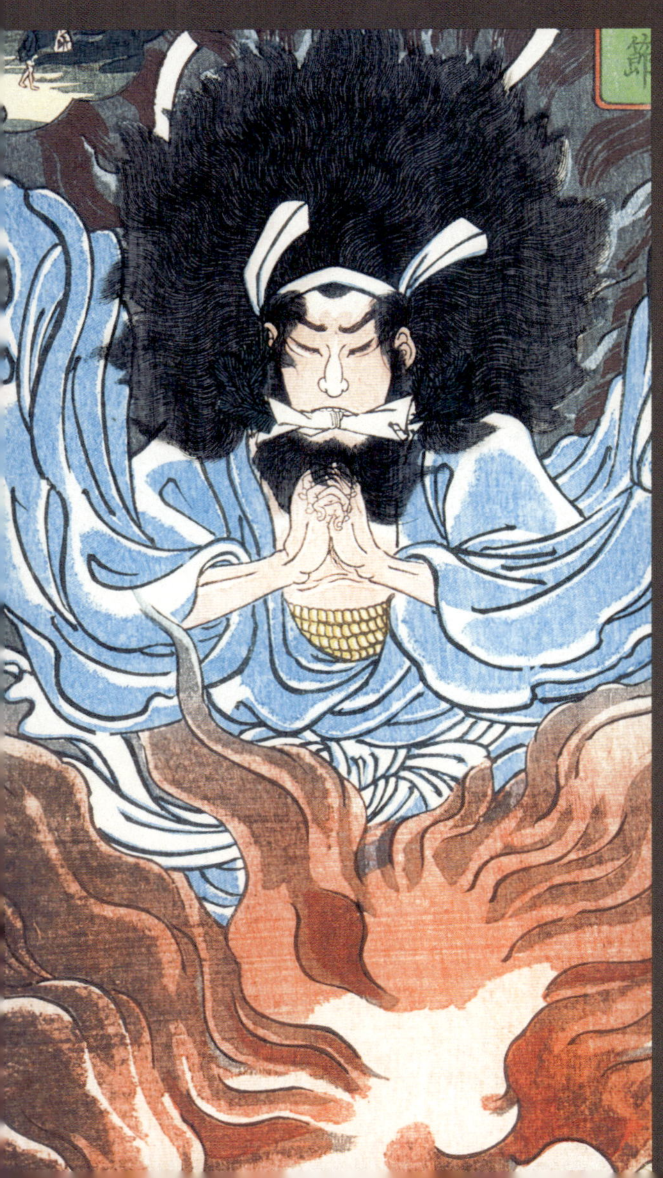

木曽街道六十九次之内 蕨 犬山道節 / 歌川国芳

嘉永 5 年（1852） / 中山道広重美術館蔵

木曽街道の 69 の宿場に日本橋と京都を加えた 71 図からなる本シリーズは、単なる名所風景画ではなく、各宿場名から語呂合わせで連想される伝説や歌舞伎の名場面を描く、国芳の機知に富んだ連作。本図は宿場名の「蕨」から、「藁の火」を連想し、『南総里見八犬伝』に登場する八犬士の一人、火遁の術を使う犬山道節を描く。凄まじい炎が、黒煙と化しながら立ち昇る。『八犬伝』にちなんで、画面右上のタイトルを子犬が囲んでいる。

Kamitsukeno Yatsunata and Sahohime, from the series
A Mirror of Famous Generals of Great Japan / Tsukioka Yoshitoshi

1879 / Tokyo Metropolitan Library

"A Mirror of Famous Generals of Great Japan" consists of 51 pictures, featuring famous generals such as Amaterasu Ōmikami (the Sun Goddess), a shogun Tokugawa Iemitsu of Edo Bakufu, other shogun, heroic figures, and feudal warlords. This picture features the story of the famous warrior Yatsunata in Japanese mythology, but the real starring character would be Empress Sahohime who is almost swallowed by blazing fire. She is the wife of Emperor Suinin. Her close elder brother Sahohiko orders her to assassinate the emperor. She accepts and tries to kill him, but fails to do so, because of her attachment to her husband. She confesses the conspiracy to the emperor and goes back to her brother's place. Then, Yatsunata sets fire to Inagi Castle where Sahohiko and Sahohime are holed up in. Sahohime passes her and the emperor's baby to people outside the castle. Then, she goes back into the fire and is burned to death. The blazing fire fills the entire frame and creates a bold composition. The contrast between the dark colors of Yatsunata's army and the bright colors of Sahohime produces a dramatic impression.

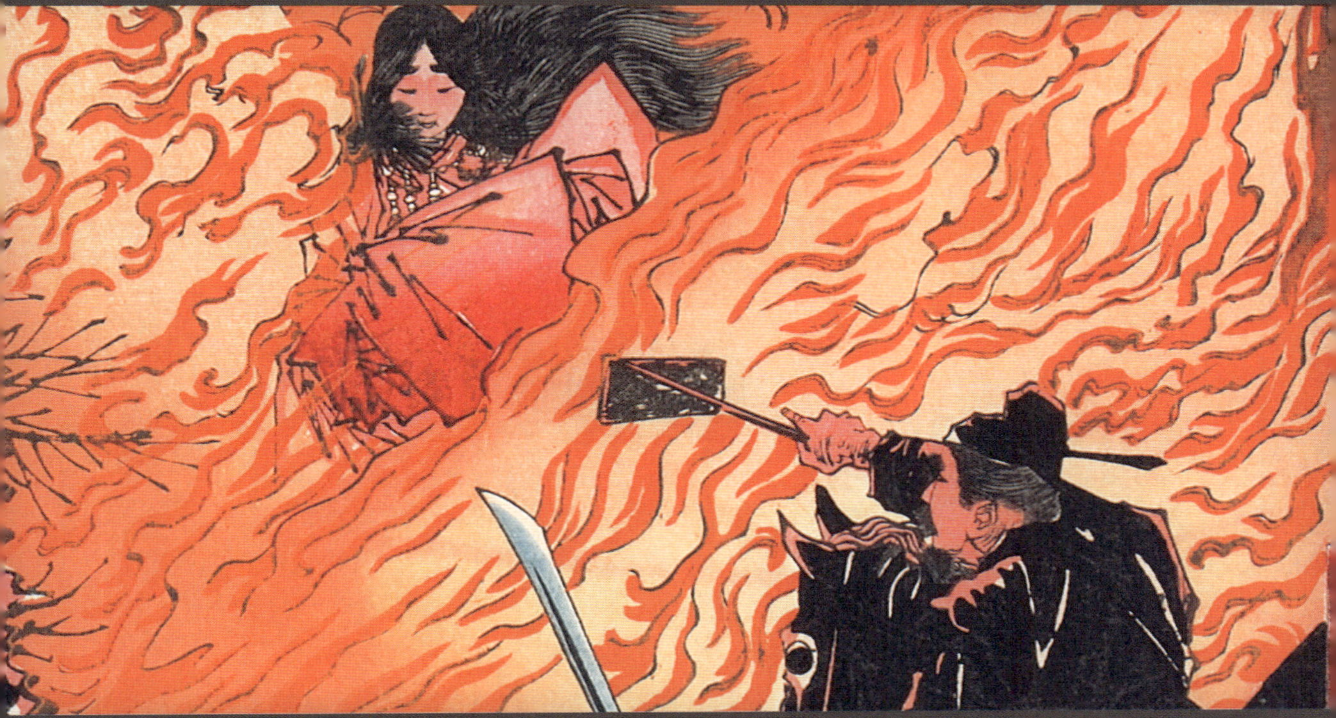

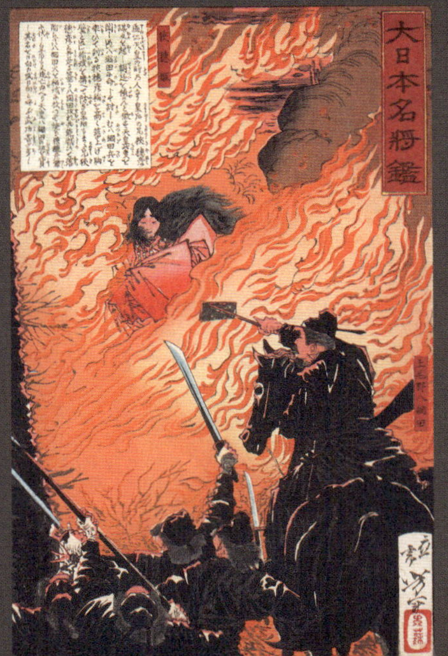

大日本名将鑑 上毛野八綱田 狭穂姫 ／
月岡芳年

明治 12 年（1879） ／ 東京都立中央図書館蔵

『大日本名将鑑』は、天磐戸の天照大神から徳川家光まで、将軍・英雄・戦国大名などの「名将」を描いた 51 図のシリーズ。本図が描く「名将」は記紀神話に登場する武人八綱田であるが、主役は燃え盛る火に呑み込まれようとする狭穂姫だろう。垂仁天皇の妻・狭穂姫は、兄の狭穂彦から天皇暗殺を命じられるが果たせず、天皇に兄の謀計を白状し、兄が立て籠る稲城に去る。火を放たれた狭穂姫は、身籠もっていた天皇の子を城の外へ預け、再び火の中へ戻り兄と共に焼死したという。画面のほとんどを燃え盛る炎が占める大胆な構図。敵味方の明暗の対比も劇的な効果を高めている。

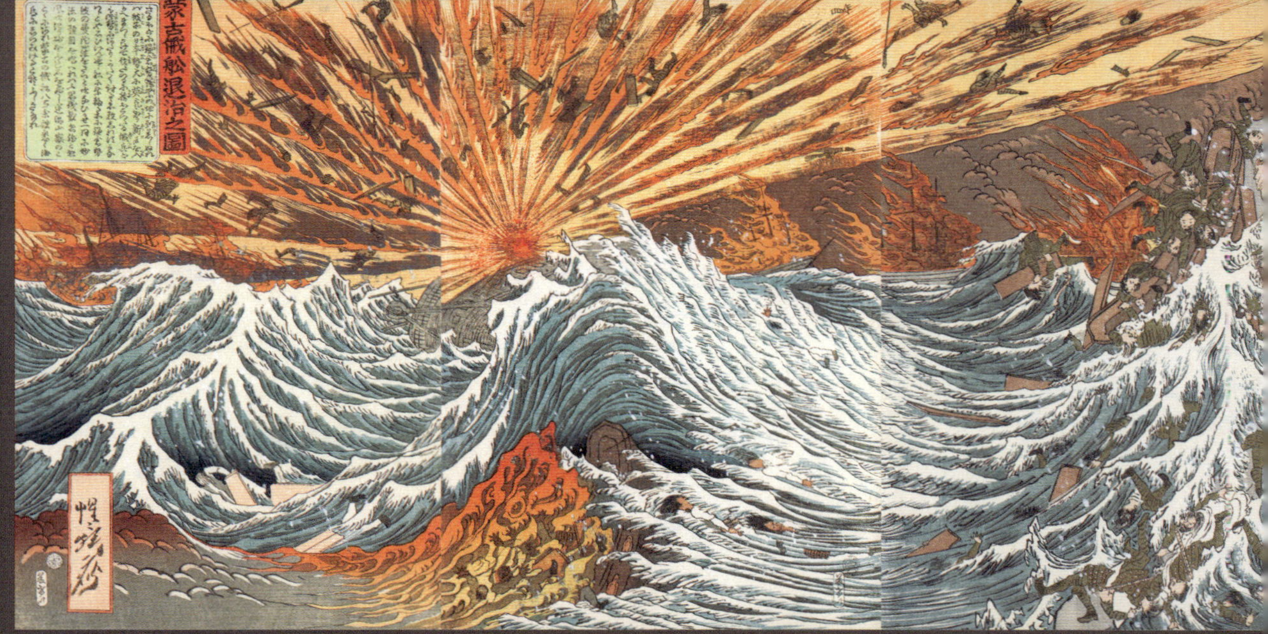

Extermination of Mongolian Ships /
Kawanabe Kyōsai

1863 / Israel Goldman Collection, London
Photo：Art Research Center, Ritsumeikan University

The Mongolian army attempted to invade Japan from the sea in the Kamakura period of the 13th century, but thanks to strong winds, it resulted in failure. Japanese people called the winds "Kamikaze," meaning "Divine Winds." Under the title of the legendary old battle, this picture depicts a coeval incident which happened in May 1863. Choshu Domain attacked American, French and Dutch ships with gunfire in the Kanmon Straits. Here, debris and people are flying off from a bombarded ship, while others are thrown out into the sea from a sinking burning ship. Kyōsai did not only spectacularly depict, but also scrupulously illustrated in order to express the brutality of the scene.

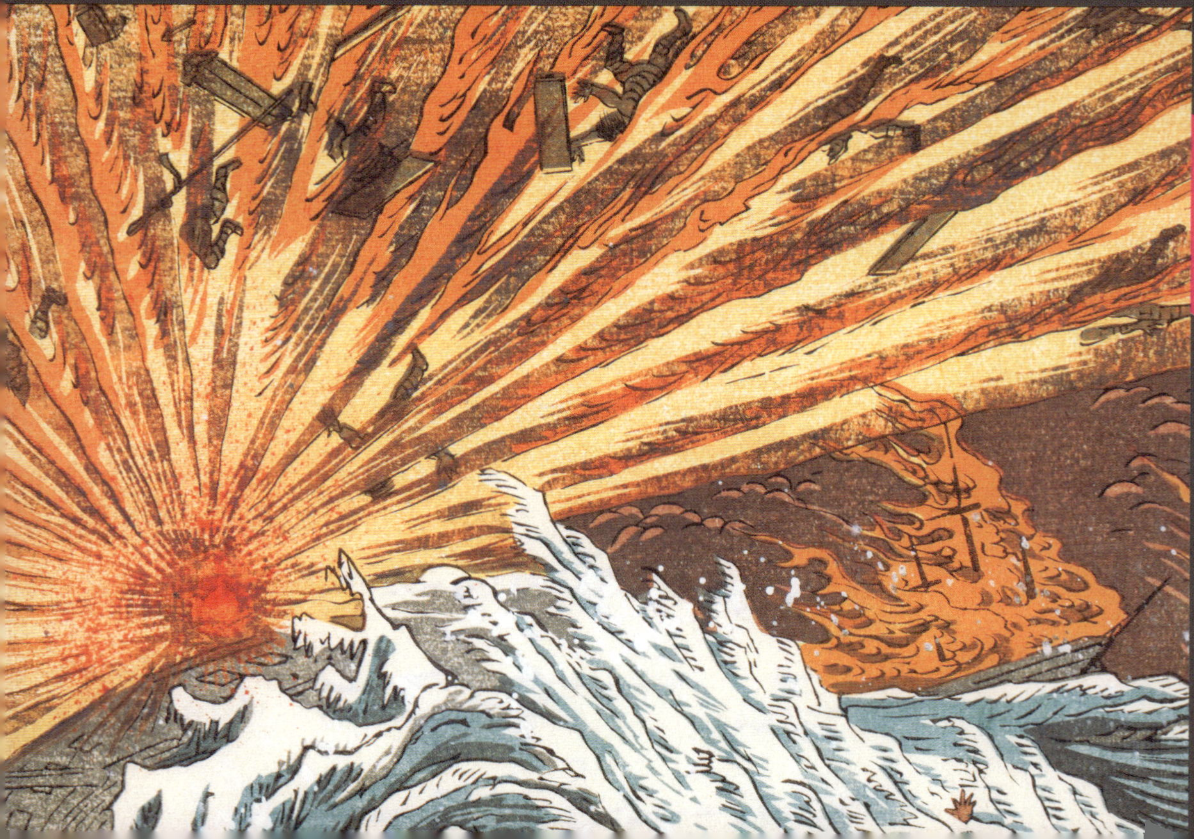

蒙古賊船退治之図 ／ 河鍋暁斎

文久 3 年（1863）／ イスラエル・ゴールドマン・コレクション
Photo：立命館大学アート・リサーチセンター

「神風」による勝利と伝説化された鎌倉時代の元軍の日本侵攻「蒙古襲来」の名を借りて、同時代の事件 —— 文久3年（1863）5 月に長州藩が馬関海峡（現関門海峡）を航行する米仏蘭船を砲撃した事件 —— を描いたもの。砲撃を受けた船から火炎や破片や人が飛び散り、燃えながら沈みゆく船からは、人がこぼれ落ち溺れて波に消えていく。壮観でありながら、生々しく残酷な状況が克明に描かれる。

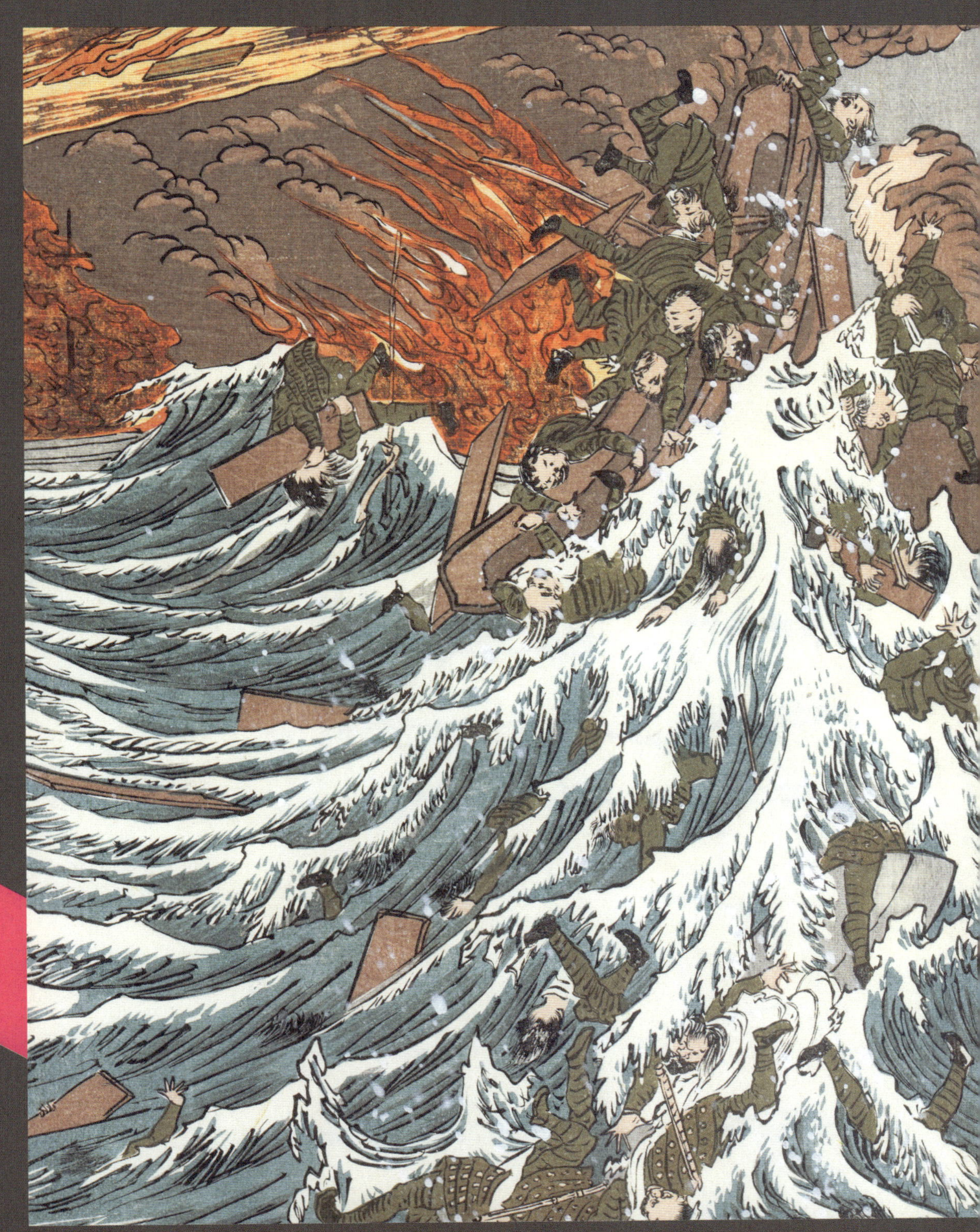

怪異の

爆発、落雷、雲煙、波濤。えも言われぬ怪異のおぞましさや凄まじさを表現するために、絵師たちはこれらの現象を利用した。先行作例を巧みに引用し、固定した形を持たないこれらの現象に、さまざまな形を与えていった。特殊な効果を駆使して物語や心情を伝える技術は、今日の漫画やアニメにも受け継がれている。

Monstrous Energy

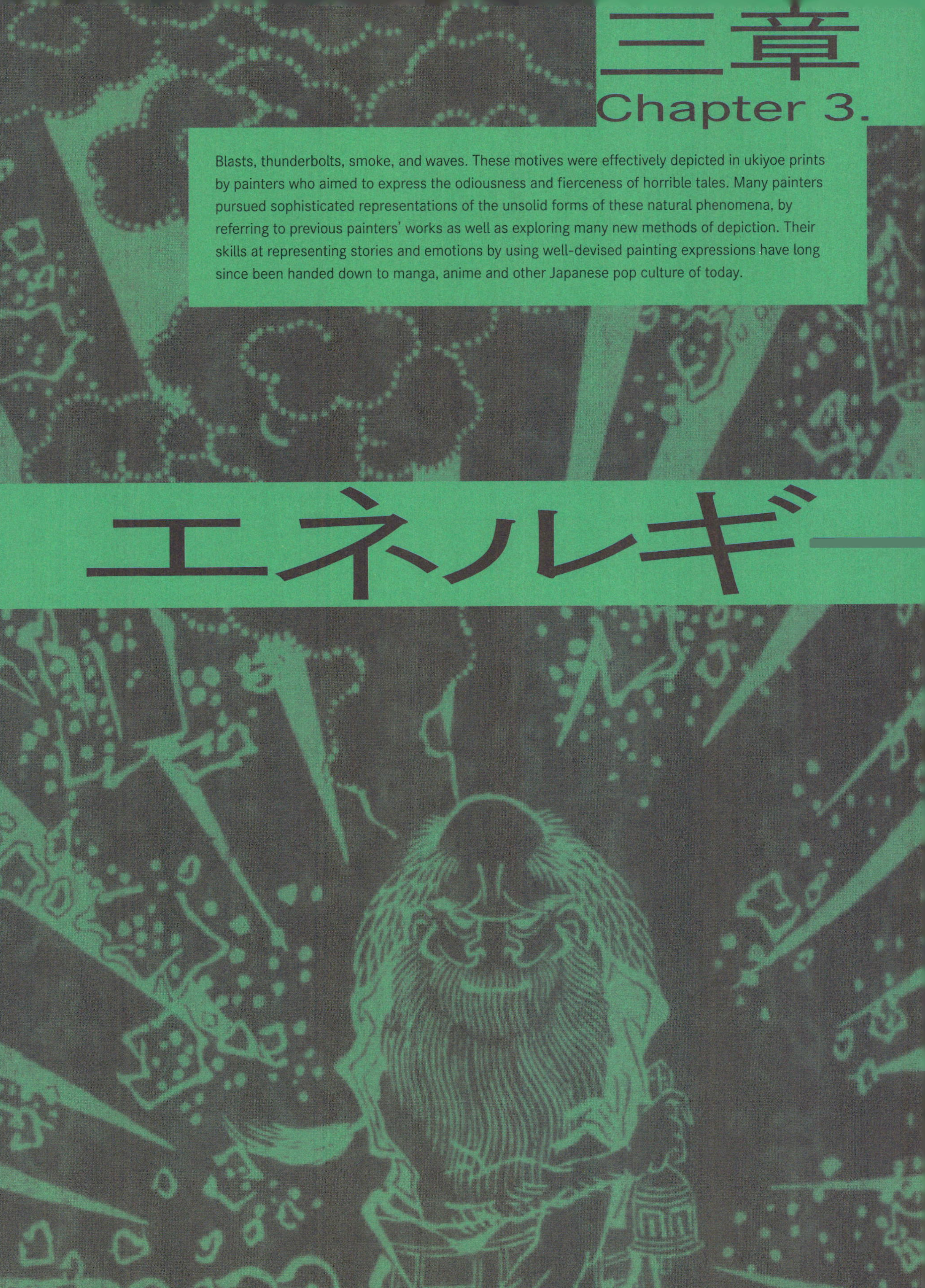

三章
Chapter 3.

Blasts, thunderbolts, smoke, and waves. These motives were effectively depicted in ukiyoe prints by painters who aimed to express the odiousness and fierceness of horrible tales. Many painters pursued sophisticated representations of the unsolid forms of these natural phenomena, by referring to previous painters' works as well as exploring many new methods of depiction. Their skills at representing stories and emotions by using well-devised painting expressions have long since been handed down to manga, anime and other Japanese pop culture of today.

エネルギー

The Strange Tales of the Bow Moon, The Side Story of Chinzei Hachirō Tametomo
The third volume of the first part Mōun Blasts a Stone Coffin and Emerges
Texts by Kyokutei Bakin / Print illustrations by Katsushika Hokusai

Published in 1808 / National Diet Library, Japan

"The Strange Tales of the Bow Moon" were published during 1807 to 1811. It is a fantastical lengthy novel featuring the warrior Minamoto-no Tametomo who is believed to have been exiled to Izu-ōshima Island where he eventually killed himself. But in this novel, he leaves Izu-ōshima alive and moves to Ryukyu islands (another name for Okinawa), where he re-establishes a kingdom. This picture depicts Mōun awakening from a long sleep and blasting a stone coffin open. In a later episode called The Ryukyu Kingdom in this novel, he becomes a constant enemy of Tametomo. Mōun practices sorcery to take over a country, and his true identity is revealed to be the monster Kyūryū. Here, the emergence of Mōun who is, so to speak, the end boss of the story, is spectacularly depicted with radial lines, flying debris, blast waves, as well as exaggerated gestures and facial expressions of people.

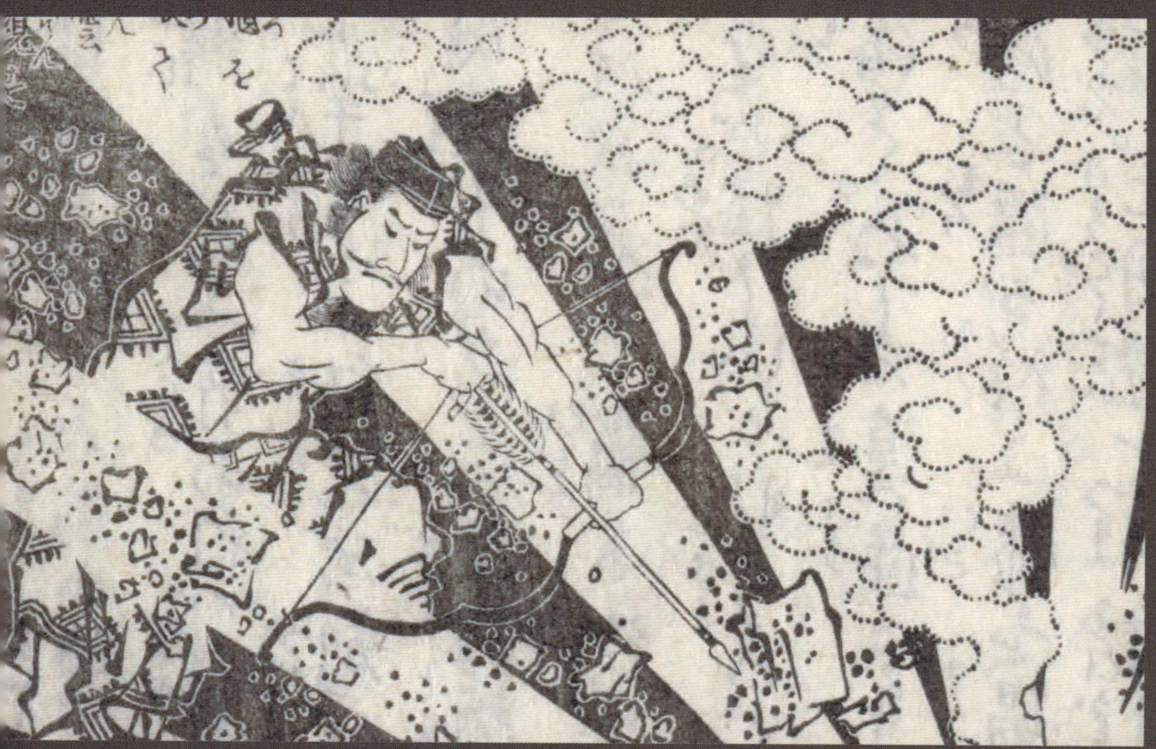

Print illustrations by Katsusika Hokusai

When he was around 45 years old, Hokusai started working on print illustrations for lengthy novels, and increasingly got into it. Around that time, lengthy novels became a voguish genre of literature and was called Yomihon. Especially, the lengthy novels Hokusai worked on with the popular author Kyokutei Bakin (1767-1848) became huge hits one after another. Hokusai is even regarded as a key person in the creation of the popularity of Yomihon. He worked on over 1,100 print illustrations, which were for over 200 lengthy novels. Hokusai dynamically depicted complicated stories in limited paper frames, by using only black ink. His print illustrations greatly influenced many future generation ukiyoe painters. One of which was the younger painter Kuniyoshi who took inspirations from Hokusai's lengthy novel "New Suiko-gaden" and created his own Suikoden series.

北斎の挿絵

北斎は45歳ころから、江戸で流行しはじめた「読本」と呼ばれる長編小説の挿絵に取り組み、傾注していく。とりわけ曲亭馬琴（1767-1848）とタッグを組んで次々とヒット作を手がけ、北斎によって読本は大いに流行したとさえいわれる。手がけた読本挿絵は200冊1100図にも及ぶという。国芳の水滸伝シリーズの範となった『新編水滸画伝』はじめ、複雑な内容を限られた画面に墨一色で臨場感たっぷりに伝える挿絵の数々は、後世の浮世絵師たちに絶大な影響を与えた。

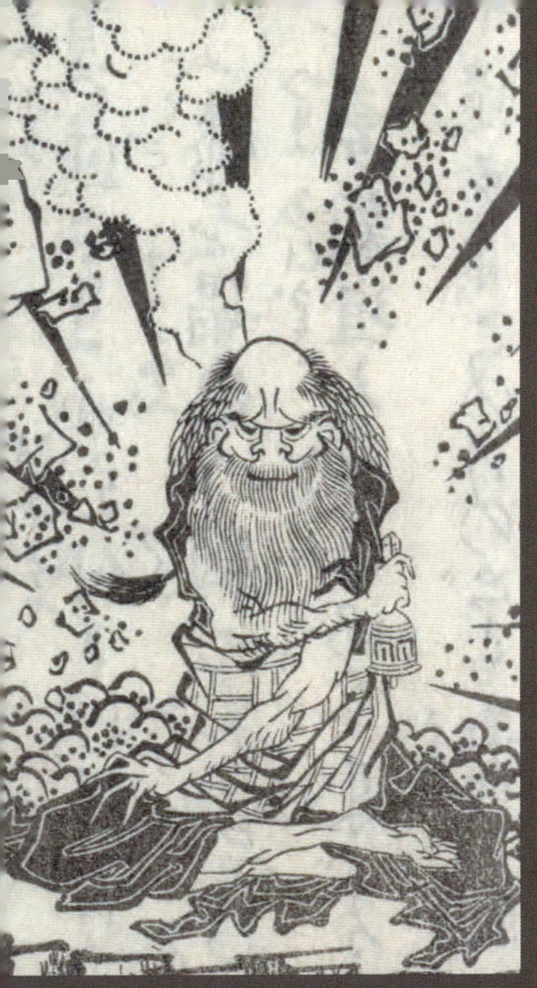
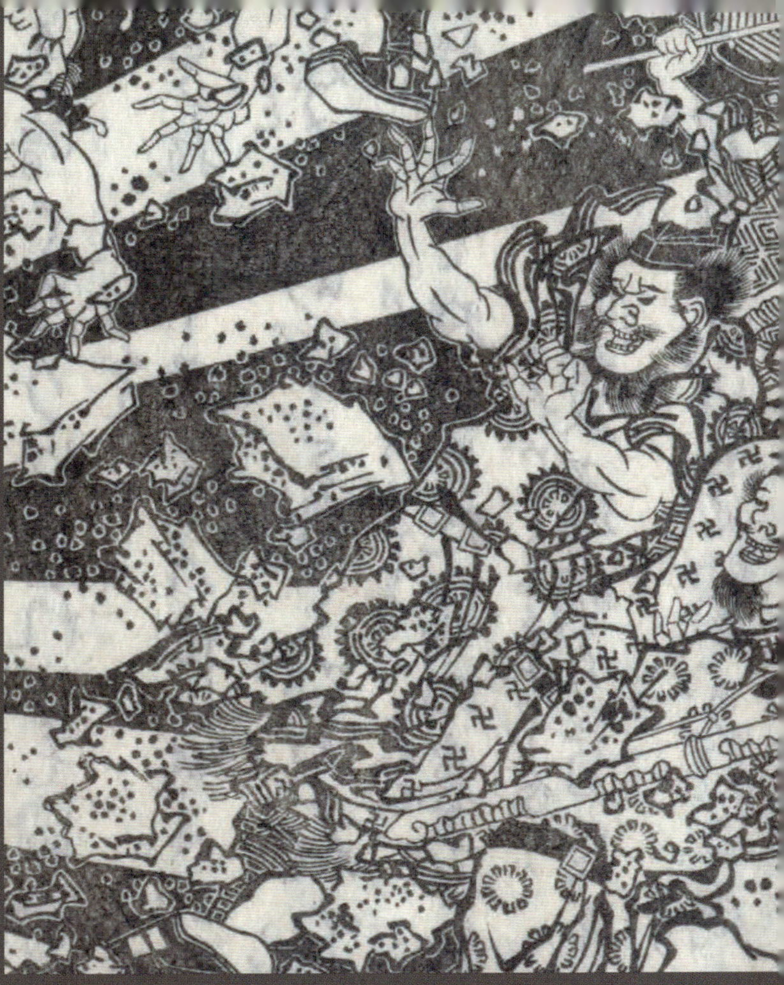

『鎮西八郎為朝外伝 椿説弓張月』前編巻之三より
「石柩を破り矇雲出現す」曲亭馬琴著 ／ 葛飾北斎画

文化 5 年（1808）刊 ／ 国立国会図書館蔵

『椿説弓張月』（1807-1811年刊行）は、配流先の伊豆大島で自害したと伝えられる平安時代の武将源為朝が、生きて琉球に渡り王国を再建するという長編の伝奇小説。本図は琉球王国篇で宿敵となる矇雲が、石棺を爆発して長い眠りから復活する場面。妖術を駆使して国を乗っ取る矇雲の正体は、虹竜と呼ばれる化物だった。放射状の線と飛び散る破片、爆風を受ける人たちの大袈裟な身振りや表情が、ラスボスの登場を彩る。

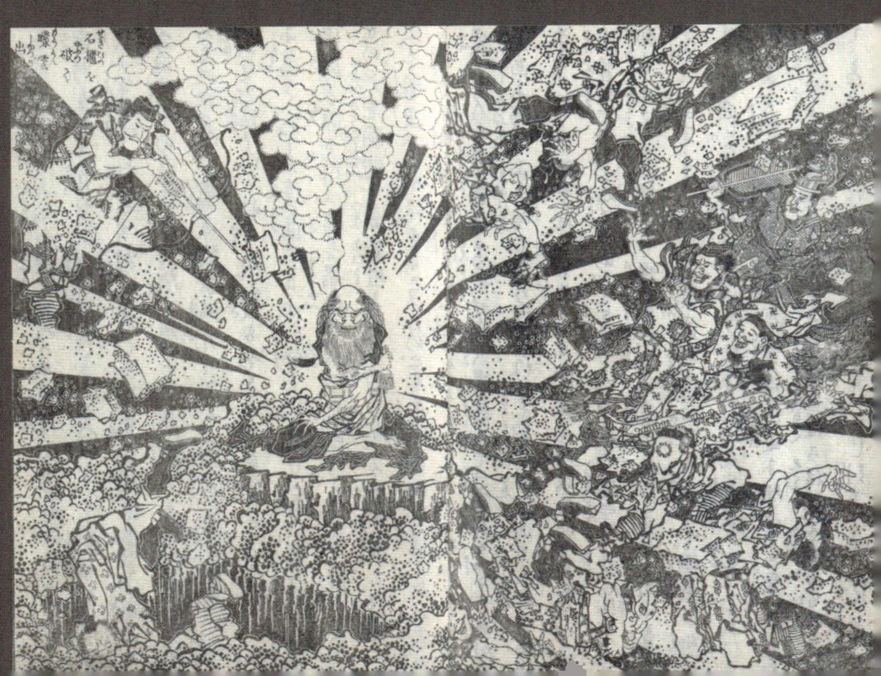

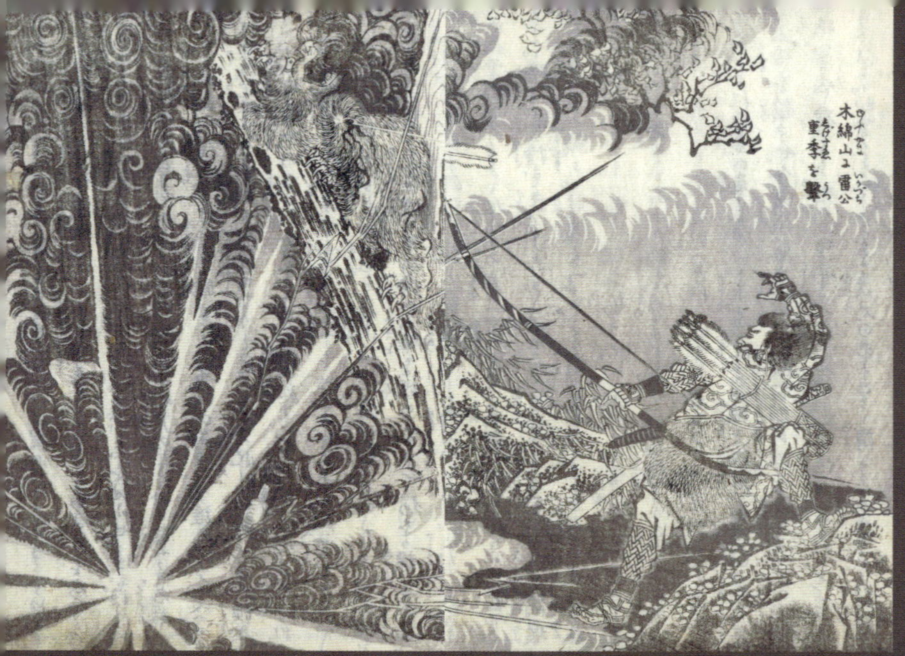

The Strange Tales of the Bow Moon, The Side Stories of Chinzei Hachirō Tametomo,
The first volume of the first part Ikazuchi Defeats Shigesue at Mount Yufu
Texts by Kyokutei Bakin / Print illustrations by Katsushika Hokusai
Published in 1807 / National Diet Library, Japan

In this story, Minamoto-no Tametomo and his vassal Sudō Shigesue are attacked by a giant snake in Mount Momiji.
Shigesue cuts the snake's body open and takes a treasure ball out from inside. The thunder god Ikazuchi aspires to deprive
Shigesue of the ball, and drops ground-breaking thunder on him. Tametomo, who is good at shooting, instantaneously shoots
at Ikazuchi, but it does not help Shigesue to avoid being smashed up by thunder. In the bottom left of the picture, Shigesue only
shows his face, hand and foot among the pervasive smoke. The radial lines express the huge power of thunder.

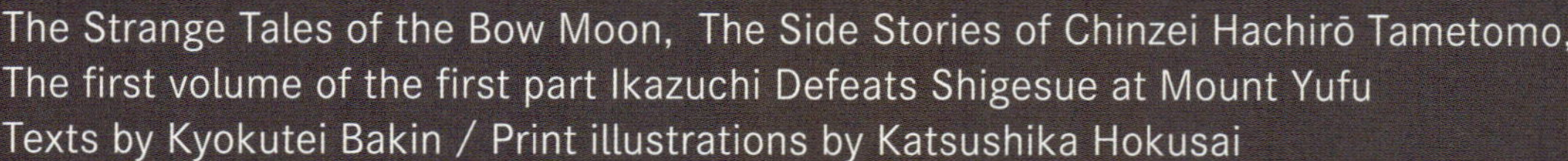

『鎮西八郎為朝外伝 椿説弓張月』
前編巻之一より
「木綿山に雷公 重季を撃」
曲亭馬琴著 ／ 葛飾北斎画
文化 4 年（1807）刊 ／ 国立国会図書館蔵

源為朝と須藤重季の主従は紅葉山で蟒蛇（巨大な蛇）
におそわれる。重季が蟒蛇の体を割き、その体内か
ら玉を取り出すと、玉を狙って訪れた雷公が天地を
震わせるほどの雷を重季目がけて落とす。為朝はと
っさに得意の弓で雷公を射るが、重季はばらばらに
砕け散る。立ちこめる煙に覆われながら、重季は顔
と手、足をわずかに覗かせる。死にゆく重季の身体
は薄墨であらわされ、雷の威力は放射状の線で表現
されている。

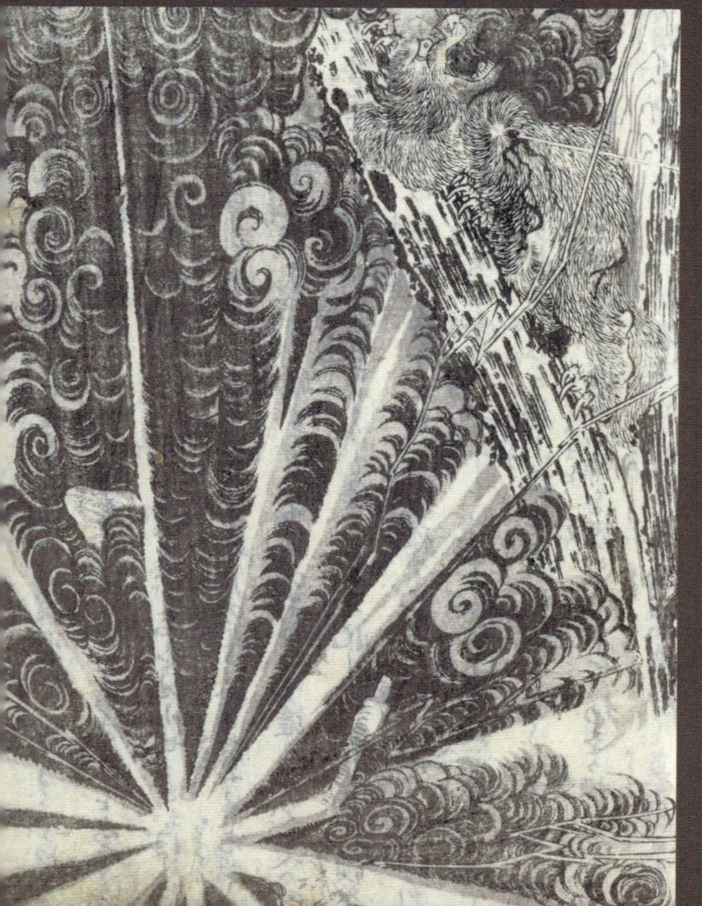

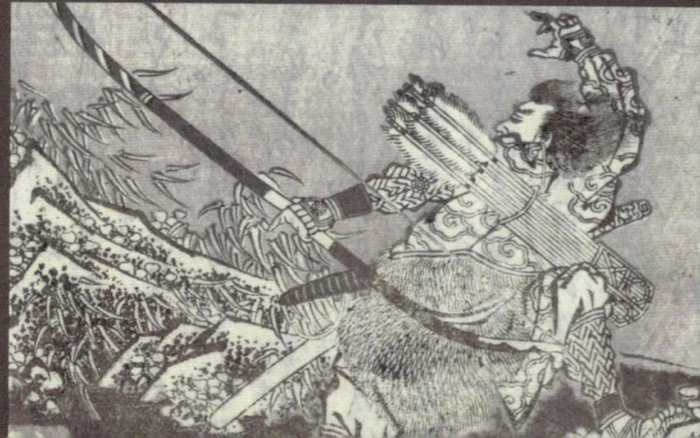

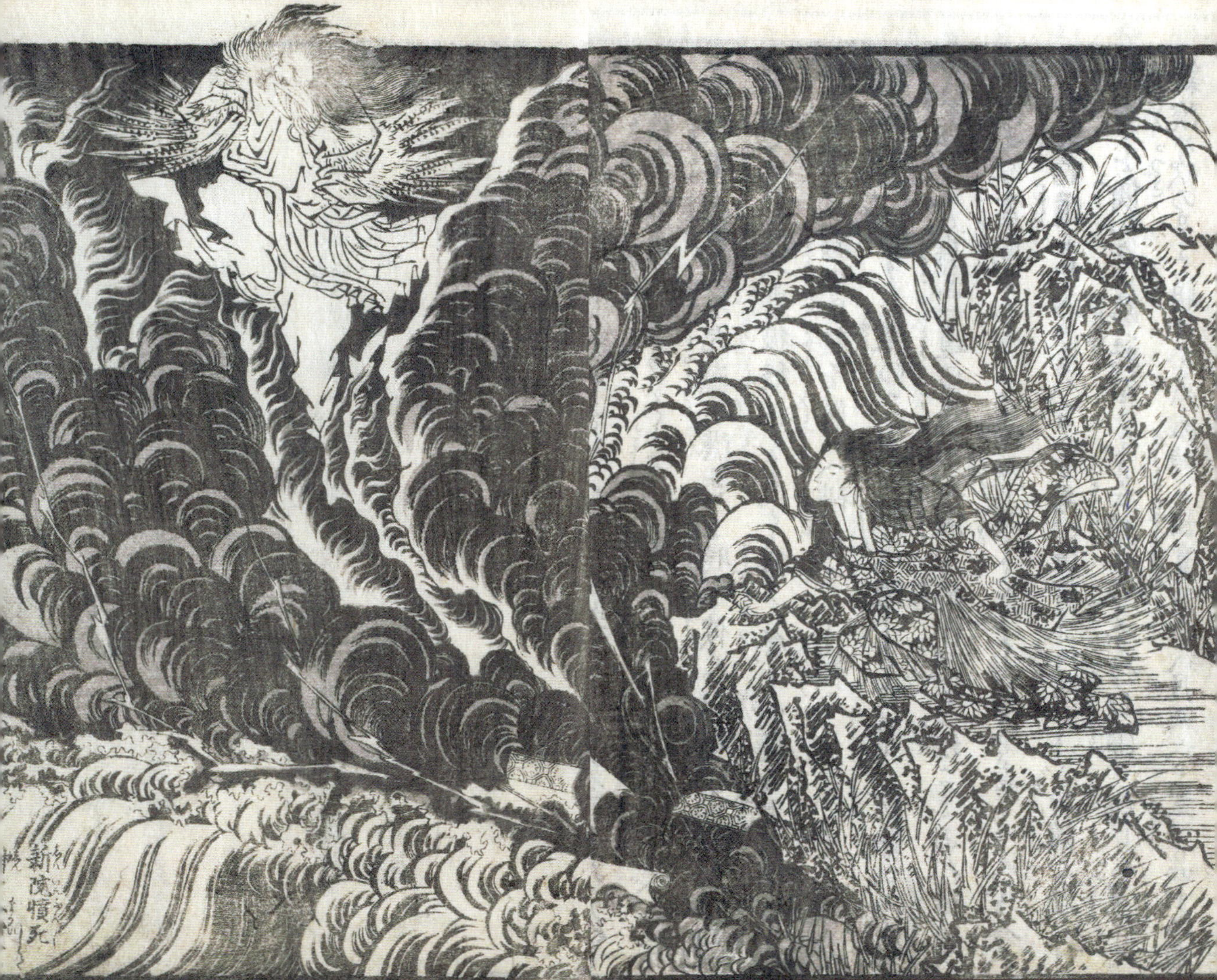

The Strange Tales of the Bow Moon, The Side Stories of Chinzei Hachirō Tametomo, The sixth volume of the first part The Retired Emperor Sutoku Devotes His Soul to Devildom

Texts by Kyokutei Bakin / Print illustrations by Katsushika Hokusai

Published in 1807 / National Diet Library, Japan

Legends say that the retired emperor Sutoku transformed into a long-nosed goblin in Sanuki Province, where he was exiled to. He is regarded as the most frightening vengeful spirit in Japanese history. In "The Strange Tales of the Bow Moon," Sutoku transforms into the goblin, after declaring himself to be a protective deity of the warrior Tametomo and his wife Shiranui, which she is there to witness. Here, as a goblin with a beak and wings, Sutoku flies up and goes outside the picture frame. He generates heavy clouds and lightning, which strongly blow Shiranui's kimono and hair.

『鎮西八郎為朝外伝 椿説弓張月』前編巻之六より
「新院憤死 神を魔界に投ず」曲亭馬琴著 ／ 葛飾北斎画

文化 4 年（1807）刊 ／ 国立国会図書館蔵

日本史上もっとも恐れられる怨霊の一人、崇徳院は、配流先の讃岐国で生きながら天狗になったと伝えられる。『椿説弓張月』に登場する崇徳院は、源為朝の妻・白縫の前で、為朝と白縫の守り神になることを宣言しながら天狗へ変化する。嘴と羽を持つ天狗姿となり、画面の枠外へと舞い上がる崇徳院。猛烈な雲気と稲光を発生させ、白縫の衣や髪を激しくなびかせている。

The Strange Tales from Hokuetsu Region The Author Konron Struck by a Tornado in Niigata Texts by Tachibana Konron / Print illustrations by Katsushika Hokusai

1812 / University of Toyama Library

A book of essays written by Tachibana Konron, a literary man in Echigo Province, a part of Hokuetsu. It includes tales of dragons, seven wonders of the region, tales of ghosts, and other strange stories. With well-liked Hokusai's print illustrations of ominous scenes, the book gained enormous popularity.

『北越奇談』より
「編者崑崙新潟にて竜巻にあふ」
橘崑崙著 ／ 葛飾北斎画

文化9年（1812）刊 ／
富山大学附属図書館蔵

越後の文人・橘 崑崙による北越地方にまつわる随筆集。龍の話、越後七不思議、怪談・奇談などが、北斎の得意とするおどろおどろしい光景とあいまって、評判を呼んだ。

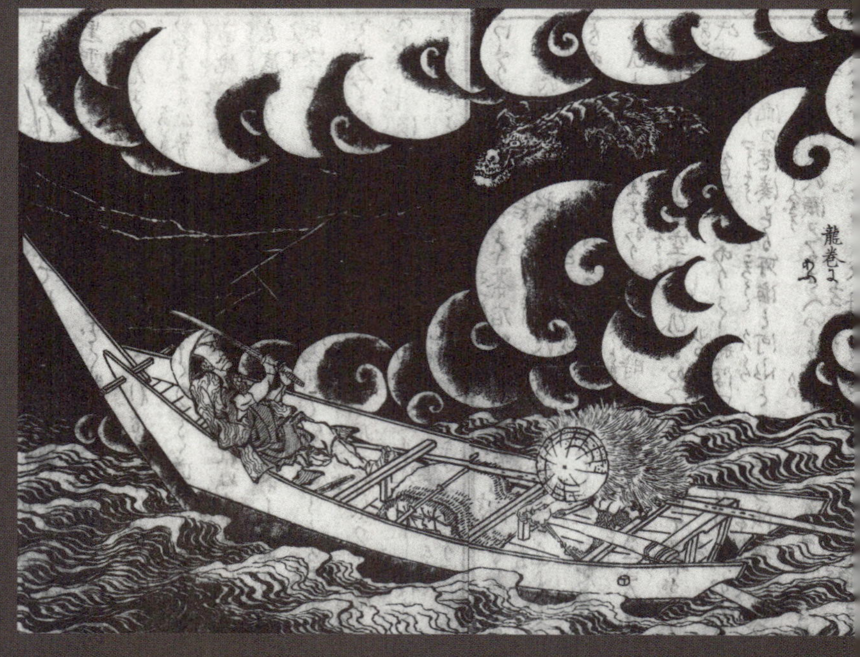

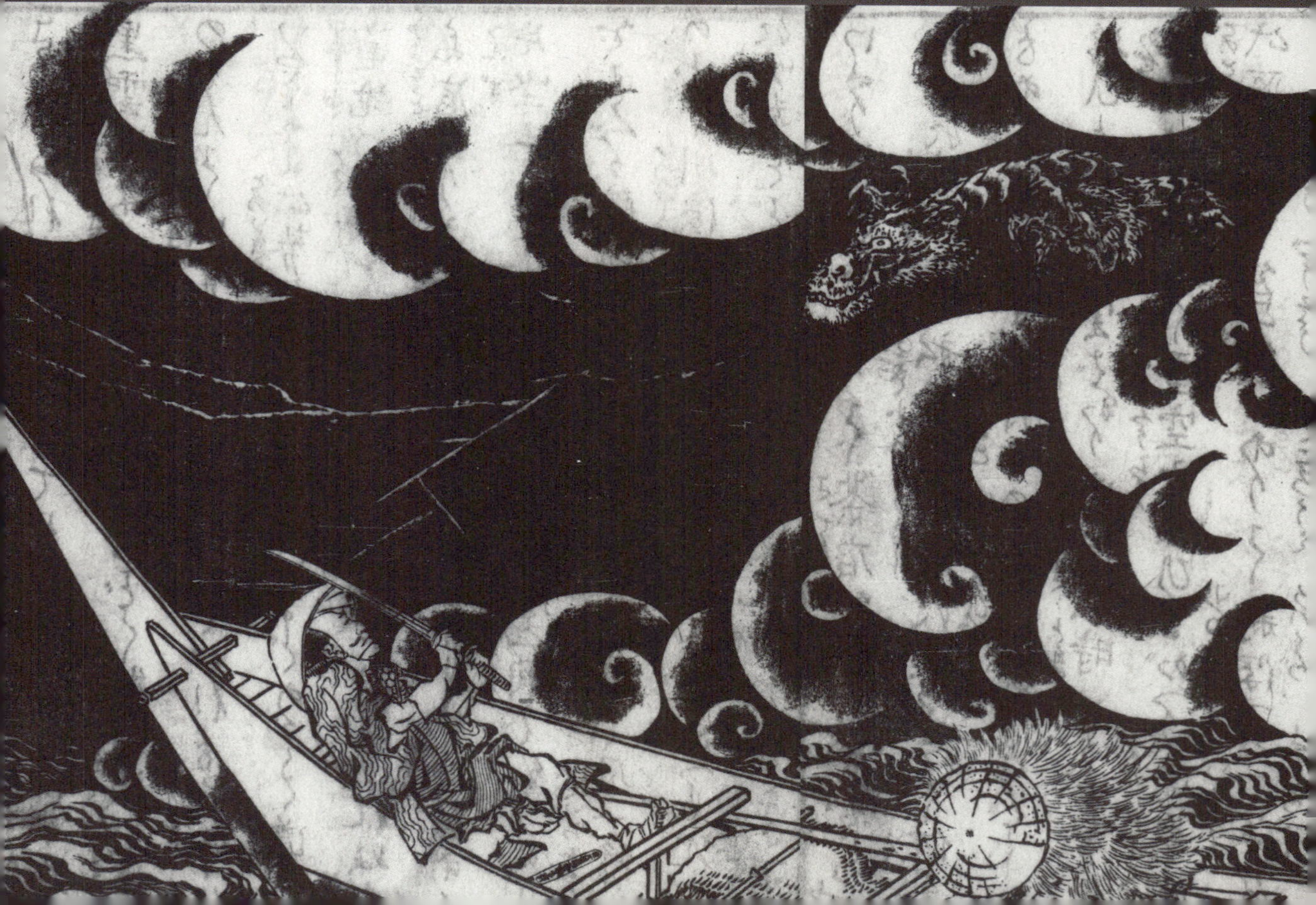

The Life of Shakyamuni Illustrated, Volume Six
The King Ruriō Fired the Palace and Killed the Shakya Clan and their Vassals
Texts by Yamada Isai / Print illustrations by Katsushika Hokusai

1812 / Shinshiro City Public Library

This is a scene from the life history book of Shakyamuni. It is one of Hokusai's print illustration works for lengthy novels called Yomihon which he did in his final years. Ruriō is a king who attempted to destroy the Shakya clan in ancient India. As Shakyamuni predicted that the clan would be judged by the heavens, every last one of them including the king as well as the palace buildings were smashed up by hundreds and thousands of thunderbolts, according to the legend. The picture depicts the thunder god lifting a drum onto his back, and the swirls which emerged from the impact of thunder dropped by a dragon god. The swirls and debris of the palace represent the disastrous destruction.

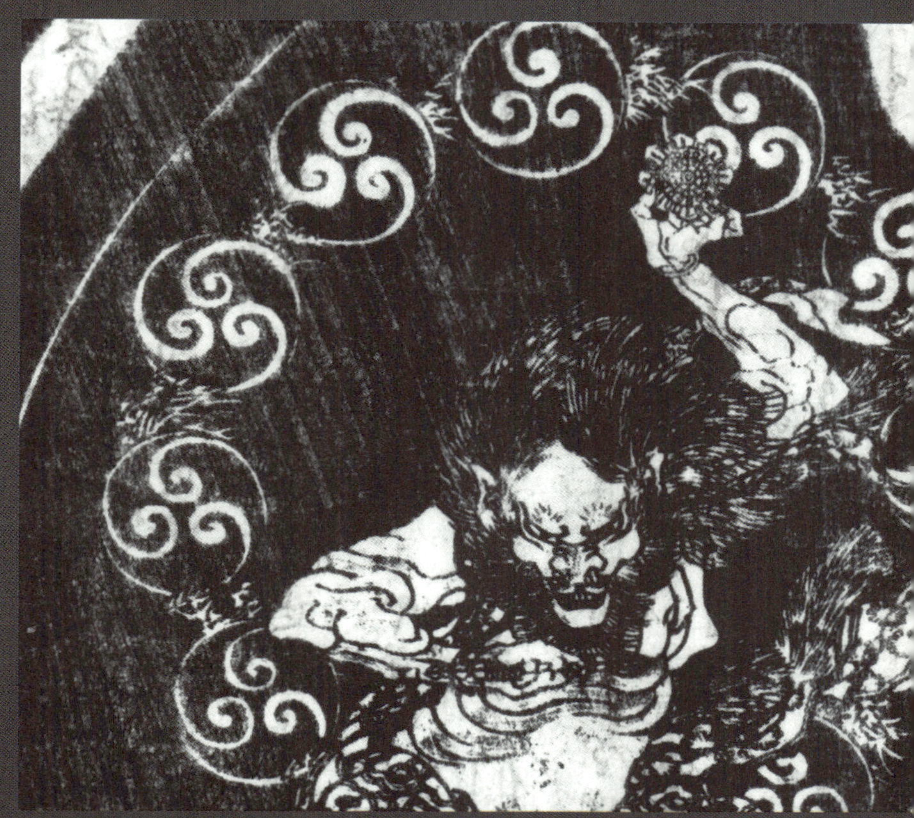

『釈迦御一代記図会』六より「暴悪を罰して天雷流離王が王宮を焼君臣を撃殺す図」
山田意斎著　／　葛飾北斎画

弘化2年（1845）／ 新城図書館ふるさと情報館蔵

北斎が晩年に手がけた読本挿絵のうち、釈迦の伝記の一場面。「流離王」は古代インドで釈迦の一族を滅ぼそうとした王。釈迦が「天に裁かれるだろう」と予言した通り、王のみならず王宮とそこにいた人々は一人残らず「百千の雷」により微塵に砕け散ったという。描かれるのは、雷太鼓を背負う雷神と、竜神が落とした雷の衝撃だ。渦巻きと、そこに巻き込まれる王宮の破片によって、絶望的な破壊が表現されている。

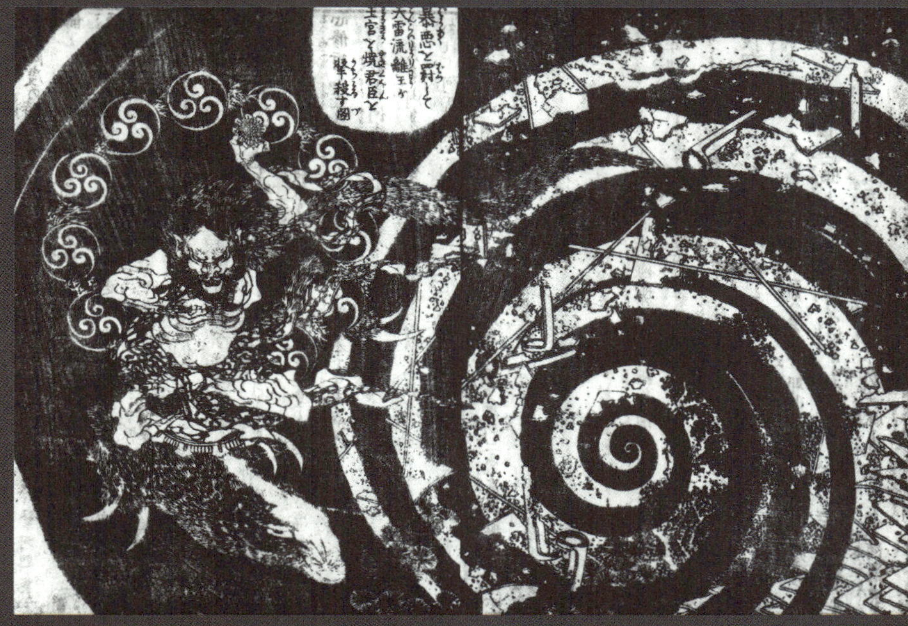

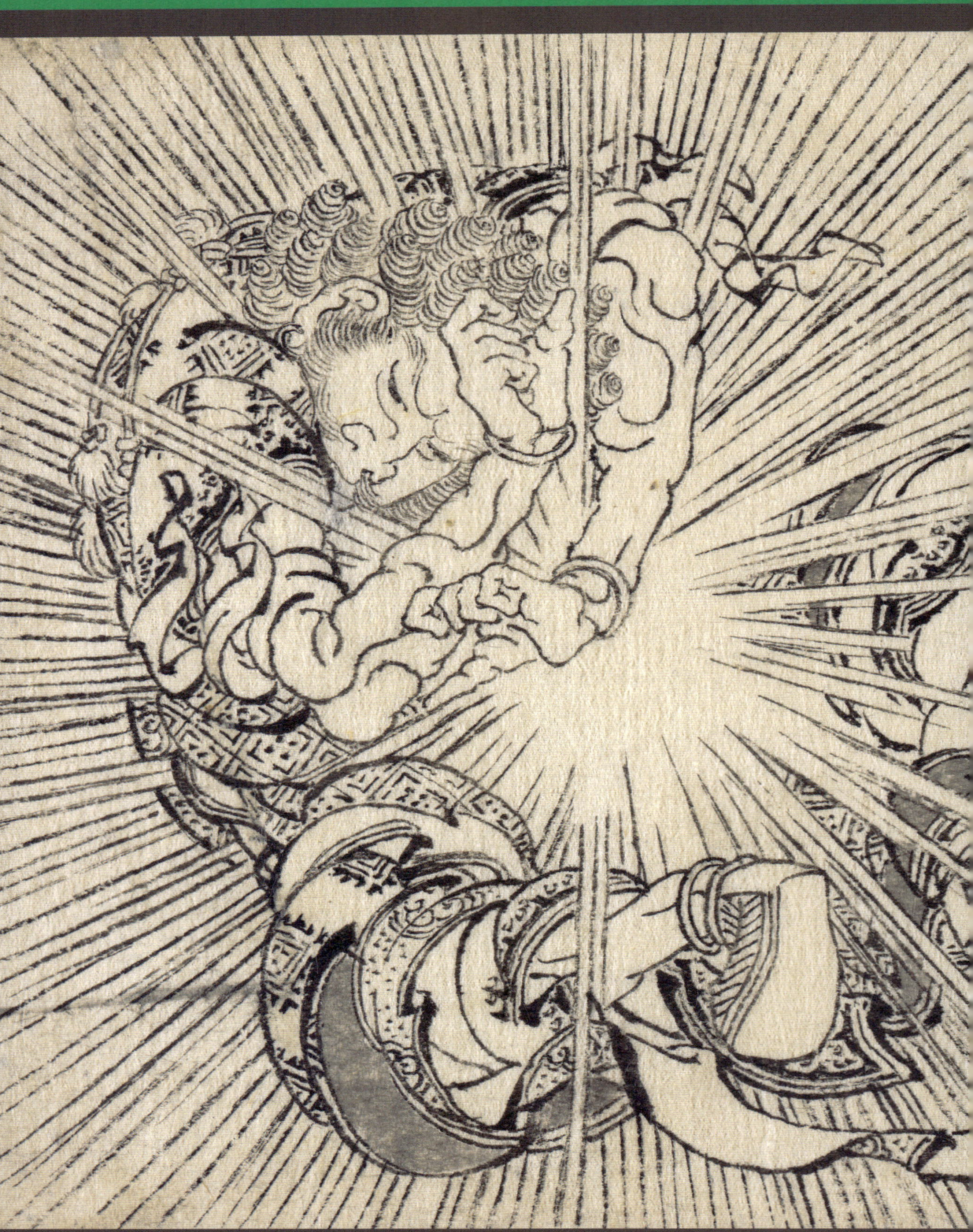

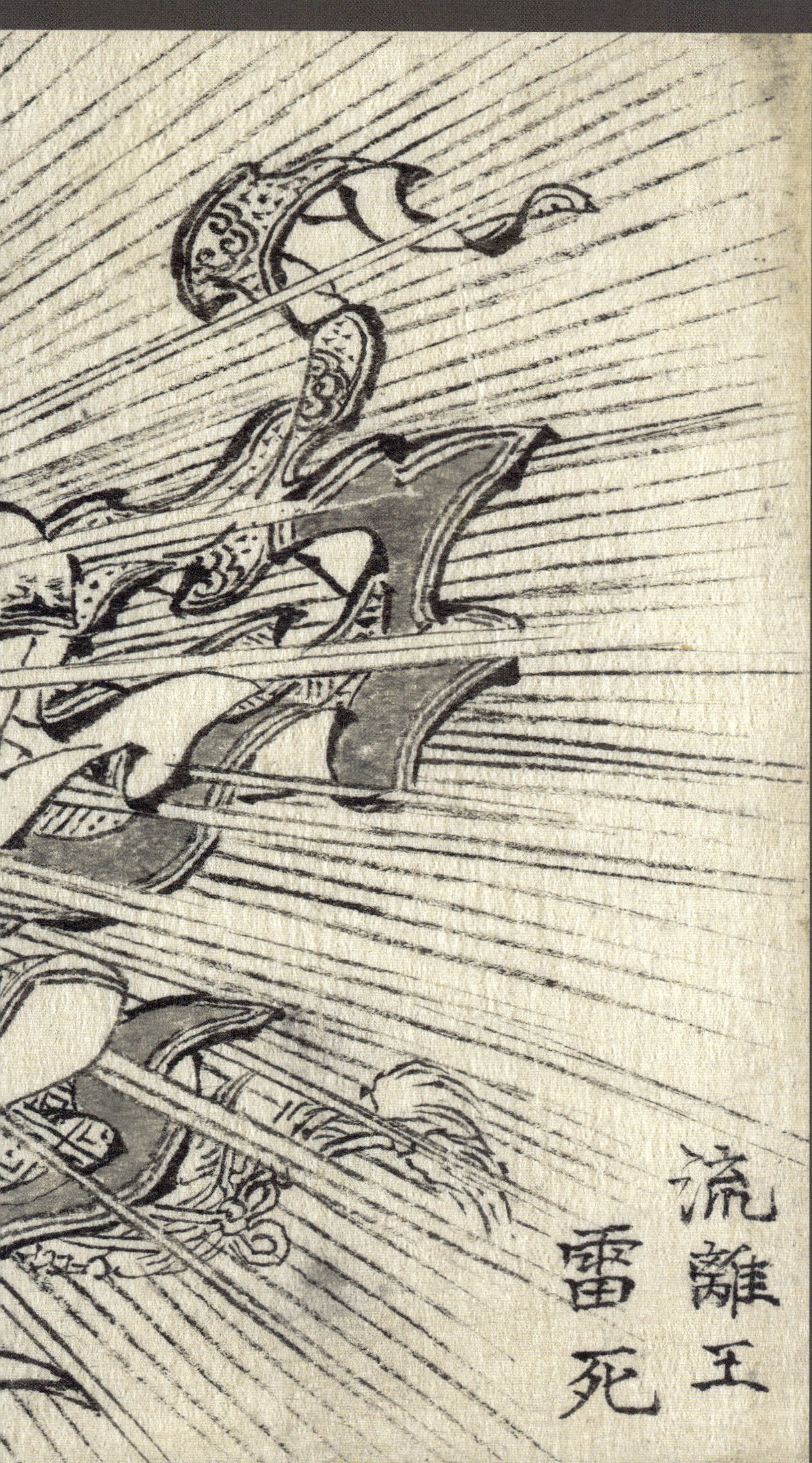

The Great Picture Book of Everything Ruriō Killed by a Lightning Strike / Katsushika Hokusai

1829 / British Museum

The picture depicts Ruriō dying by lightning strike. The expression is applicable to concentrated lineworks seen in Japanese contemporary manga. This picture is one of the Hokusai's 103 original drawings for print illustrations of his unfinished work "The Great Picture Book of Everything." He might have envisioned creating an illustrated encyclopedia including various deities and Shakyamuni's disciples in Buddhism, Chinese mythologies and legends.

『万物絵本大全図』より「流離王 雷死」/ 葛飾北斎

文政 12 年（1829）/ 大英博物館蔵

雷によって死にゆく流離王。現代の漫画の効果線の一種である「集中線」に通じる表現である。本図は、北斎の未刊原稿で、103枚の図譜の下絵からなる『万物絵本大全図』の一枚。本書で北斎は、仏教の諸尊や釈迦の弟子たち、中国の神話や伝説などを含む、絵入百科事典を構想したと考えられている。

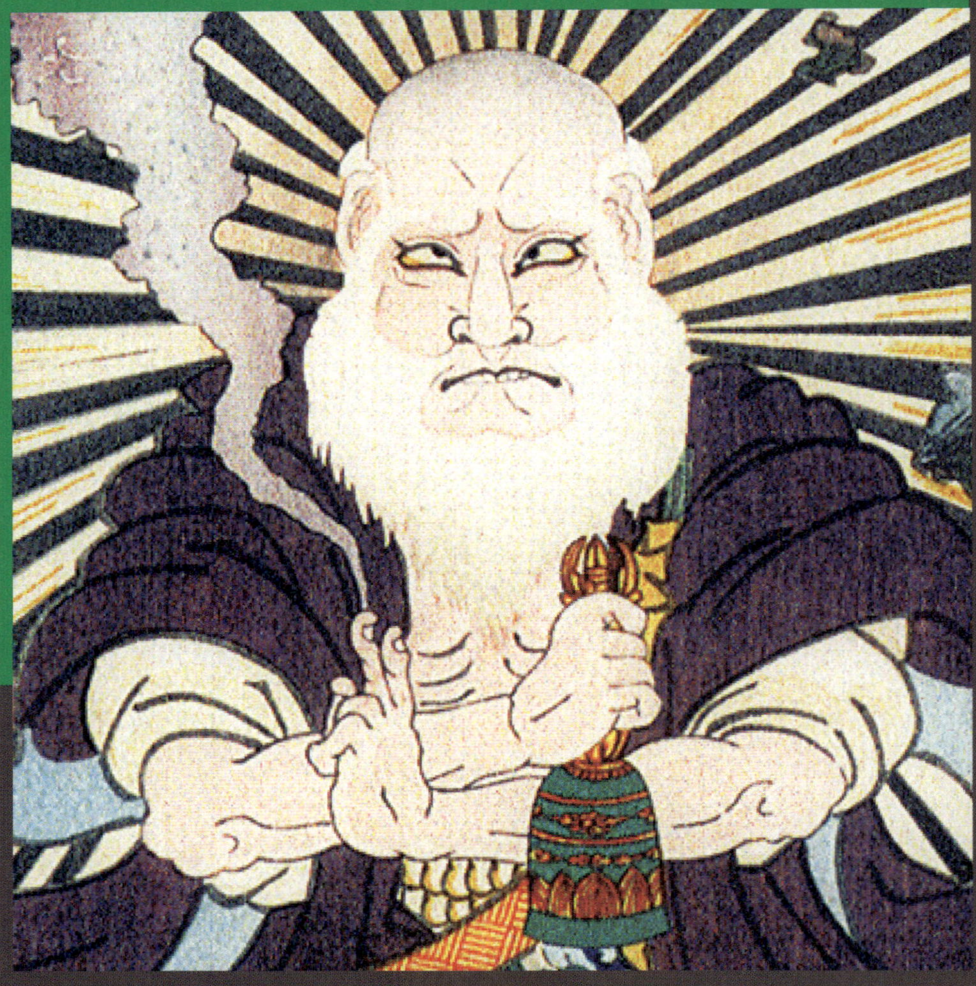

Reverend Priest Mōun, from the series Toyokuni's Comparison of Magics / Utagawa Toyokuni III, also known as Utagawa Kunisada I

1863 / Tokyo metropolitan library

Among a series of 37 print illustrations, each of which depicting a sorcerer, this picture features Mōun from the novel "The Strange Tales of the Bow Moon." To depict the scene, Toyokuni III referred to a Hokusai's print illustration (P.44), but changed the composition by getting rid of the surrounding people, zooming in on Mōun, and placing him in the center of the picture. Many radial lines in yellow resemble halos seen in many Buddhist paintings, but they look much flashier. The picture suggests that "The Strange Tales of the Bow Moon" was still popular at that time, even half a century after its publication.

豊国揮毫奇術 競 蒙雲国師 ／ 歌川豊国（3代）（初代国貞）

文久3年（1863）／ 東京都立中央図書館蔵

妖術師を描いた 37 枚の連作のうち、『椿説弓張月』の曚雲を描く一枚。北斎の挿絵（P.44）をもとに、周囲の人々を取り去り、曚雲にクローズアップして中央に配置している。放射状に伸びる線をいく筋もの黄色い線で彩色し、後光をいただく仏画を思わせながらも、飛び散る破片が爆発を伝え、ど派手な一枚となっている。出版から半世紀を経てもなお『椿説弓張月』人気は健在だったようだ。

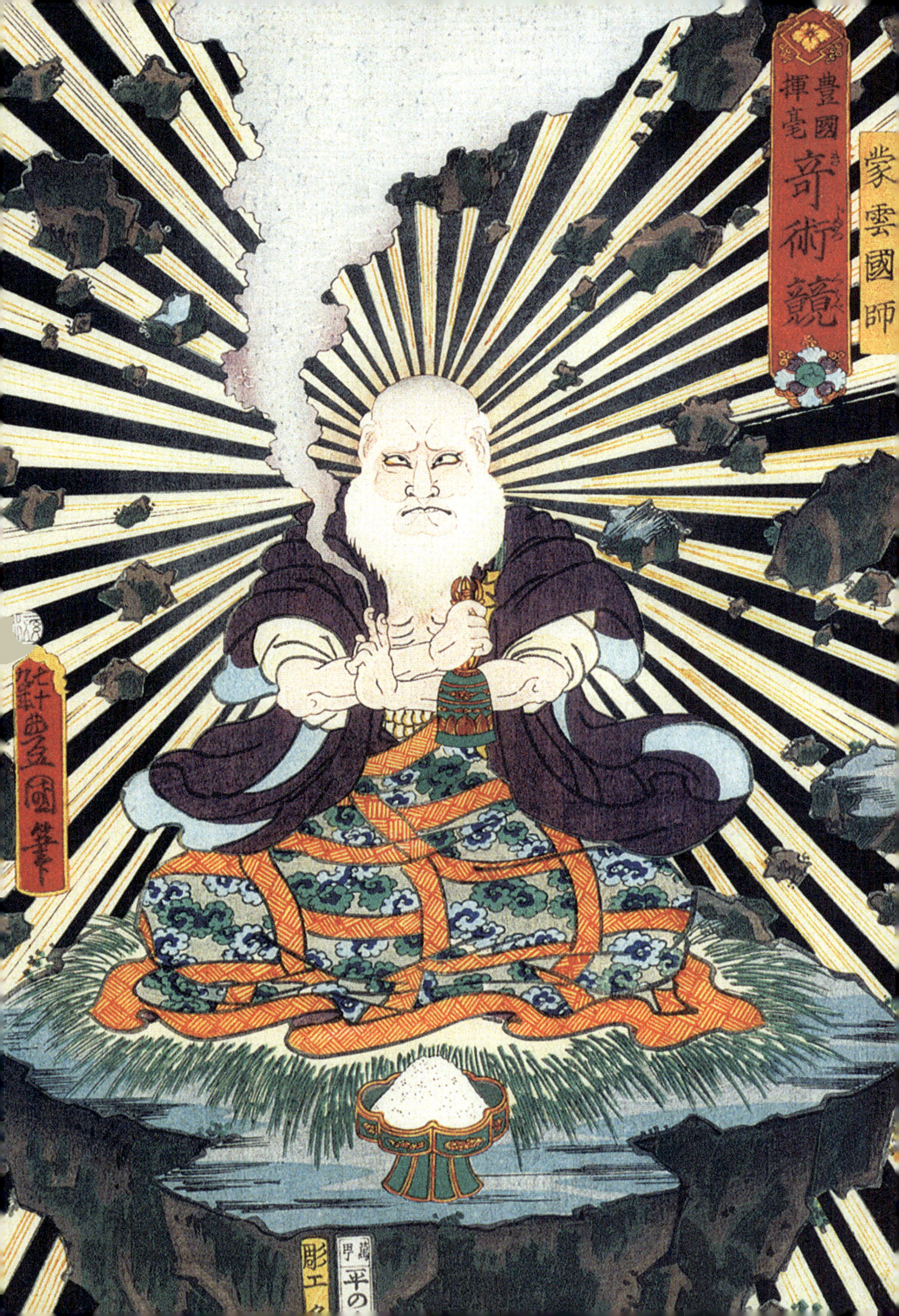

豊國揮毫
奇術競
蒙雲國師
七十余齡
五
國
筆

Inuyama Dōsetsu, from the series Toyokuni's Comparison of Magics / Utagawa Toyokuni III, also known as Utagawa Kunisada I

1861 / Tokyo Metropolitan Library

The picture depicts the warrior Inuyama Dōsetsu from the novel "Nansō Satomi Ha'kkenden," who is an expert at using fire in ninja martial arts. The novel features eight warriors including him, each of them possessing a treasure ball. Each ball is engraved with a different kanji character, which respectively means humanity, justice, courtesy, wisdom, loyalty, sincerity, filial piety and obedience. They fight to save the Satomi clan, the feudal warlord in Bōsō Province. The author Kyokutei Bakin wrote this lengthy novel after his former novel "The Strange Tales of the Bow Moon," and took 28 years to finish. It gained popularity and was adapted into kabuki theater plays. This picture depicts Dōsetsu's kimono with a tasseled hem called Baren and slits in both sides called Yoten, both features are unique to a kind of kabuki stage costume. The kimono has the pattern of a dragon holding a treasure ball, which might suggest that Dōsetsu has the ball of loyalty.

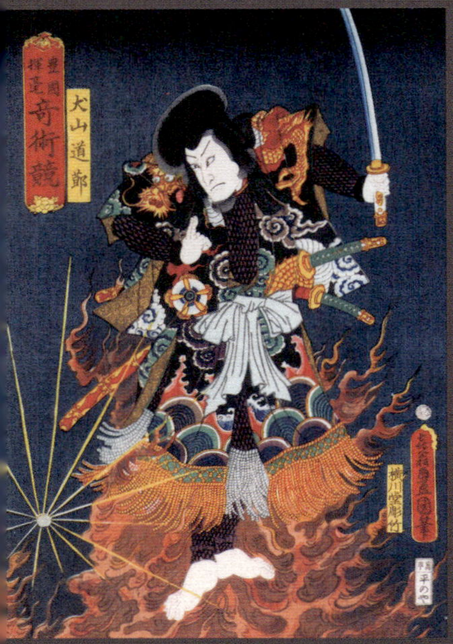

豊国揮毫奇術競
犬山道節 ／
歌川豊国（3代）（初代国貞）

文久元年（1861）／
東京都立中央図書館蔵

「仁・義・礼・智・忠・信・孝・悌」の八つの玉をそれぞれ持つ八犬士が、房総の戦国大名・里見氏の危機を救う物語『南総里見八犬伝』。登場する八犬士の一人、火遁の術を使う犬山道節。馬琴が『椿説弓張月』に続いて手がけたこの物語は、28年の歳月をかけて仕上げた長編小説で、人気を博し、歌舞伎でも上演された。裾に房飾り（馬簾）が垂れ下がる四天（両脇に切れ目が入った着物）は、歌舞伎独特の衣装。龍が玉を掴む着物の柄は、玉を持つ八犬士に因んだものだろう。

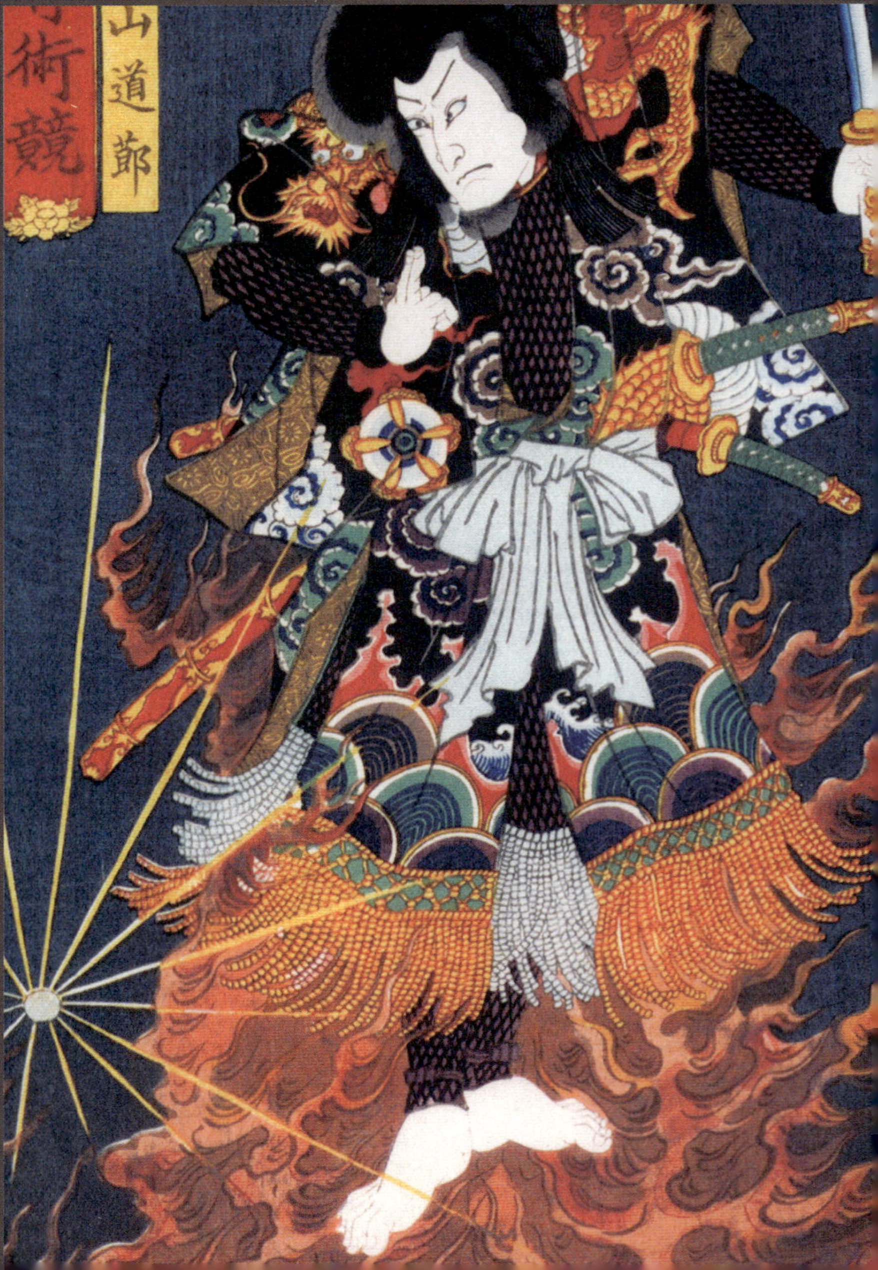

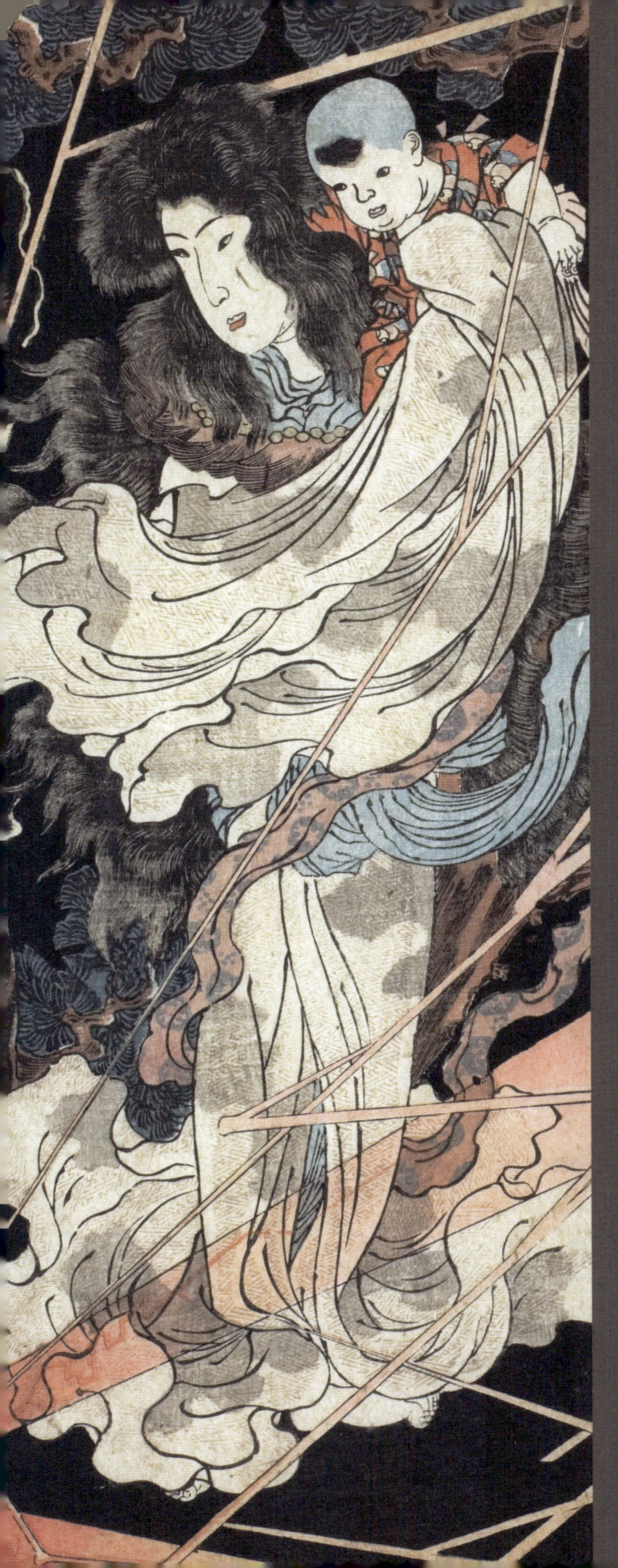

Inue Shinbē Masashi, from the series The 800 Heroes of the Japanese Suikoden / Utagawa Kuniyoshi

1831 / The Art Institute of Chicago

The novel "Nansō Satomi Ha'kkenden" tells that, when Fusehime, a daughter of Satomi Yoshizane, committed suicide by disembowelment, eight treasure balls miraculously flew in all directions. The balls respectively passed into eight warriors' hands. Fusehime already died, but her spirit sometimes appeared in this world to get the eight warriors out of danger time after time. Inue Shinbē was almost killed by the villain Kajikurō, when he was 4 years old, but Fusehime appeared with furious lightning and ripped the villain's body apart. Since then, Shinbē was raised in Fusehime's sacred cave until he was 9, and later became the youngest warrior among the eight, holding a superhuman strength.

本朝水滸伝剛勇八百人一個 犬江親兵衛仁 ／ 歌川国芳

天保 2 年（1831） ／ シカゴ美術館蔵

『南総里見八犬伝』の八犬士はそれぞれ、里見義実の息女・伏姫が割腹した際に飛び散った八つの玉のうちのひとつを持つ。伏姫は死してなお八犬士の前にたびたびあらわれてはその危機を救う。4歳の犬江親兵衛が悪党の舵九郎に殺されそうになったときにも、凄まじい雷光とともにあらわれ、舵九郎の身体を引き裂いた。親兵衛は伏姫の神洞でその後9歳まで養育され、人間離れした強さを持つ最年少犬士となった。

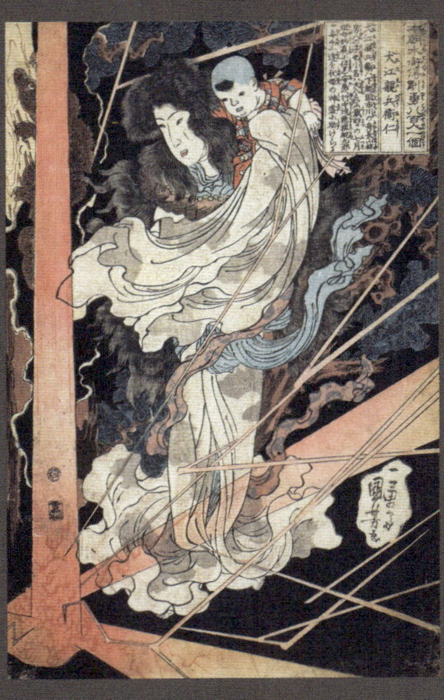

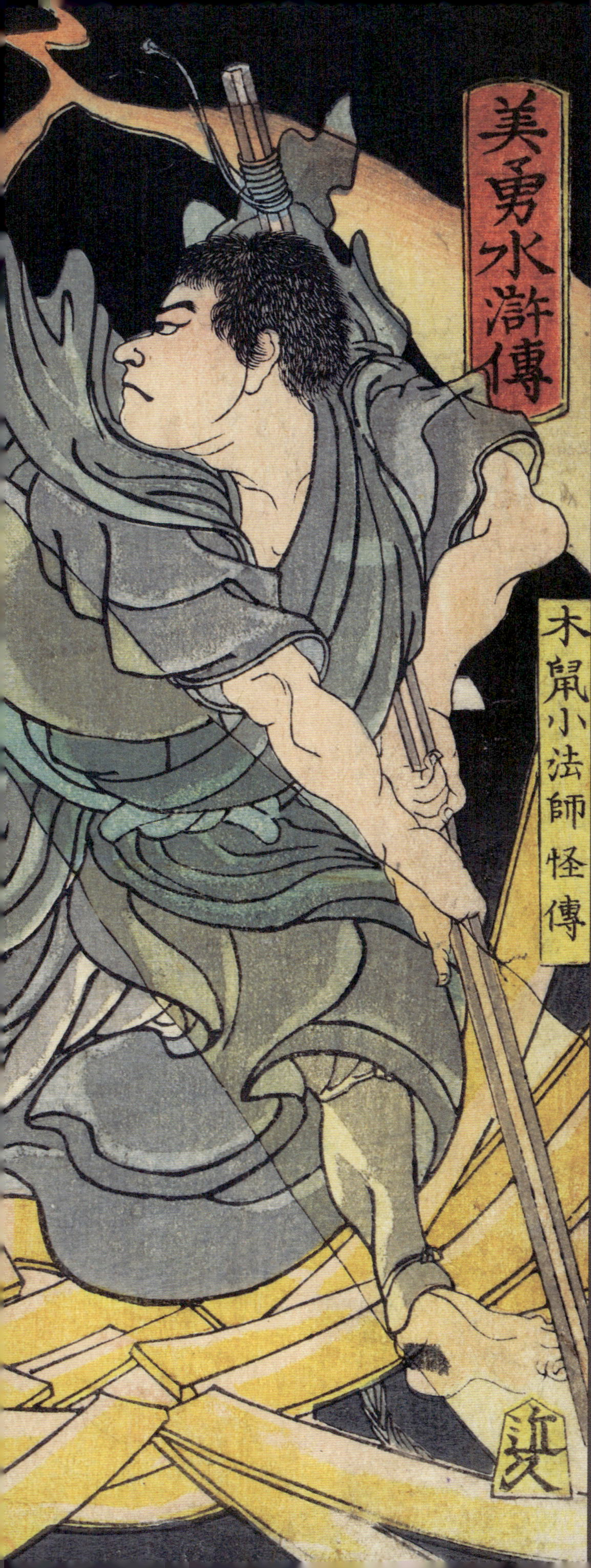

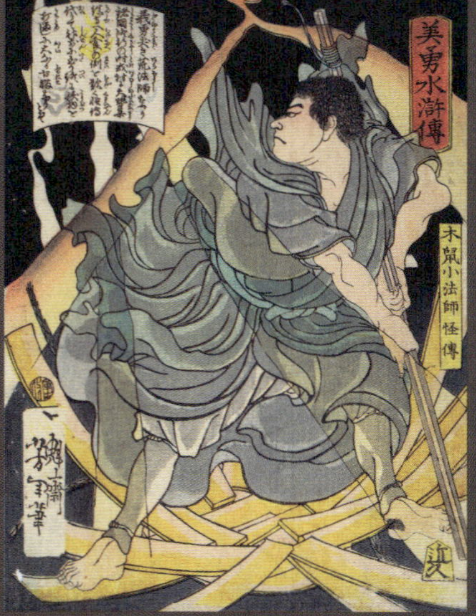

Beauty and Bravery in Suikoden
Kinezumi Kobōshi Kaiden /
Tsukioka Yoshitoshi,

1866, Art Research Center, Ritsumeikan
University

The picture depicts a warrior-priest, Kaiden, from the novel "Shunketsu Shintō Suikoden," which was written by Gakutei Sadaoka and Chisokukan Shōkyoku, and published during 1828 -1882. The novel was written based on the original Chinese Suikoden, but the story's setting was changed to Japan's early Warring States period. The text tells that while Kaiden was visiting various provinces for his Buddhist trainings, he defeated a man-eating monster and found out that the monster's true identity was an old cat. In this picture, the flashlights illuminating darkness represent Kaiden's strength against specters.

美勇水滸伝 木鼠小法師怪伝 /
月岡芳年

慶応 2 年 （1866） / 立命館大学 ARC 所蔵
（arcUP5339）

『水滸伝』に倣って日本の戦国時代初期を舞台にした『俊 傑神稲水滸伝』（岳亭定岡・知足館松旭作、1828-1882 年刊）に登場する荒法師・怪伝。天狗と取っ組み合いをしたと伝えられる。詞書には、諸国を修行するなかで人食い妖怪を退治したところ古猫だったというエピソードが書かれている。暗闇を照らす閃光で、妖魔に強い人物像を表現する。

Nyūunryū Kōsonshō, from the series One Hundred Ghost Stories from China and Japan / Tsukioka Yoshitoshi

1865 / Hagi Uragami Museum

Nyūunryū Kōsonshō is a member of the 108 heroes of "Suikoden." The text tells that he mastered magical powers and could appear and disappear anywhere at his will.He also has a power to create clouds and rains. When he holds his hands in a prayer position in front of water, storms would start swirling and waves would stir up. A dragon would emerge from the storm, and ascend to heaven.His nickname Nyūunryū means "a dragon enters into clouds."Here, Kōsonshō not only stirs waves up, but also makes his hair and kimono stand, and glares at viewers. It is more intense compared to Kuniyoshi's picture (P.22) on the same theme.

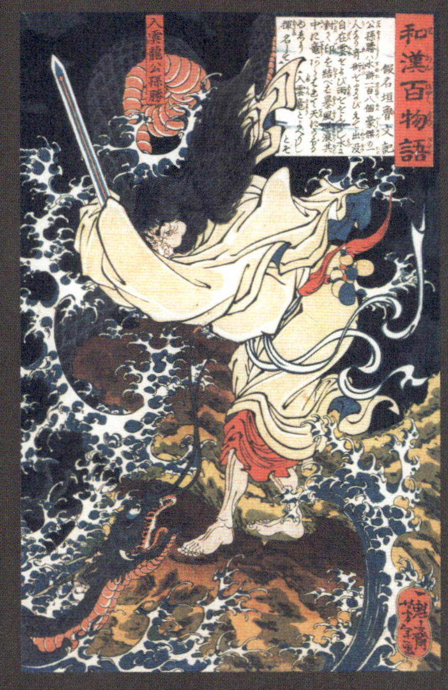

和漢百物語 入雲龍公孫勝 ／ 月岡芳年

慶応元年（1865）／ 山口県立萩美術館・浦上記念館蔵

『水滸伝』の豪傑108人のうちの一人、入雲龍公孫勝。詞書によれば彼は、奇術を学んで出没自在。雲を呼び雨を降らし、ひとたび水に向かって印を結んで唱えると、暴風が吹き荒れ、逆立つ浪が起こり、その中に龍が現れて天に昇る。よってあだ名を「入雲龍」という。波のみならず、髪も衣服をも逆立てこちらを睨みつける公孫勝。国芳の絵（P.22）から、一層激しさを増している。

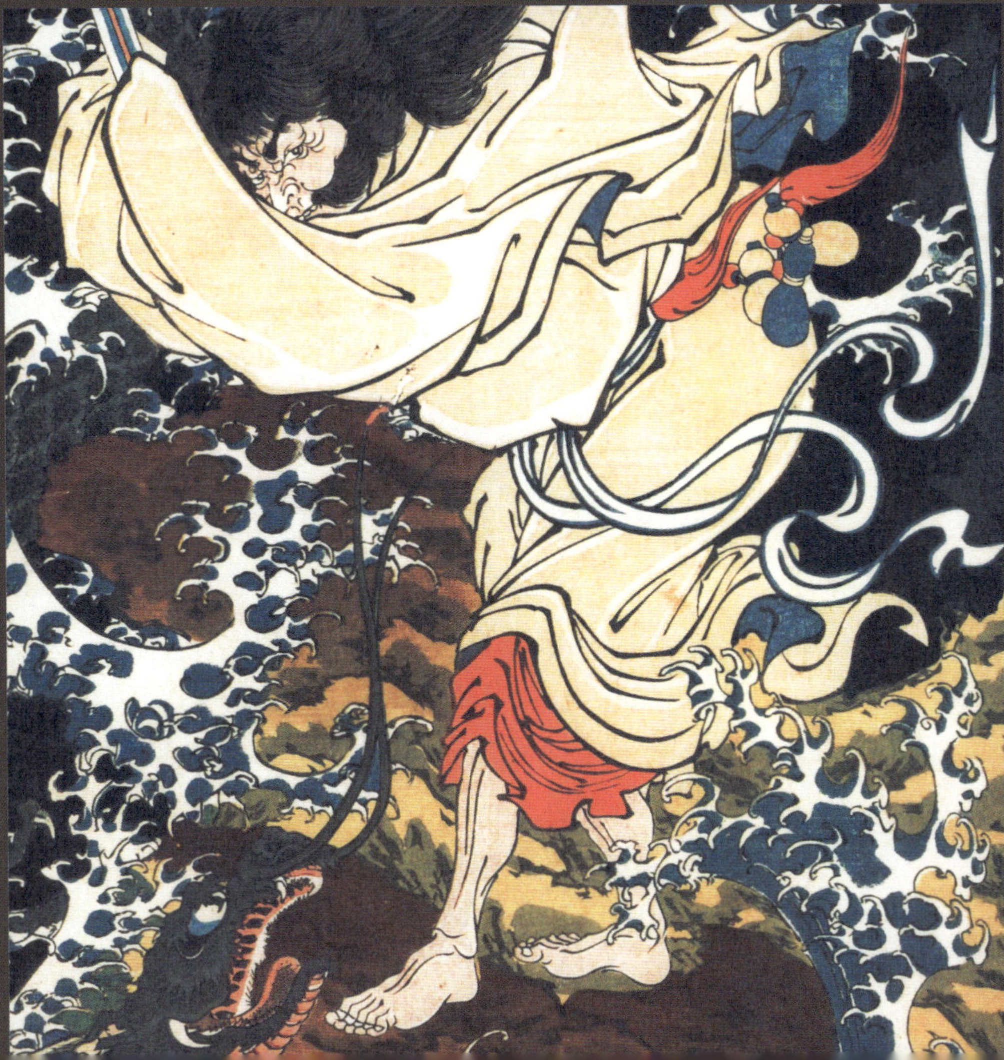

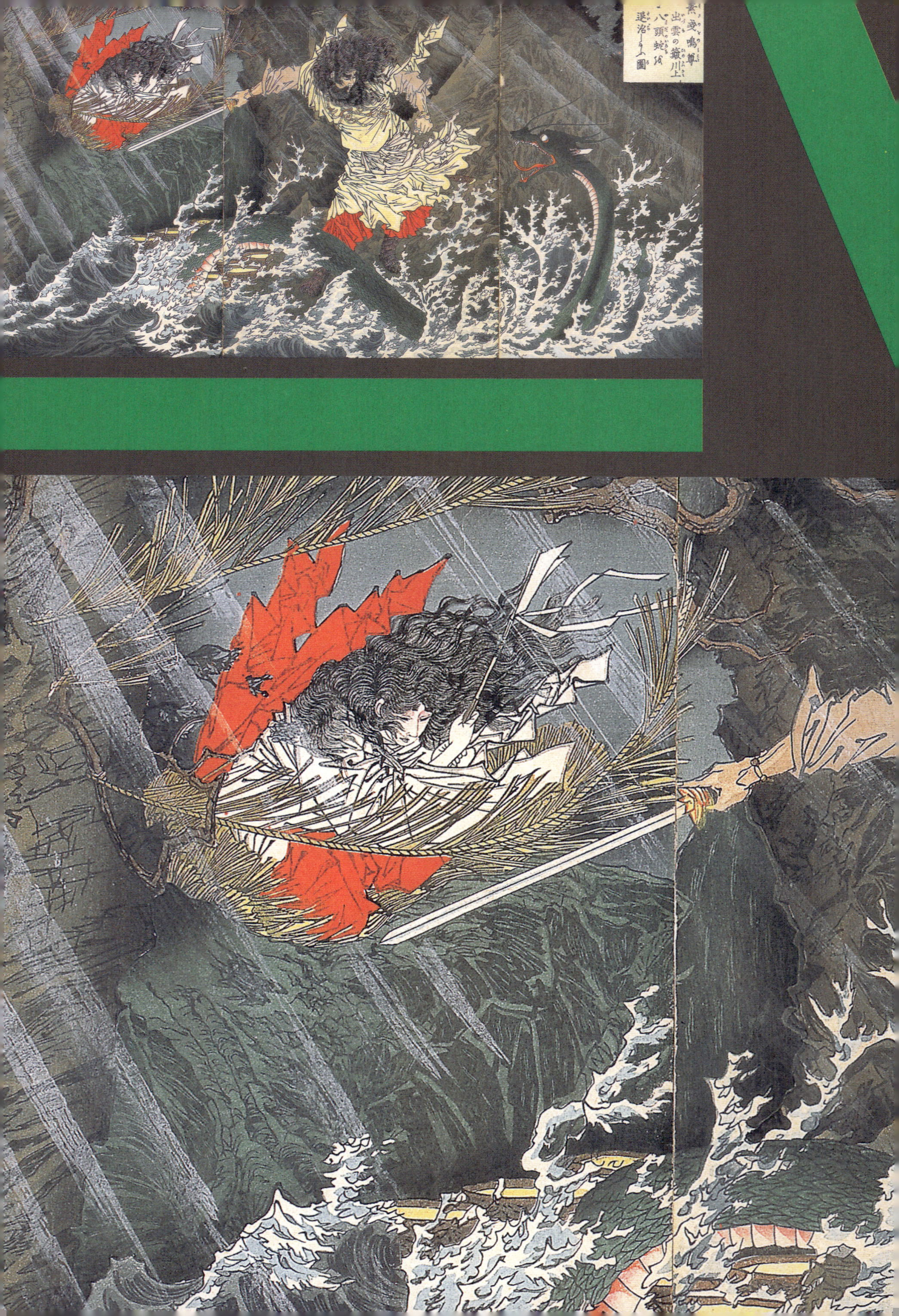

素戔嗚尊
出雲の簸川上
八頭蛇渕
退治之図

Susanoo-no Mikoto Defeating an Eight-headed Snake at Hikawajō in Izumo Province, from the series A Brief History of Japan in Pictures / Tsukioka Yoshitoshi

1893 / Shimane Museum of Ancient Izumo

According to the oldest history book in Japan called "Kojiki" (A Record of Ancient Matters), once a year, a big snake with eight heads and eight tails called Yamata-no Orochi appeared in Izumo Province to eat a young girl. When the snake came to eat the last surviving girl, Kushinada-hime, a god, Susanoo-no Mikoto, who had gotten thrown out of heaven and descended onto earth, defeated the snake. The picture's depiction of Kushinada-hime being surrounded by rice plants might refer to kanji characters of her name in the second oldest Japanese history book "Nihonshoki" (Chronicles of Japan), which includes " 稲 " meaning rice plants. All the motions including the stirring waves and standing hair and kimono are depicted in fine lines. The size of the snake gives some reality to the mythological theme, as it is not too big.

日本略史之内 素戔鳴尊出雲の簸川上に八頭蛇を退治したまふ図 / 月岡芳年

明治 26 年（1893）/ 古代出雲歴史博物館蔵

『古事記』によれば、八岐大蛇は頭と尾が八つずつある大蛇で、毎年出雲に訪れては年ごとに一人ずつの娘を食い、最後に残った櫛名田姫を食いに来たとき、高天原から追放されこの地に降った須佐之男命に退治された。この絵で姫が稲に囲まれているのは、『日本書紀』の「奇稲田」の表記に因んだものだろう。逆立つ波、髪、衣服には、皺や襞が執拗に描き込まれ、劇的な効果を高めている。巨大すぎない八岐大蛇が、神話に信憑性を与えている。

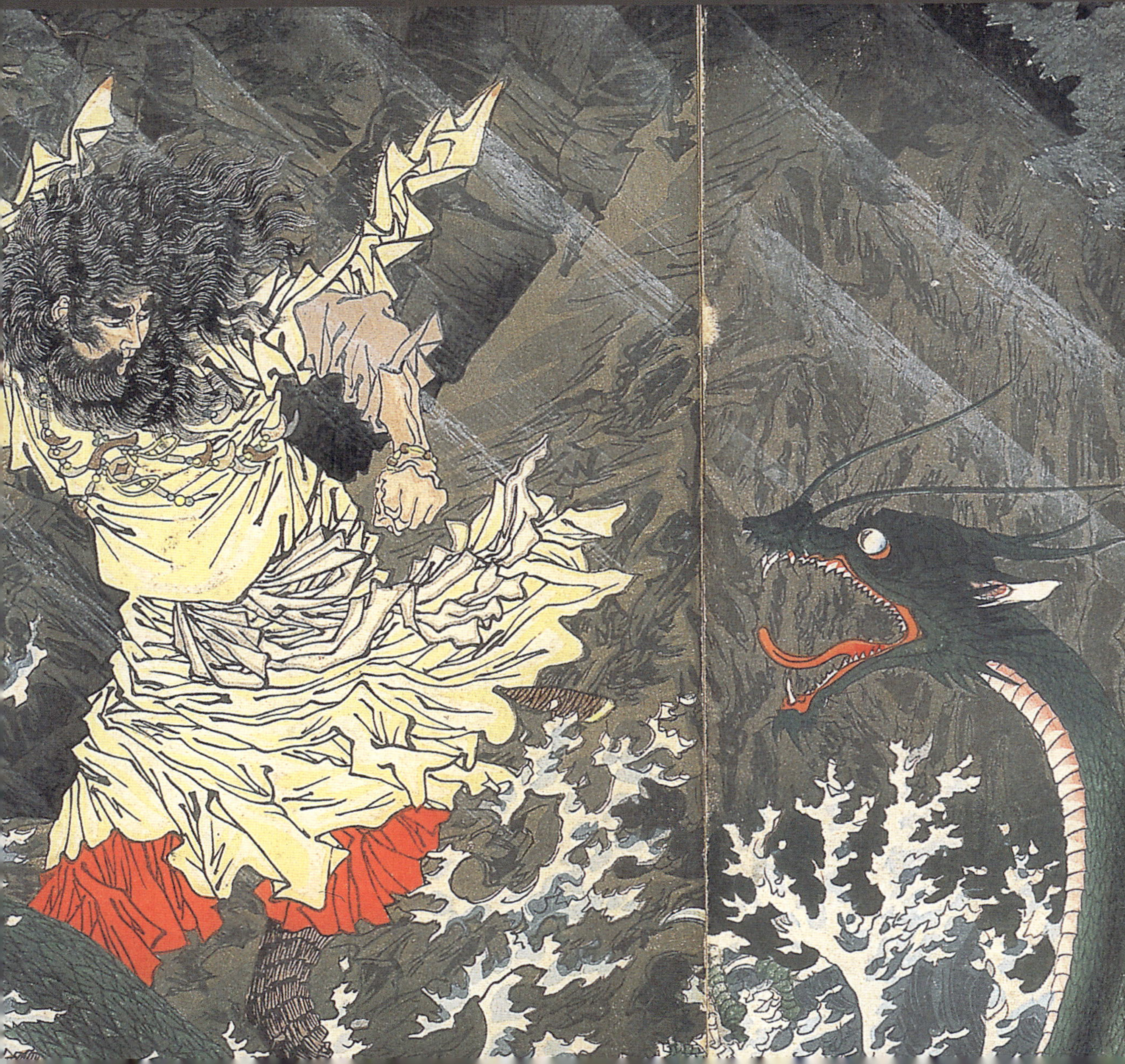

Roaring Specters

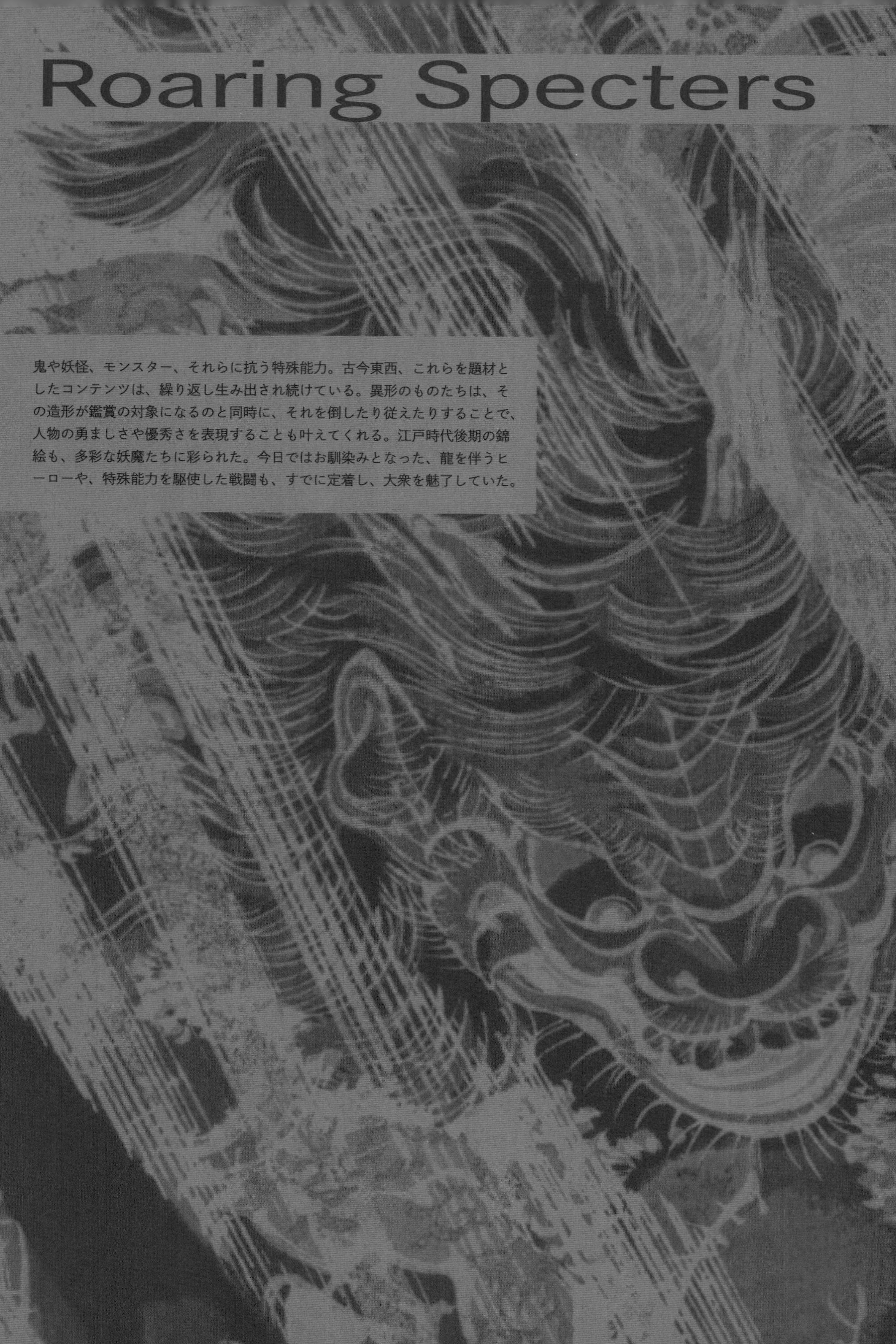

鬼や妖怪、モンスター、それらに抗う特殊能力。古今東西、これらを題材と
したコンテンツは、繰り返し生み出され続けている。異形のものたちは、そ
の造形が鑑賞の対象になるのと同時に、それを倒したり従えたりすることで、
人物の勇ましさや優秀さを表現することも叶えてくれる。江戸時代後期の錦
絵も、多彩な妖魔たちに彩られた。今日ではお馴染みとなった、龍を伴うヒ
ーローや、特殊能力を駆使した戦闘も、すでに定着し、大衆を魅了していた。

妖魔の狂騒

Ogres, specters and monsters, as well as the psychics who resist them. Various stories featuring these creatures and people can be found in all ages and countries. Viewers would not only enjoy seeing the appearances of these strange creatures, but also appreciate the bravery and distinction of the heroes who defeat or control them. Many different kinds of specters can be found in Nishikie, or polychrome ukiyoe prints, of the late Edo period. At that time, heroes with dragons and battles involving psychics were already popular and fascinated the public, which is still the same today.

四章
Chapter 4.

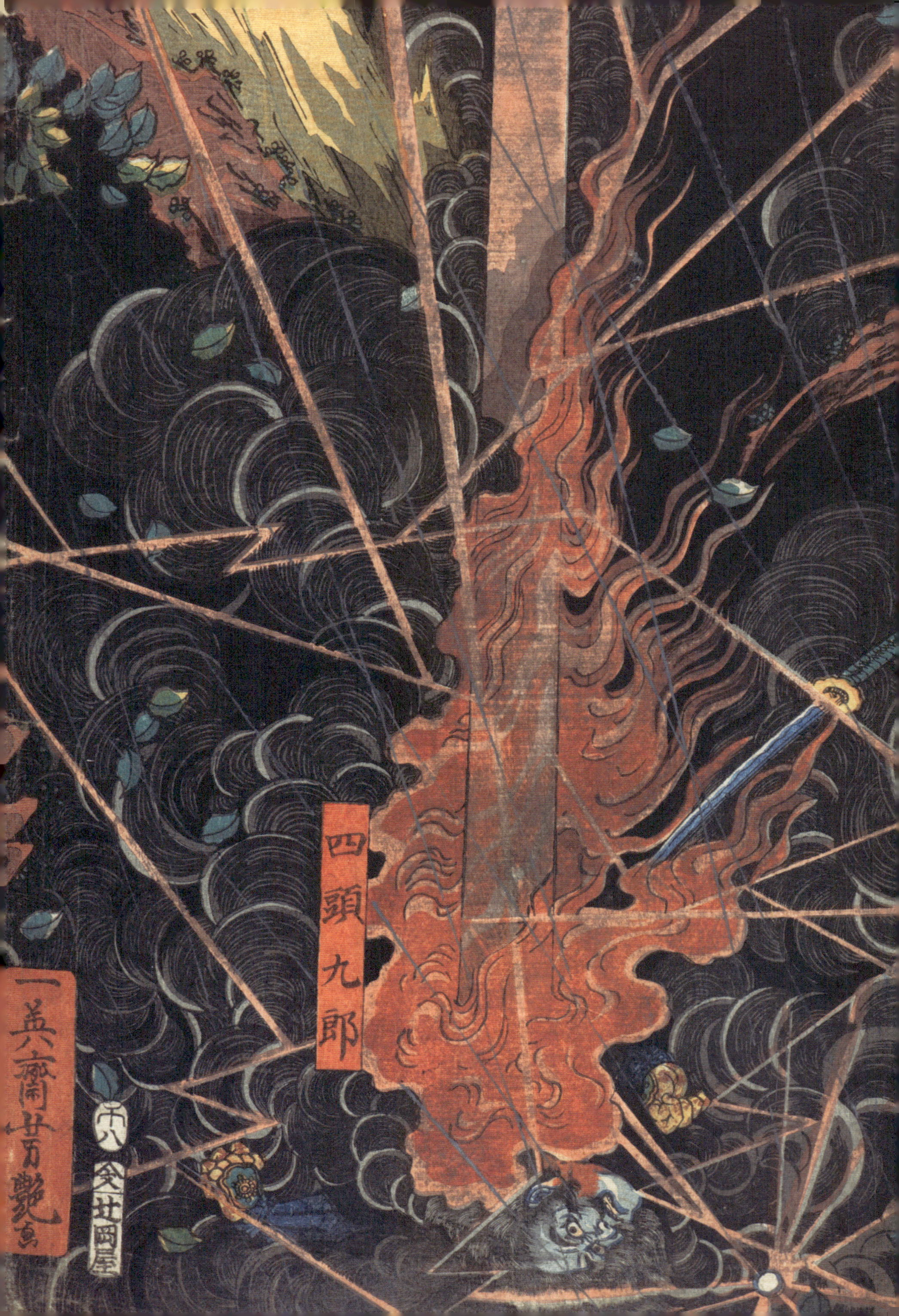
四頭九郎
一英斎芳艶画

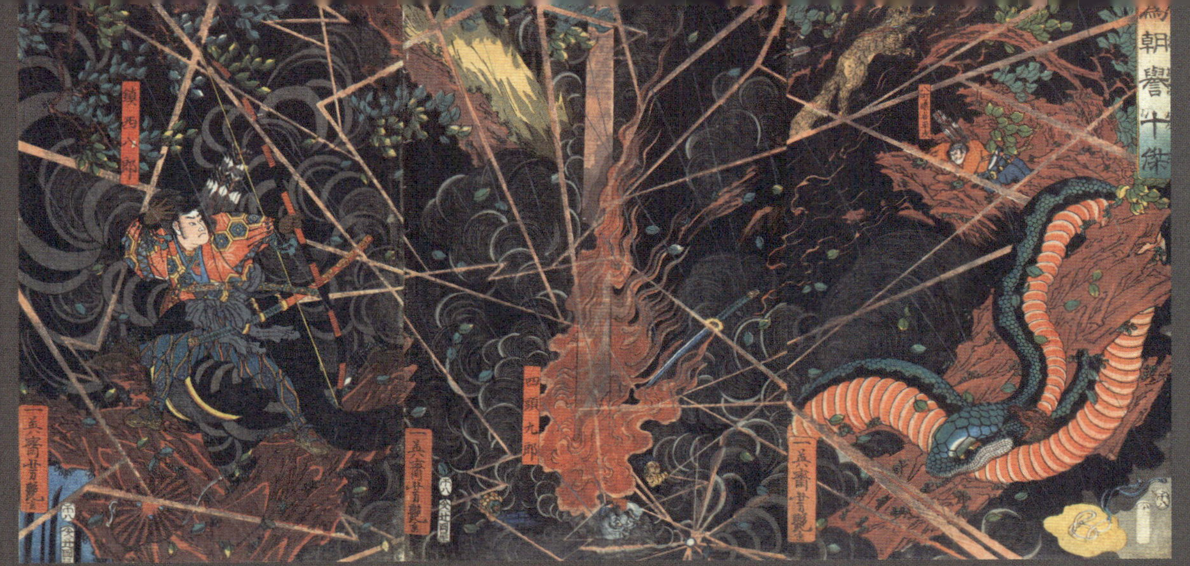

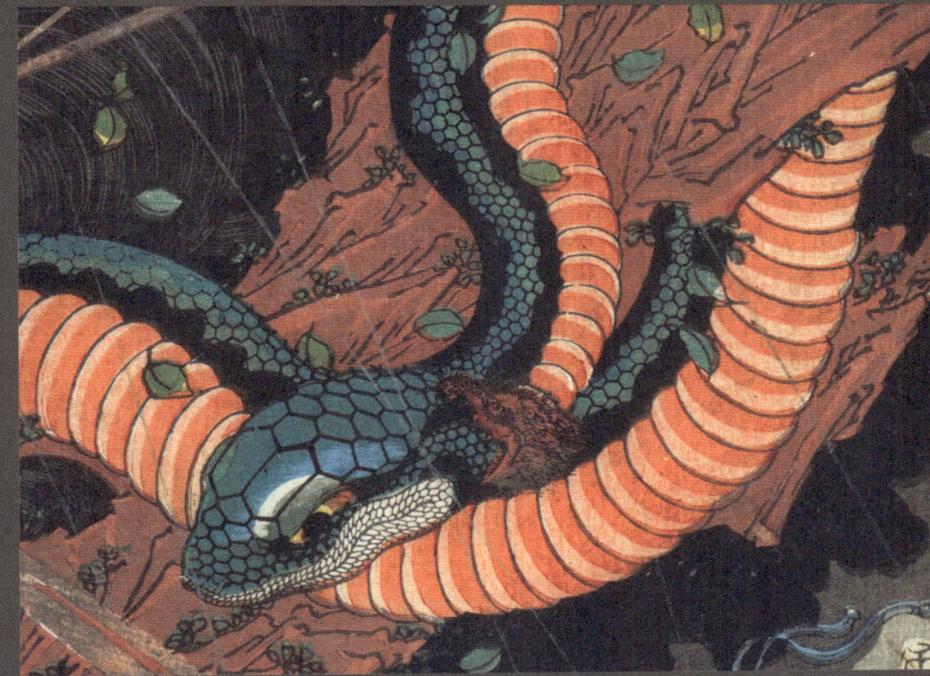

Ten Famous Excellences of Tametomo / Utagawa Yoshitsuya

1858

The triptych panoramic picture depicts a scene from the novel "The Strange Tales of the Bow Moon." Minamoto-no Tametomo and his vassal Sudō Shigesue are attacked by a giant snake, and soon after that, by the thunder god Ikazuchi (P.46). The middle frame depicts Shigesue being killed by a thunderstrike. The pervasive fire smoke, the giant tree split down, and lightning sparkling in all directions. All of these effectively express the great shock of thunder, which shakes heaven and earth.

為朝誉十傑 / 歌川芳艶

安政5年（1858） / 個人蔵

『椿説弓張月』で、源為朝と須藤重季の主従が蟒蛇（巨大な蛇）と雷公に立て続けにおそわれる場面（P.46）を、3枚続きのワイド画面に展開したもの。中央では雷に打たれ絶命する重季。立ちこめる火煙と、雷で引き裂かれた大木、画面を四方八方に散る稲光で、天地を震わす雷の衝撃をあらわす。

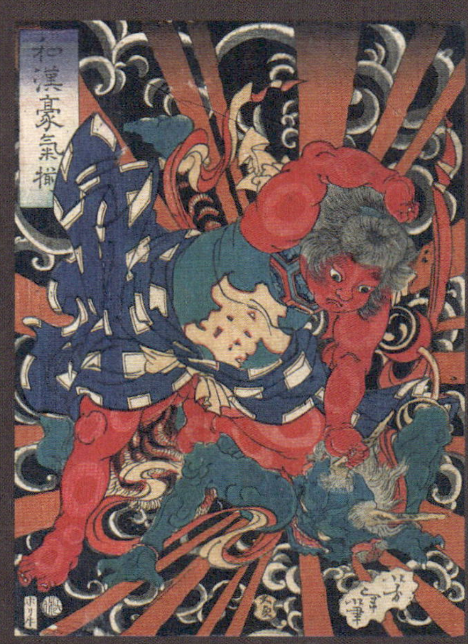

Kintarō, from a series Valor in China and Japan / Tsukioka Yoshitoshi

1868 / Photo : Morimiya

It depicts the legendary red-skinned boy Kintarō. He rides on a specter's back, grabs one of its horns and seems to be bringing his fist down in a punching motion. The specter has horns and wears leather pants. The appearance is based on a general image of Japanese ogres, but his small drums tied in a circular form are an attribute of the thunder god. In the book "Biography of Kintoki," published in 1767, there is a scene where Kintarō, also known as Kintoki, catches the thunder god and roars at him to show his anger against the noise of growling thunder. This episode represents the uncanny superhuman strength of Kintarō, who is believed to be a child of a red dragon.

和漢豪気揃 金太郎 ／ 月岡芳年

慶応 4 年（1868） ／ 提供：古美術もりみや

真っ赤な肌の金太郎。何者かに乗りかかり、その角を掴んで拳を下ろさんとしている。虎の皮のパンツに角。お馴染みの鬼の姿だが、小さな太鼓を輪に連ねた連鼓は雷神のアイテムだ。『金時一代記』（1767 年刊）には、金太郎が雷神を捕まえて「ごろごろ鳴ってやかましい」と怒る場面がある。赤い龍の子と言われる金太郎の、神をも恐れぬ人並外れたエピソードだ。

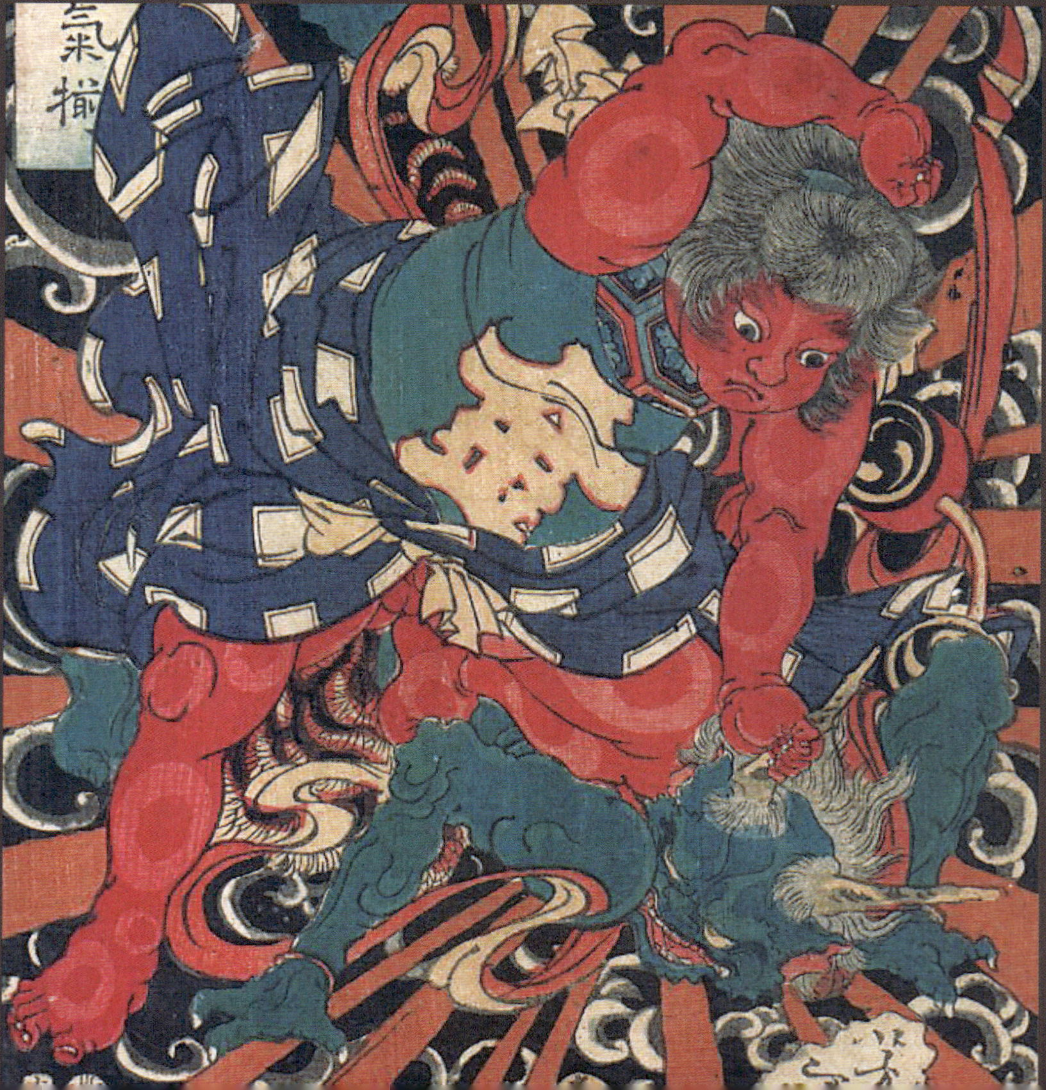

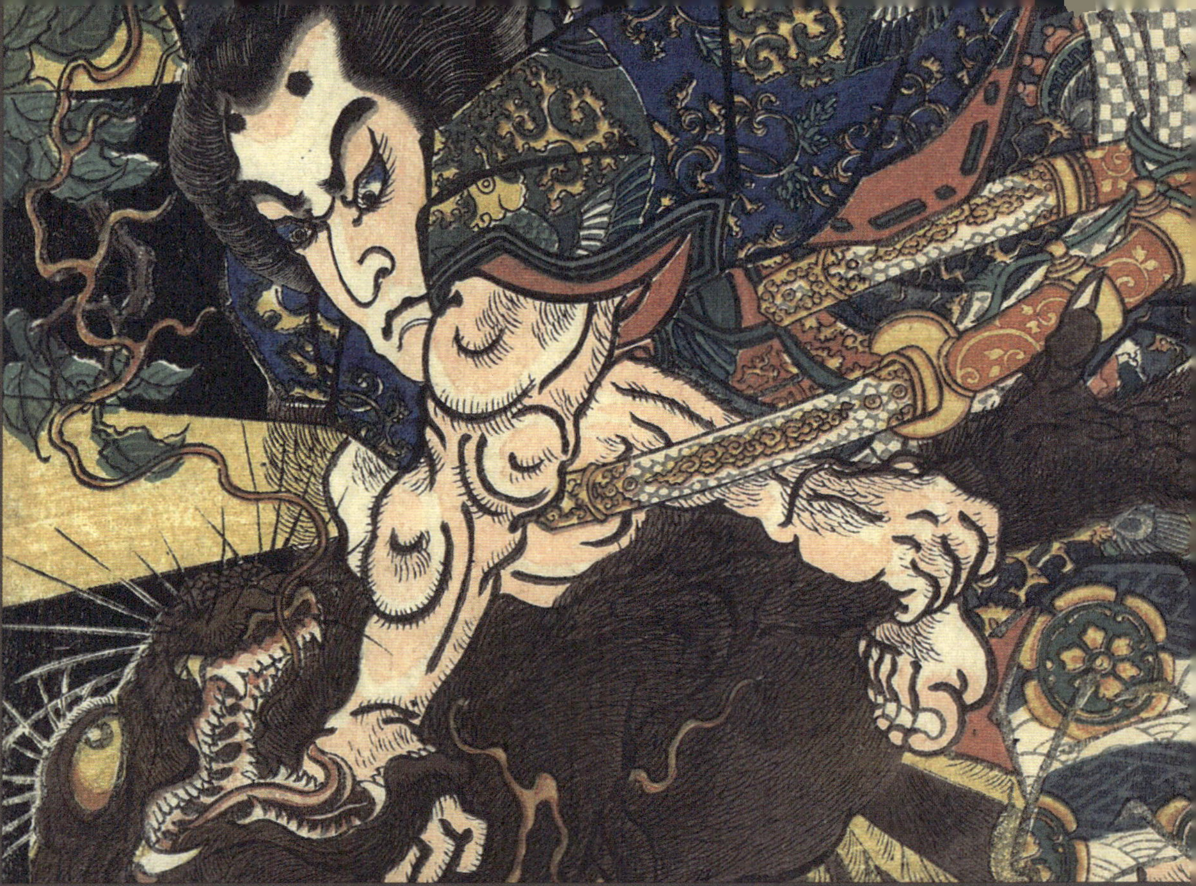

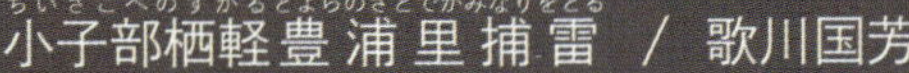

Chiisakobe-no Sugaru Catching Lightning at Toyorano-sato / Utagawa Kuniyoshi

1834–1835 / Photo : Morimiya

Legends tell that Chiisakobe-no Sugaru, a vassal of Emperor Yūryaku, caught the thunder god by order of the emperor. Later, after Sugaru's death, the emperor built a memorial pole with an inscription which reads "The grave of Sugaru, who caught the thunder god." The thunder god was angered by it and dropped lightning on the pole, but got wedged in the pole's cleft and trapped. The emperor then changed the inscription to "The grave of Sugaru, who caught the thunder god while he was alive and even after his death." This story is included in the book "Miraculous Stories from the Japanese Buddhist Tradition" written in the early Heian period. Here, the thunder god is illustrated as a beast. The radial straight lines and curved lines in different thicknesses and sizes effectively express his fierce resistance. Sugaru crosses his thickly muscled arms and grabs the thunder god. His bold look represents that he is a truly dependable retainer.

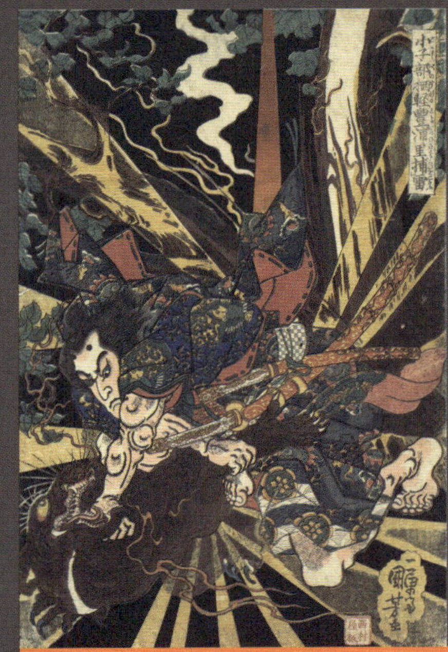

小子部栖軽豊浦里捕雷 / 歌川国芳

天保 4 年（1833）/ 提供：古美術もりみや

雄略天皇の侍者・小子部栖軽は、天皇の命で雷鳴する雷神を捕えた。栖軽の死後、天皇はその墓に「雷を捕えし栖軽が墓」と記したところ、怒った雷神がそこに雷を落とし、柱に挟まり捕まった。「生きても死にても雷を捉えし栖軽」と、天皇は書き改めた。平安初期の仏教説話集『日本霊異記』の初めに載る話だ。筋骨隆々の腕をクロスさせ、獣姿の雷神をむんずと掴む栖軽。雷神の激しい抵抗が、画面を縦横無尽に走る線によってあらわされている。

Abe-no Yasuchika Prayed for Tamamono-mae / Utagawa Kuniyoshi

1833 / British Museum

In the late Heian period, the Cloistered Emperor Toba became sick, and
a yin-yang master was ordered to find out the cause of his sickness.
According to his psychic reading, it was attributed to the beauty
Tamamono-mae, to whom the cloistered emperor loved tenderly. Yasunari
also read her true identity as a fox monster with nine tails, which had
previously committed bad acts in India and China, and then flew to Japan.
The picture depicts a magical mirror which can unmask one's true identity.
It shows a silhouette of a fox with nine tails. The lights beamed from the
mirror shine on some parts of Tamamono-mae's hair, and only these parts
change their color into gold, the color of the fox fur. Additionally, the fox's
tails are depicted in the upper left of this picture. Her true identity as a fox
monster was discovered and she was shot dead. Her soul flew to Nasuno in
Shimotsuke Province and transformed into a stone called Se'sshō-seki. This
tale was adapted into a Noh song "Se'sshō-seki" in the medieval period,
and became a widely known legend.

阿部安近祈玉藻前 ／ 歌川国芳

天保4年（1833）／ 大英博物館蔵

平安時代後期、鳥羽法皇の具合が優れないので陰陽師に調べさせると、法王
が寵愛する美女・玉藻前が原因だという。その正体は、天竺（インド）と中
国で悪行をかさねて日本に飛来した、九本の尾がある狐だという。本図で正
体を暴く鏡には、九尾の狐のシルエットが浮かびあがる。そこから発する光
が当たったところだけ、玉藻の髪が黄金色の狐の毛に変わり、画面左上には
尾も見える。正体を見破られた狐は射殺され、その霊は飛んでいき、下野（栃
木県）那須野の殺生石となった。謡曲『殺生石』をはじめ、さまざまに伝説
化され広まった話。

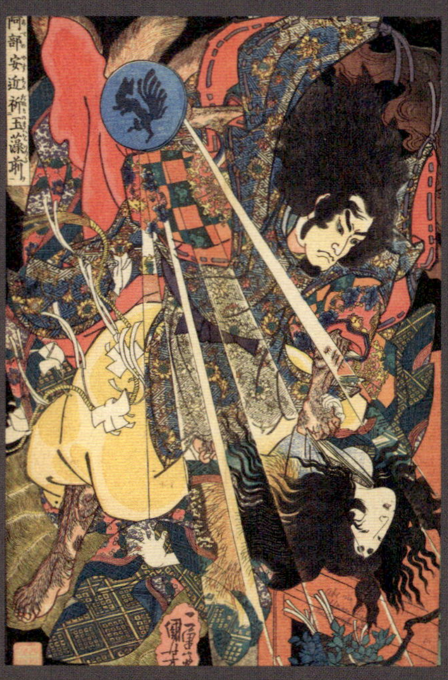

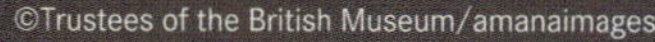

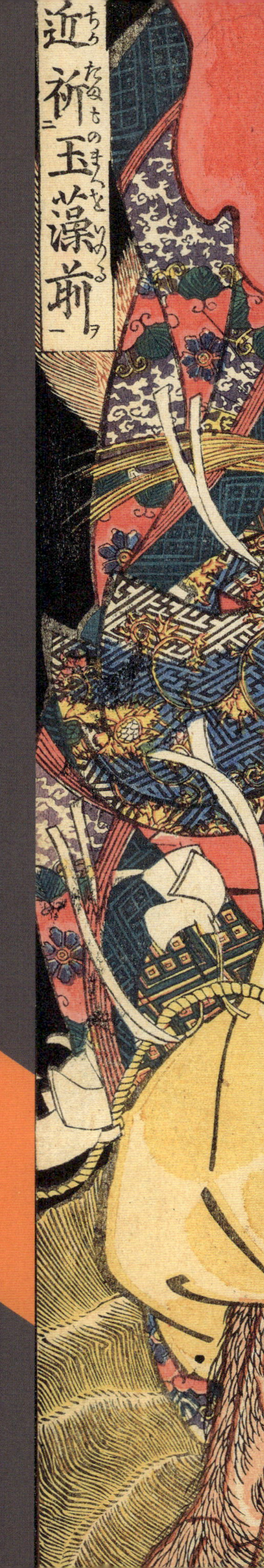

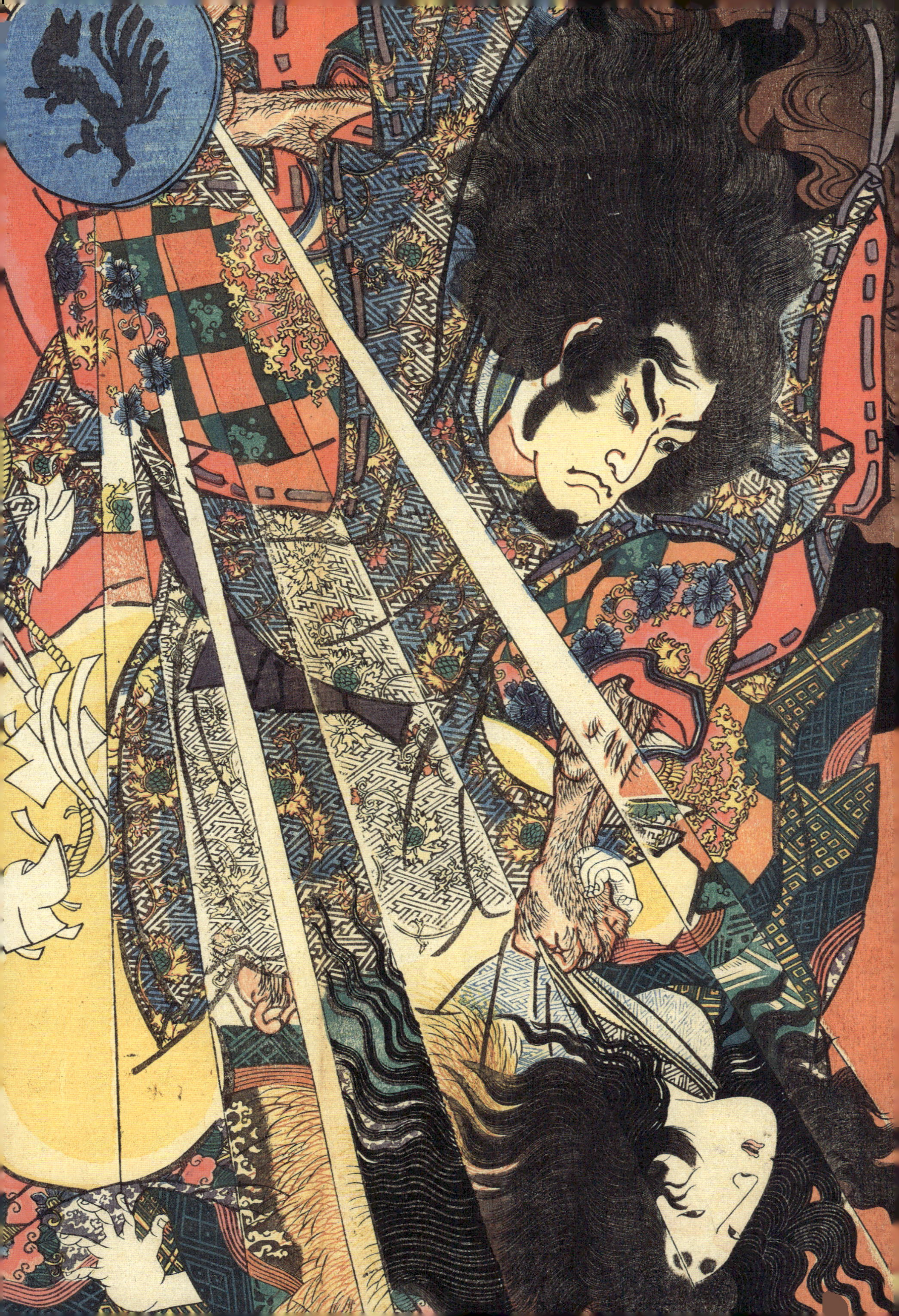

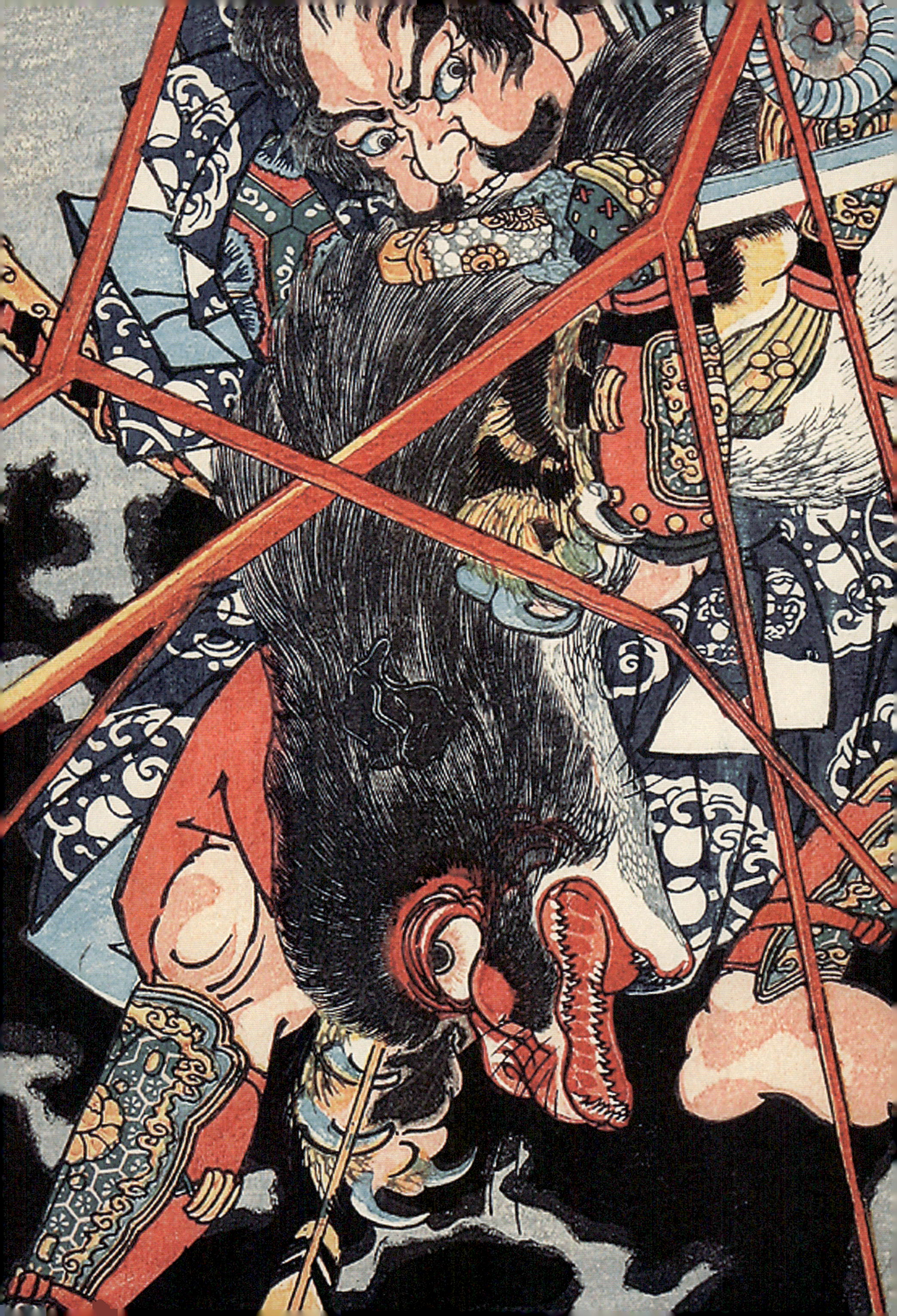

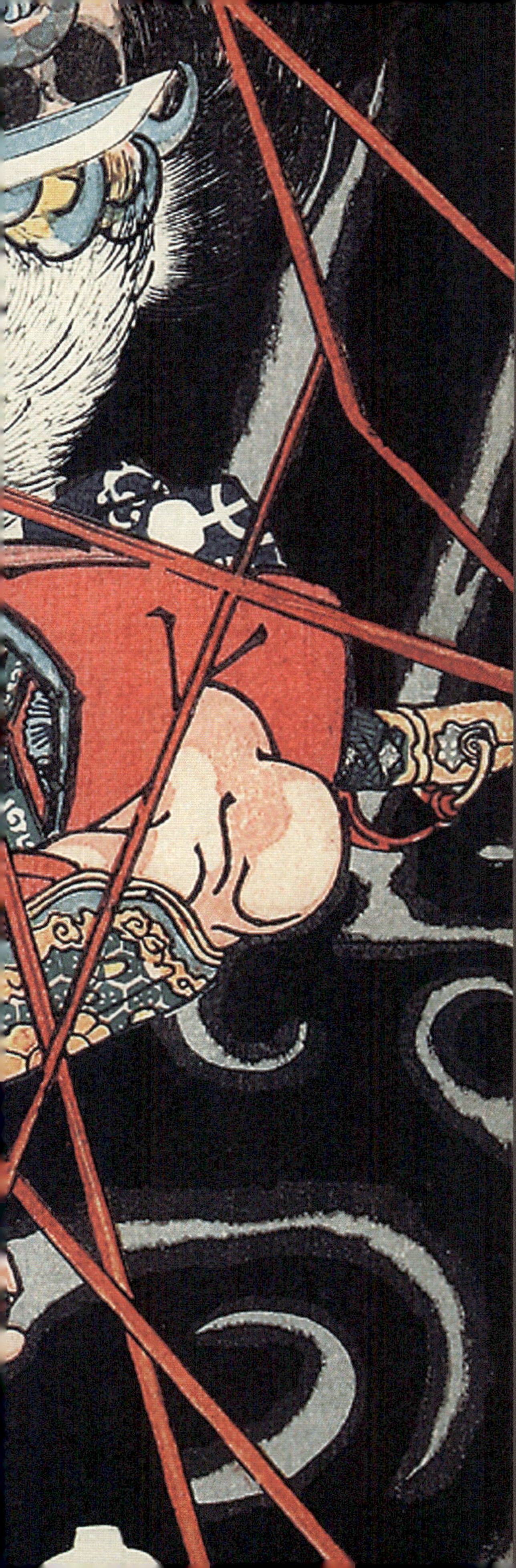

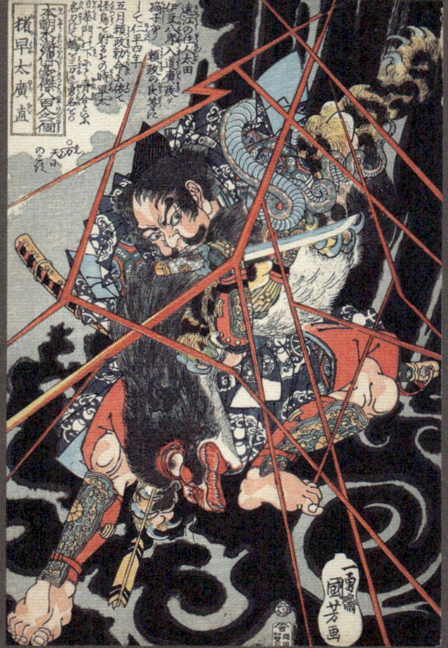

Ino Hayata Hironao, from the series
The 800 Heroes of the Japanese Suikoden /
Utagawa Kuniyoshi

1831 / Photo : Morimiya

The picture depicts a tale of Minamoto-no Yorimasa defeating
a monster called Nue. It is a popular legend of monster killings
in Japan. Yorimasa is a warrior in the late Heian period, and a
descendant of Minamoto-no Yorimitsu who also successfully
defeated monsters. The story tells that dark clouds emerged
night after night to frighten the emperor. After it was
discovered that the one who sent these clouds was a monster,
Yorimasa was ordered to kill it. Using excellent marksmanship,
he shot the monster with arrows, and his dependable vassal,
Ino Hayata, immediately caught the monster. According to
"Heike Monogatari" (The Tale of the Taira Clan), the monster
had a monkey's head, a raccoon dog's body, a snakes' tail,
tiger's paws and feet, and its cry resembled that of Nue. Here,
the figure is depicted based on the above descriptions, as well
as looking like Chimera.

本朝水滸伝豪傑八百人一個 猪早太広直 / 歌川国芳

天保 2 年（1831）/ 提供：古美術もりみや

よく知られる妖怪退治伝説のひとつ、源頼政の鵺退治を描いた
もの。頼政は平安時代後期の武将で、やはり妖怪退治で活躍し
た源頼光の子孫でもある。天皇を夜な夜な悩ます黒雲が妖怪の
仕業だと知れたことから、その退治を頼まれた頼政。それを見
事に弓で射たところを、頼りの家来・猪早太がすぐさま捕まえ
た。『平家物語』によればその姿は、頭は猿、胴体は狸、尾は蛇、
手足は虎、鳴き声は鵺のようだったという。本図の鵺は、その
説明の通りのキメラのごとき姿である。

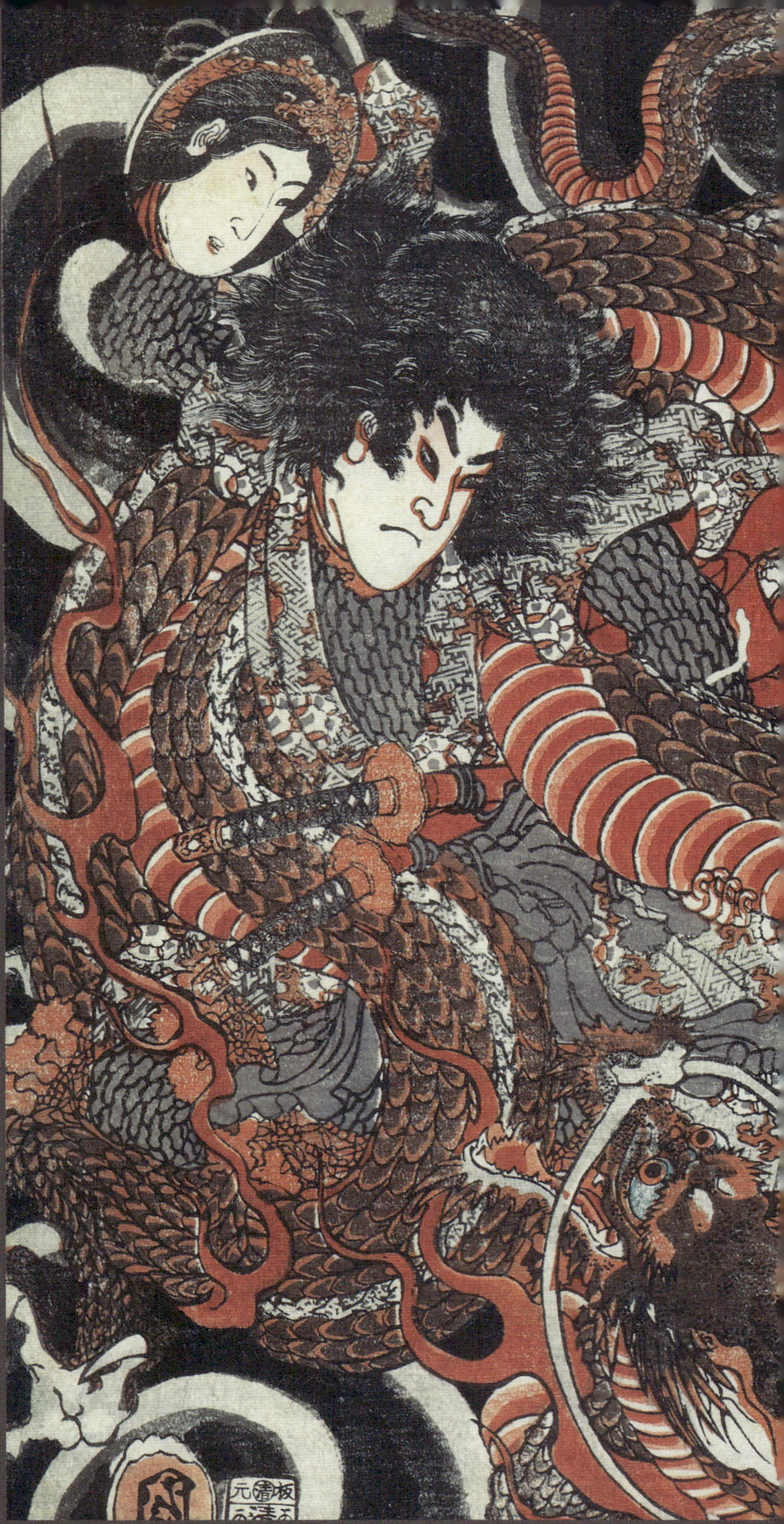

Ryūō Tarō, from the series Heroes of China and Japan / Utagawa Kuniteru

1847–1848 /
The Tsubouchi Memorial Theatre Museum

The picture depicts Tatsumaru Masatatsu, also known as Ryūō Tarō, who successfully fought in the illustrated novel "The Heroic Tale of Ryūō Tarō" written by Shikitei Kosanba. It was released around the same time as the publication of the novel. The painter Utagawa Kuniteru also worked on parts of the print illustrations for the novel. The pairing of a dragon and a hero was a standard theme for such novels, which targeted young readers.

和漢英雄伝 龍王太郎 ／ 歌川国輝

弘化4年 - 嘉永元年（1847-1848） /
早稲田大学演劇博物館蔵

式亭小三馬による絵入り小説『竜王太郎英雄譚』で活躍する龍丸正辰、通称龍王太郎。小説の出版と並行して販売されたものだろう。本図の作者・歌川国輝は、この小説の挿絵を一部担当している。年少の読者向けの小説で、ドラゴンとヒーローは定番の組み合わせになっていた。

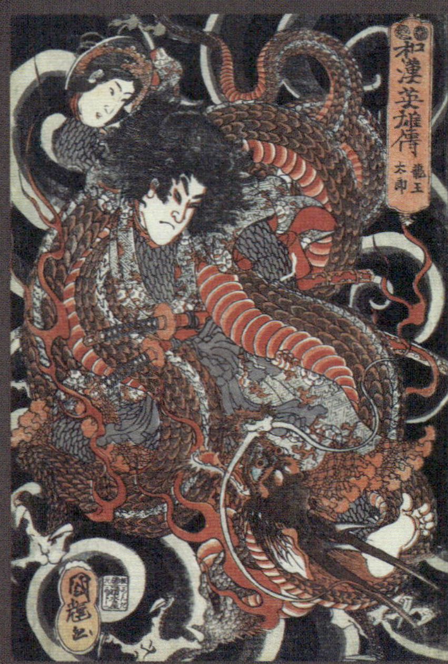

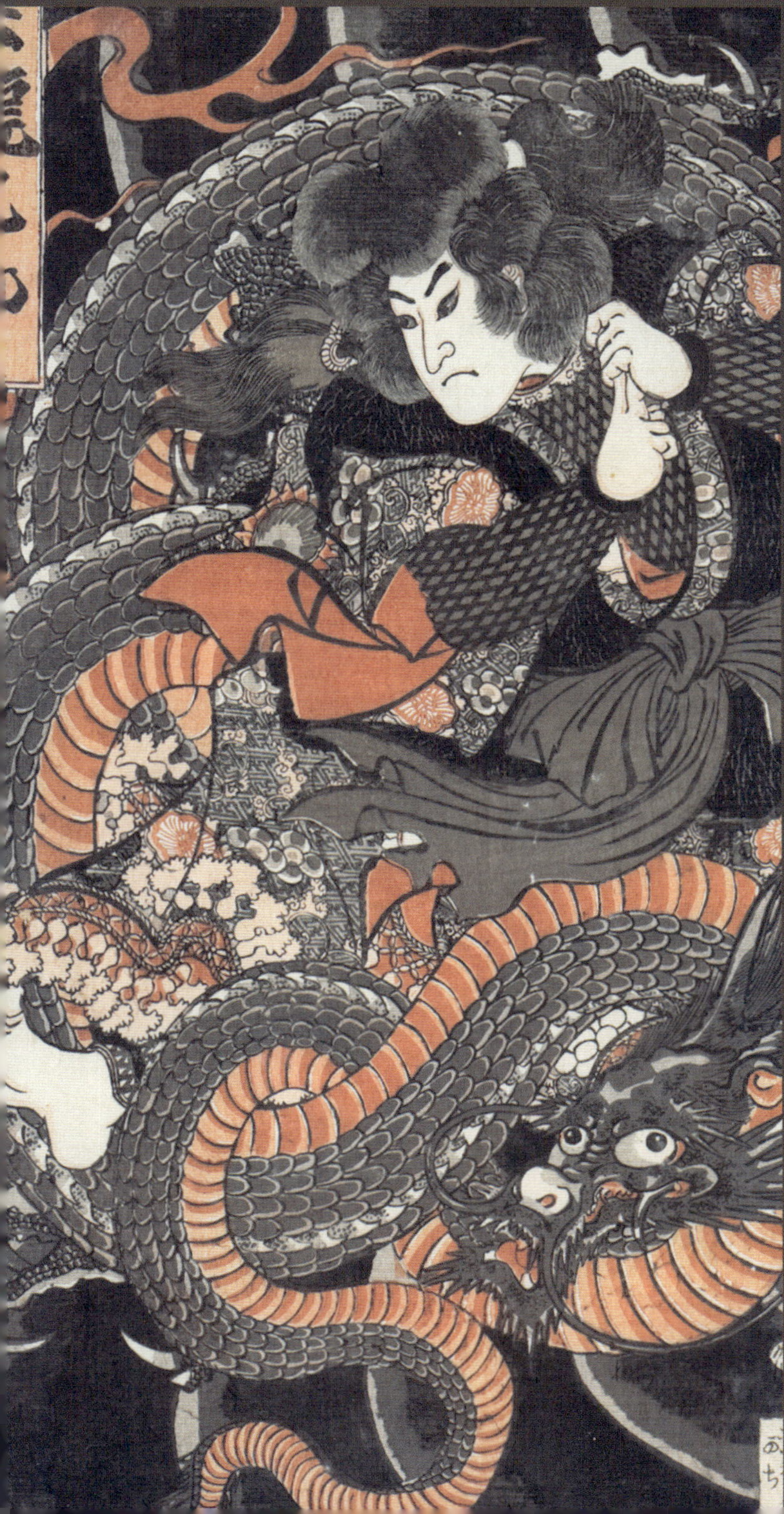

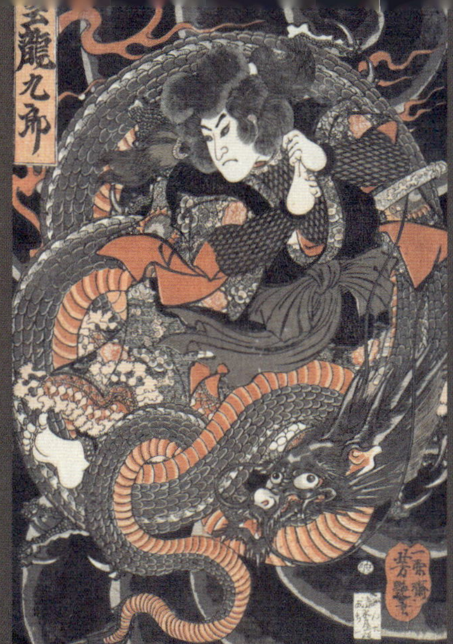

Unryū Kurō / Utagawa Yoshitsuya
The Tsubouchi Memorial Theatre Museum

This picture is based on the illustrated novel "The Tale of a Theft Unryū Kurō" written by Shikitei Sanba. The story is about the crimes of Unryū Kurō and Toraō-maru, captains of two different robber bands. The atrocious tales of the villains became popular among young people in the late Edo period.

雲龍九郎 ／ 歌川芳艶
早稲田大学演劇博物館蔵

式亭三馬による絵入り小説『雲竜九郎 偸盗伝』は、雲竜九郎と虎王丸、二人の盗賊の頭の悪行を描いた物語。悪のヒーローによる残酷な物語が、江戸時代後期の若者たちのあいだで人気を集めた。

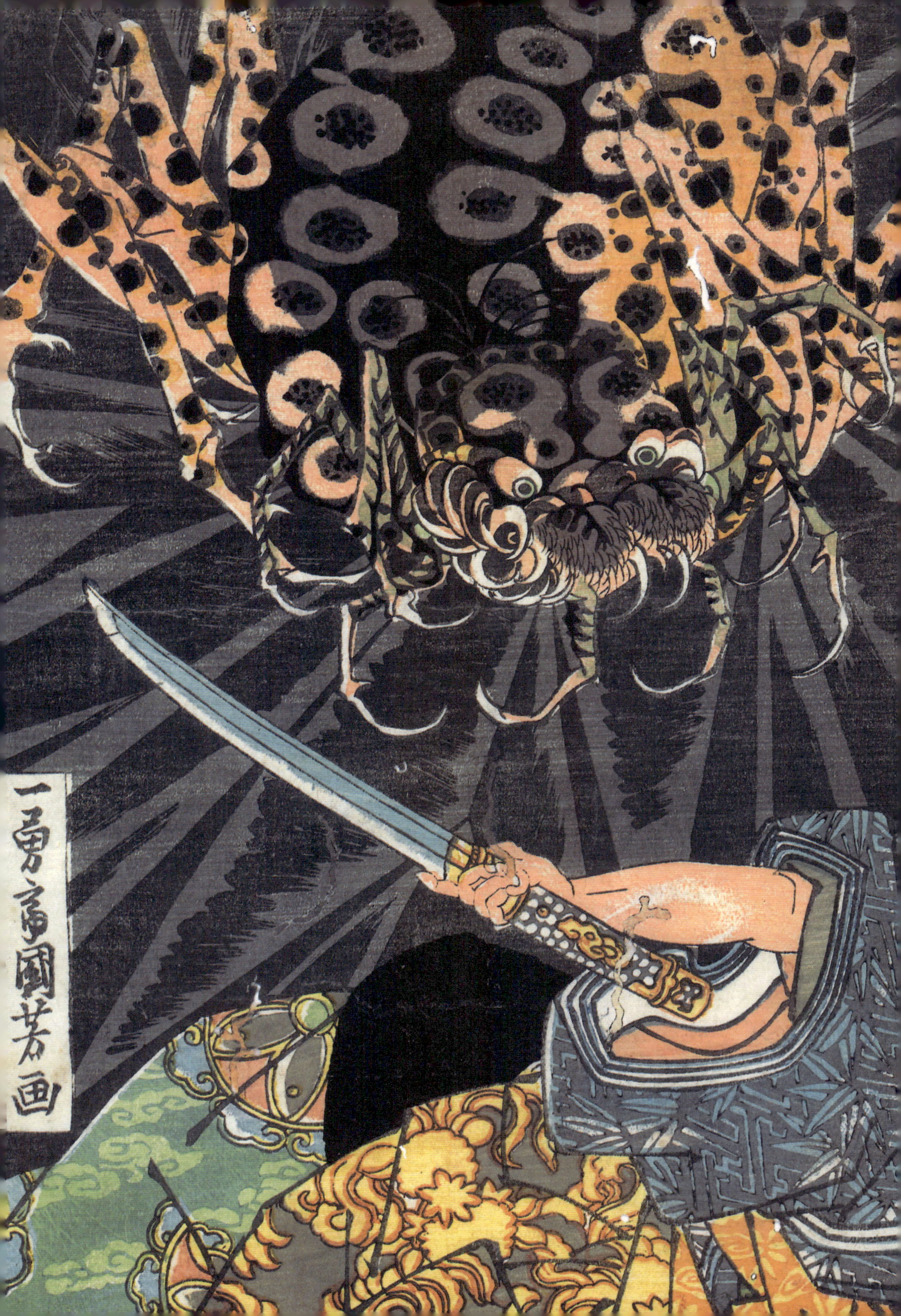
一勇斎國芳画

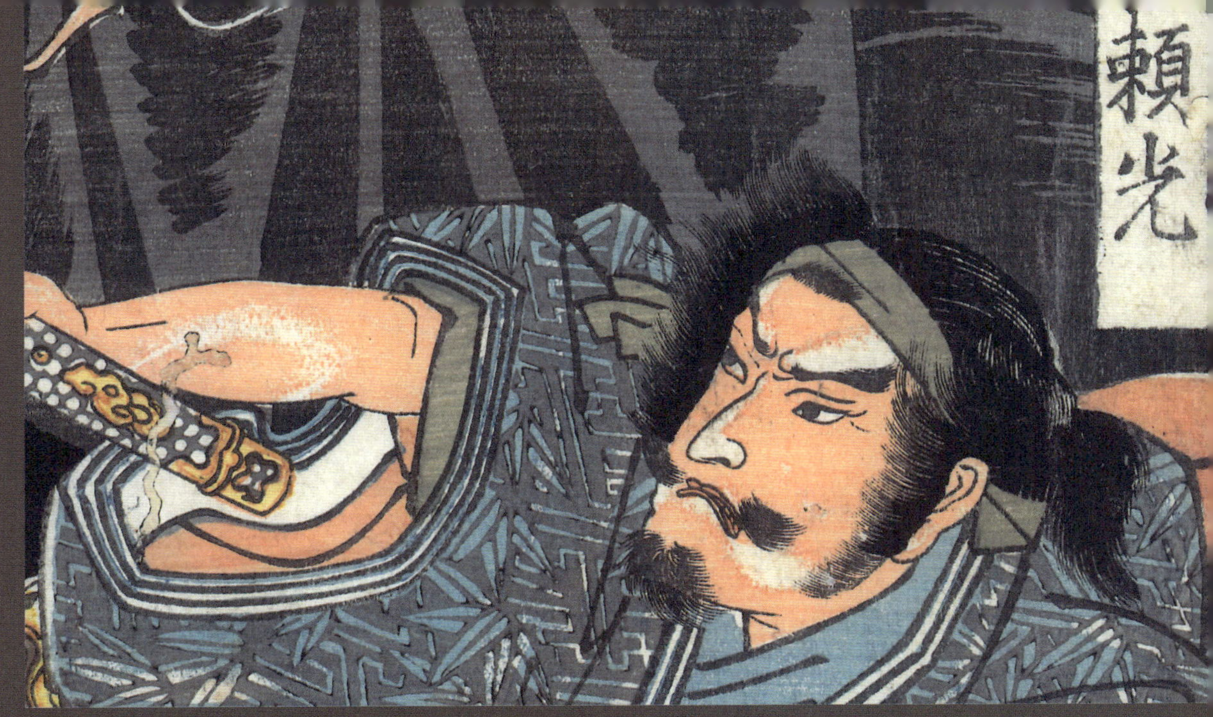

Minamoto-no Yorimitsu and His Four Retainers Defeating the Spider Monster Tsuchigumo / Utagawa Kuniyoshi

1815–1842 / Touken World Foundation

Minamoto-no Yorimitsu was a warrior in the Heian period. Various legends of him and his vassals are widely known. This picture depicts a legend of Yorimitsu and his four retainers eliminating a spider monster called Tsuchigumo. While Yorimitsu was laid up and his four retainers were playing a game of Go at a feudal lord's mansion, Tsuchigumo emerged. Here, Yorimitsu wearing a Hachimaki head band draws a bedside sword and attacks the monster. Among various paintings on the same theme, this spider has an especially lurid look.

源頼光 四天王 土蜘蛛退治之図 ／ 歌川国芳

文化 – 天保期（1815~1842） ／ 刀剣ワールド財団（東建コーポレーション）蔵

平安時代の武将・源頼光と配下の武者たちは、さまざまな「頼光伝説」で、人口に膾炙してきた。本図は、頼光と四天王による土蜘蛛退治の場面。屋敷で寝込む頼光と碁を打つ四天王のもとに土蜘蛛が現れ、頼光は病鉢巻の姿で枕元の刀を抜いて斬りかかる。数多くある土蜘蛛退治の絵の中で、とりわけ毒々しい蜘蛛が描かれる。

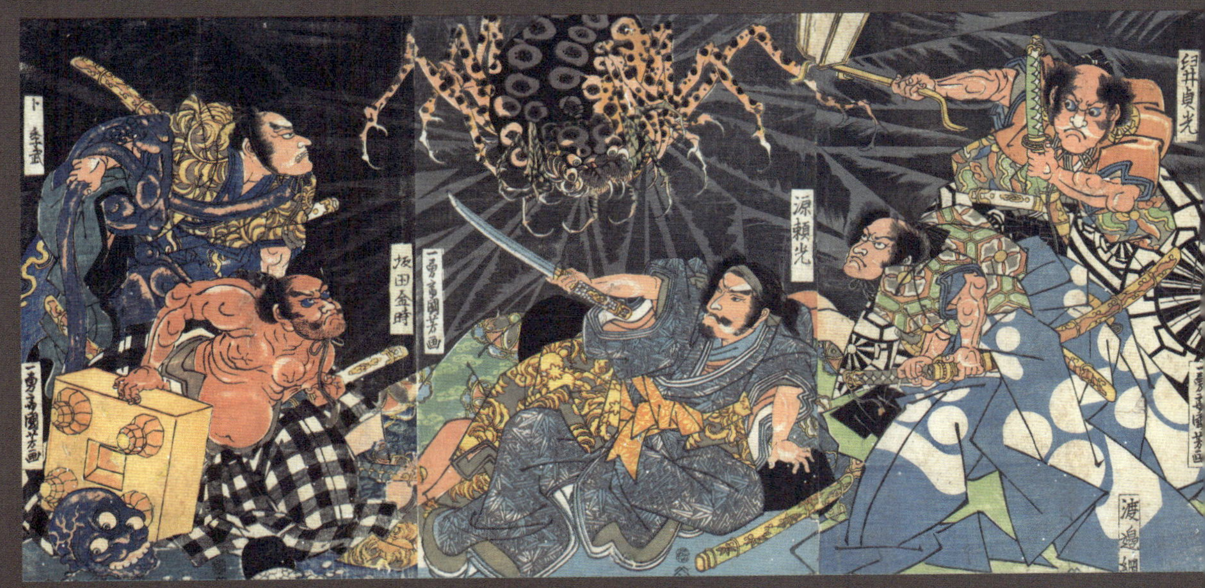

Minamoto-no Yorimitsu, the Spider Monster Tsuchigumo and Other Monsters / Utagawa Kuniyoshi

1843 / Keio University

This picture depicts the same scene as P.72 In this picture, shadows of uncanny creatures are cast onto the curtain. The shadows lead to the spider's webs in the upper right of the picture. Minamoto-no Yorimitsu is now in great danger. The man in front of Yorimitsu is a warrior Urabe-no Suetake. His kimono is emblazoned with his family crest, a patten of a plant called Omodaka. It resembles the family crest of Mizuno Tadakuni who led the Tenpō Reforms as a senior councilor of the Tokugawa shogunate. When this ukiyoe print was published, it was regarded as a caricature, featuring Tokugawa Ieyoshi, a shogun of the Edo Bakufu, as Yorimitsu, Mizuno and other senior councilors as Yorimitsu's four retainers, and many people punished during the Tenpō Reforms as the monsters on the curtain.

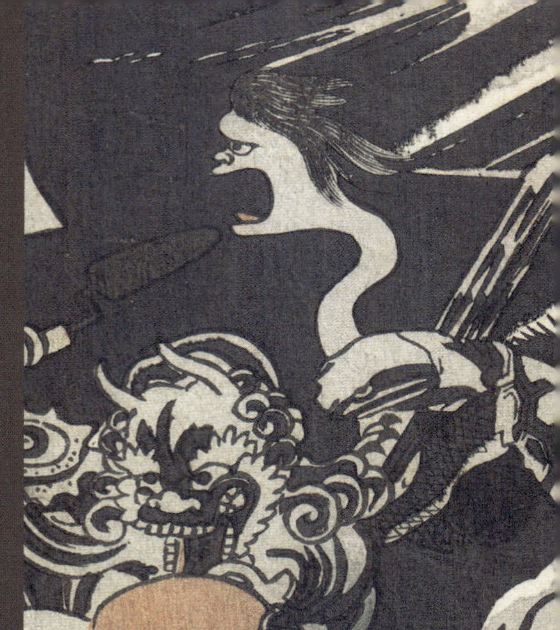

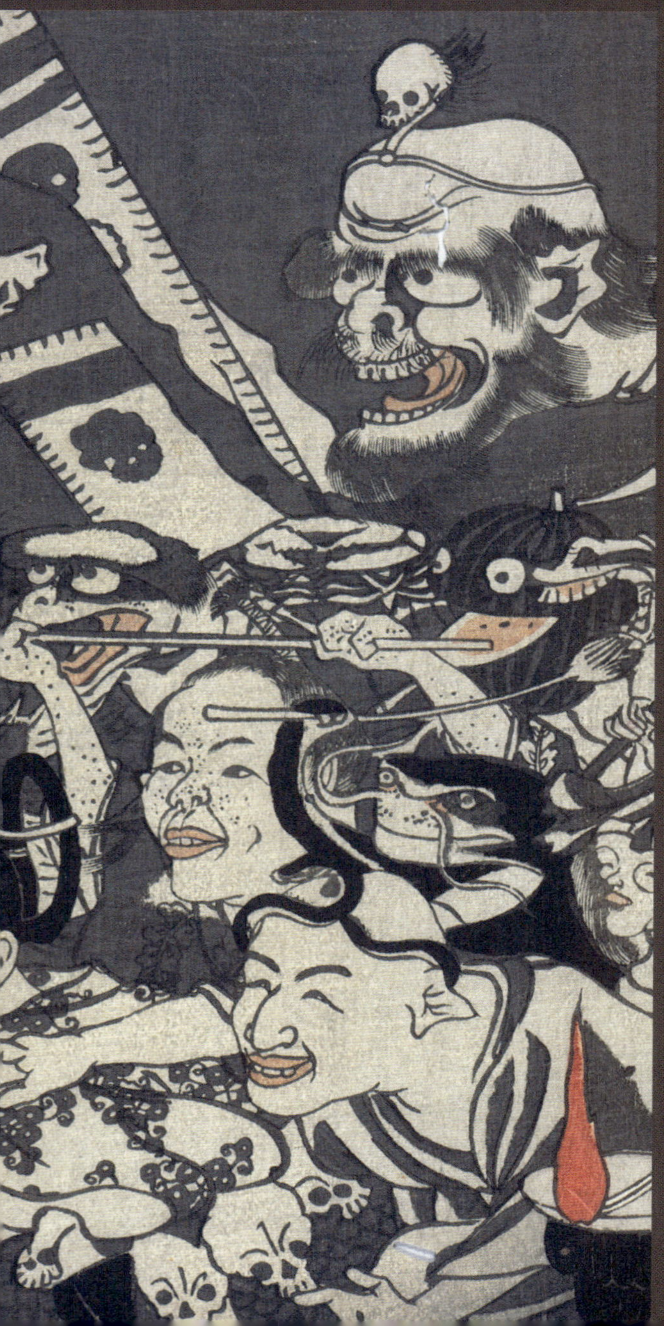

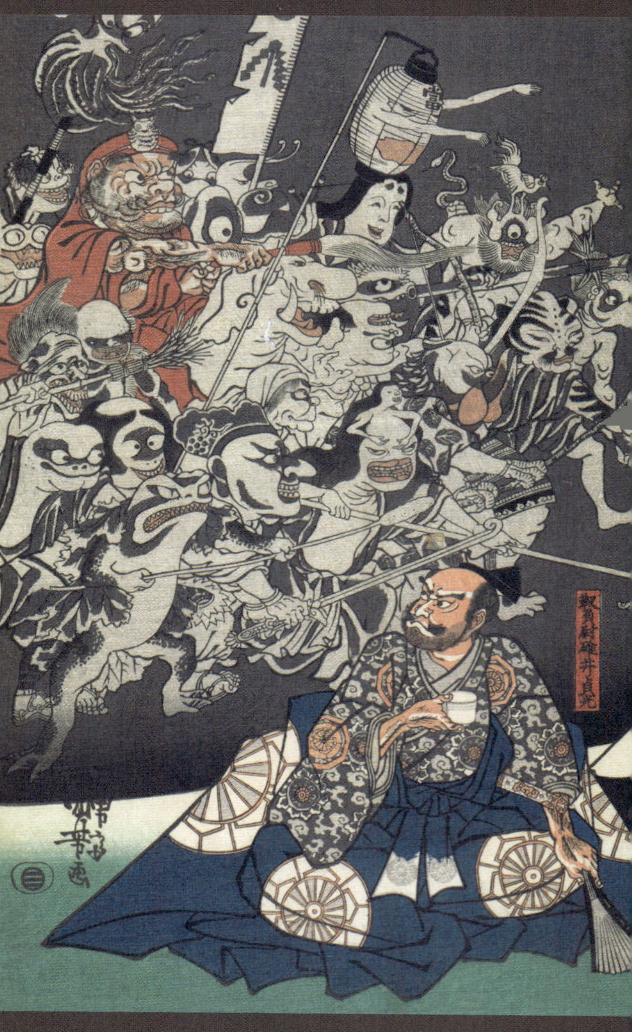

源頼光公舘土蜘作妖怪図 ／ 歌川国芳

天保 14 年（1843）／ 慶應義塾大学蔵
P.72 と同じ場面を描いたもの。大勢
の異形のものたちが浮かび上がる天幕
が、右上では土蜘蛛の糸と化し、頼光
に危機が迫っている。頼光の手前に
配された卜部季武の家紋は、当時天保
の改革を主導した水野忠邦と同じ沢潟
紋である。この絵は、頼光を将軍徳川
家慶に、四天王を水野ほか時の老中に、
天幕に描かれた妖怪たちを改革で処罰
された怨みを持つものたちに見立てた
改革の風刺絵だろうと噂を呼んだ。

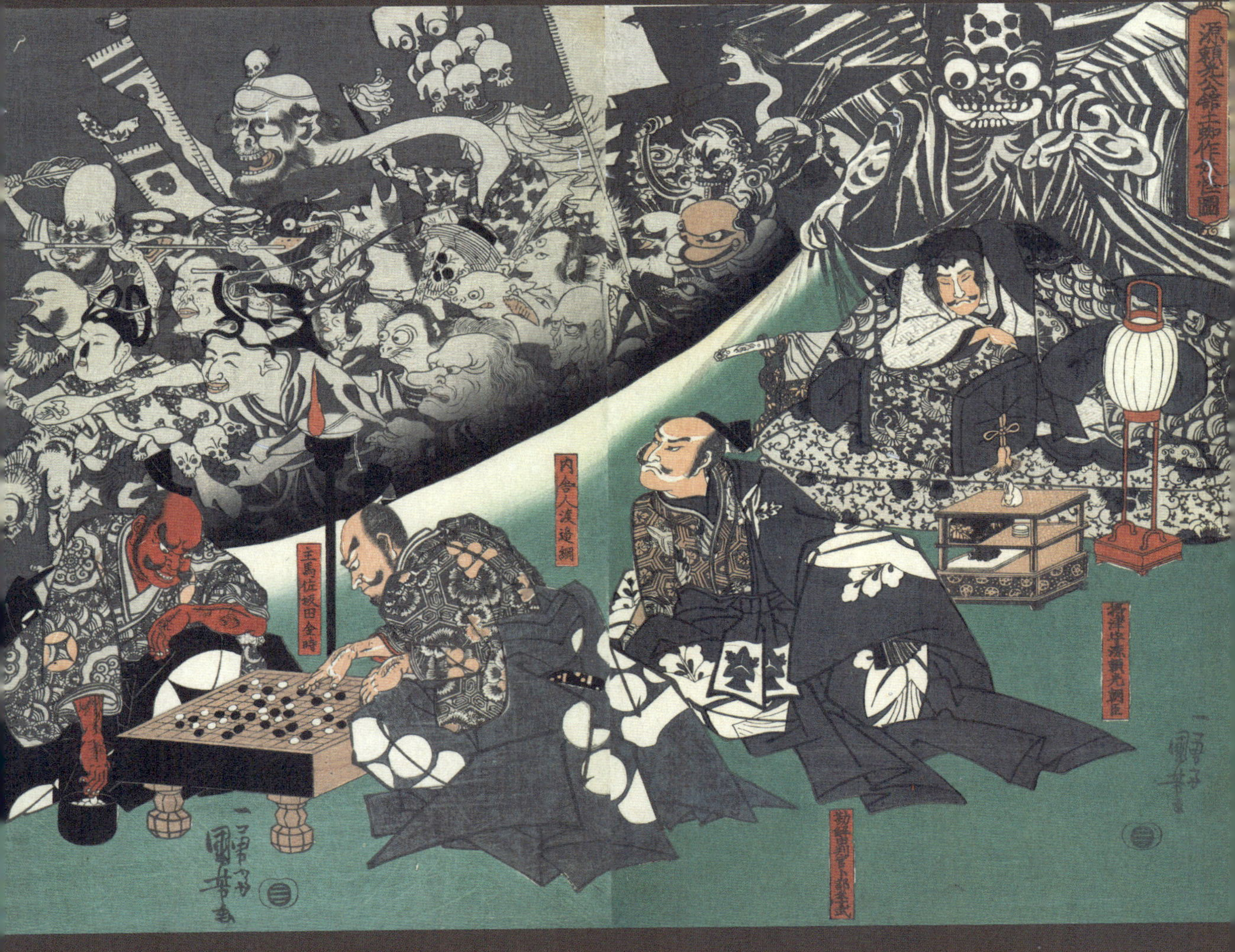

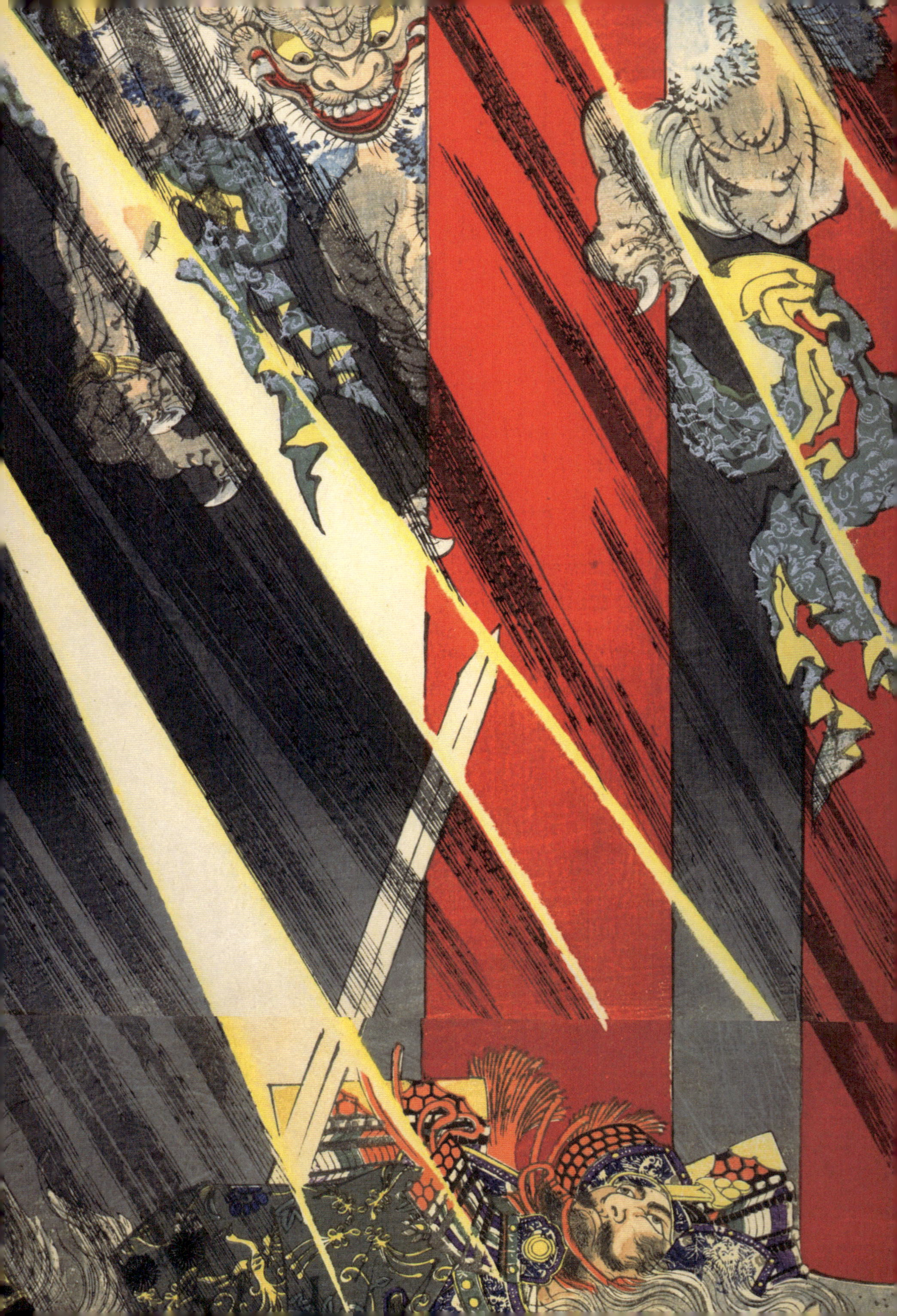

Watanabe-no Tsuna Cutting an Ogre's Arm at the Rajōmon Gate / Tsukioka Yoshitoshi

1888 / National Diet Library, Japan

The picture depicts the tale of Watanabe-no Tsuna, one of the four retainers of the warlord Minamoto-no Yorimitsu, defeating an ogre at the Rajōmon Gate. Tsuna hears a rumor that an ogre lives at the Rajōmon Gate on the border of the old capital Kyoto. He visits the gate to know if the rumor is true or not, bringing a card called Kinsatsu, which works as an official testament of his visit. Here we see the ogre emerging in the dark night and trying to beat on Tsuna. In the next moment, Tsuna would draw his long sword and cut the ogre's arm off. This tale was adapted into a Noh song "Rajōmon," which tells that the praised hero Tsuna is stronger and more frightening than the ogre.

羅城門渡辺綱 鬼 腕斬之図 / 月岡芳年

明治 21年（1888） / 国立国会図書館蔵

頼光四天王の一人、渡辺綱による羅生門の鬼退治を描く。都の境界となる羅城門に鬼が棲むという噂を聞いた綱は、真偽を確かめるために見に来た印となる「禁札」を持って訪れる。風雨とともに闇夜にあらわれた鬼が、綱に襲い掛かろうとしている。この後、綱は太刀を抜いて斬り掛かってその腕を斬り落とす。謡曲『羅城門』では、綱は鬼よりも恐ろしいと称えられる。

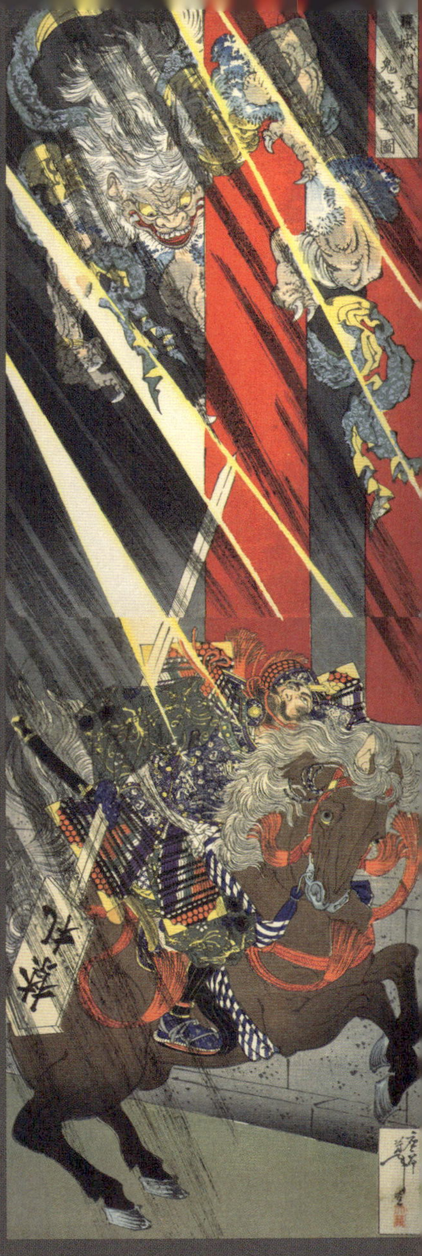

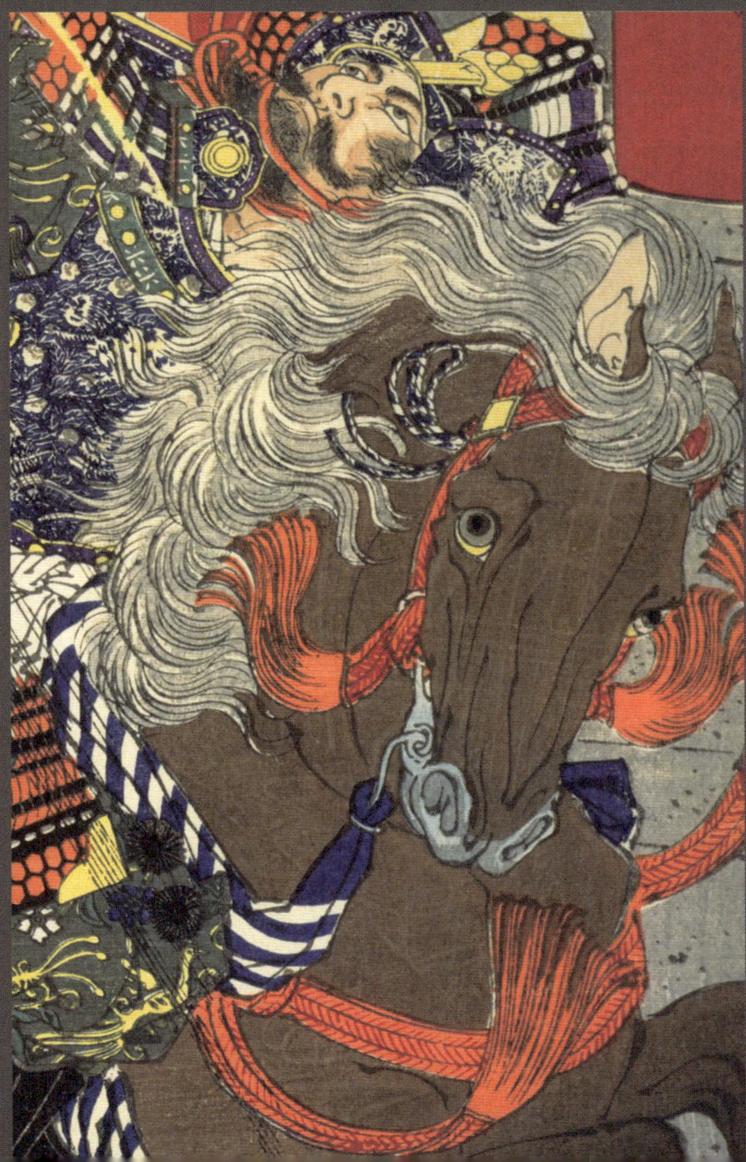

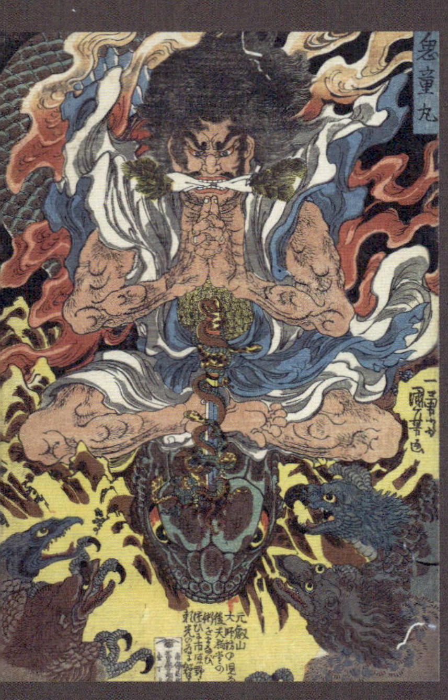

Kidōmaru / Utagawa Kuniyoshi

1839–1841 / The Tsubouchi Memorial Theatre Museum

Kidōmaru is known as a son of the ogre Shuten Dōji in some legends. He ambushes Minamoto-no Yorimitsu at Ichiharano to kill him, but Yorimitsu reads his attempt and kills Kidōmaru instead. The text in this picture reads that Kidōmaru lived in Mount Hiei in his childhood, and mastered martial arts from long-nosed goblins. This description is based on the book "The Former Taihei-ki." Kidōmaru sits on a giant snake's head, and sticks a sword with five small coiled snakes into its head, and practices sorcery in a blazing fire. By his sorcery, several specters come from outside the picture frame and show their faces.

鬼童丸 ／ 歌川国芳

天保 10 -12 年（1839-1841） ／ 早稲田大学演劇博物館蔵

酒呑童子の子という伝承もある鬼童丸は、源頼光の命を狙い市原野で待ち伏せしていたところを、頼光に見抜かれ斬られるエピソードが知られる。本図には、もとは比叡山の稚児であり、天狗の術を修めたという『前太平記』が伝える設定が記されている。大蛇の上に座り、5匹もの蛇が巻き付いた刀をその頭に突き立て、妖術を発し火炎をまとう。引き寄せられた妖魔たちが、画面外から顔をのぞかせている。

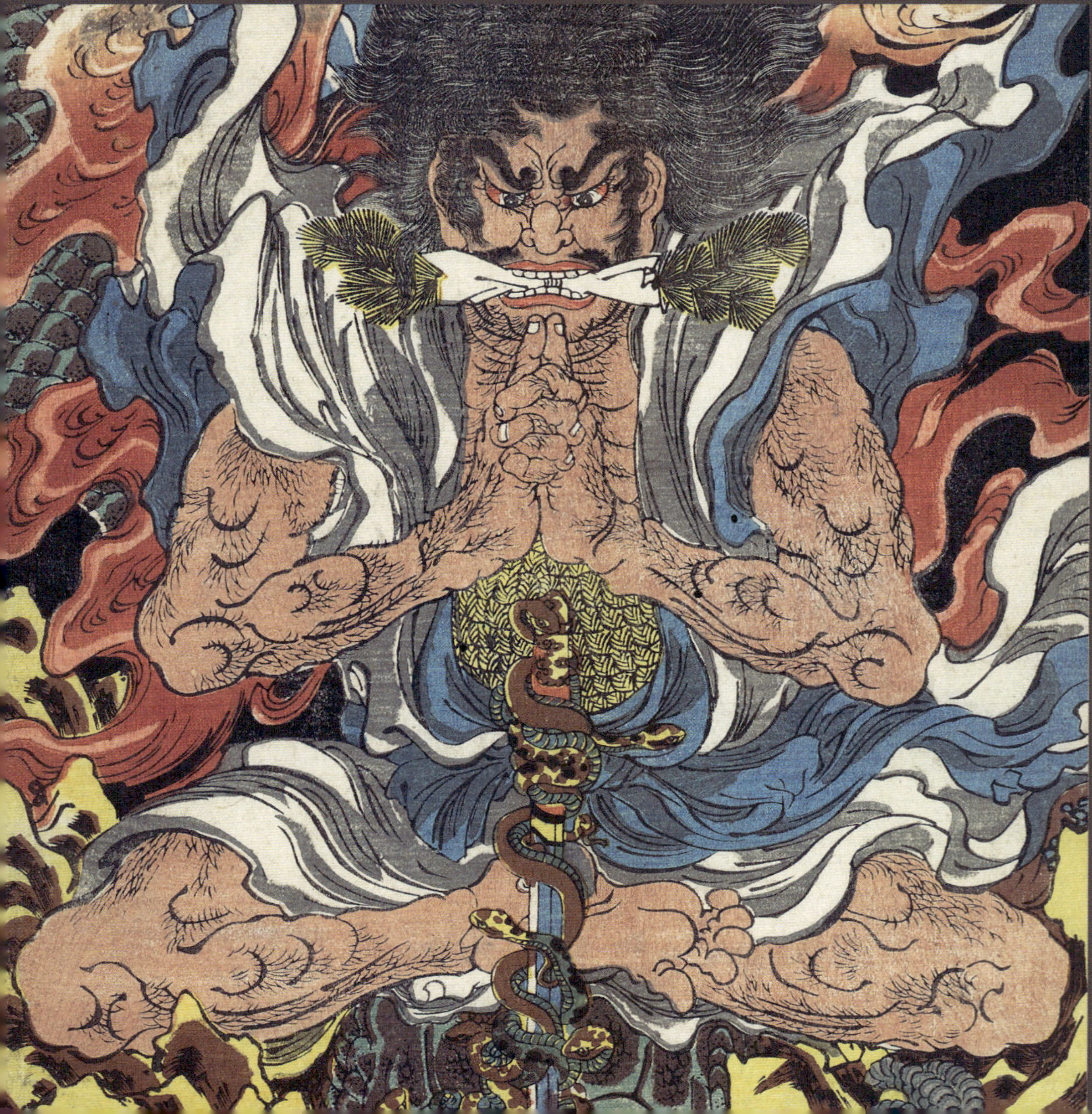

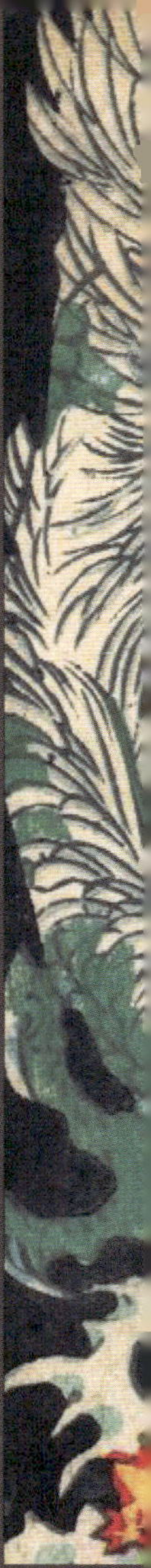

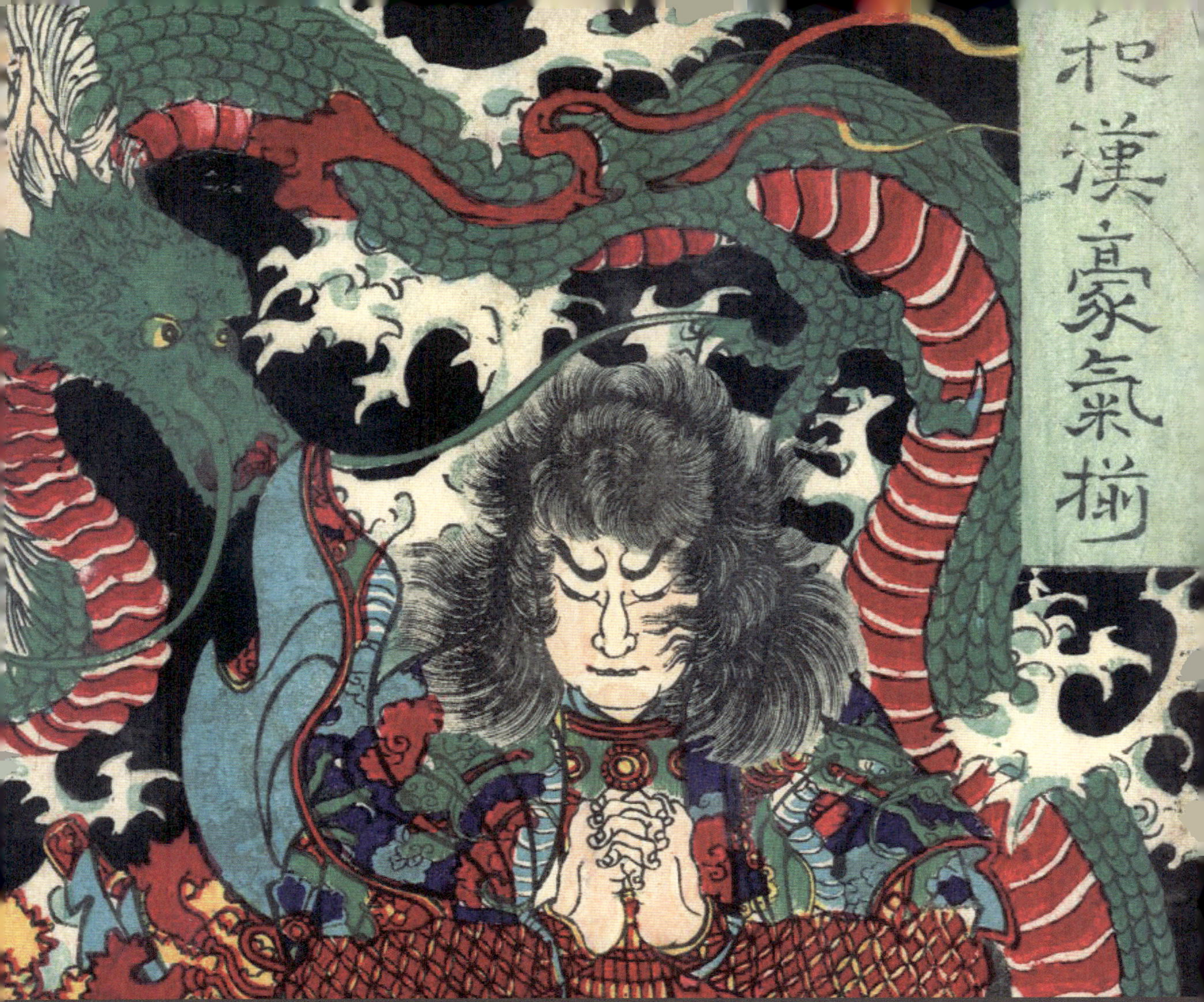

Hakamadare Yasusuke, from a series Valor in China and Japan / Tsukioka Yoshitoshi

1866 / Photo : Morimiya

This picture is based on the novel "A Strange Record of Four Elite Robbers" written by Kyokutei Bakin, published in 1805. A great robber Hakamadare Yasusuke practices sorcery and leads Minamoto-no Yorimitsu and his vassals around by the nose. The story plot revolves around Hakamadare's bad acts. The following episode was later adapted into ukiyoe prints and became popular. Hakamadare scares Yorimitsu and his vassals during their unguarded moments, by practicing sorcery to create an illusion of a battle between a great snake and a bear. This picture depicts Hakamadare reciting magic words to call upon a dragon. The dragon and stirring waves brilliantly color the antihero.

和漢豪気揃　袴垂保輔 ／ 月岡芳年

慶応2年（1866）　／　提供：古美術もりみや

曲亭馬琴の『四天王剿盗異録』（1805 年刊）は、妖術を使う大盗賊・袴垂保輔が、源頼光一行を翻弄する物語。袴垂の悪事を中心にストーリーが展開する。幻術によって蟒蛇と熊が戦う光景を見せ、頼光一行を驚かせて虚をつく場面が、錦絵の人気の題材となった。本図の袴垂は、術を唱えて龍を召喚している様子だ。優雅に体をくねらせる龍と沸き起こる水が、ダークヒーローを華麗に彩っている。

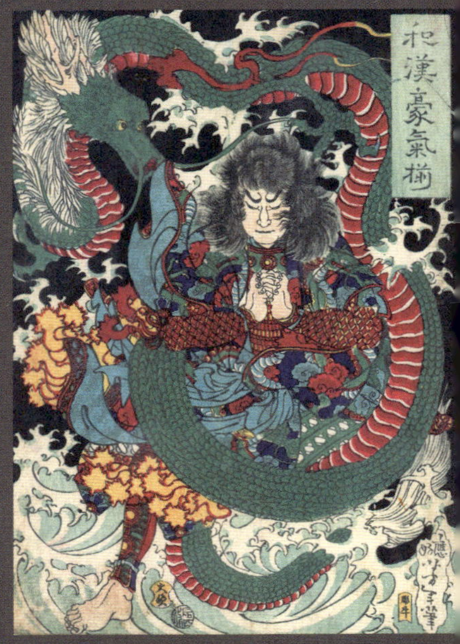

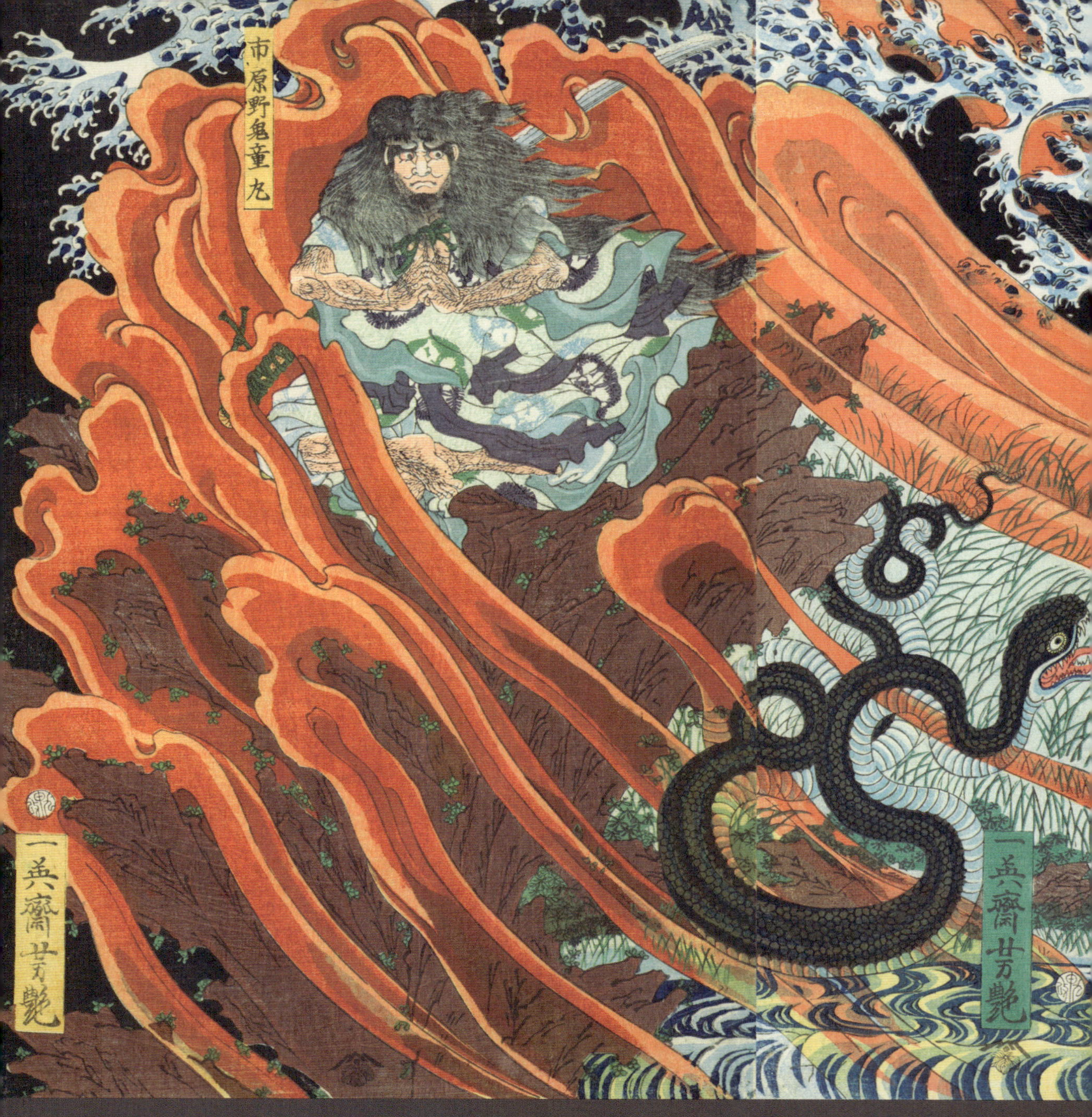

Two Robbers' Competition in Sorcery Practices in Deep Mountains / Utagawa Yoshitsuya

1860

The climax of the novel "A Strange Record of Four Elite Robbers" is a sorcery battle between Hakamadare Yasusuke and Kidōmaru. This picture depicts Kidōmaru on the upper left and Hakamadare on the lower right, in order to make a diagonal composition. While Hakamadare puts their surrounding area on fire, Kidōmaru makes heavy rain fall. Kidōmaru summons a poisonous snake and uses it to attack Hakamadare, then Hakamadare calls upon an eagle to let it catch the snake. It effectively expresses their fierce battle. The poisonous snake and the eagle are locked into each other's gazes. Their eye lines intersect with the motions of spouting flame and water.

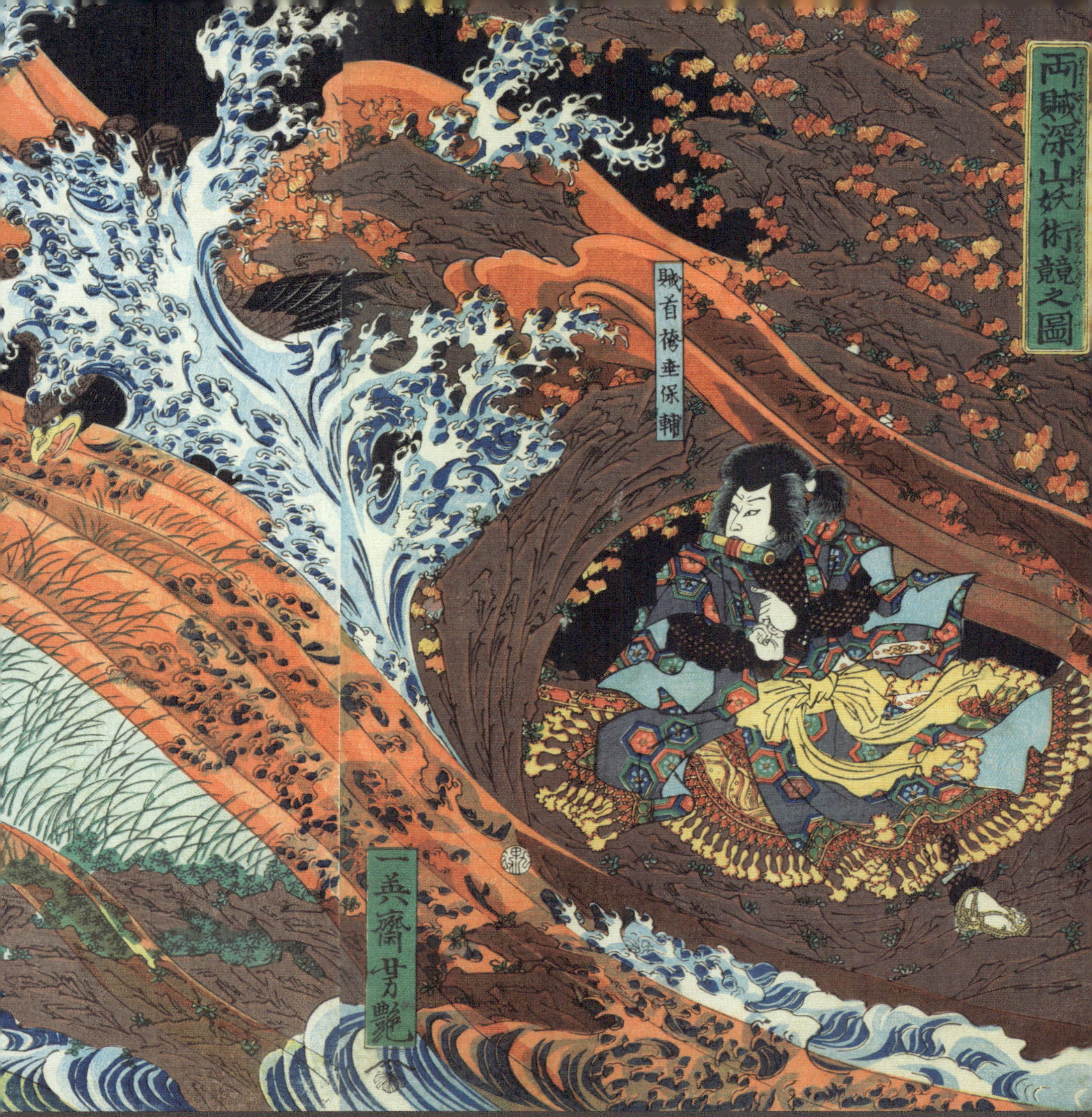

両 賊 深 山 妖 術 競之図 ／ 歌川芳艶

万延元年（1860）／ 個人蔵

『四天王剿盗異録』最大の見せ場は、袴垂保輔と鬼童丸の妖術合戦。本図では画面左上に鬼童丸、右下に袴垂と、対角線上に二者を配置して術のぶつかり合いを描いている。袴垂が炎であたりを燃やそうとすると、鬼童丸は豪雨を降らす。鬼童丸が毒蛇を呼び出して攻撃を仕掛けると、袴垂が召喚した鷲が毒蛇を捕える。お互いに向かってほとばしる炎と水、その動きと交差するように、毒蛇と鷲がにらみ合う。

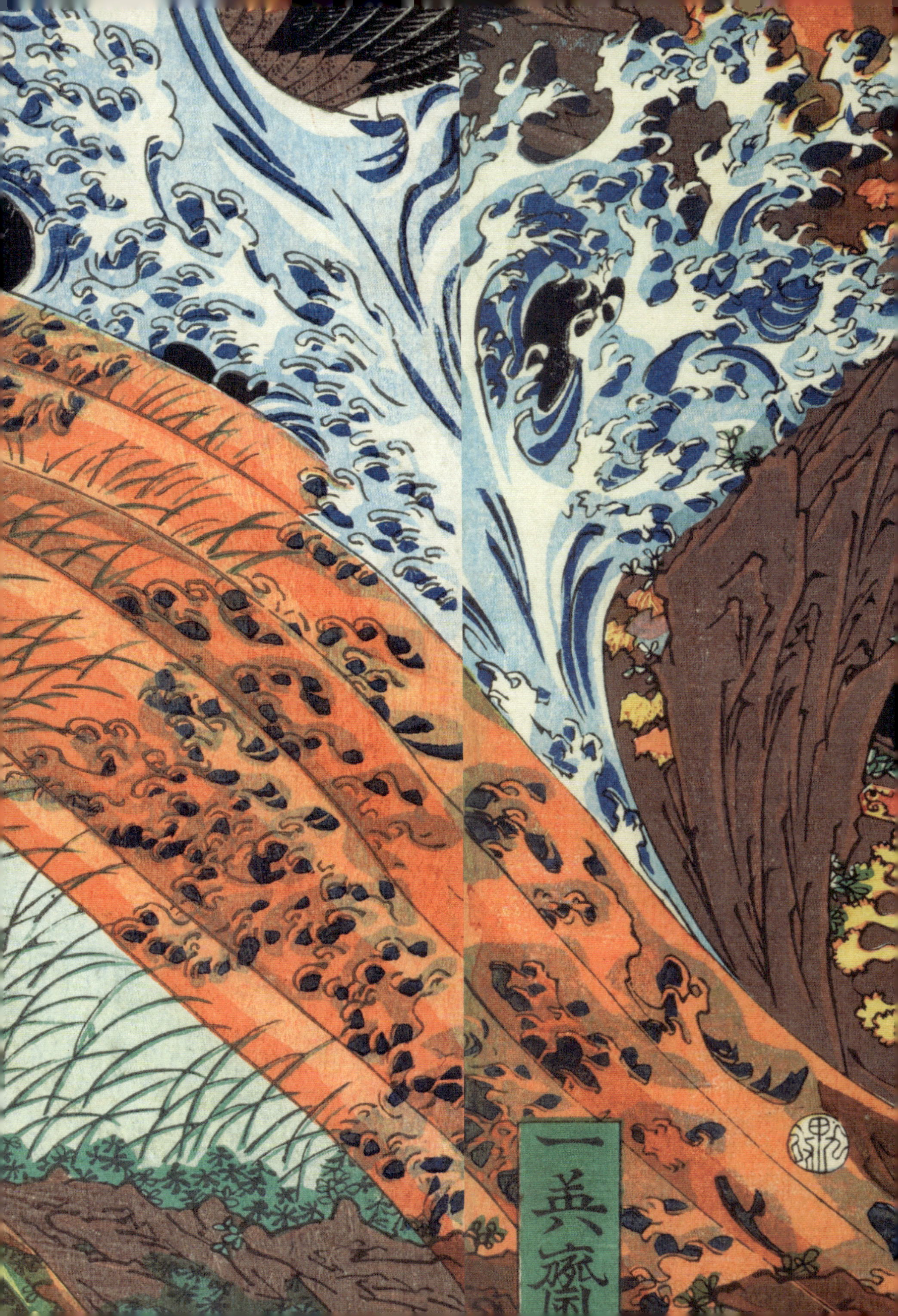

一勇齋國芳

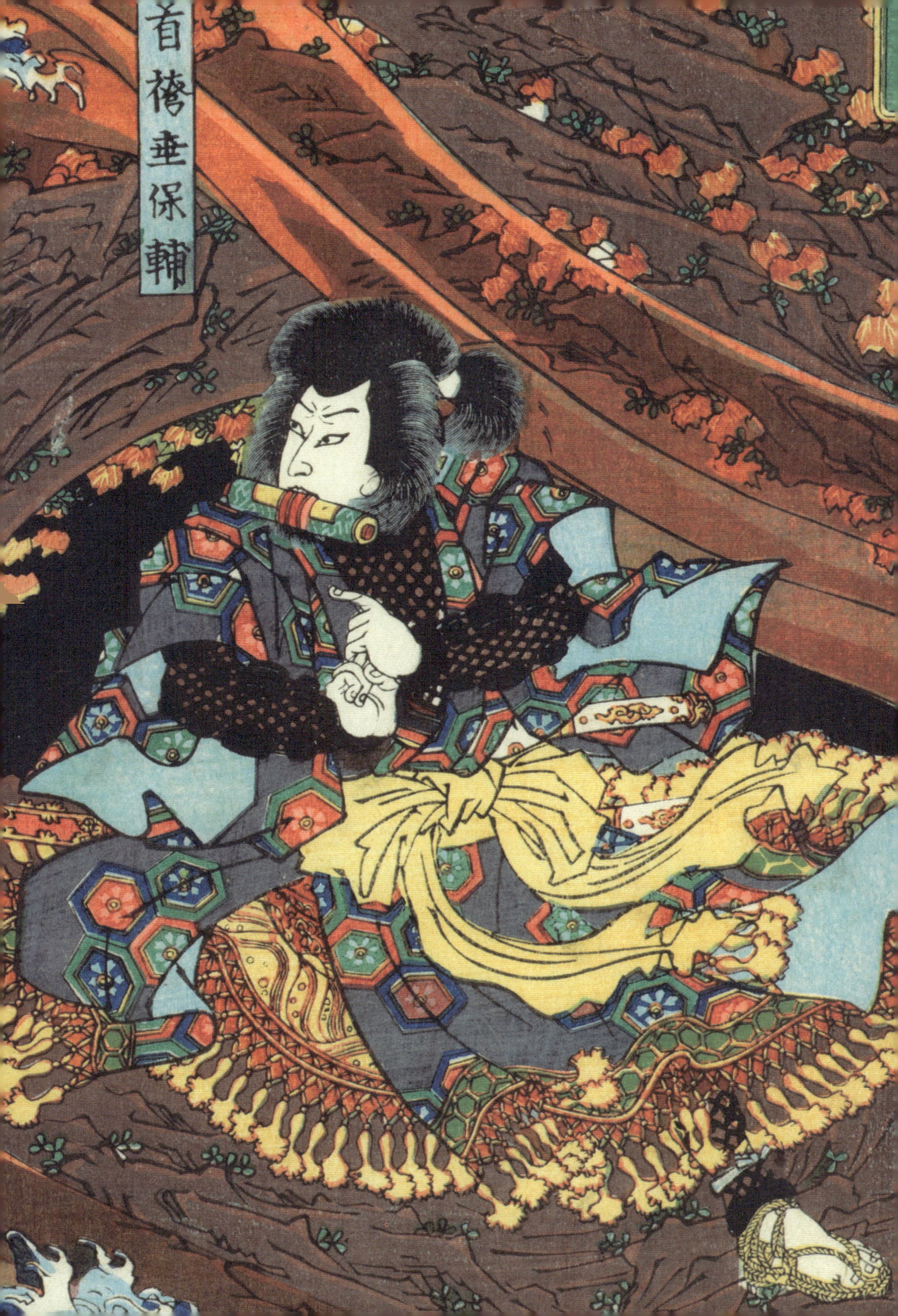
百椊垂保輔

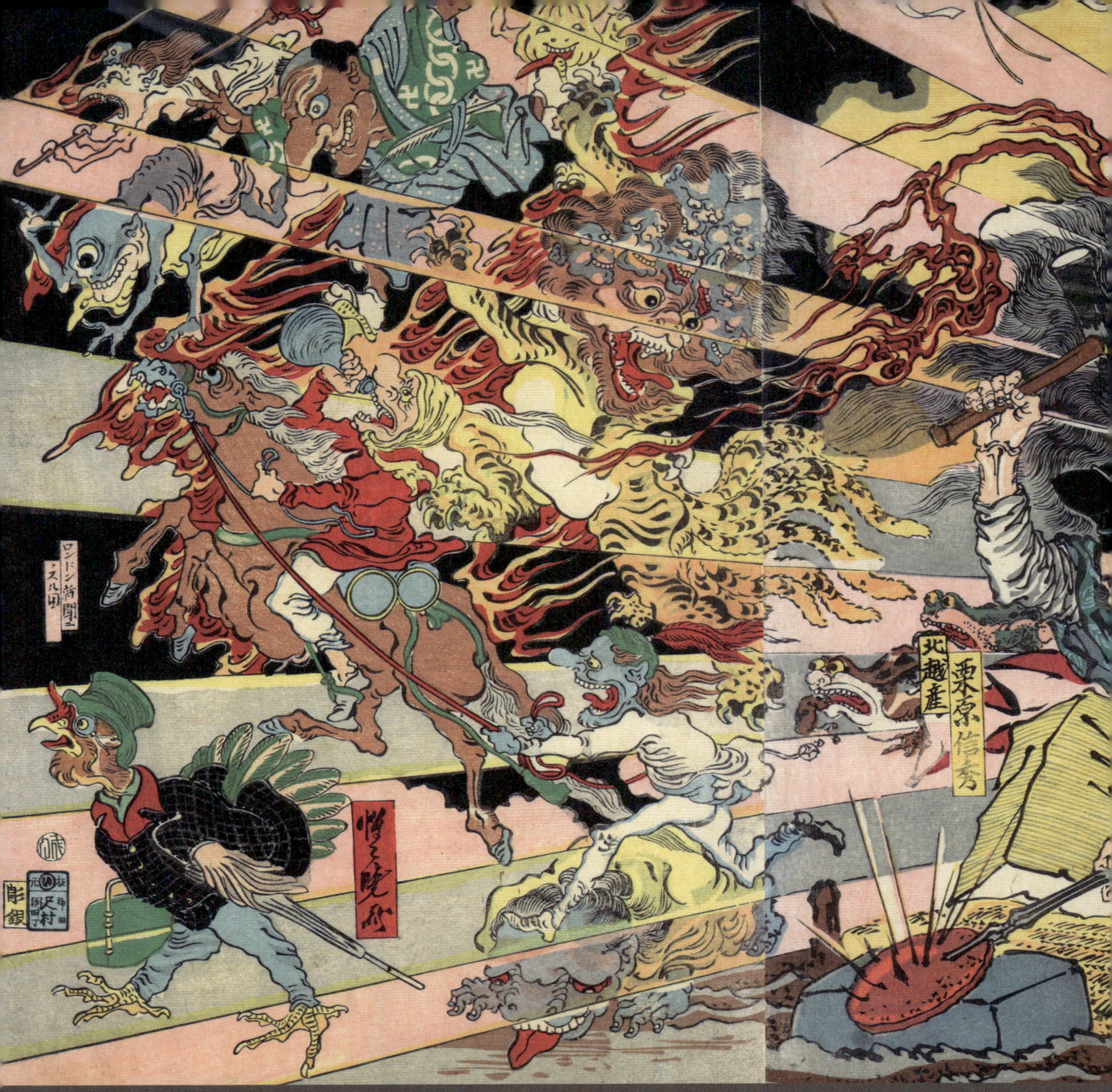

Famous Mirror: The Spirit of Japan, Newly Published / Kawanabe Kyōsai

1874 / Israel Goldman Collection, London
Photo : Art Research Center, Ritsumeikan University

The picture might depict devils and infidels being terrified of the special mirror's brilliance and running away. There are not only strange monsters but also people looking like foreign nationals who wear western clothing. A foreign man on the upper left has an especially long nose and wears a formal kimono. He resembles a character called Mr. Punch from "Japan Punch," which was a satirical comic magazine at that time and was published by an English painter Charles Wirgman in Yokohama. The man polishing the mirror is Hon'ami Narishige, the fifteenth of the Hon'ami clan. The family had long been a sword polishing and appraisal purveyor to Edo Bakufu. The other man producing a mirror in the center of the picture is Kurihara Nobuhide, who was a purveyor to Emperor Meiji. The composition expresses the friction between Japanese traditional culture against newly imported foreign culture.

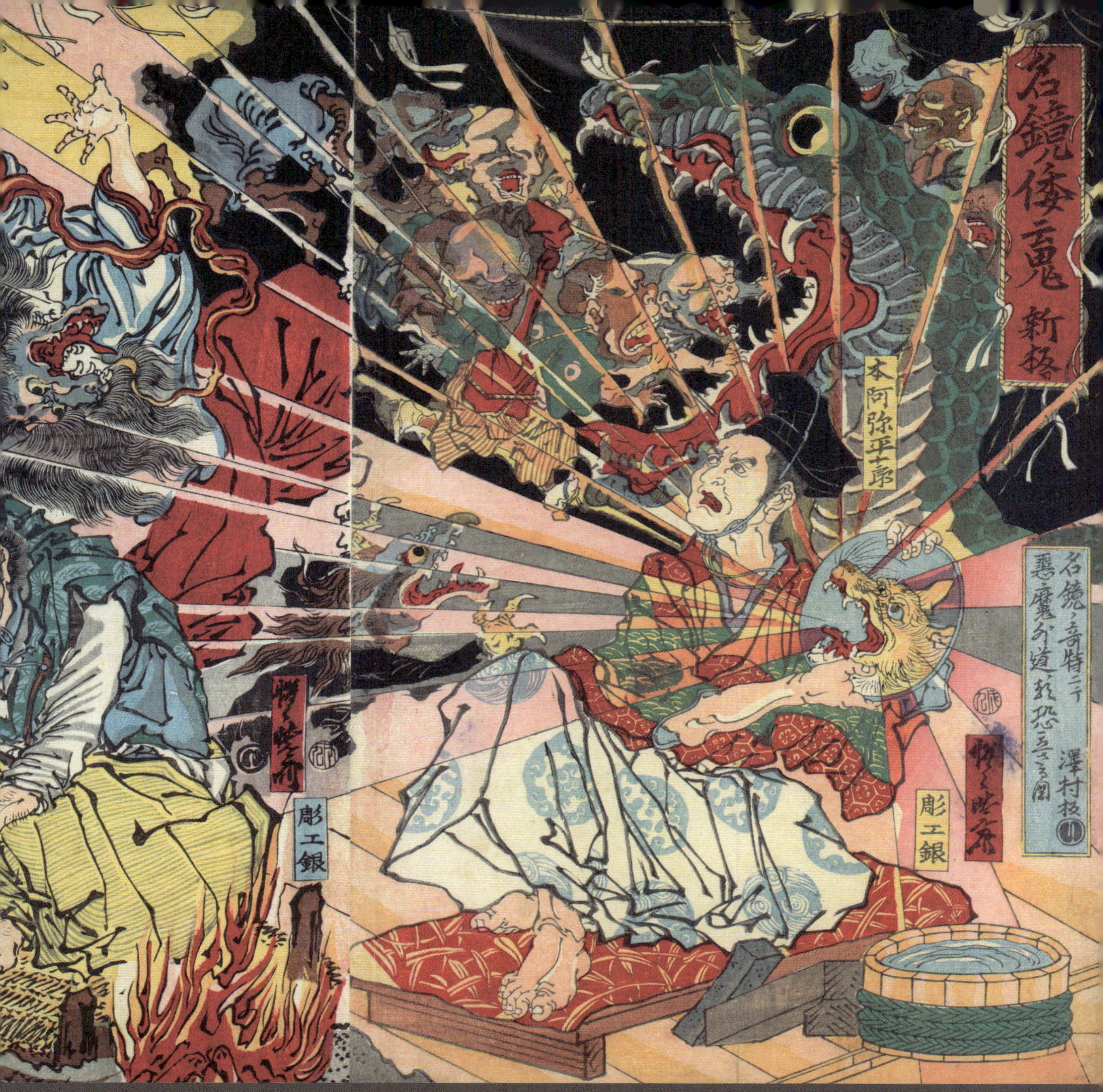

名鏡倭魂 新板 / 河鍋暁斎

明治 7 年（1874）／ イスラエル・ゴールドマン・コレクション

Photo：立命館大学アート・リサーチセンター

名鏡の輝きに、悪魔外道が恐れ退散する図とされる。異形の妖怪たちに、洋服に身を包む外国人を思わせる者たちが混ざっている。左上の異様に大きな鼻の裃姿の外国人は、イギリス人画家チャールズ・ワーグマンが横浜で発行していた風刺漫画雑誌『ジャパン・パンチ』のマスコット「ミスター・パンチ」。鏡を磨くのは刀剣の研磨・鑑定で幕府御用を務めた本阿弥家の 15 代成重、中央で鏡を鍛えるのは明治天皇の御用を務めた刀工栗原信秀。新興の外国文化に対抗する日本の伝統文化という構図になっている。

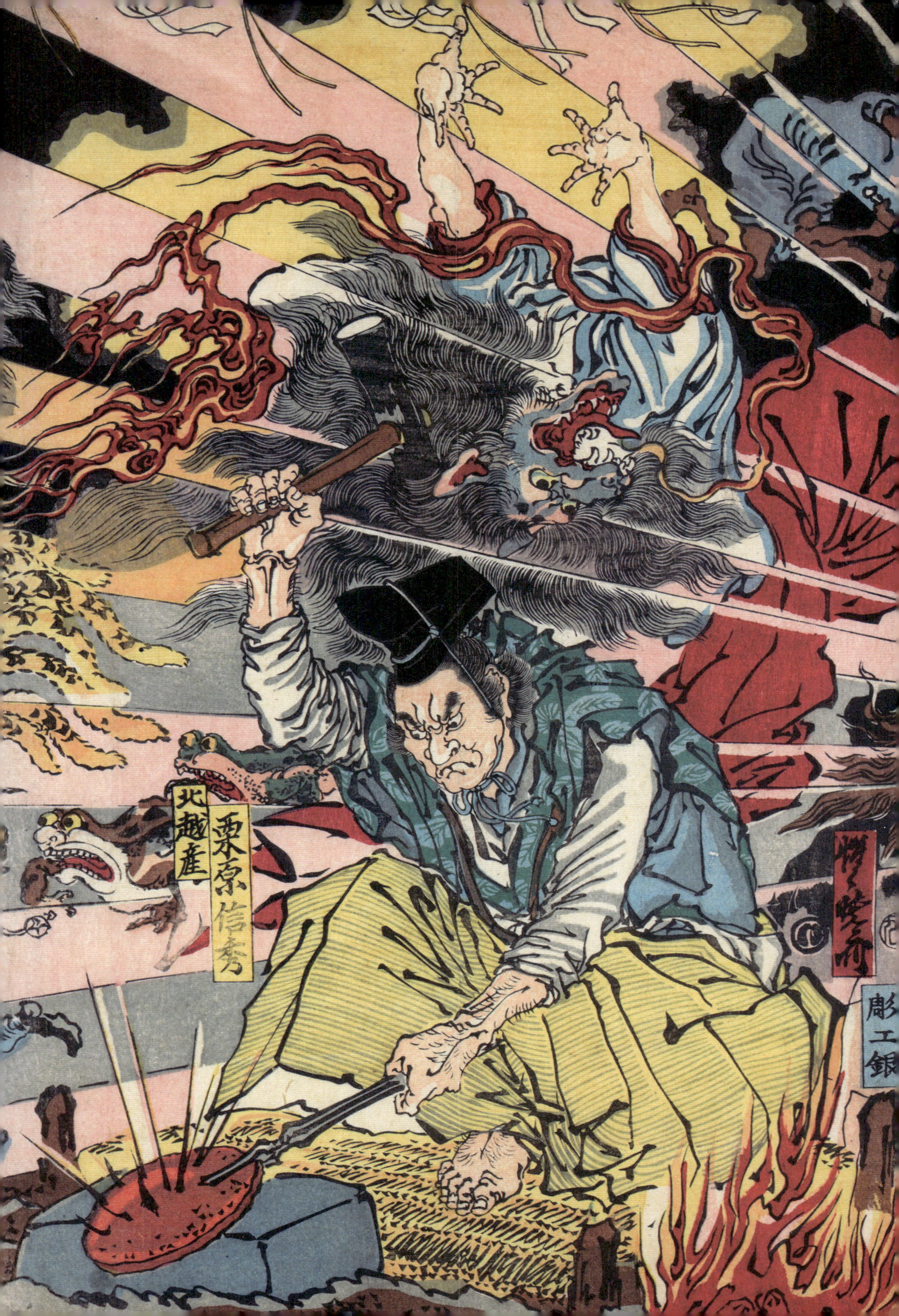
北越産
栗原信秀
惺々暁斎
彫工銀

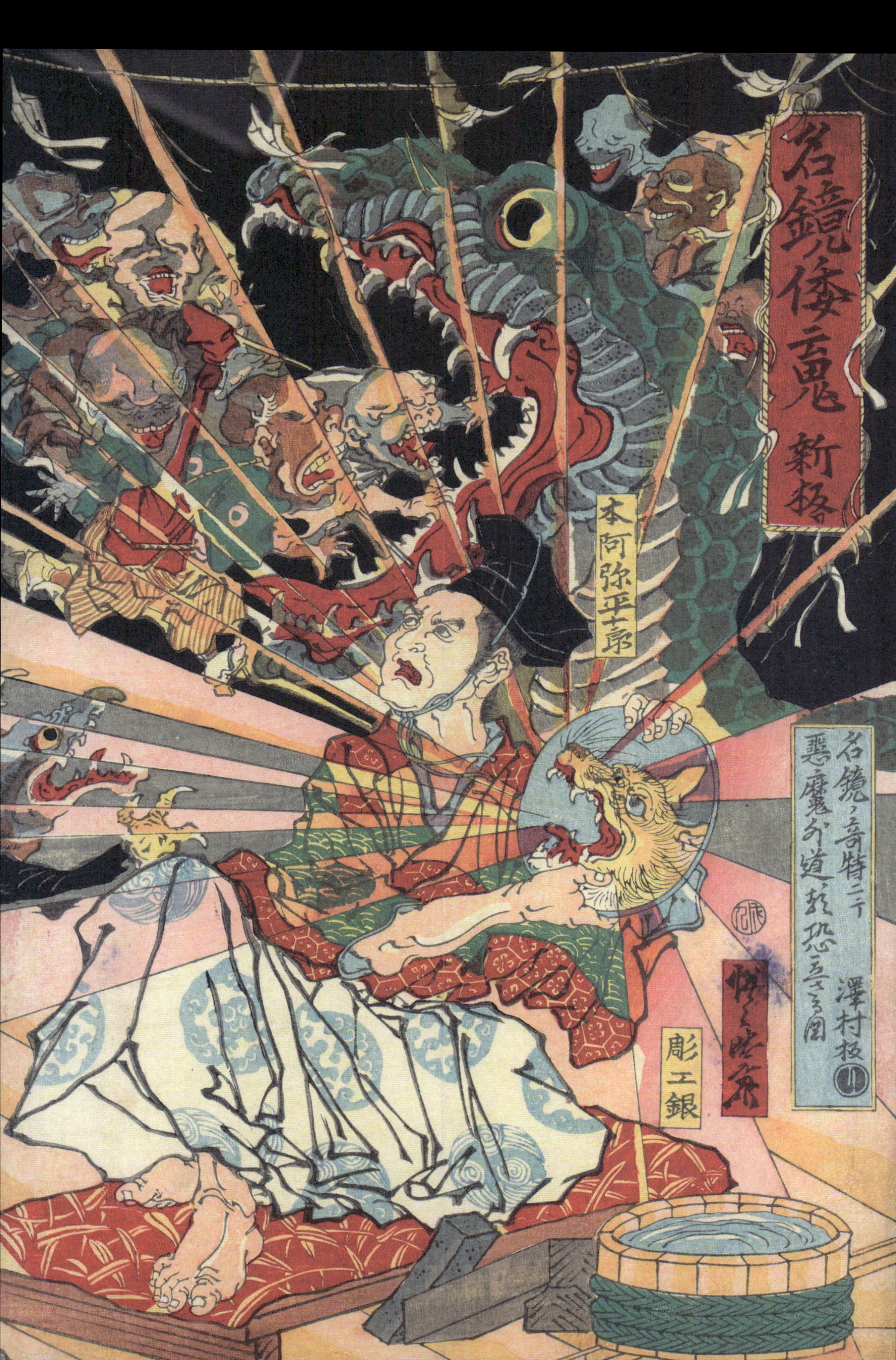

名鏡倭三鬼　新撰
本阿弥平吉
名鏡ノ奇特ニて　澤村板
悪魔が道理恐さ々を圖
彫工銀
惺々暁斎

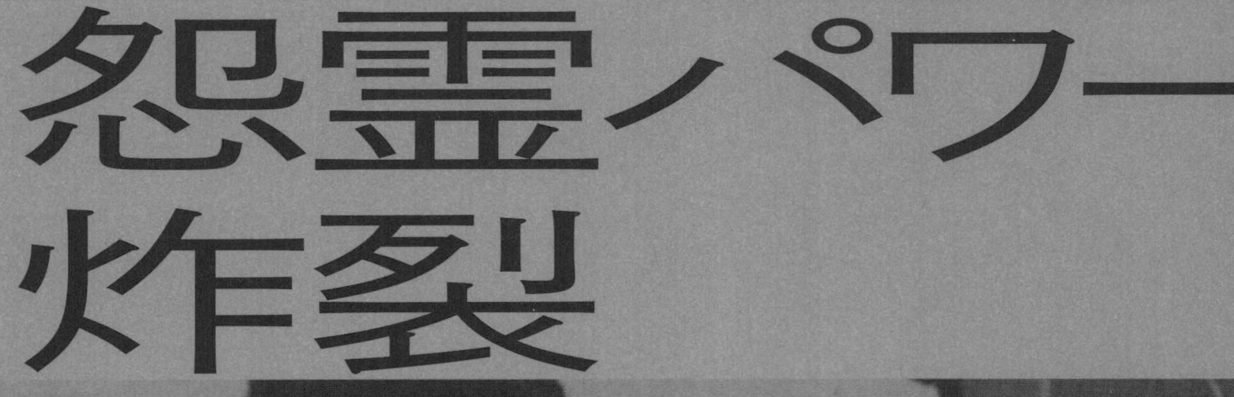

怨霊パワー炸裂

In Japan, since ancient times, natural disasters were regarded as phenomenon caused by vengeful spirits of people who died with grudges or by violent acts. People were in awe of those spirits, which drove them to create various festivals, observances, literature and other forms of entertainment. Many Nishikie, or polychrome ukiyoe prints, featuring vengeful spirits lively and vividly represent their fierce powers.

古来日本では、人々を脅かす天災や疫病は、恨みを持って死んだり、非業の死を遂げた人の怨霊の仕業と考えられてきた。怨霊への畏怖の念が、行事や慣習、文学や芸能をかたちづくってきた。凄まじい怨霊の力を表現した錦絵には、鮮烈な印象を与えるものが少なくない。

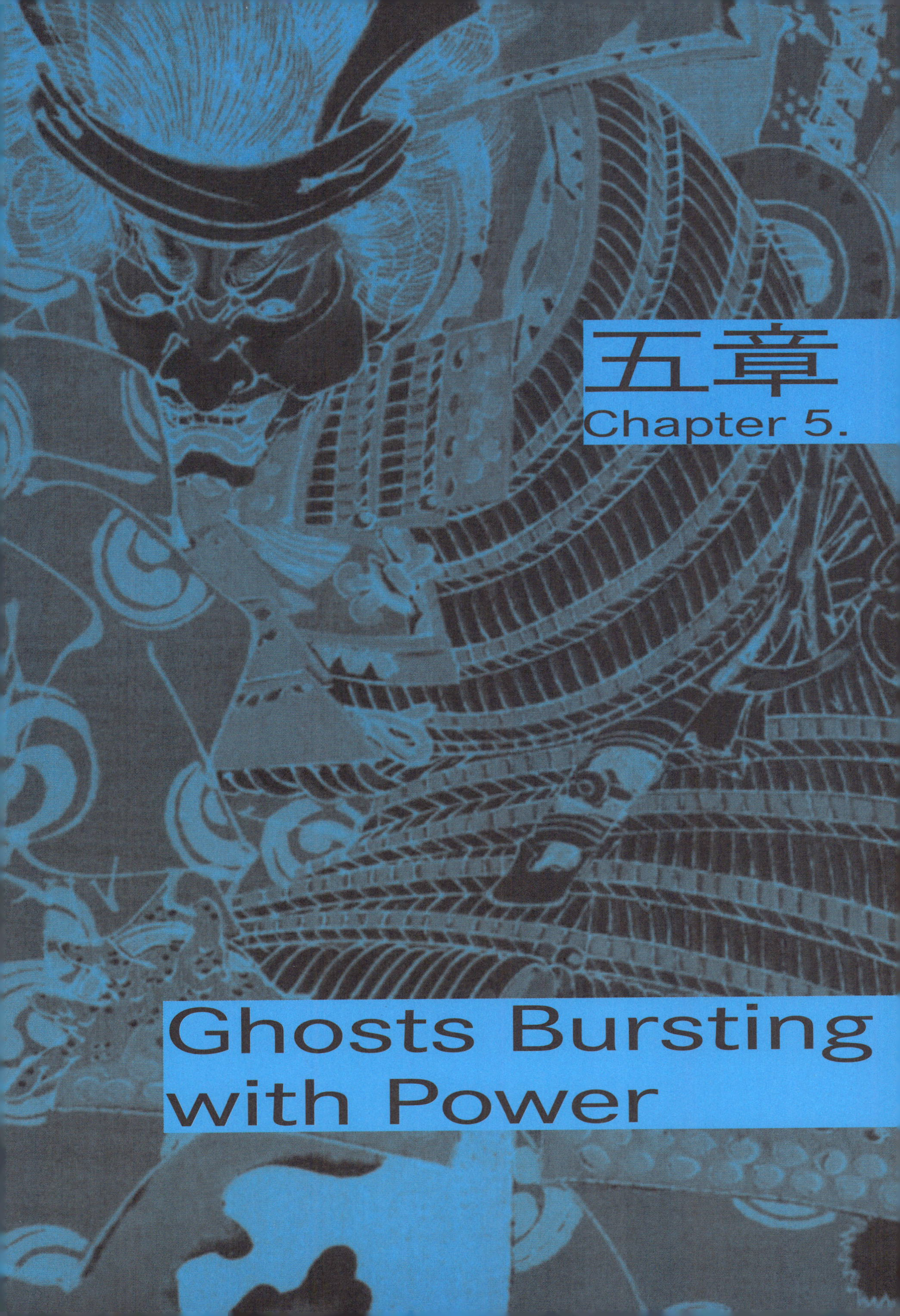

五章
Chapter 5.
Ghosts Bursting with Power

Ten Famous Excellences of Tametomo / Utagawa Yoshitsuya
1858

This picture depicts a scene from "The Strange Tales of the Bow Moon," which features Emperor Sutoku transforming into a long-nosed goblin. He is one of the most frightening vengeful spirits in Japanese history. Here, he generates heavy clouds and lightning. The fierceness of the storm is represented by blustering waves, as well as a flying Buddhist sutra, and the blowing kimono and hair of Shiranui. The painter Utagawa Yoshitsuya is a disciple of Utagawa Kuniyoshi. He was given his artist name Yoshitsuya, which includes the kanji character " 艶 " meaning glamorous, referring to the glamorous coloring of his pictures. To depict the scene, he referred to Hokusai's monochrome print illustration (P.47), and added his own originalities such as deep shaded expressions and dark colorings, in order to further express the extraordinary spectacle.

為朝 誉 十傑 ／ 歌川芳艶
安政 5 年（1858） ／ 個人蔵

日本史上もっとも恐れられる怨霊の一人、崇徳院が天狗へと変化を遂げる、『椿説弓張月』の一場面。猛烈な雲気と稲光。荒れ狂う波、吹き飛ばされた経文、白縫の髪や衣服が、その凄まじさを伝える。歌川芳艶は国芳の門下で、その彩色の艶麗なことから「芳艶」の号を与えられたという。北斎によるモノクロームの挿絵（P.47）が、独特の陰影表現や濃い彩色によって、一層異様に表現されている。

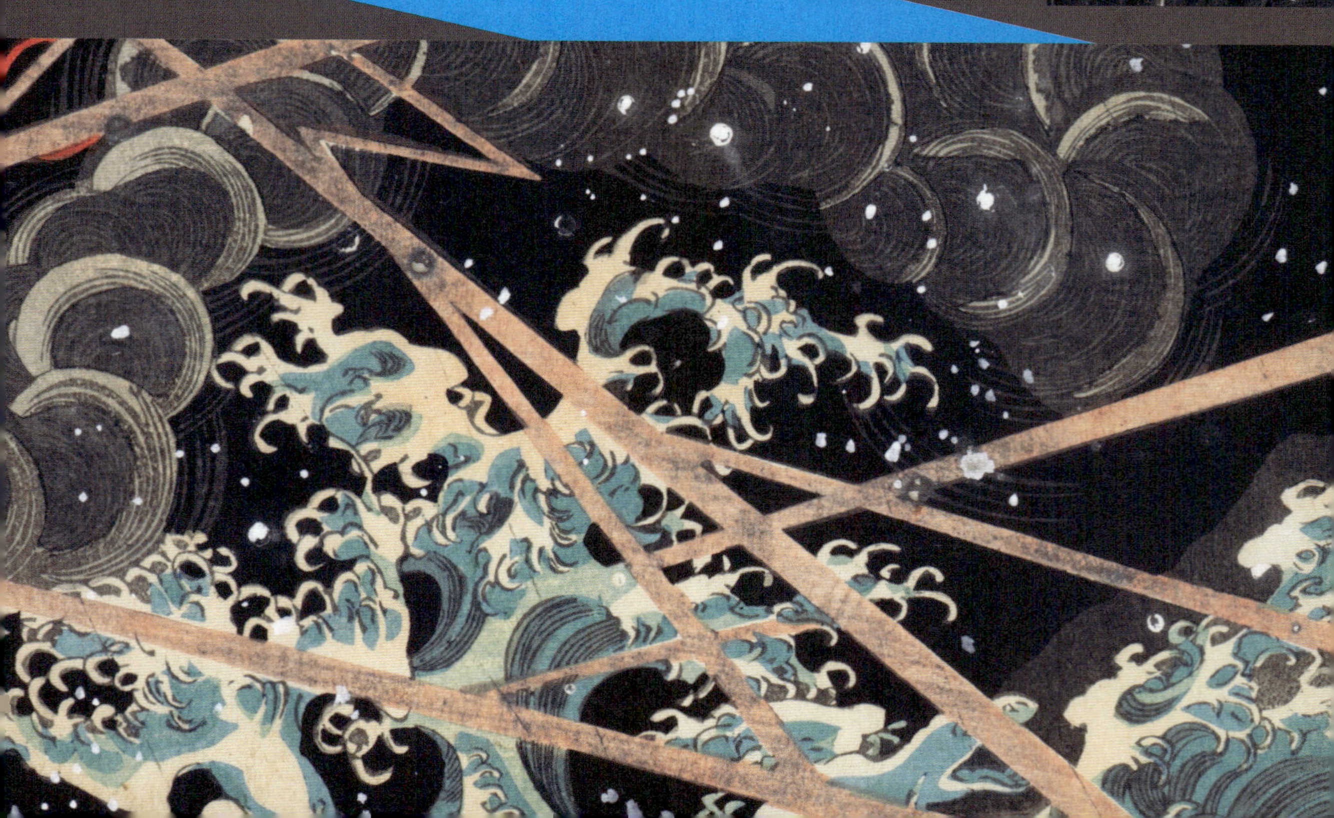

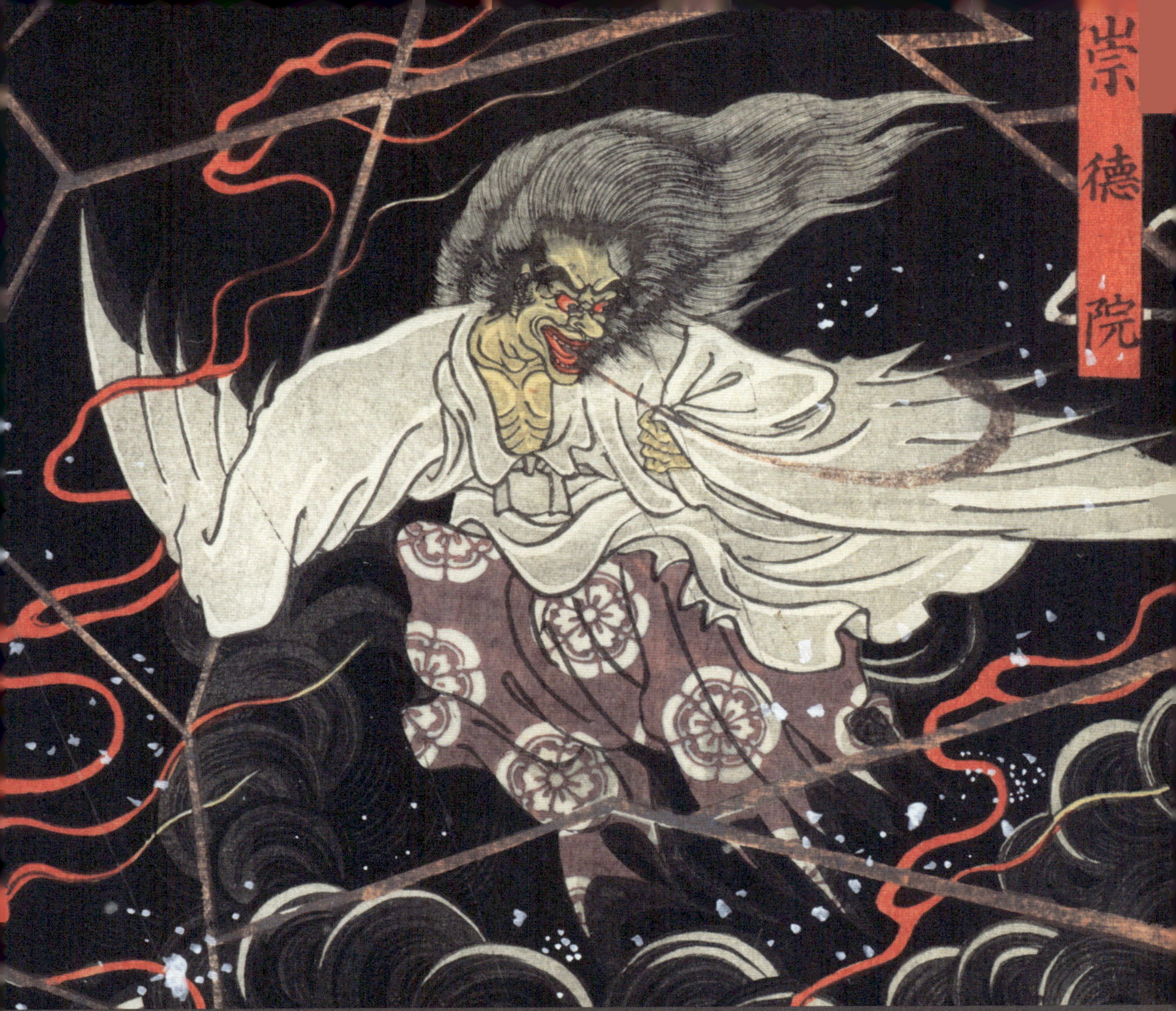

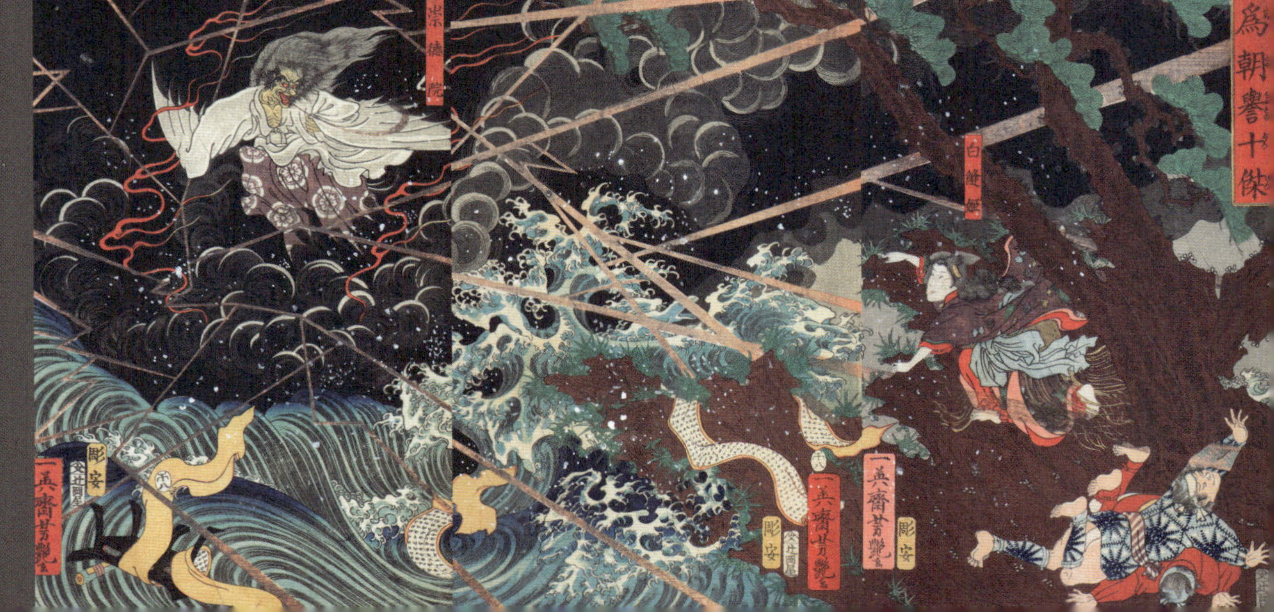
崇徳院
為朝譽十傑

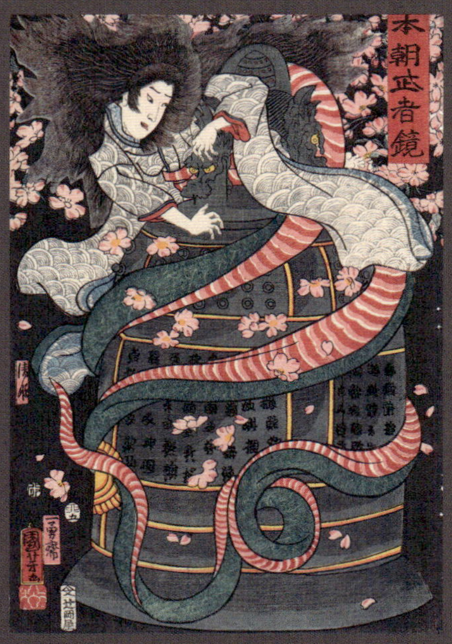

Kiyohime, from the series
A Mirror of Japanese Warriors /
Utagawa Kuniyoshi

1855 / Museum of Fine Arts, Boston

This picture depicts Kiyohime gazing lovingly at the temple bell. Cherry blossoms are falling during a dark night, and her black hair is monstrously blowing in the wind. With her obi belt coming untied, she gradually transforms into a serpent and enwinds the bell. Her kimono has traditional wave patterns called Seigaiha, and it transforms into the serpent's scales with the same patterns. Likewise, stripe patterns on her belt transform into the same patterns on the serpent's belly. The dragon-shaped crown of the bell also seems to be the head of the serpent.

本朝武者鏡 清姫 ／ 歌川国芳

安政 2 年（1855）／ ボストン美術館蔵

満開の桜が散る闇夜で、黒髪を異様に舞い上げながら、梵鐘を愛おしそうに見つめる清姫。赤い縞の帯が解けて、次第に蛇の姿となって梵鐘に巻きついていく。清姫の着物の青海波文様が蛇の鱗へ、帯の縞が蛇の腹へと成り変わる。梵鐘の上部の竜の頭をかたどった装飾が、あたかも蛇体の頭部であるかのように見える。

Kiyohime

There is a legend about a girl Kiyohime who wholeheartedly gave her heart to a priest Anchin. She followed him but he kept fleeing. Over the course of time, Kiyohime transformed into a serpent. In the end, Anchin escaped into the large bell of Dōjōji Temple, but the serpent enwound itself around the bell and burned him to death. This tragic drama is all caused by the woman's obsession. It is a part of the passed-down historical legends of Dōjōji Temple, and has been widely adapted into various art forms, including literature, painting, and theater plays such as kabuki, Noh (masked dance-drama) and Jōruri (puppet play).

清姫

思いを寄せながらも去ってしまった僧の安珍を追いかける清姫は、ひたすら彼を追ううちに、いつの間にか蛇の体となっていた。 道成寺の梵鐘の中に逃げ込んだ安珍であったが、清姫は鐘に巻きつき、安珍を焼き殺す。道成寺の縁起に基づくこの、女の執念が巻き起こす悲劇の伝説は、文学や絵画、能や歌舞伎や浄瑠璃などで、多彩に展開された。

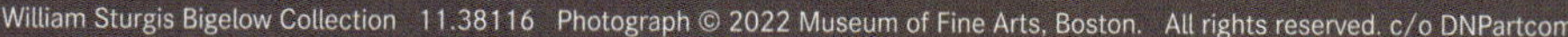

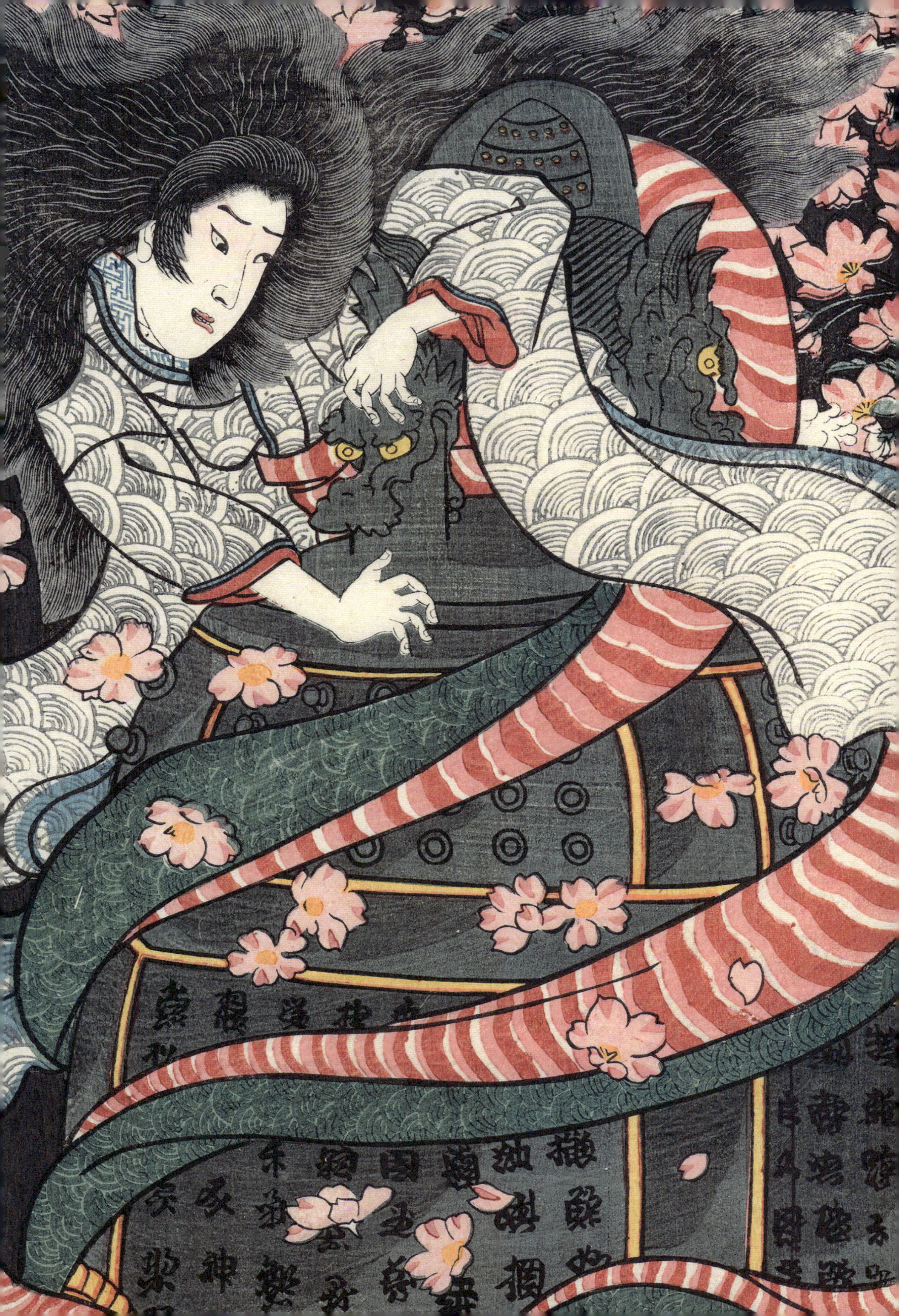

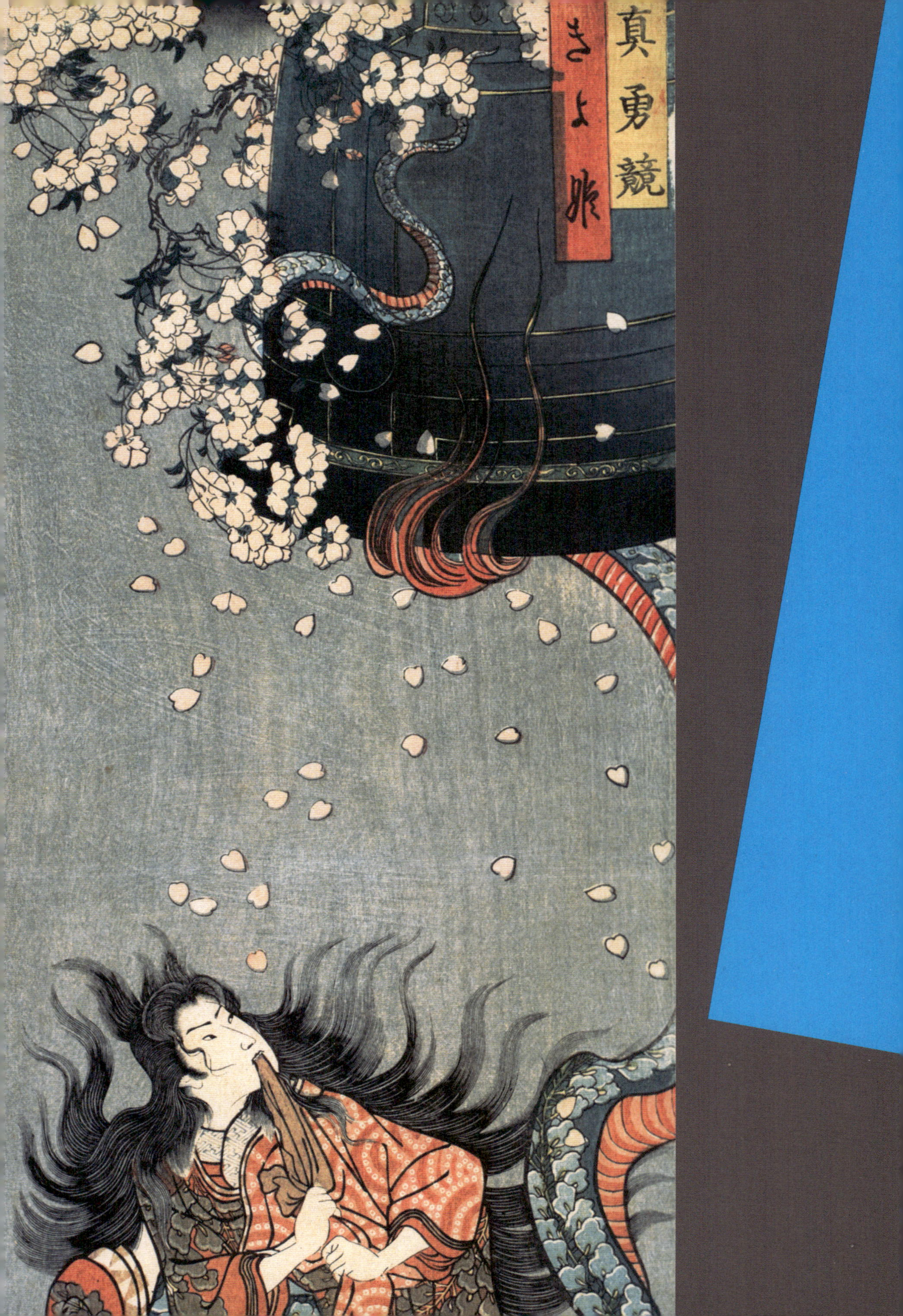

真勇競
きよ姫

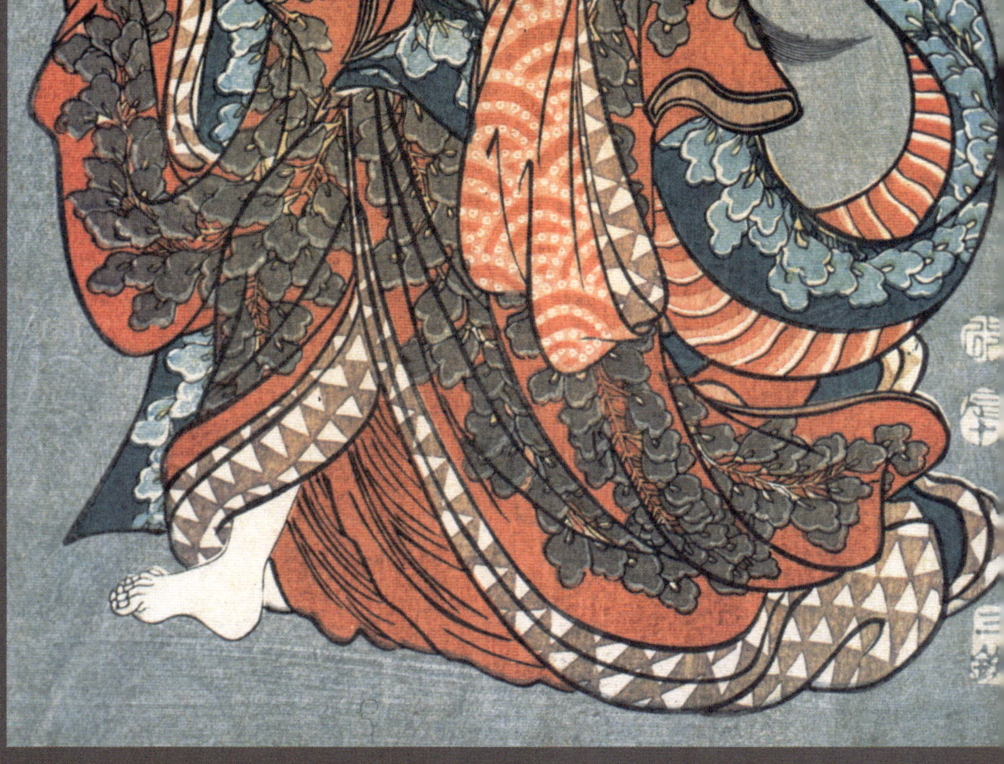

Kiyohime, from the series Comparisons of True Courages / Utagawa Kuniyoshi

Edo period, 19th century / Tokyo National Museum

Kiyohime chews a towel and gazes at the temple bell with grudge on her face. Her long hair stands like a flame and her obi belt gradually transforms into a serpent. The serpent's tail enters the temple bell, which is hanging in the upper part of the picture. The flames which are escaping from inside the bell suggest that the tail is burning within. The wisteria flower patterns on her kimono and obi belt continue on the serpent's scales. She takes off her upper kimono from the left shoulder and shows her under kimono with Seigaiha wave patterns. The bottom hem of the kimono has scale patterns. Both patterns suggest the story of Kiyohime transforming into a serpent and swimming across the Hidaka River. The tragic drama is spectacularly depicted under falling cherry blossoms on a dark night.

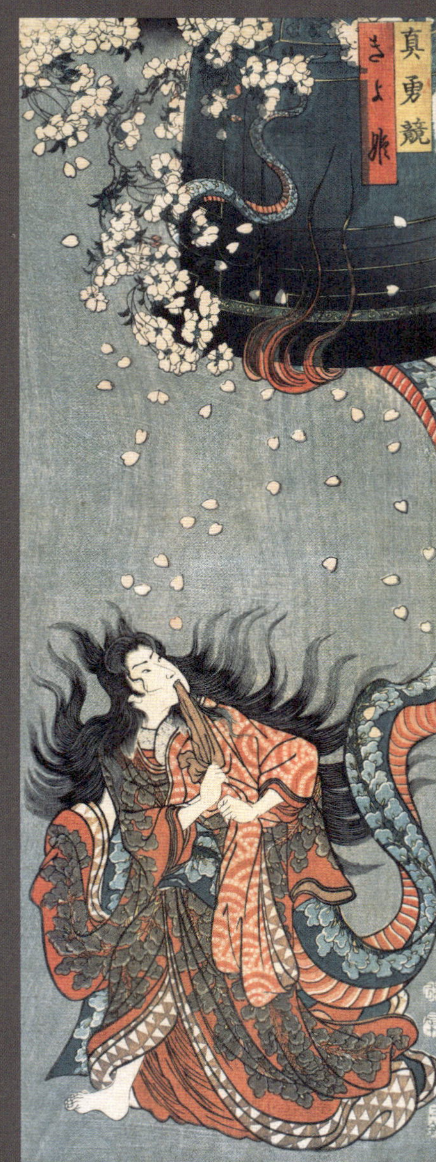

真勇競 きよ姫 / 歌川国芳

江戸時代・19 世紀 / 東京国立博物館蔵

手拭いを噛んで恨めしそうに梵鐘を睨みつける清姫。長い髪は炎が立ち上るように逆立ち、帯が次第に蛇体となる。画面上部に吊り上がる梵鐘にまで到達したその尾が、鐘の中を燃やしていることを、漏れ出た炎が伝える。着物と帯の藤の花が、蛇の鱗へ連続していく。肩脱ぎした左上半身には水をあらわす青海波文様、裾には鱗文様、いずれも蛇と化し日高川を渡った清姫の物語に関わる文様が施される。闇夜に満開の桜が散るなか、残酷な悲劇が、華やかに繰り広げられている。

Image: TNM Image Archives

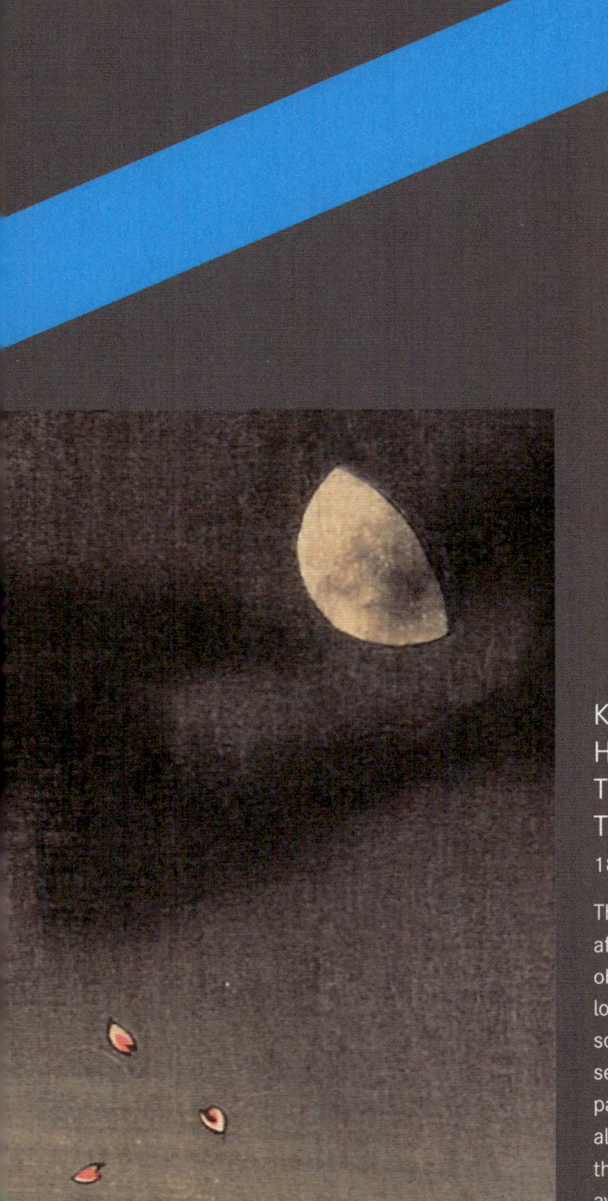

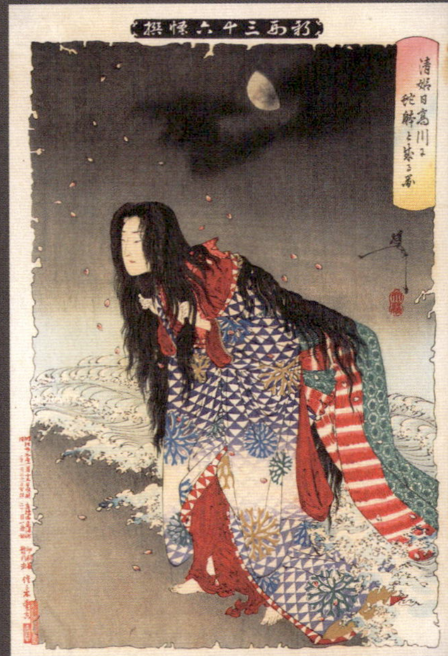

Kiyohime Transforming into a Serpent at the Hidaka River, from the series New Forms of Thirty-six Ghosts /
Tsukioka Yoshitoshi

1890 / Tokyo Metropolitan Library

This picture depicts Kiyohime emerging from the Hidaka River, after she transformed into a serpent and swam across it. Her obi belt disappears into the water, so how the tip of the belt looks is left unseen and is up to viewers' imaginations. The scales have triangular chain patterns, which represent the serpent. In several Noh and kabuki theater plays, the same pattern can be seen on the bodies of ogresses or serpents. It also symbolizes some female characters' true identities before their transformations, as well as their obsessions. Yoshitoshi avoided excess in his expression and instead, he realistically drew the surreal story. The falling cherry blossoms in the moonlit night seem sorrowful, since they seem to represent Kiyohime's failing love.

新形三十六怪撰 清姫日高川に蛇体と成る図 /
月岡芳年

明治 23 年（1890） / 東京都立中央図書館蔵

日高川を蛇体となって泳いで渡ったと伝えられる清姫が、川から出てきた様子。水の中に伸びる帯の先がどうなっているのかは見る者の想像に委ねられている。三角形を連ねた鱗文様は蛇体をあらわし、能や歌舞伎でも鬼女、蛇の化身に使用され、さらには女の本性や執念をあらわす記号ともなっていく。過剰な演出を抑えることで、現実離れしたストーリーに現実味を与えている。月夜に散る桜は、清姫の散りゆく恋をあらわすように、悲しげである。

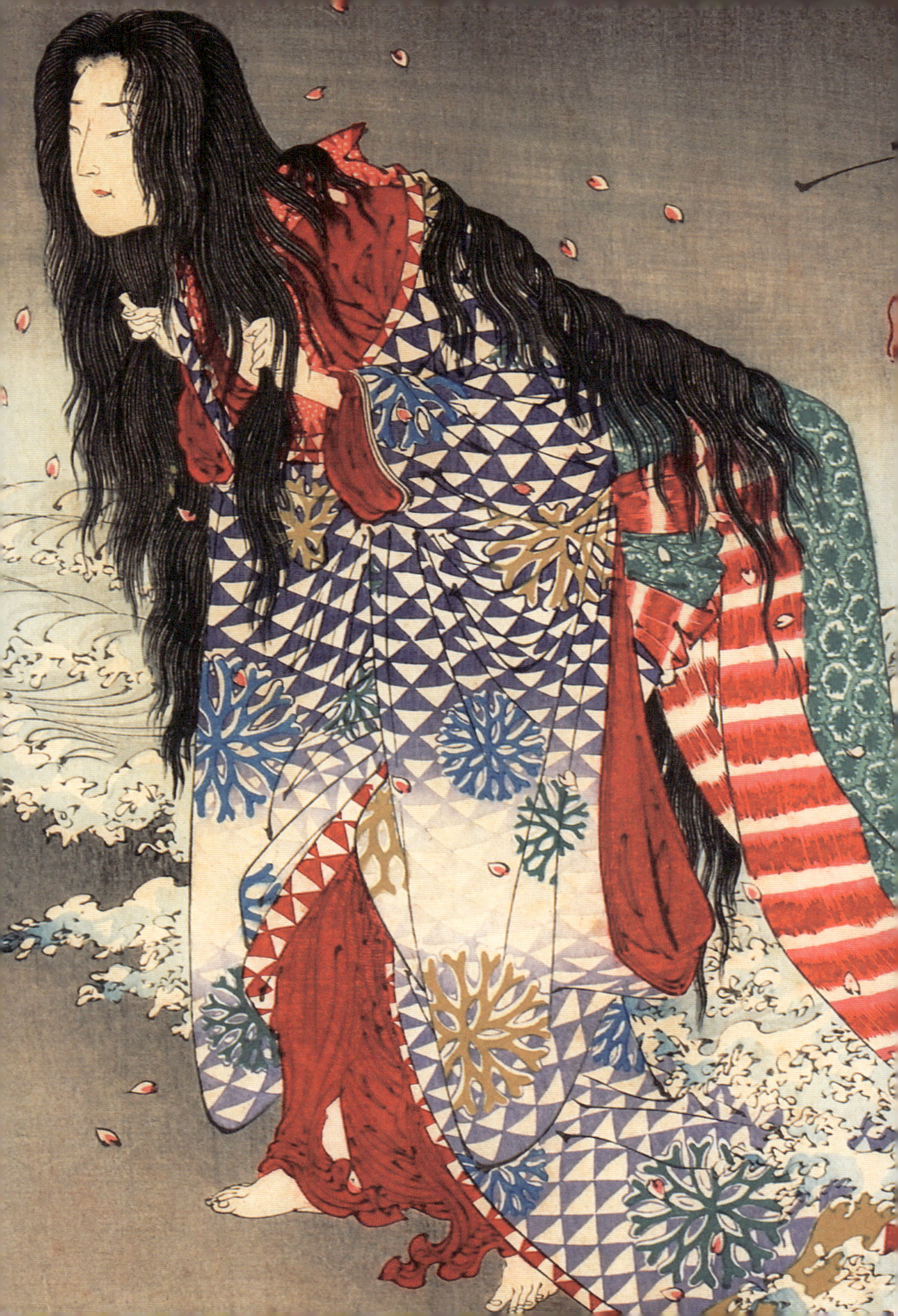

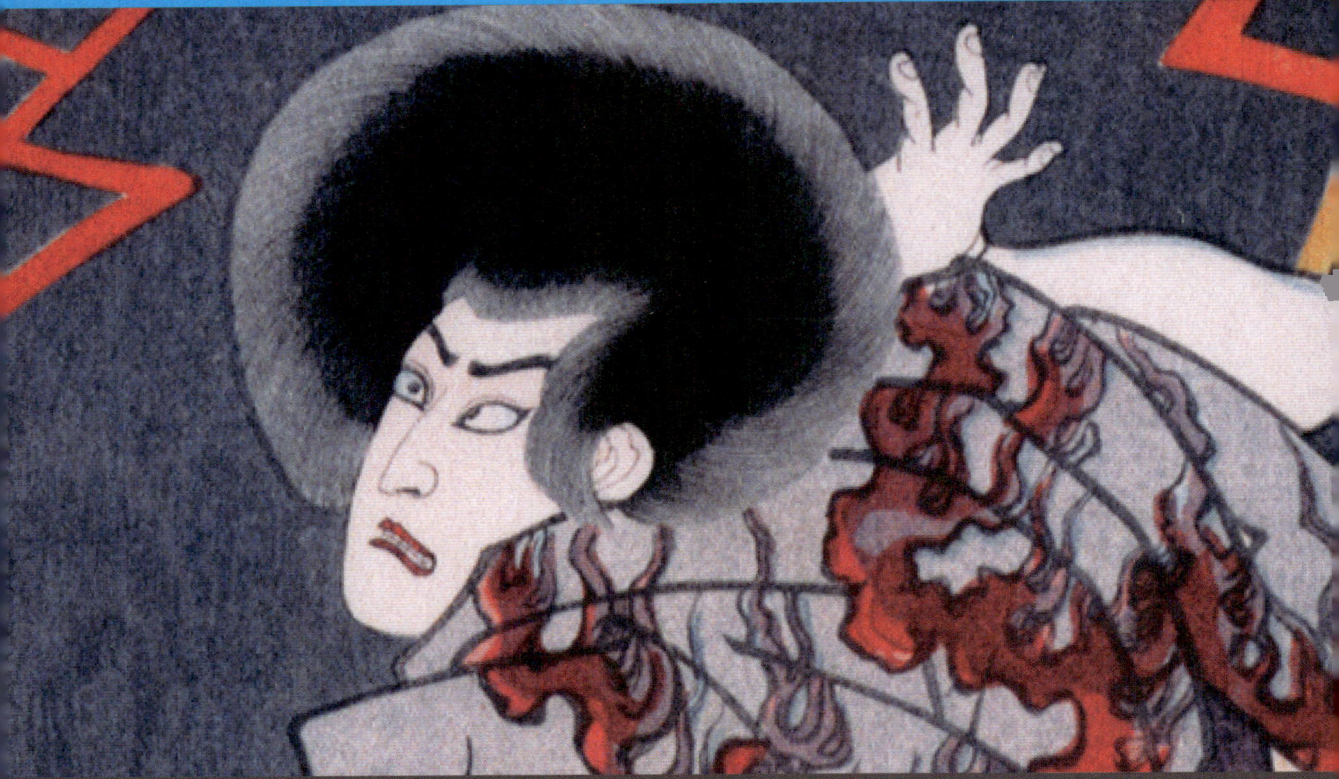

Priest Narukami, from the series Toyokuni's Comparison of Magics / Utagawa Toyokuni III, also known as Utagawa Kunisada I

1862 / Tokyo Metropolitan Library

The picture depicts a scene from "Narukami", which is one of the Kabuki Jūhachiban, or the eighteen best plays of the Ichikawa family of kabuki actors. In the story, Priest Narukami gets angry at the Imperial Court of the time, which leads him to confine a dragon in a waterfall basin. This dragon was a god who could make rain fall, but with his capture, no rainfall would come. To save the people from the drought, the Imperial Court ordered the beauty Kumonotaema-hime to tempt the priest and lead him to unseal the confinement. With her success, it started raining again, but the priest noticed her trap and got angry. In a glow of anger, he transformed into thunder and started to chase her. Here, Priest Narukami is depicted as a powerful deity with a flame-patterned white kimono and a standing hair-style called Igaguri.

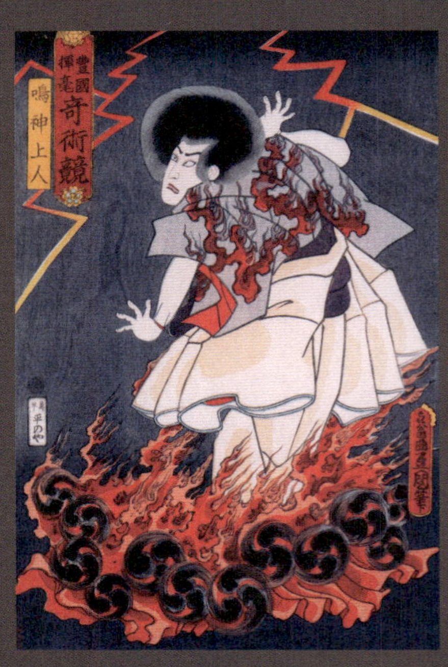

とよくに き ごう き じゅつくらべ なるかみしょうにん
豊国揮毫奇術 競 鳴神上人 ／
歌川豊国（3代）（初代国貞）

文久 2 年（1862）／ 東京都立中央図書館

歌舞伎十八番『鳴神』を描く。朝廷に腹を立てた鳴神上人が滝壺に竜神を封じこめたので、雨が降らなくなった。旱魃を救うため、朝廷は雲の絶間姫という美女に上人を誘惑させ、封印を解かせた。再び雨が降るようになったが、上人は偽られたことを知り激怒する。怒りのために、生きながら雷となって、姫を追う。白地に火炎模様の衣装と、逆立った髪・
いがぐり
毬栗で、荒人神があらわされている。

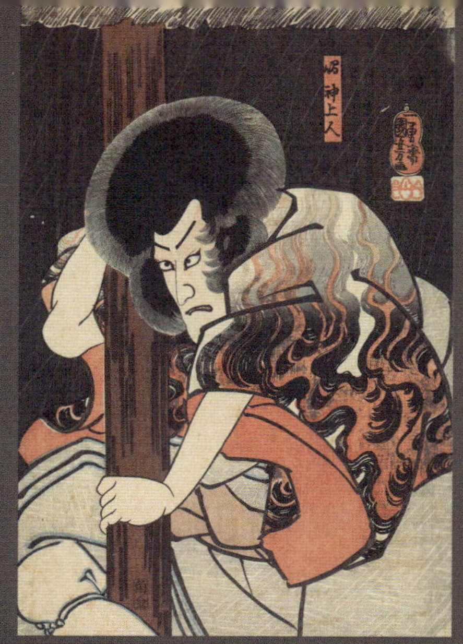

Priest Narukami / Utagawa Kuniyoshi

1851 / The Tsubouchi Memorial Theatre Museum

This picture depicts an Aragoto scene from the kabuki program "Narukami". Aragoto is a generic term for scenes which feature exaggerated postures, makeup, and costumes in kabuki. Here, Priest Narukami strikes a pose with his hands holding a cave's pillar and a foot hooking around it. With his eccentric hair-style and flame-patterned kimono, this pose represents his fierce anger. The thick and clear outlines effectively represent the powerful stage performance.

鳴神上人 ／ 歌川国芳

嘉永 4 年（1851） ／ 早稲田大学演劇博物館蔵

『鳴神』の「荒事」の所作のひとつ。岩屋の柱を両手でつかみ片足をからませる「柱巻の見得」。そうした所作が、異様な髪形と火炎をまとう衣装を伴うことで、激しい怒りの表現となる。舞台の荒々しさを、太く明快な輪郭線によって力強く表現する一枚。

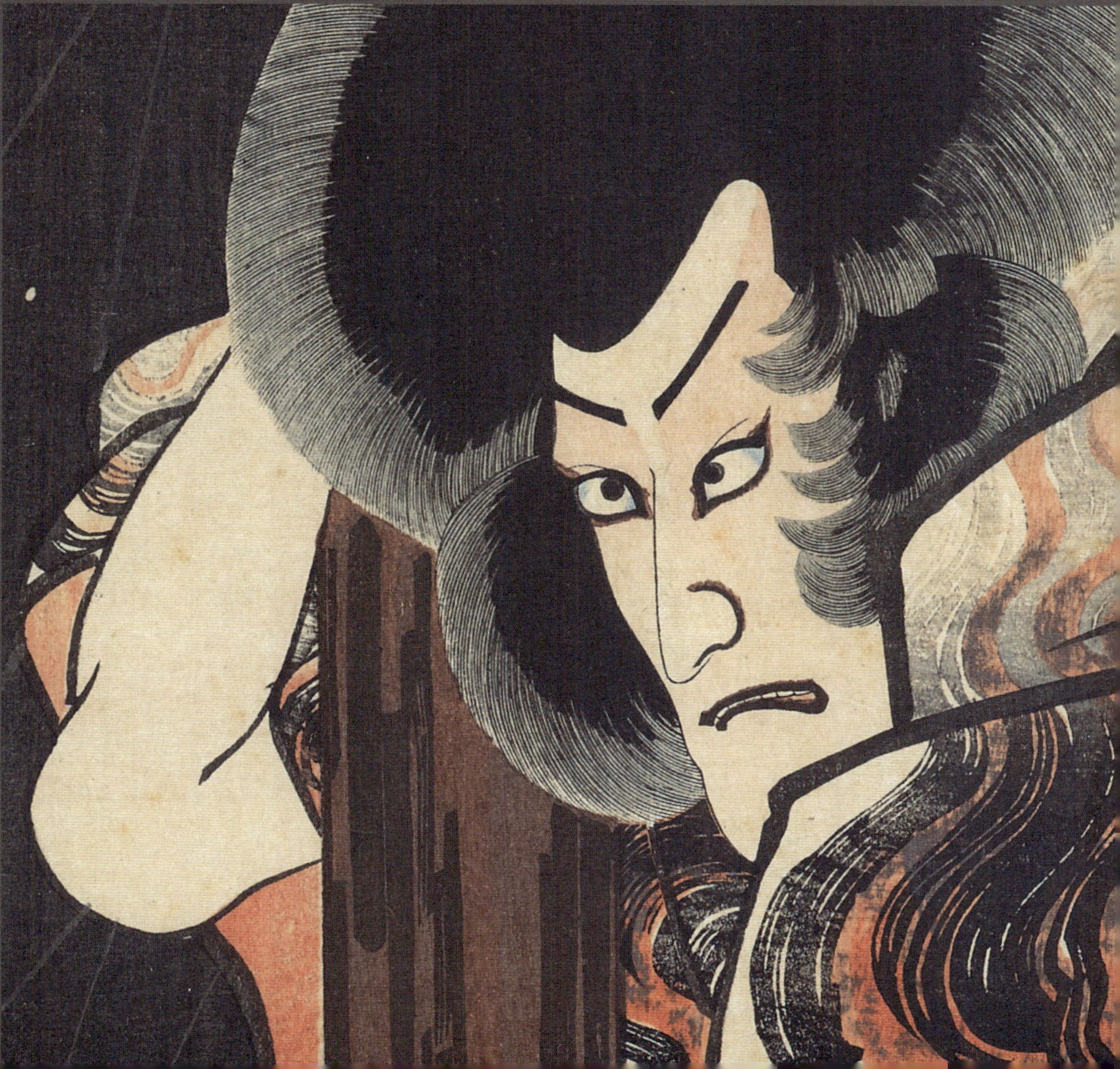

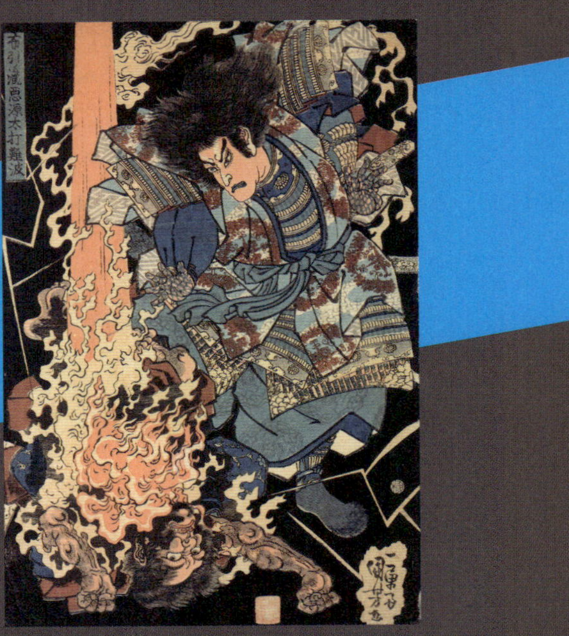

Akugenta Defeating Nanba at the Nunobiki Waterfall / Utagawa Kuniyoshi

1833 / British Museum

This picture depicts the legend of Nanba Tsunefusa being burnt in a blaze of fire. Akugenta Yoshihira, who transformed into a vengeful spirit, with his hair standing up straight, bangs his right leg down on Nanba, as he previously declared, "I will kick you to death." The lightning and blazing flames are depicted to vividly express the dreadful catastrophe.

布引ノ瀧悪源太打難波 ／ 歌川国芳

天保 4 年（1833） ／ 大英博物館蔵

燃え盛る火炎に焼かれゆく難波経房。髪を逆立て怨霊と化した義平は、「蹴殺さん」との宣言の通り、右足を難波経房に振り下ろしている。落下する雷の軌道や燃え盛る炎が、残虐な場面を華々しく盛り立てている。

Minamoto-no Yoshihira

Minamoto-no Yoshihira was a warrior at the end of the Heian period. His nickname Akugenta represents his fierce temperament and immense strength. He had a failed assassination attempt on Taira-no Kiyomori, and was therefore decapitated in the Rokujō-gawara Riverside at the age of 20. Legends tell that, just before Nanba Tsunehusa cut his head off, Yoshihira declared, "After my death, I will arise as thunder to kick you to death." Ten years later, as the celebration of Kiyomori's full recovery from his illness took place at the Nunobiki Waterfall, a nationally popular place of scenic beauty, thunder came over and killed Nanba Tsunehusa by a lightning explosion.

源義平

源義平は平安時代末期の武将で、気性が激しく恐ろしいほどに強い荒武者であったために「悪源太」の異名があった。平清盛暗殺に失敗した義平は、20歳にして六条河原で打ち首となる。『平治物語』によれば義平は、難波経房によって斬首される瞬間、「必ず雷となって蹴殺さんずるぞ」と、復讐を宣言したという。10年後、清盛の病気全快を祝う宴が、天下の名勝地・布引の滝で行われたとき、雷が一行を襲い、難波経房は爆死したという。

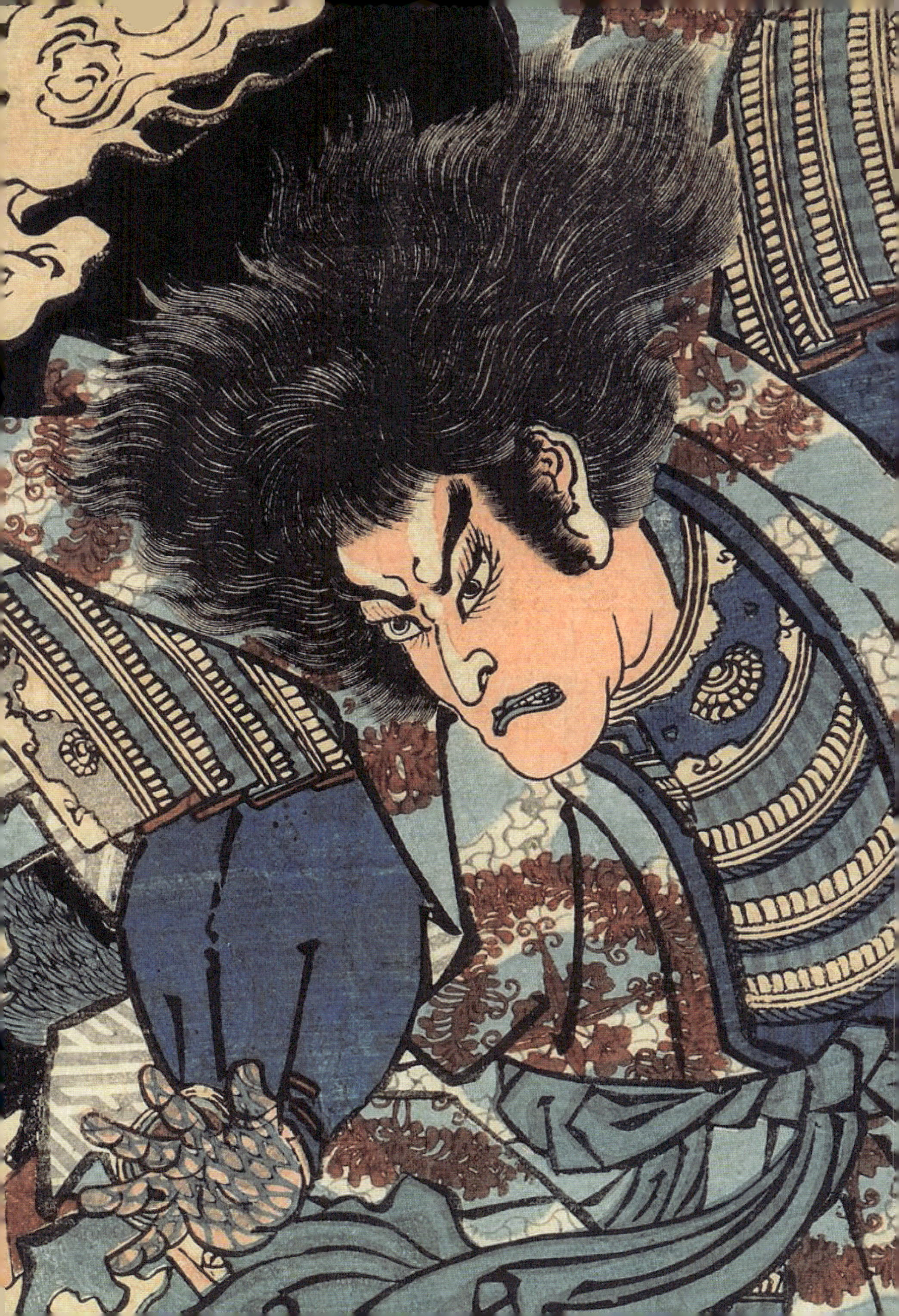

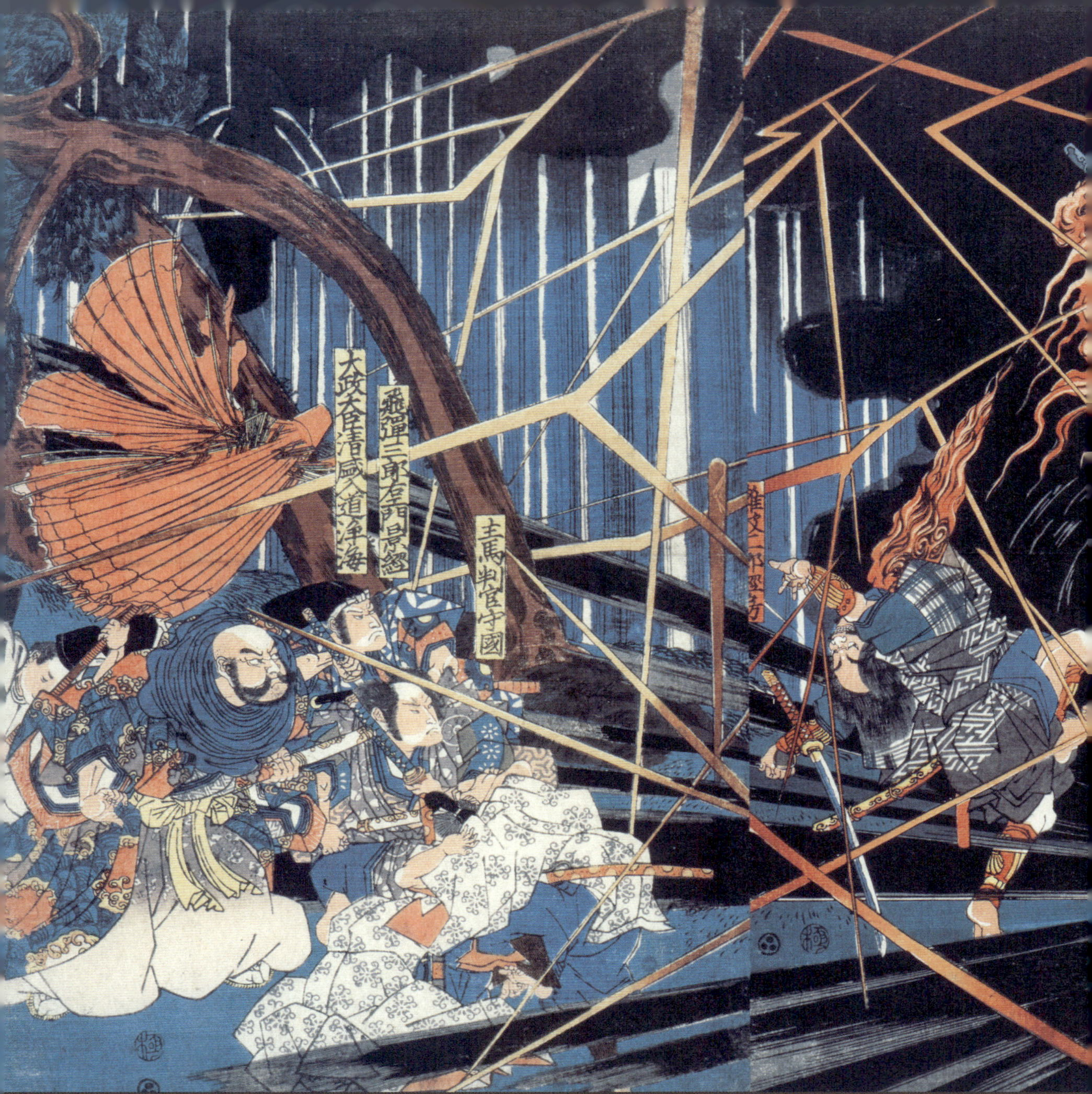

太政大臣清盛入道淨海
飛彈三郎左衛門景綱
主馬判官守國
難波二郎經方

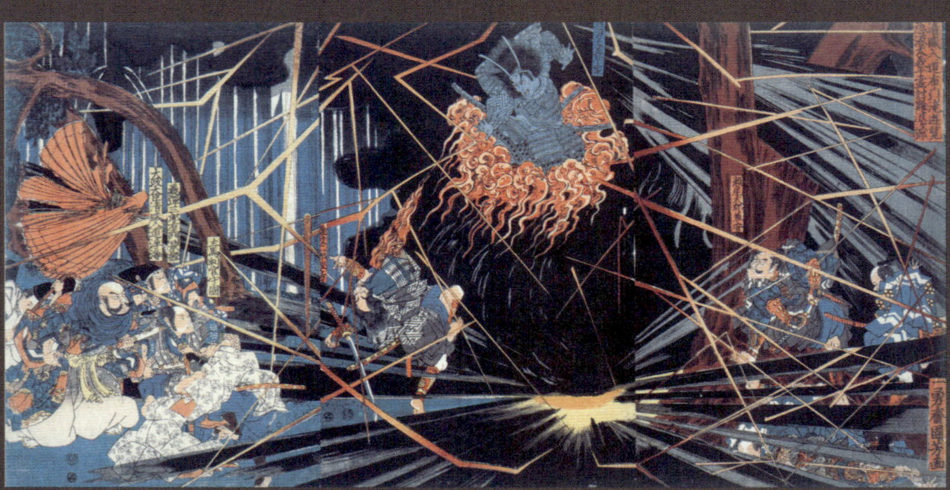

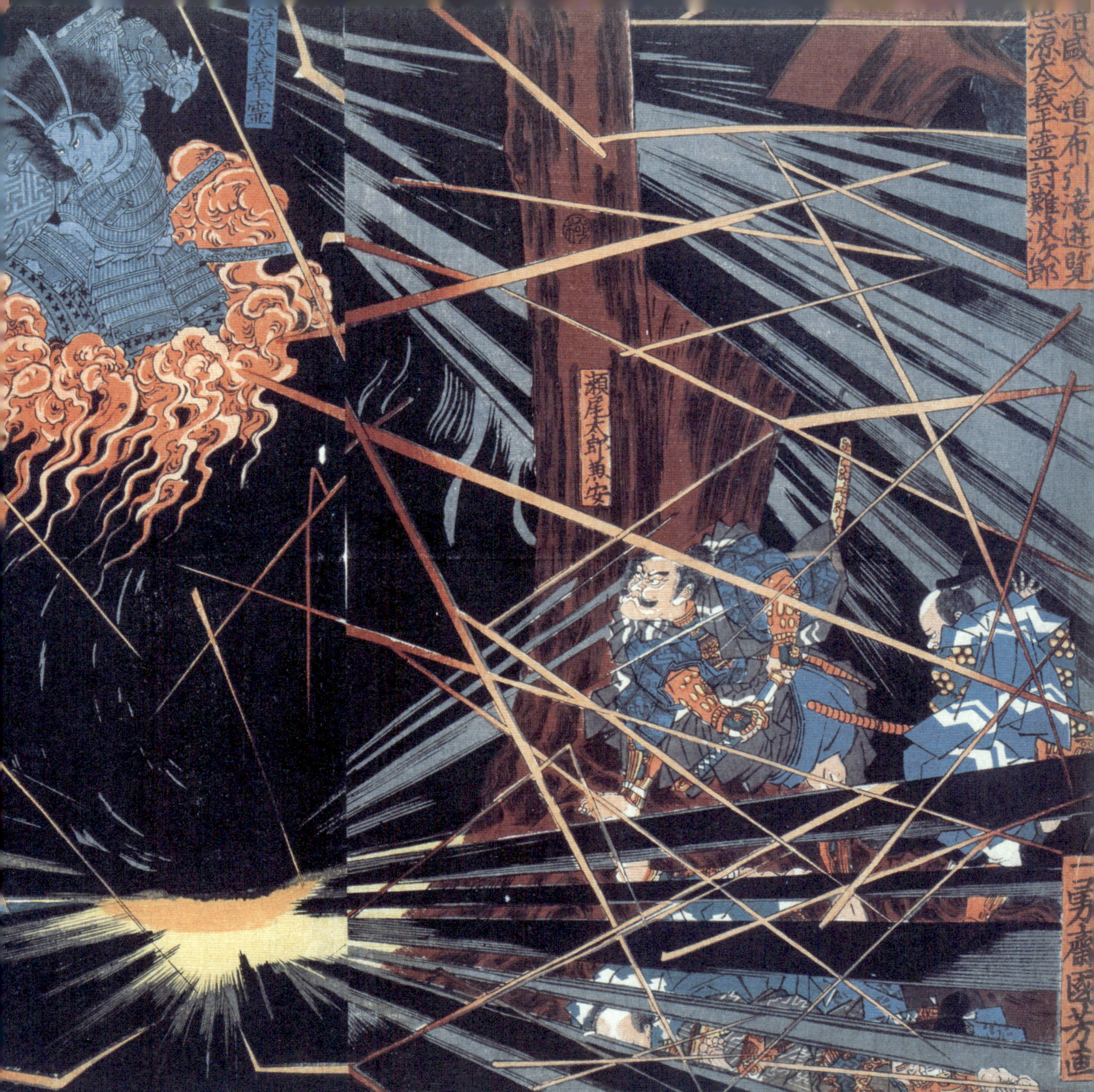

The Spirit of Akugenta Yoshihira Defeating Nanba Jirō
at the Nunobiki Waterfall during a Party for Kiyomori Nyūdo / Utagawa Kuniyoshi

1827-1830 / Kobe City Museum

This picture depicts the sounds of exploding thunder with red zigzagging lines which extend in all directions, as well as the air blasts with thick black lines. A ball of flame is sent to Nanba Tsunefusa from the hand of Yoshihira, who stands on a giant flame ball, and is depicted in monochrome. The blown Nanba, a bent tree, and a broken umbrella of Kiyomori's vassal represent the fierce storm.

きよもりにゅうどうぬのびきのたきゆうらん　あくげんたよしひらのれいなんばじろうをうつ
清盛入道布引滝遊覧悪源太義平霊討難波次郎　/　歌川国芳

文政年間末期（1827-1830年）/ 神戸市立博物館蔵

炸裂する雷鳴を、画面を四方八方に散る赤く折れ曲がる線と、黒い衝撃波で表現している。巨大な火の玉に乗る色を失った義平の手からは、難波経房に向かって、火の玉が発せられている。吹き飛ばされる難波経房に加えて、ぐにゃりと反り返る木や清盛の従者の持つ傘が、暴風の激しさを物語る。

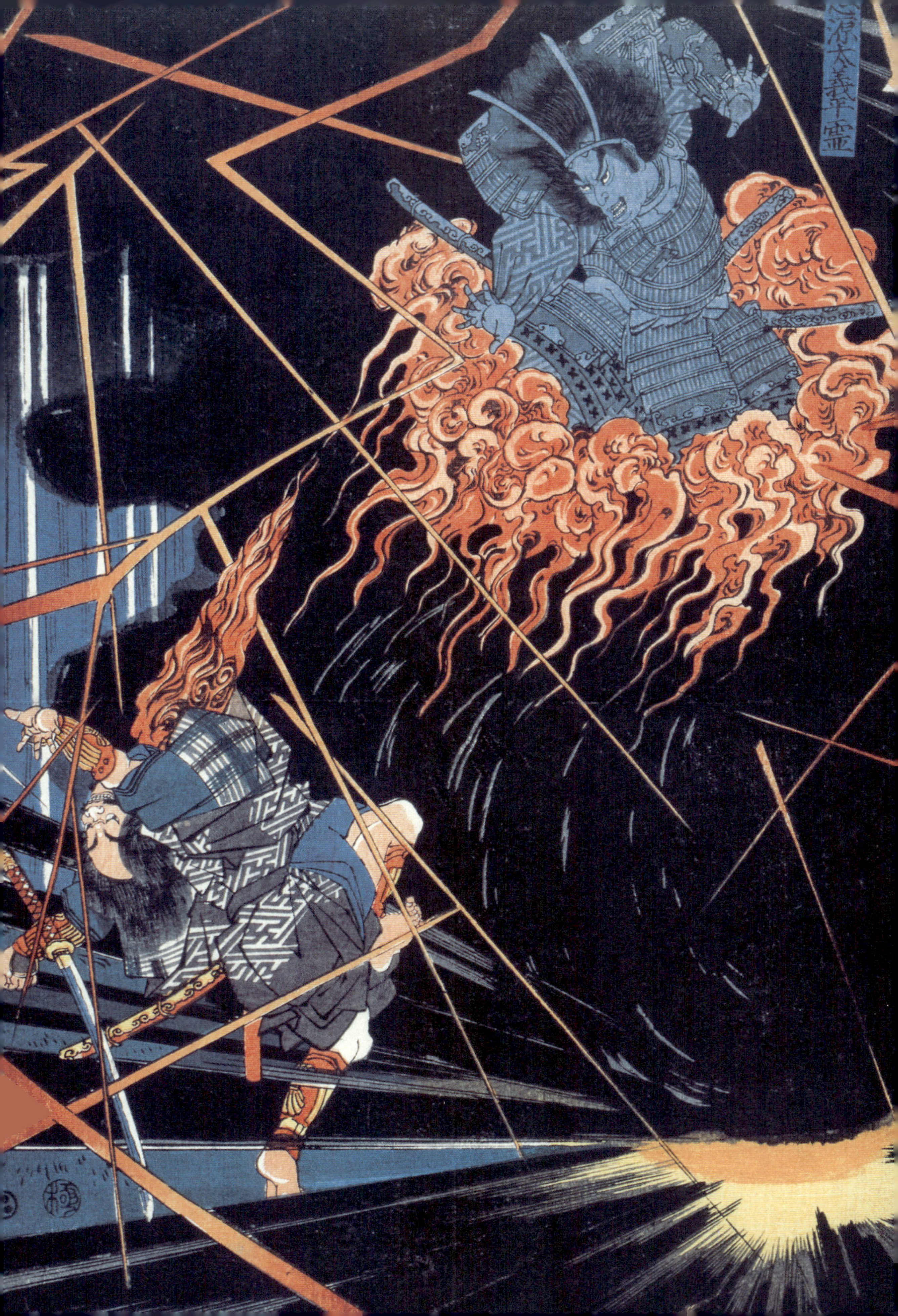

源太義平霊

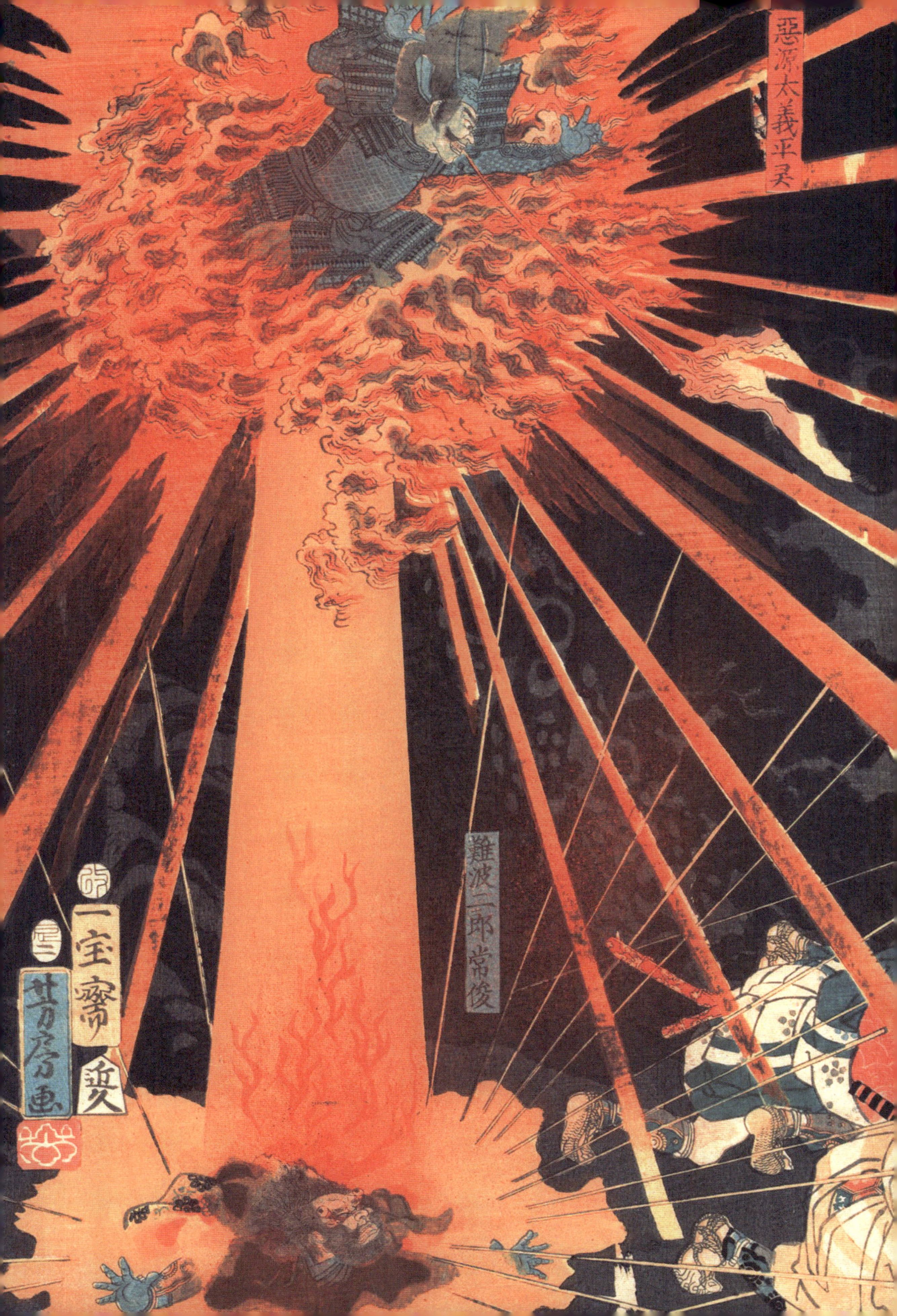

惡源太義平霊
難波二郎常俊
一宝齋
芳幾画

The Spirit of Yoshihira Defeating Nanba at the Nunobiki Waterfall during a Party for Kiyomori / Utagawa Yoshifusa

1856 / The Metropolitan Museum of Art

Among many pictures featuring vengeful spirits, this one has the most devastating expression. Yoshihira in a blazing fire shoots thunder vertically onto the ground. Nanba Tsunefusa is unable to put up any resistance and his protruding eyes stare into space. The radial lines are sent from both the sky and the ground, which express the huge power of the exploding thunder.

清盛布引滝遊覧 義平霊難波討図 / 歌川芳房

安政3年（1856） / メトロポリタン美術館蔵

怨霊の怒りを描く絵のなかで、もっとも絶望的なもののひとつ。燃え盛る炎につつまれる義平から、地面に向かって垂直に落とされた雷。難波経房はひとたまりもなく、飛び出した目が虚空をさまよっている。天からも地からも雷鳴の衝撃が放射状に発せられる。

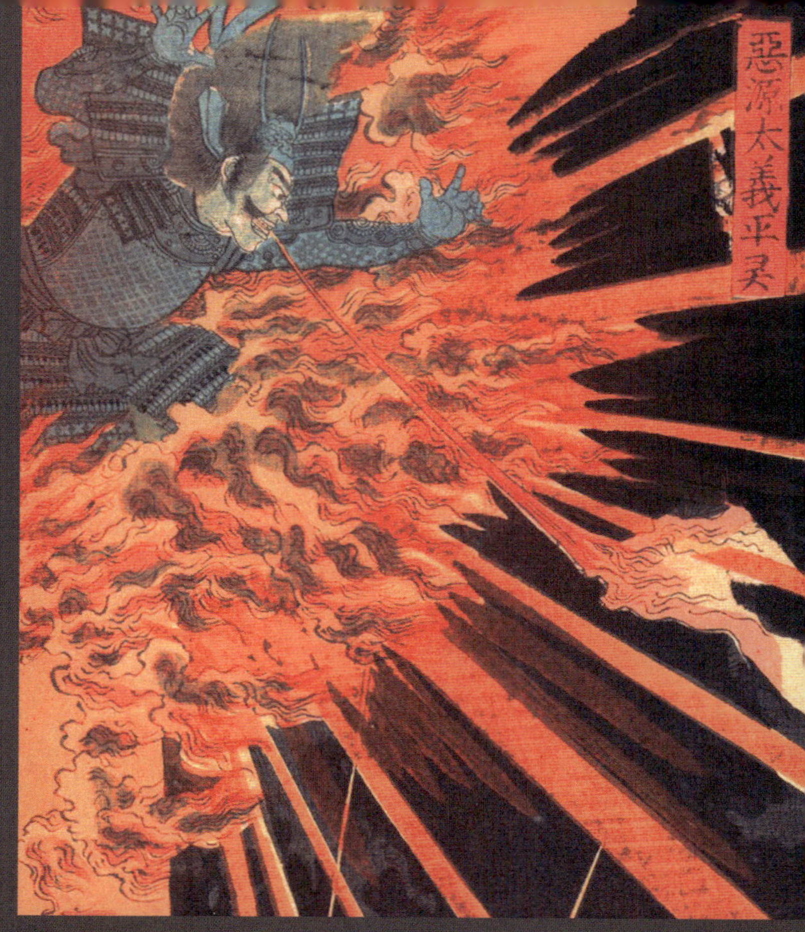

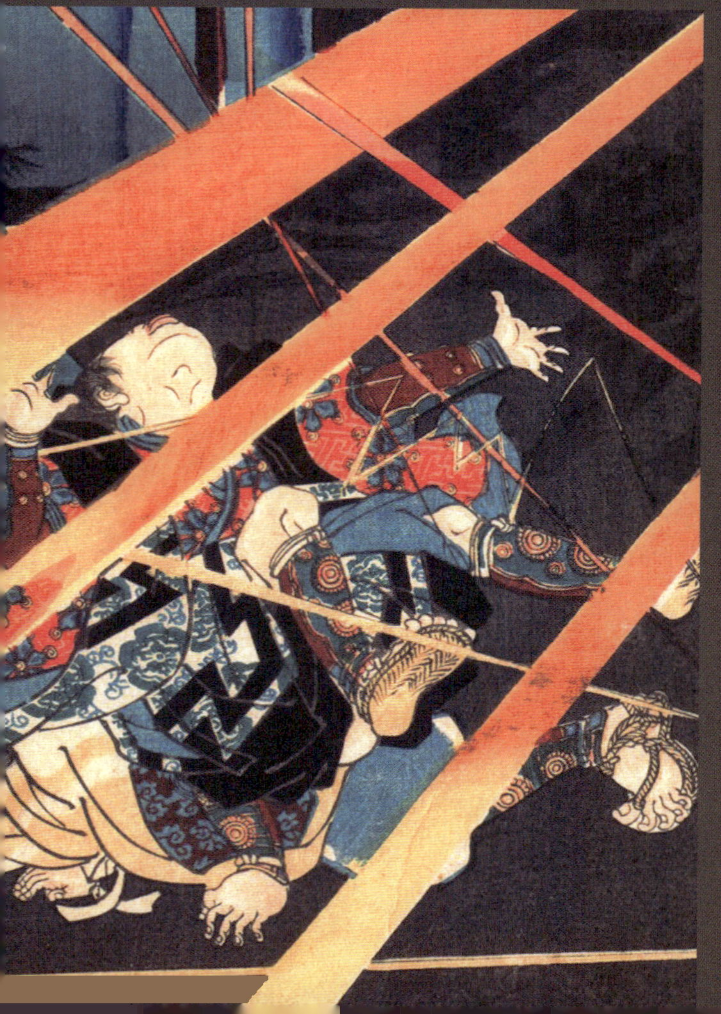

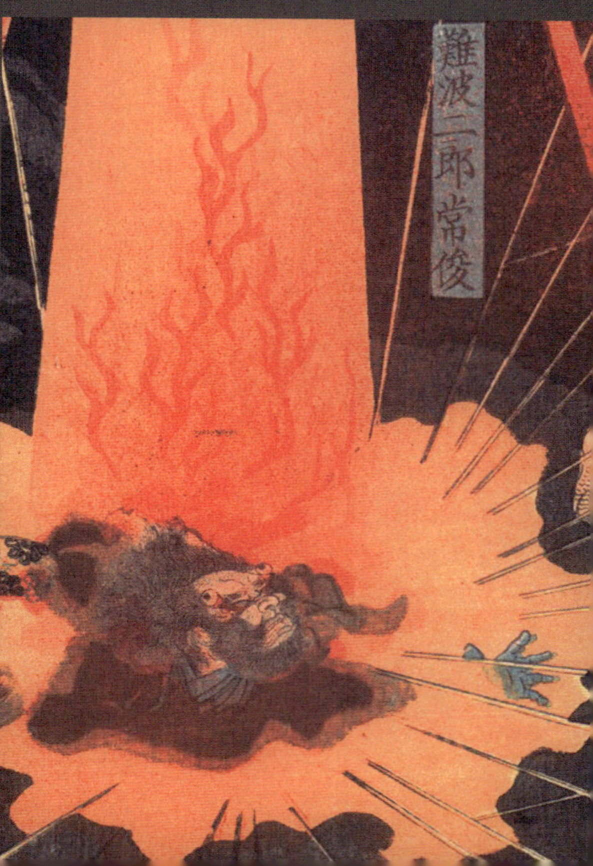

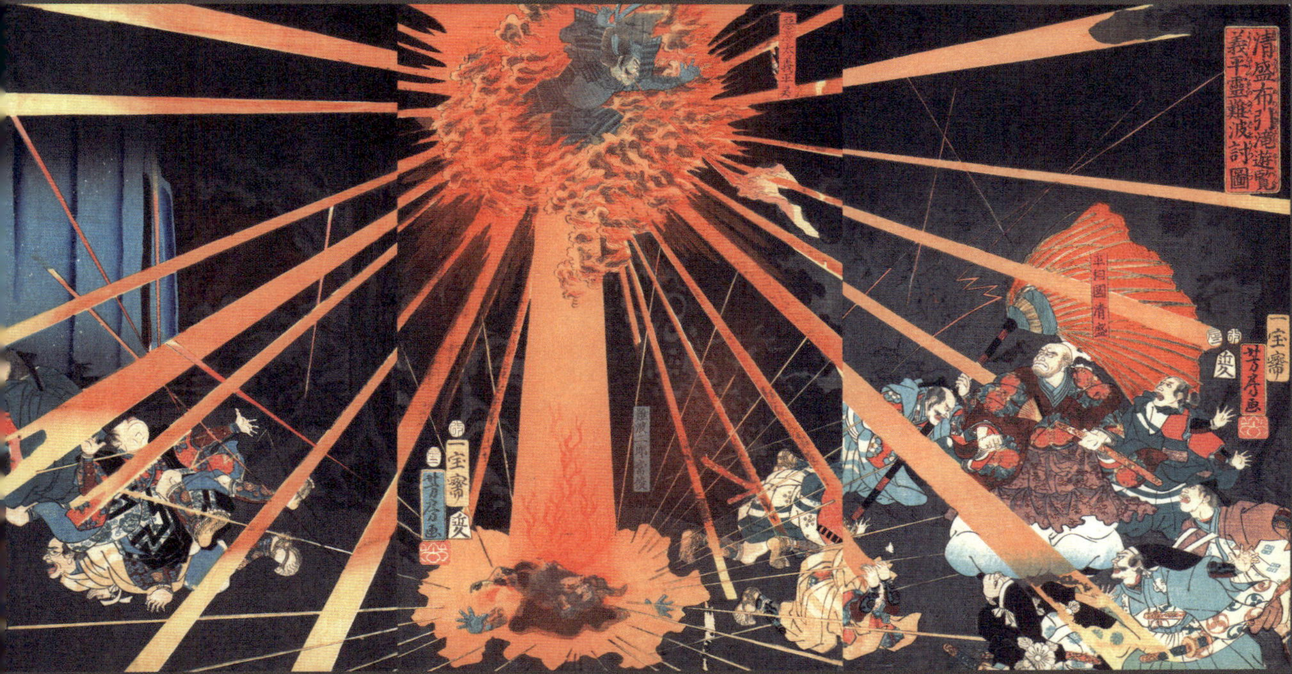

清盛布引滝遊覧義平霊難波討図
平相國清盛
一宝斎
芳虎画

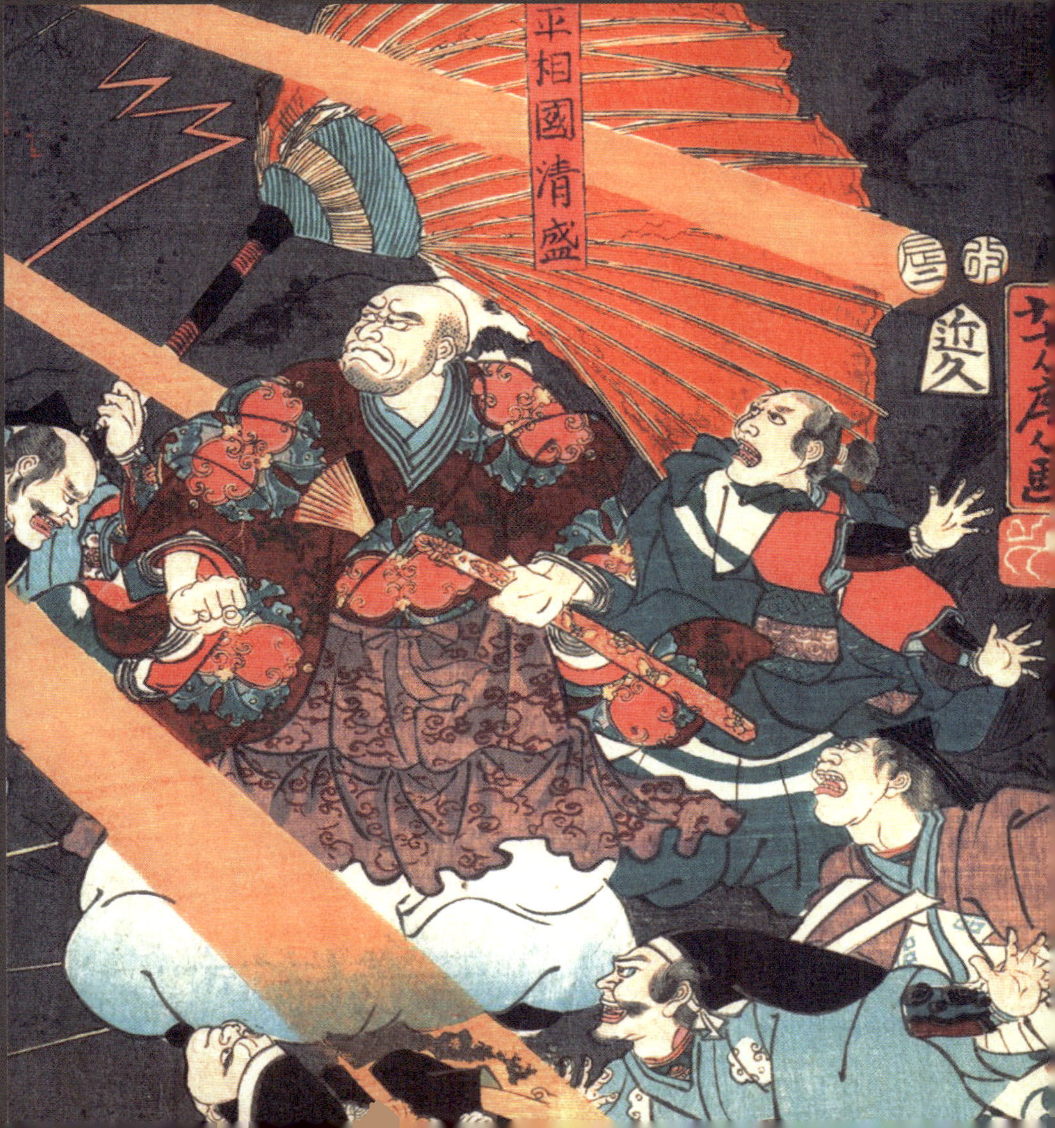

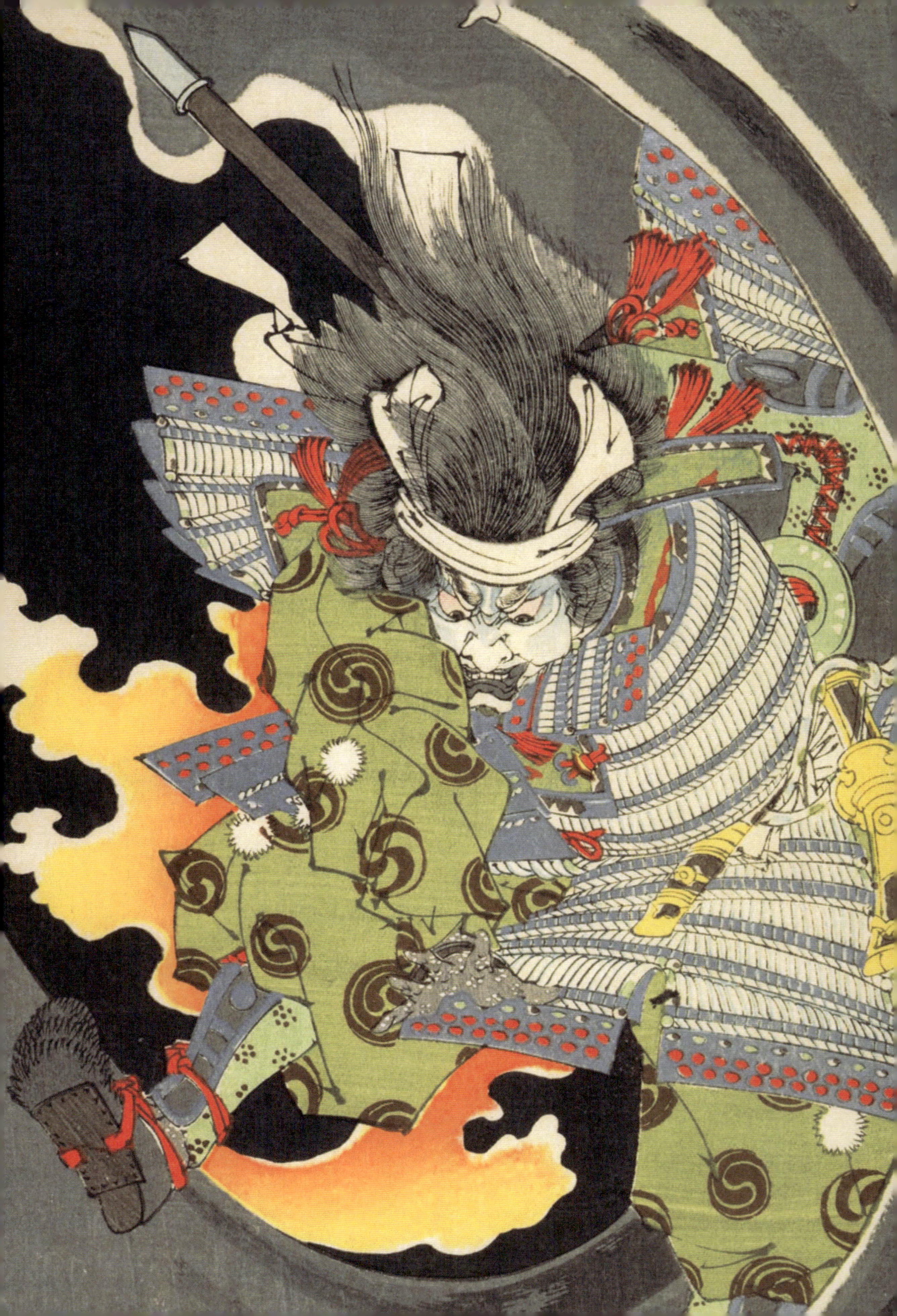

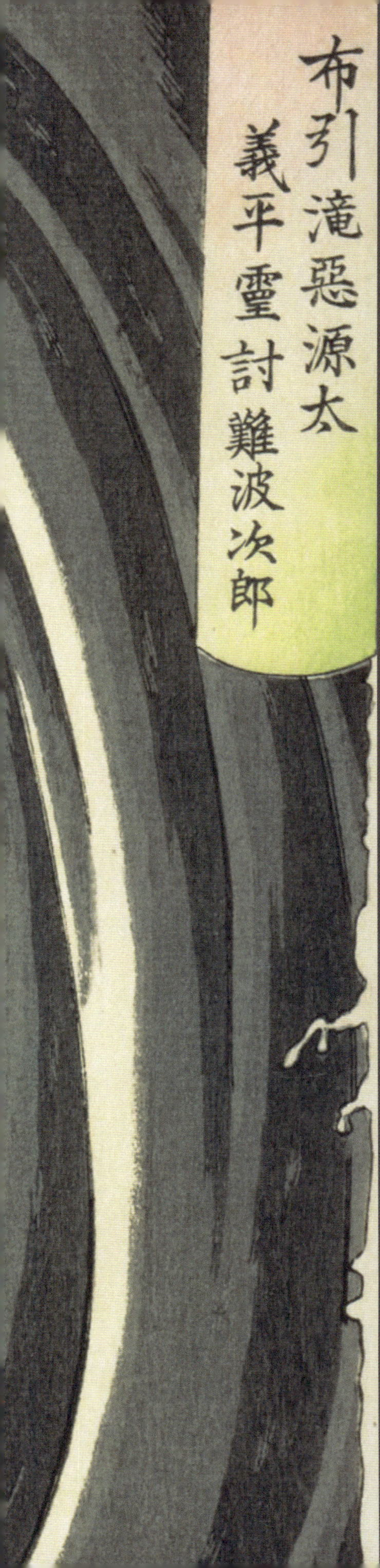

The Spirit of Akugenta Yoshihira Defeating Nanba Jirō at the Nunobiki Waterfall, from the series New Forms of Thirty-six Ghosts / Tsukioka Yoshitoshi

1889 / Tokyo Metropolitan Library

Ripping through the dark night, Yoshihira swiftly appears with an ogre-like facial expression. He gazes straight down. The blank spaces give viewers an impression that a desperate situation would happen in the following moment.

新形三十六怪撰 布引滝悪源太義平霊討難波次郎 / 月岡芳年

明治 22 年（1889） / 東京都立中央図書館

闇夜を勢いよく切り裂いてあらわれたのは、鬼のような形相の義平。目線はまっすぐに下に向かっている。画面の余白が、これから起こる絶望的な状況を予期させる。

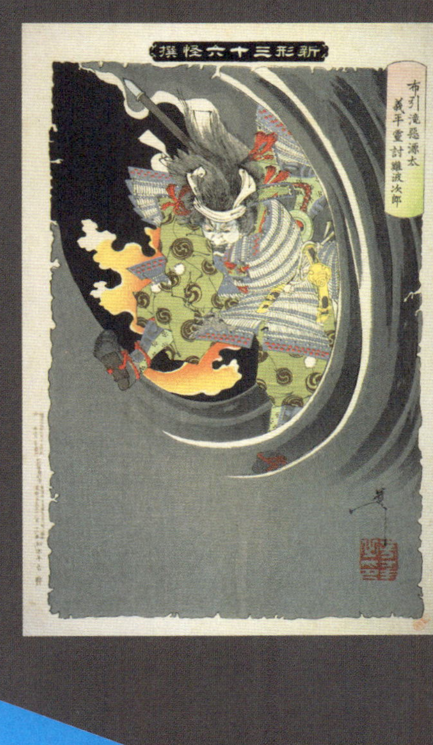

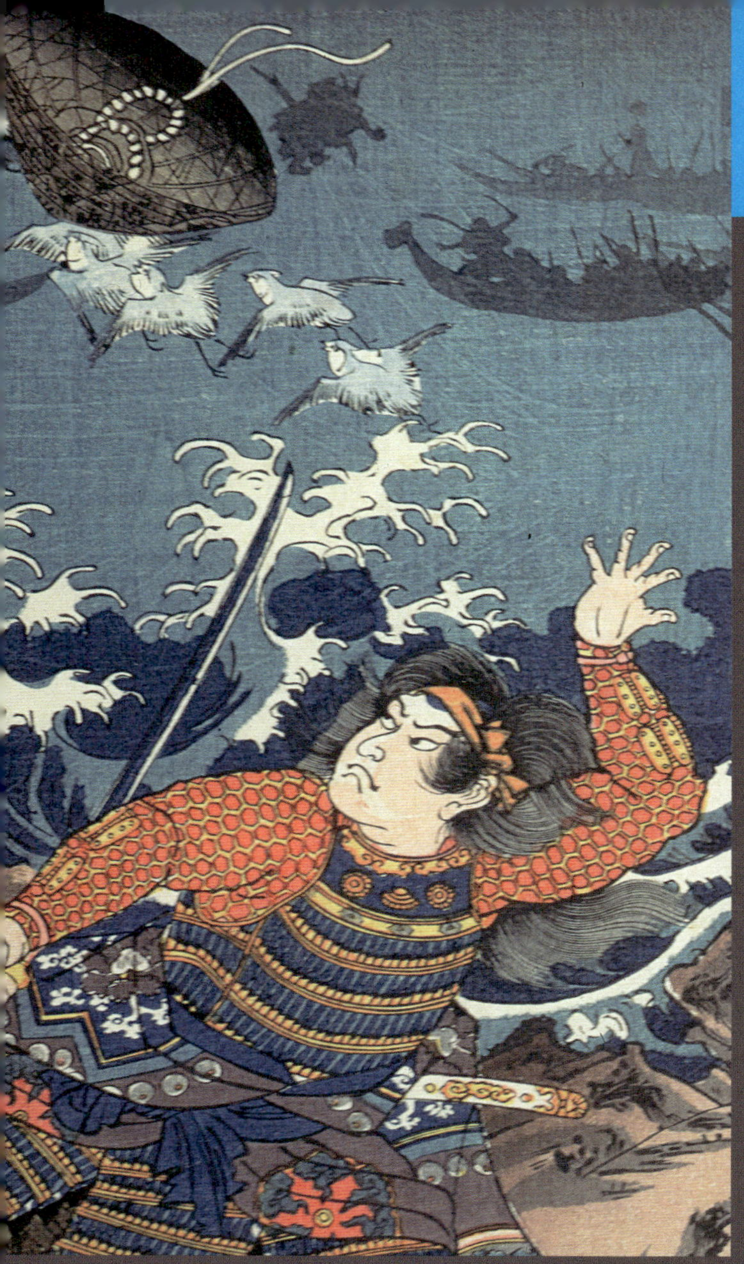

The Battle of Danno-ura / Utagawa Kuniyoshi

c.1844 / Photo : Aflo

This picture depicts the famous scene from kabuki, "Ikari Tomomori," or "Anchor Tomomori." Tomomori ties a giant anchor cable around himself, with enemy arrows planted in various parts of his body. In "Yoshitsune Senbonzakura" of kabuki and Jōruri puppet plays, Tomomori changes his name to furtively survive. When he reveals his true identity, the set changes into the scene of the Battle of Danno-ura, where the Taira clan is destroyed. The background silhouettes in the picture represent the Danno-ura Battle's symbolic scene called "Ha'ssō-tobi," where Yoshitsune jumps from one boat to another, eight boats in total, in order to escape from the Taira clan.

壇浦戦之図 ／ 歌川国芳

弘化元年（1844）頃 ／ 提供：アフロ

あちこちに弓が刺さった体に、巨大な碇を巻き付ける「碇知盛」。浄瑠璃・歌舞伎『義経千本桜』では、名を変えて生き延びた知盛が正体をあらわすと、舞台は平氏が滅んだ壇ノ浦の合戦場面へと転換する。本図の背後にも、壇ノ浦の戦いを象徴する義経の「八艘飛び」のシルエットが浮かび上がる。

Taira-no Tomomori

The picture depicts Taira-no Tomomori who was a warrior at the end of the Heian period. He witnessed the destruction of his Taira clan in the Battle of Danno-ura, and eventually threw himself into the sea. The Noh play "Funa Benkei" depicts Tomomori transforming into a vengeful spirit and chasing Yoshitsune and his vassals. They are escaping to Kyushu region by sea, but Tomomori tries to catch and sink them. In "Yoshitsune Senbonzakura" of kabuki and Jōruri puppet plays, Tomomori changes his name to furtively survive, and later pursues Yoshitsune who is setting sail from Daimotsuno-ura. The most famous scene of the theater plays is known as "Ikari Tomomori," or "Anchor Tomomori." In this scene, he is eventually defeated, ties an anchor cable around his body and throws the anchor into the sea, in order to sink himself to the sea floor.

平知盛

平安末期の武将・平知盛は、壇ノ浦の戦いで平家一門の最期を見とどけたうえで海に身を投じた。能の『船弁慶』では、怨霊化した知盛が九州へ逃走する義経主従を海に沈めんと迫る。浄瑠璃・歌舞伎の『義経千本桜』では、名を変えてひそかに生き延びた知盛が、大物浦から船出する義経の後を追う。敗れた知盛が碇の綱を体に巻きつけ、碇を海に投げ入れて海底に沈みゆく場面は「碇知盛」として名高い。

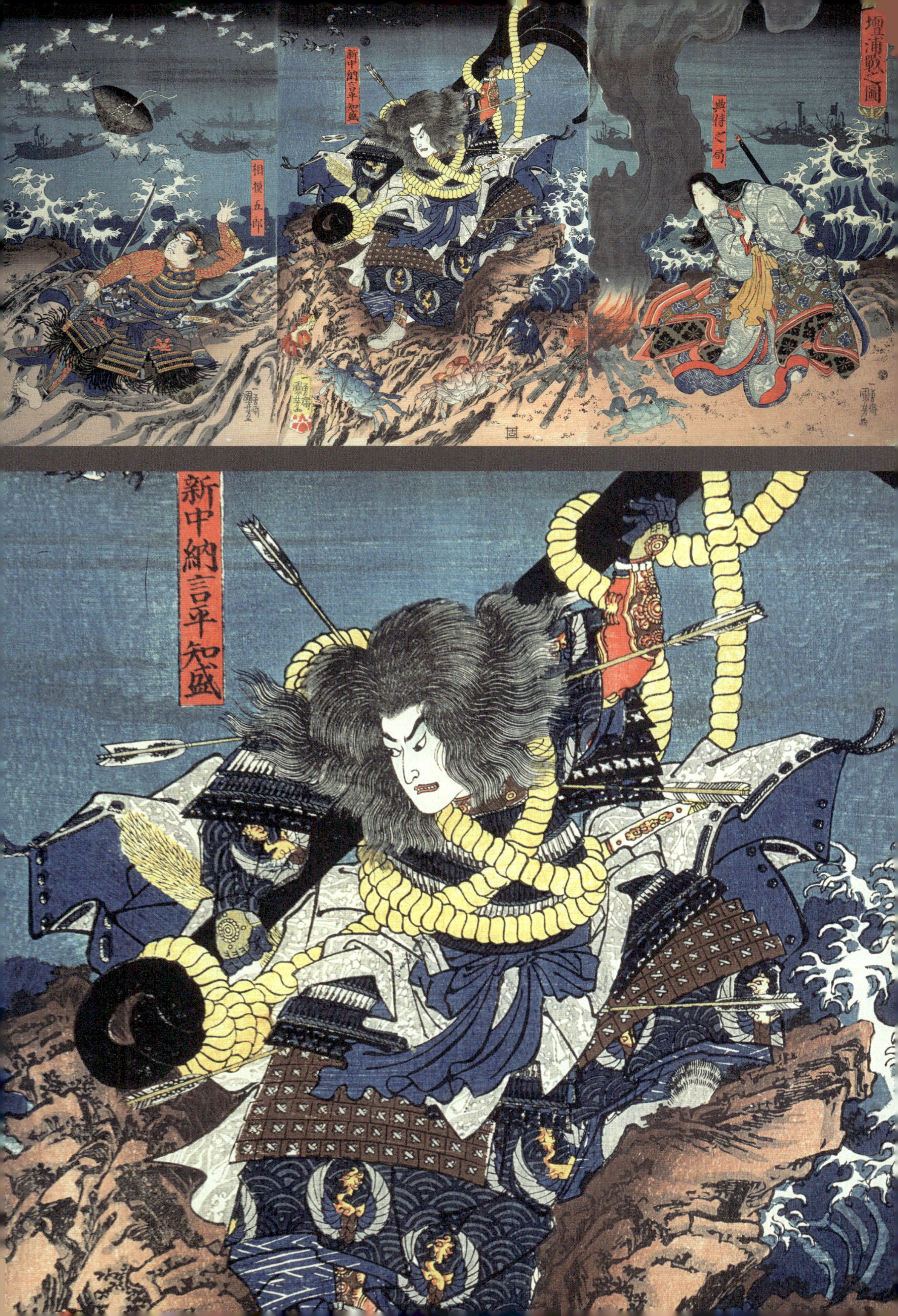

壇浦戰圖
新中納言平知盛
相模五郎
典侍之局
新中納言平知盛

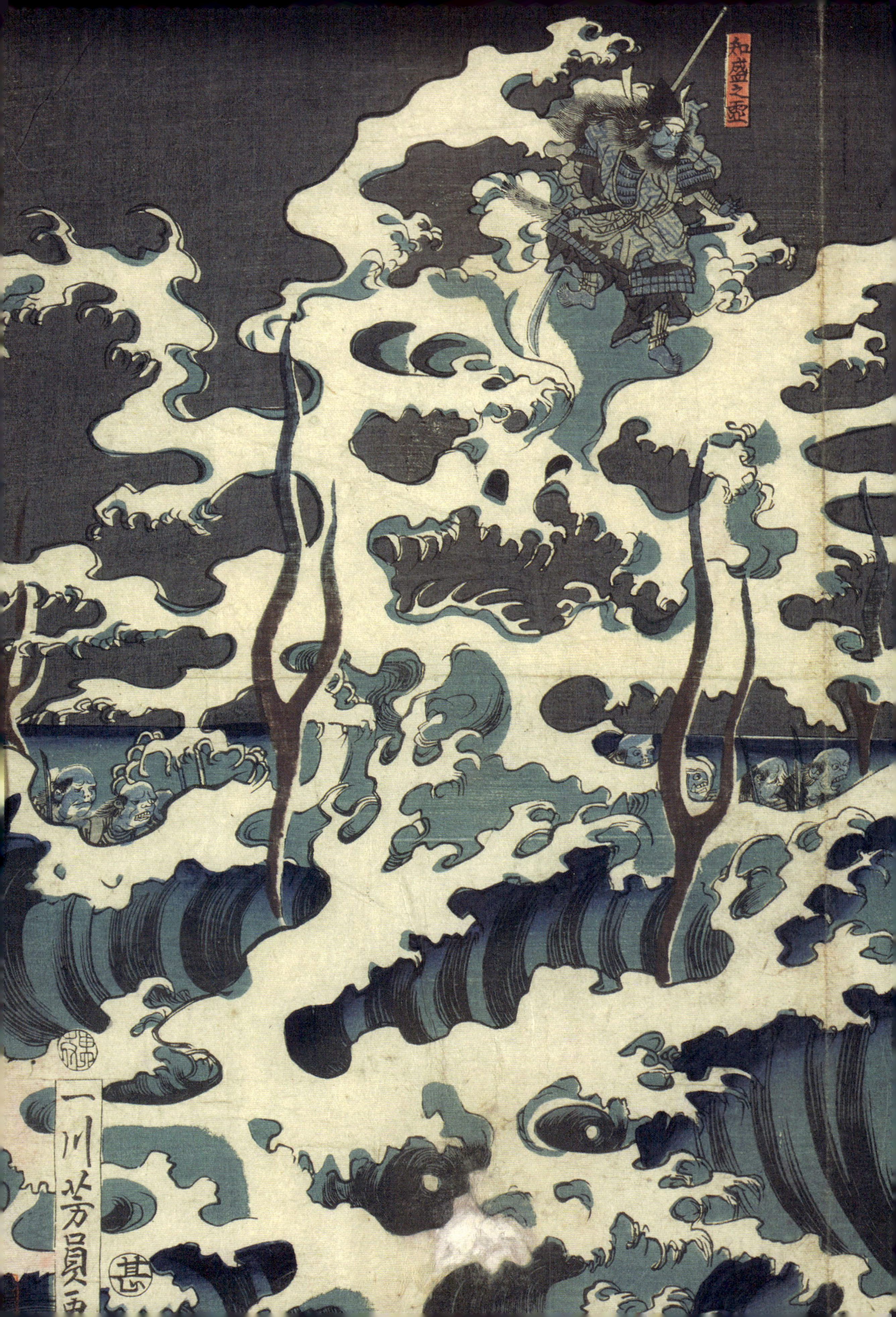
知盛之霊
一川芳員画

Caught in a Storm at Daimotsuno-ura / Utagawa Yoshikazu

1860 / Tokyo Metropolitan Library

In the Noh play "Funa Benkei," a storm catches Yoshitsune and his party, as they are setting sail from Daimotsuno-ura to escape to the west. The storm is caused by vengeful spirits of the Taira clan, who was defeated at Danno-ura and sank into the sea. This picture depicts wave splashes which form a shape resembling a giant moaning face. Tomomori stands on top of the big wave, and gazes down at Yoshitsune and his party.

大物浦難風之図 ／ 歌川芳員

万延元年（1860）／ 東京都立中央図書館

能『船弁慶』では、大物浦から西国に落ちのびようと出航した義経一行の船を暴風雨が襲う。壇ノ浦で敗れて海に沈んだ平家の怨霊の仕業である。波しぶきは、まるでうめき声をあげるような巨大な顔を形作る。その頂点に知盛が立ち、義経一行を見下ろしている。

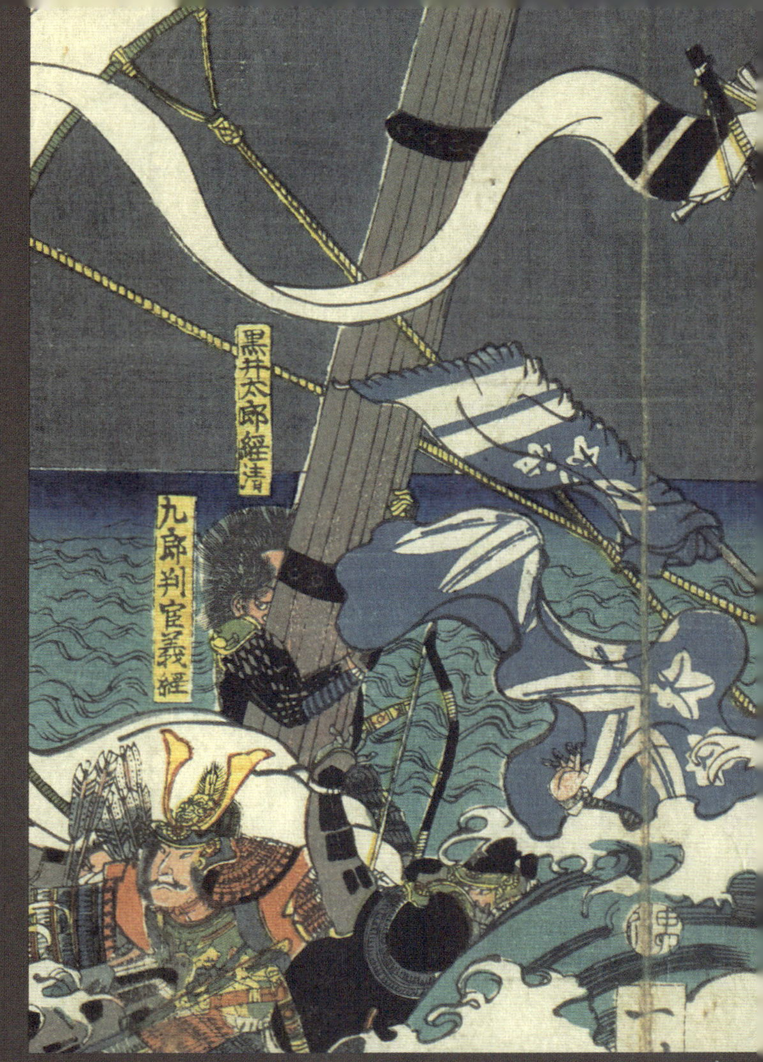

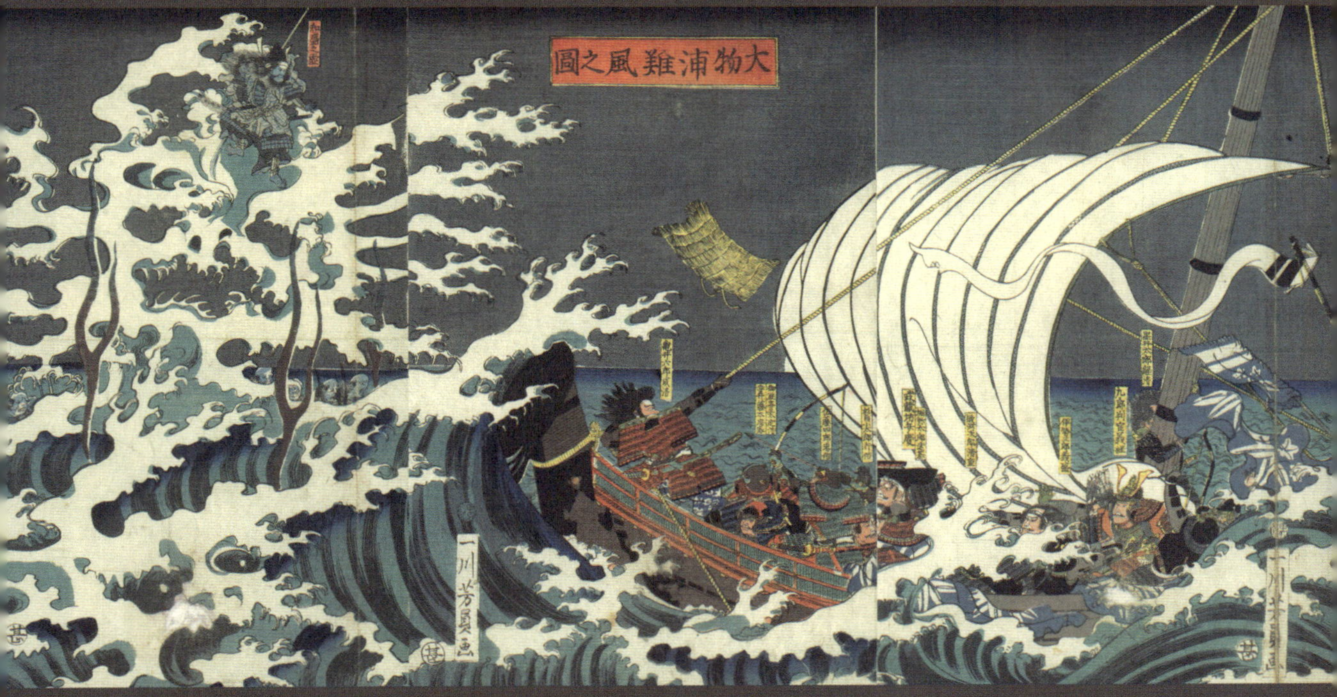

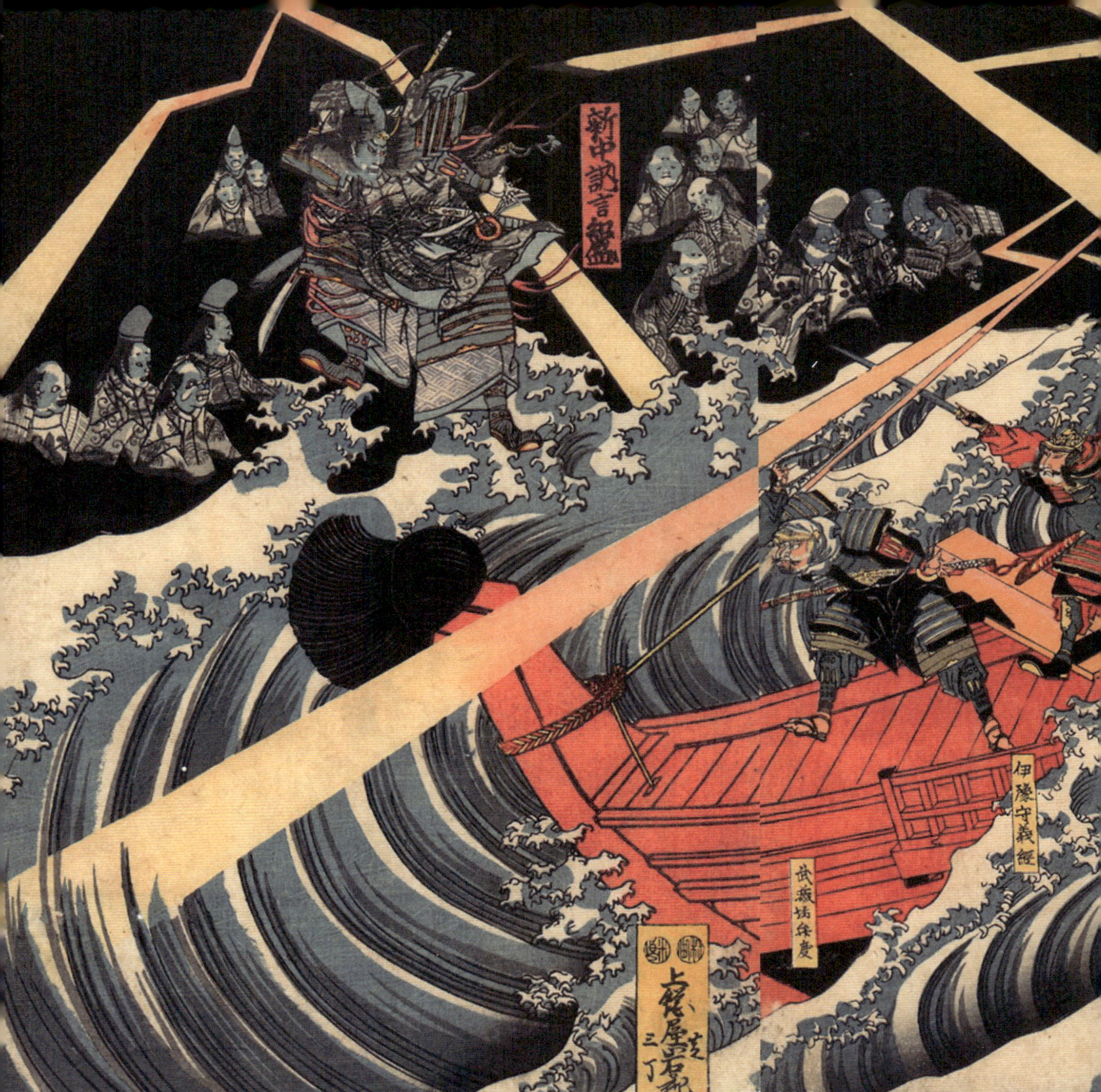

Vengeful Spirits of the Taira Clan Appearing at Daimotsuno-ura, Se'sshū Province / Katsushika Hokui

1848-1854 / Photo : Morimiya

This picture depicts vengeful spirits of the Taira clan causing a destructive storm, and threatening Yoshitsune and his party with lightning. The spirits' skin is colored in blue and white, the same colors as the waves and splashes.

摂州大物浦平家怨霊顕る図 ／ 葛飾北為

嘉永年間（1848 -1854）／ 提供：古美術もりみや

平家の亡霊が引き起こす暴風雨が雷を落とし、脅かされる義経一行。波しぶきと見紛う亡霊たちの肌色は、波と同色の青と白で彩色されている。

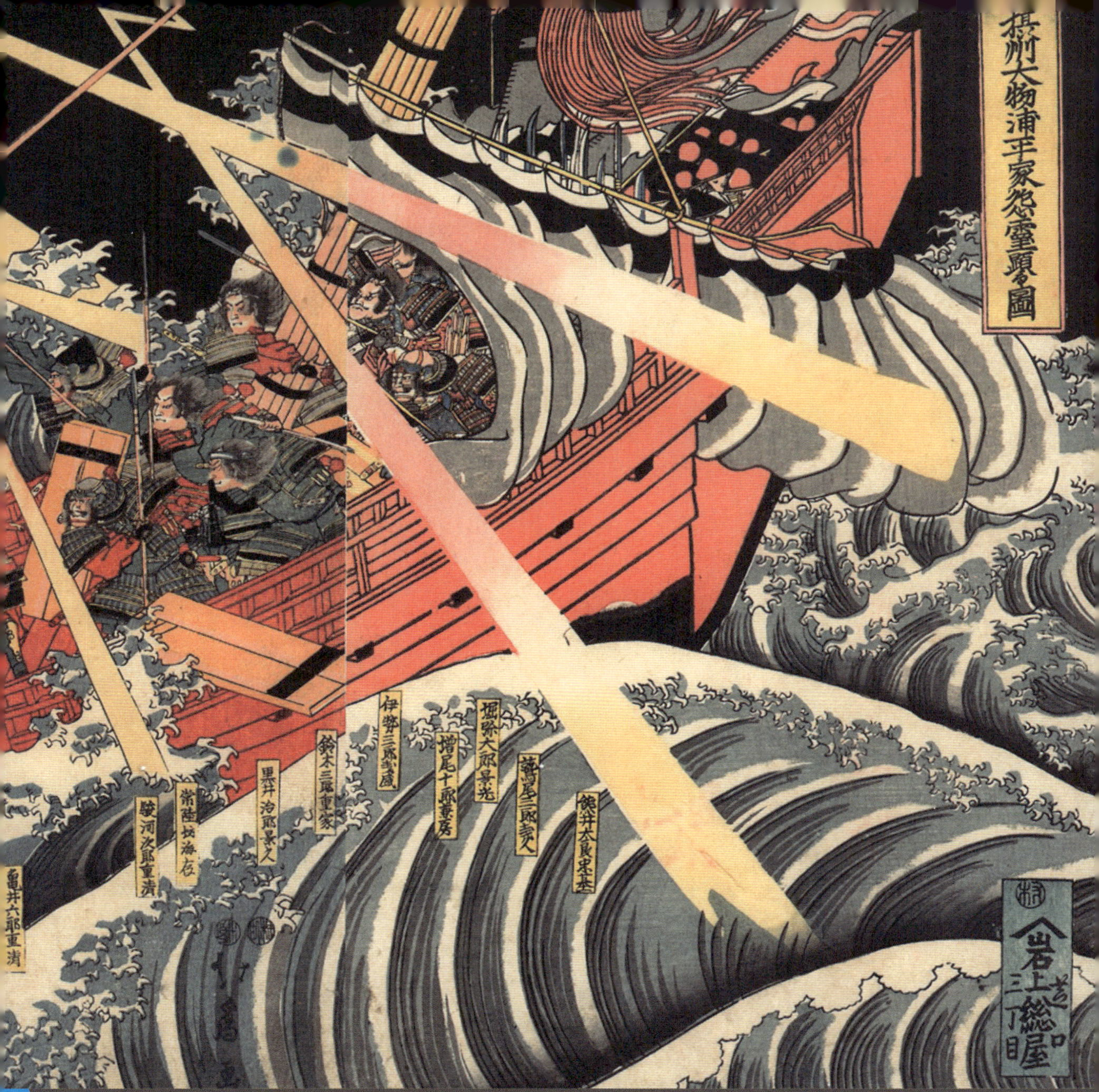

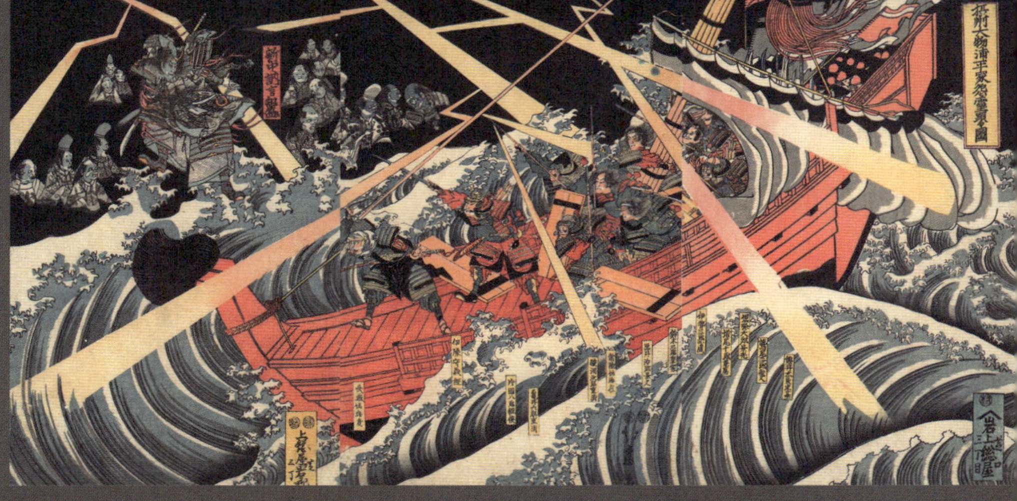

摂州大物浦平家怨霊顕る図
亀井六郎重清
駿河次郎重清
常陸坊海尊
黒井治郎景久
鈴木三郎重家
伊勢三郎義盛
増尾十郎兼房
堀彌太郎景光
滝馬屋三郎實光
鈴井太良忠基
岩上総屋

Vengeful Spirit of Taira-no Tomomori
Appearing over the Sea at Daimotsuno-
ura, from the series New Forms of
Thirty-six Ghosts / Tsukioka Yoshitoshi

1891 / Tokyo Metropolitan Library

The picture depicts the vengeful spirit of Taira-no
Tomomori causing a destructive storm. What he is
gazing at would be Yoshitsune and his party. His pale
skin represents his strong will to pay off the score of
the wiped-out Taira clan.

新形三十六怪撰
大物之浦ニ霊 平 知盛海上ニ出現之図 /
月岡芳年

明治 24 年（1891）/ 東京都立中央図書館

暴風雨を引き起こす知盛。視線の先に見据えるのは義
経一行だろう。青白い肌に、一門の怨みを晴らさんと
する意志がみなぎる。

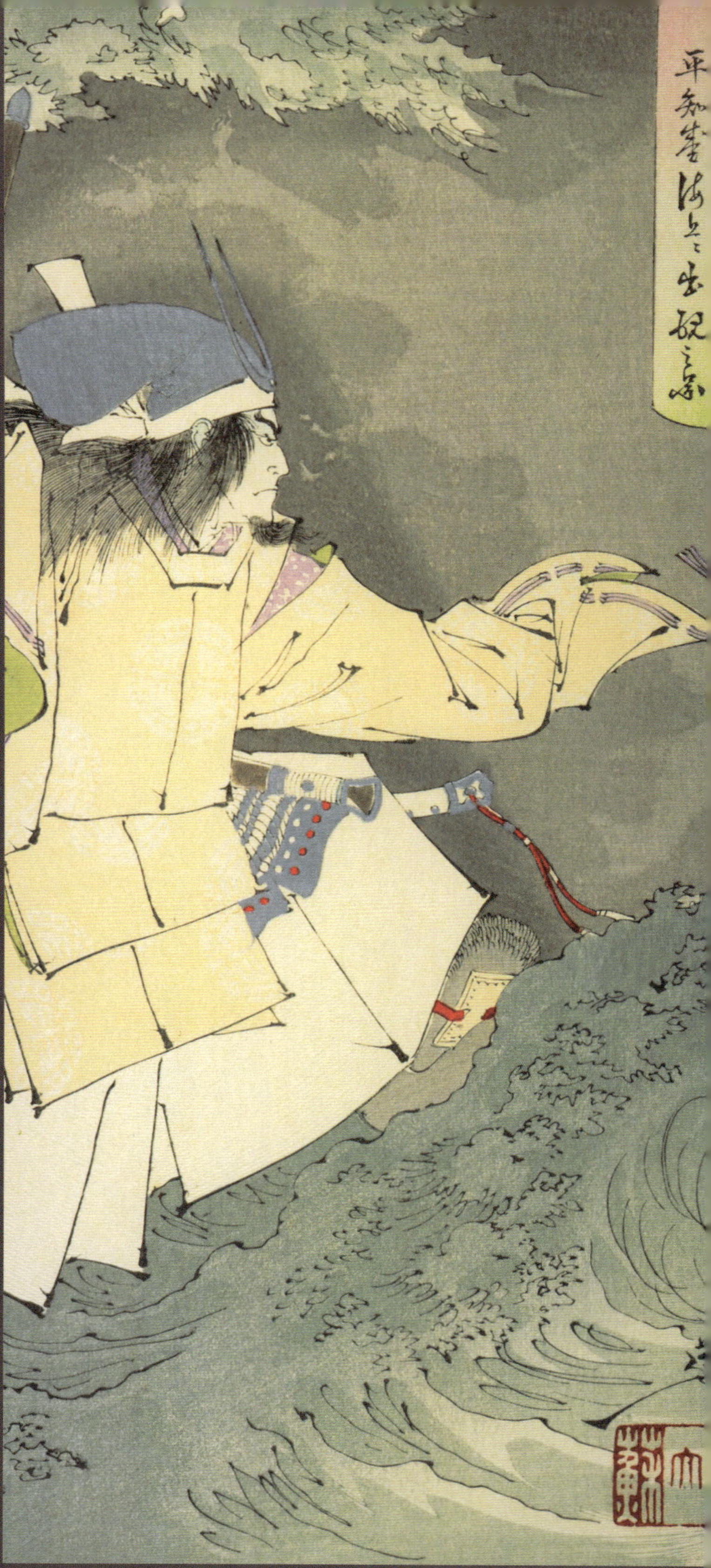

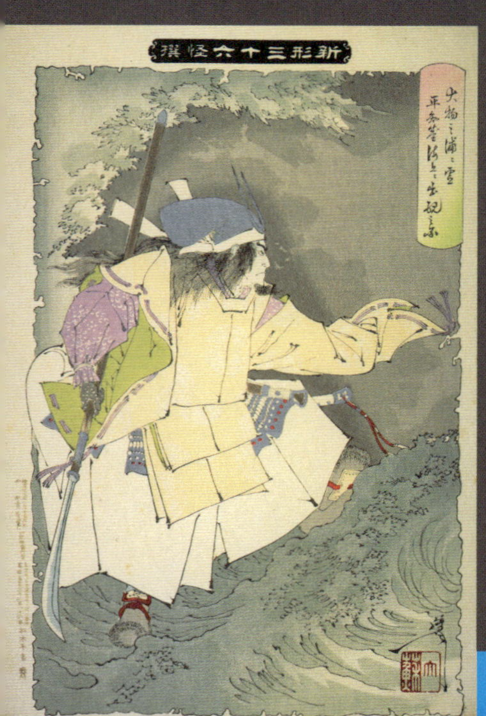

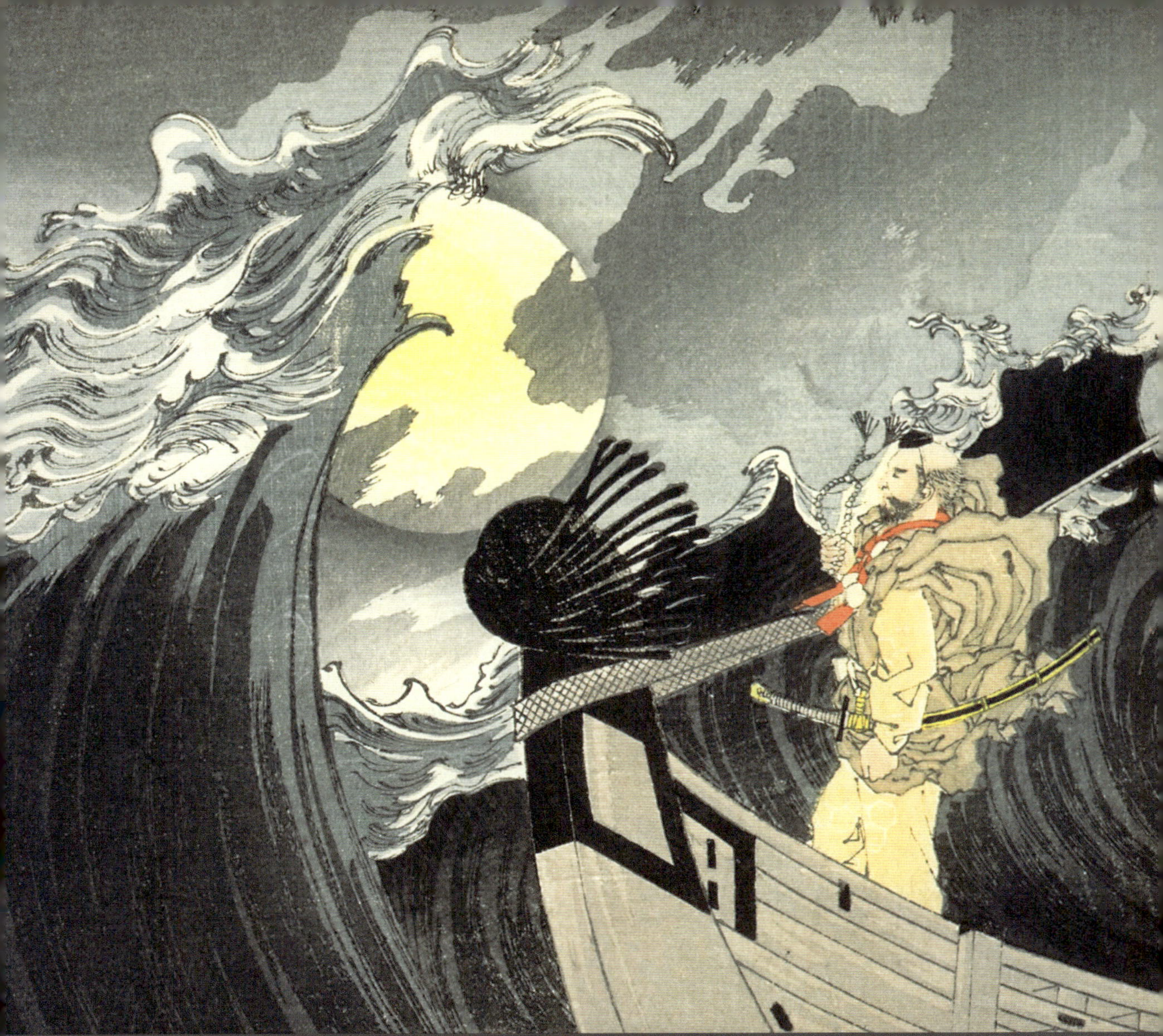

Moon Above the Waves, from the series One Hundred Phases of the Moon / Tsukioka Yoshitoshi

1886 / National Diet Library, Japan

The picture depicts dark black high waves almost covering the full moon. Benkei grasps Buddhist prayer beads and confronts vengeful spirits. His gesture is depicted in a quiet manner, which effectively expresses his unfaltering loyalty to his lord Yoshitsune.

月百姿 大物海上月 / 月岡芳年

明治 19（1886） / 国立国会図書館蔵

満月を覆い隠さんとする、どす黒い高波。怨霊に立ち向かい数珠を握る弁慶。身振りをおさえることでかえって、主君・義経への揺るぎない忠誠心があらわとなる。

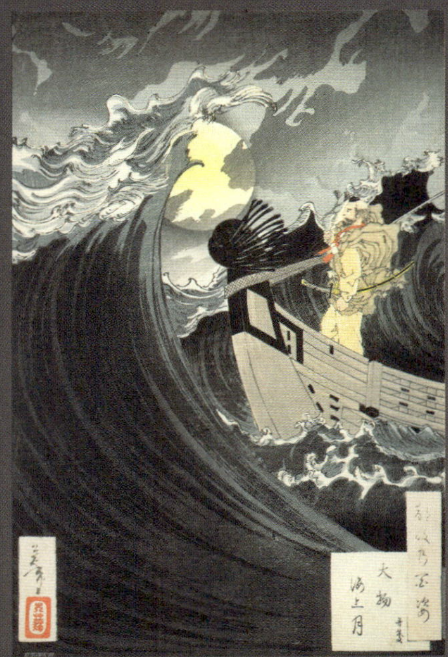

Skeletons and hell. These two motives were big sensations from the end of the Edo period and into the Meiji period. The driving force of their popularity might be attributed to the mega-selling novelist Santō Kyōden. Skeletons and hell were depicted in novels, theater plays, kimono and tattoo designs, as well as Nishikie, or polychrome ukiyoe prints. This boom probably reflects the long Japanese tradition of pictorial expressions of dead bodies, which intersected with the coeval diffusion of Western medical knowledge. It led to a change in general people's views of death, and to the creation of pop and comically represented skeletons and hell.

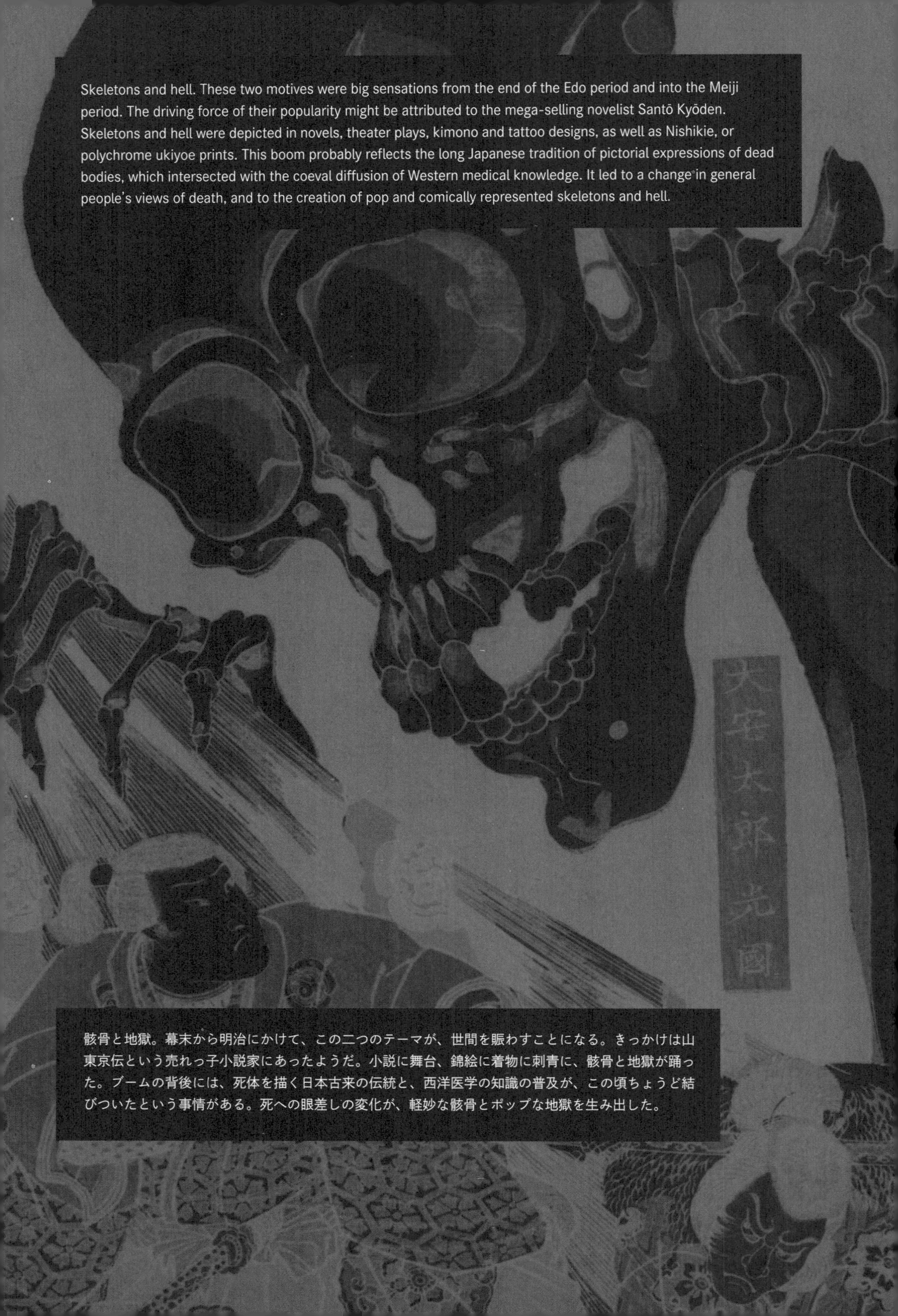

骸骨と地獄。幕末から明治にかけて、この二つのテーマが、世間を賑わすことになる。きっかけは山東京伝という売れっ子小説家にあったようだ。小説に舞台、錦絵に着物に刺青に、骸骨と地獄が踊った。ブームの背後には、死体を描く日本古来の伝統と、西洋医学の知識の普及が、この頃ちょうど結びついたという事情がある。死への眼差しの変化が、軽妙な骸骨とポップな地獄を生み出した。

Skulls Dancing in Hell

髑髏と地獄の舞踏

六章

Chapter 6.

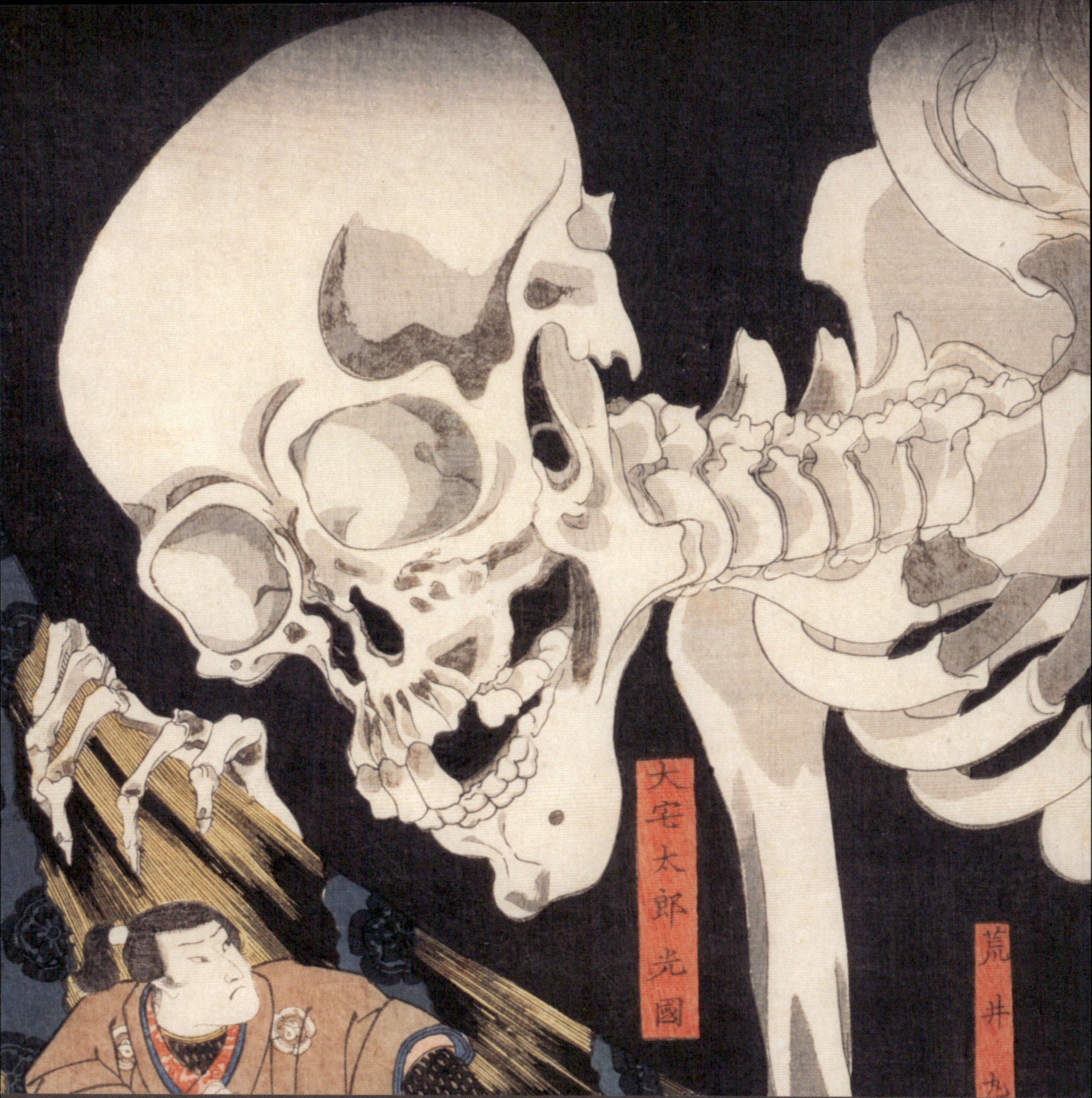

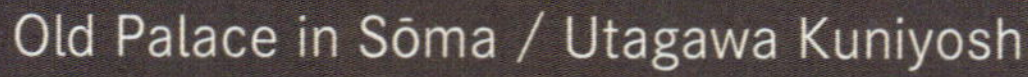

Old Palace in Sōma / Utagawa Kuniyoshi

c.1845 - 1846 / Chiba City Museum of Art

The picture depicts the same subject as P.122 Ōya Tarō Mitsukuni visits an old palace in Sōma, where Takiyasha-hime lives. The original novel writes of numerous battling skeletons, but here, Kuniyoshi depicts one giant skeleton. The white skeleton stands out against the dark night and peers into the other characters, as if it would bear down upon them.

相馬の古内裏 ／ 歌川国芳

弘化 2-3 年（1845-46）頃 ／ 千葉市美術館蔵

山東京伝による小説『善知安方忠義伝』の一場面。次頁（p.122）と同場面であるが、小説では多数の骸骨たちの合戦場面だったところを、国芳は、一体の巨大な骸骨へと変貌させた。闇夜に浮かび上がる白骨が、襲いかかるように登場人物たちを覗き込む。

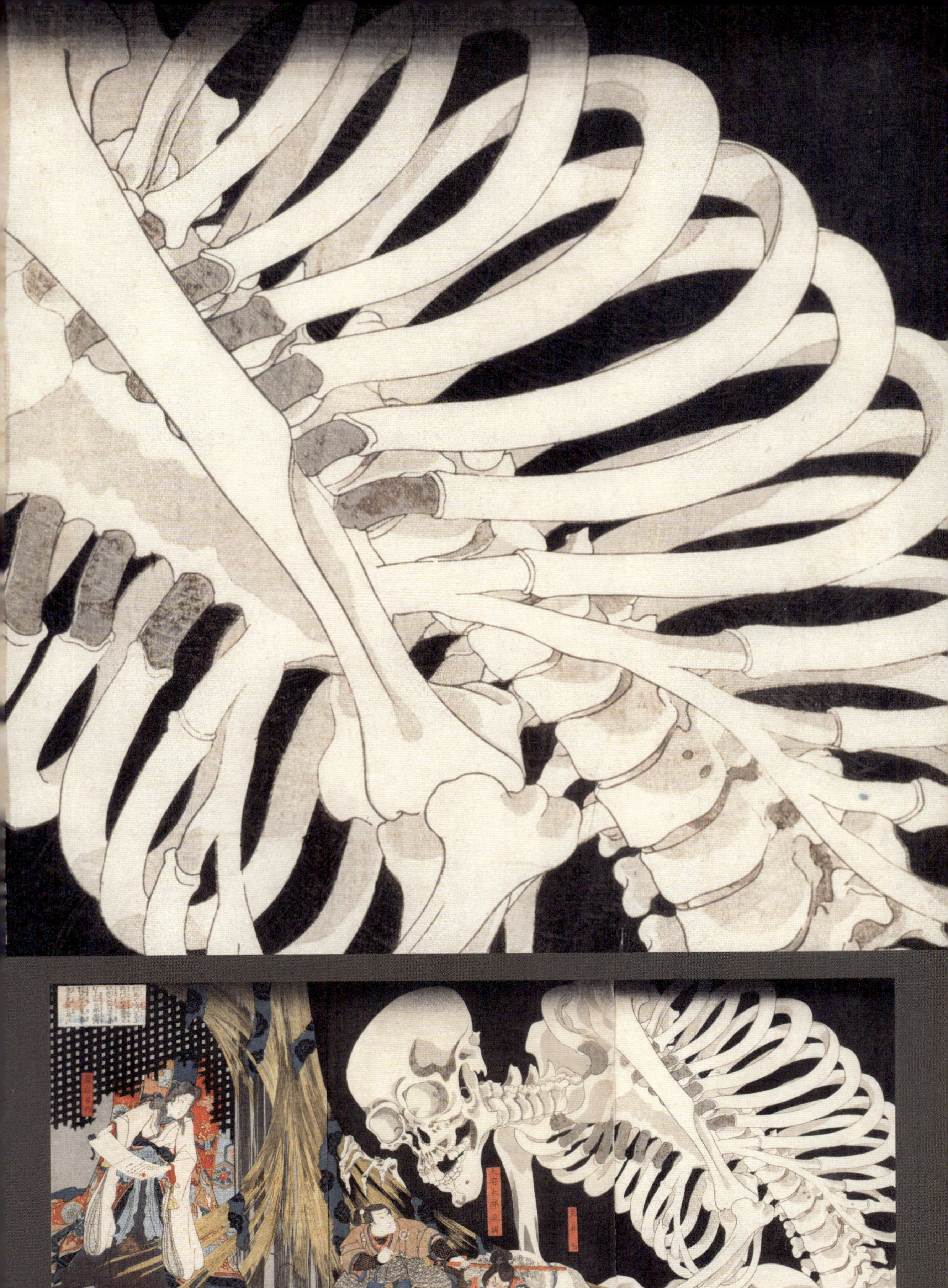

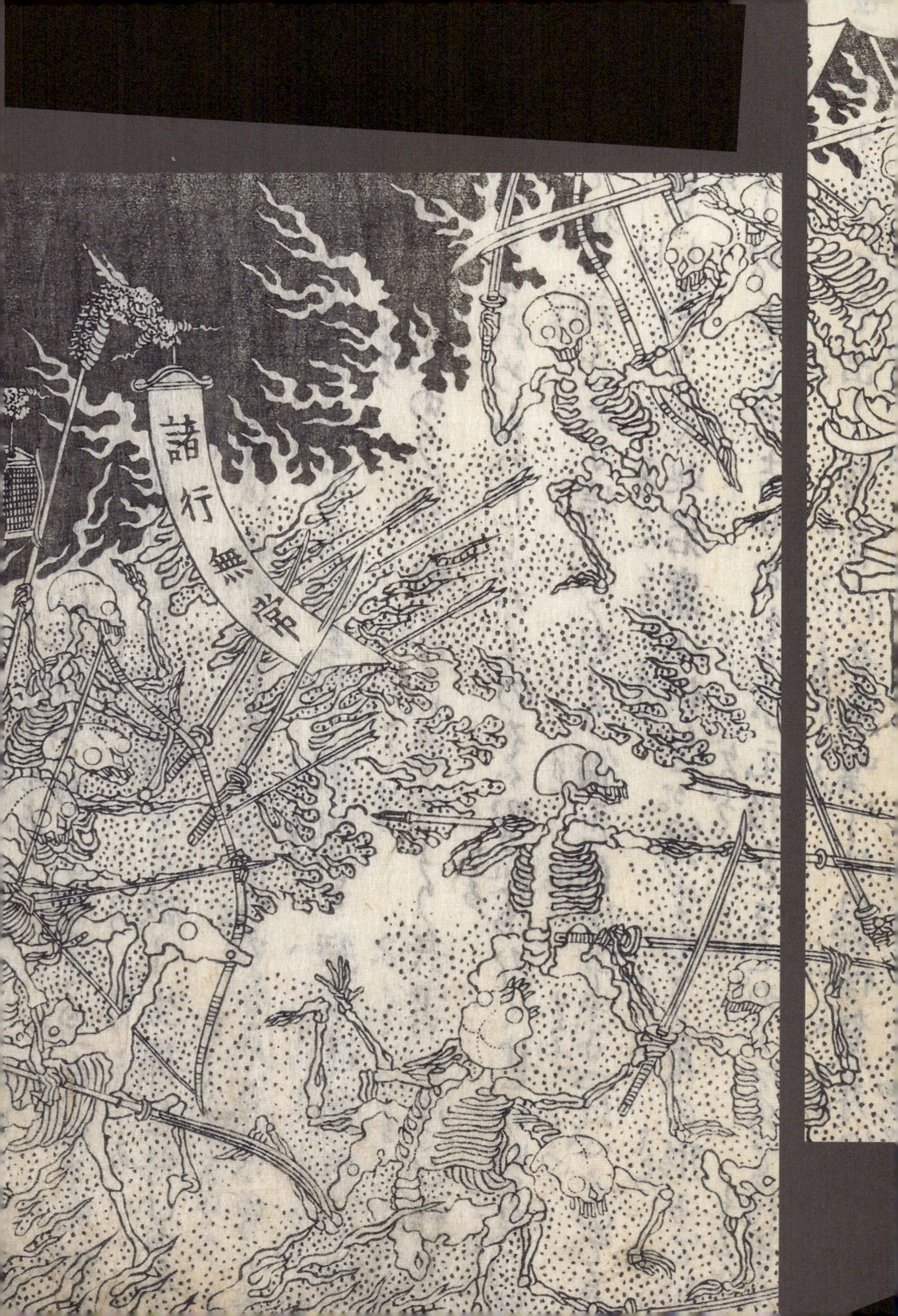

諸行無常

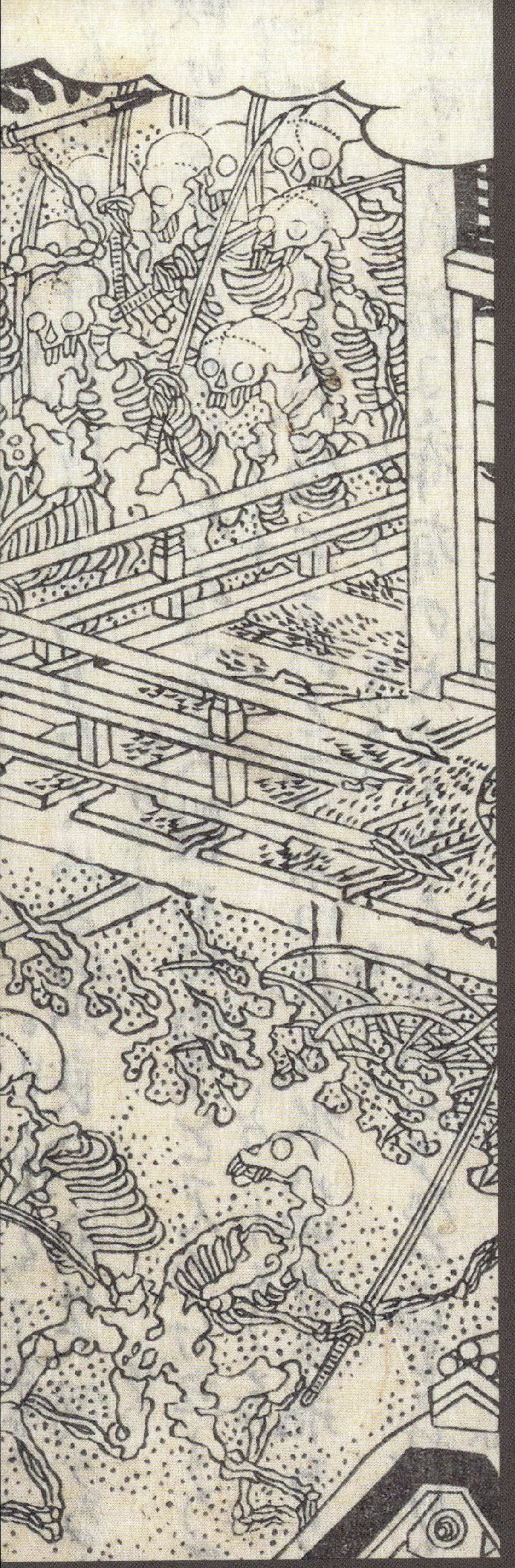

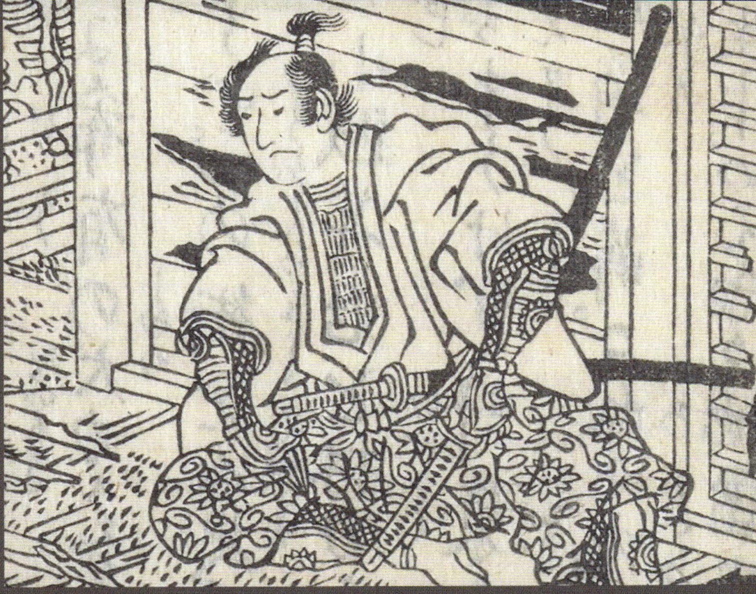

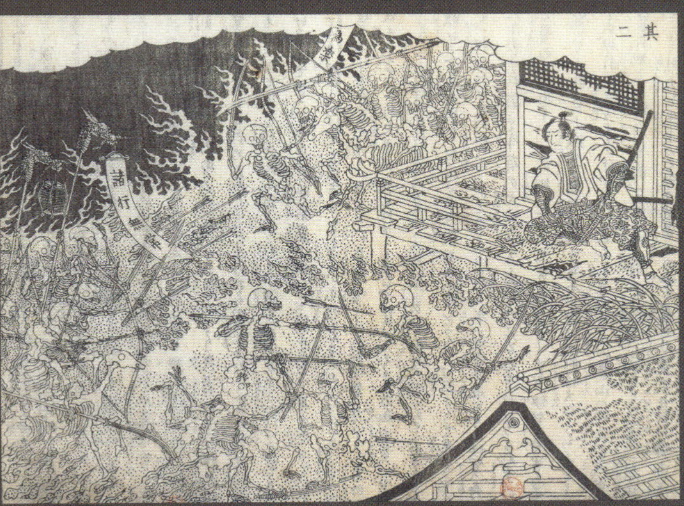

Biography of the Truly Loyal Warrior, Utō Yasukata, the first part / Texts by Santō Kyōden, Print illustrations by Utagawa Toyokuni

Published in 1806 / National Library of France

This novel was written based on the following legend of Taira-no Masakado's vengeful spirit. Masakado was a warrior who had a failed rebellion in ancient times, and was later enshrined in the eastern part of Japan. Masakado's daughter, Takiyasha-hime, could practice sorcery. She planned a rebellion in her own mansion, where monsters hung around night after night. Ôya Tarō Mitsukuni came to defeat her, but Takiyasha-hime practiced sorcery to make him encounter numerous skeletons. In this picture, each skeleton shows a different motion, including brandishing swords, or holding an arrow while riding on a skeletal horse.

『善知安方忠義伝』前編 ／ 山東京伝著、歌川豊国画

文化 3 年（1806）刊 ／ フランス国立図書館蔵

東国に祀られる怨霊・平将門の伝説をもとにした物語。将門の娘で妖術使いの滝夜叉姫が謀反を企てる屋敷には、夜な夜な妖怪がたむろする。退治に訪れた大宅太郎光国は、姫の妖術により、無数の骸骨に遭遇する。刀を振り回す骸骨に、馬の骸骨にまたがり弓矢を構える骸骨など、多彩な骸骨が群れ集う。

The Complete Legend of Drunken Enlightenment in Japan, The first volume /
Texts by Santō Kyōden, Print illustrations by Utagawa Toyokuni

Published in 1809 / Art Research Center, Ritsumeikan University

The print illustration titled "Stinky Skin Bag" depicts a beautiful woman, but if you flip the paper, you would see a skeleton illustration on the next page. It represents the Buddhist perspective that even a beautiful woman is just a skeleton wrapped with a stinky skin bag.

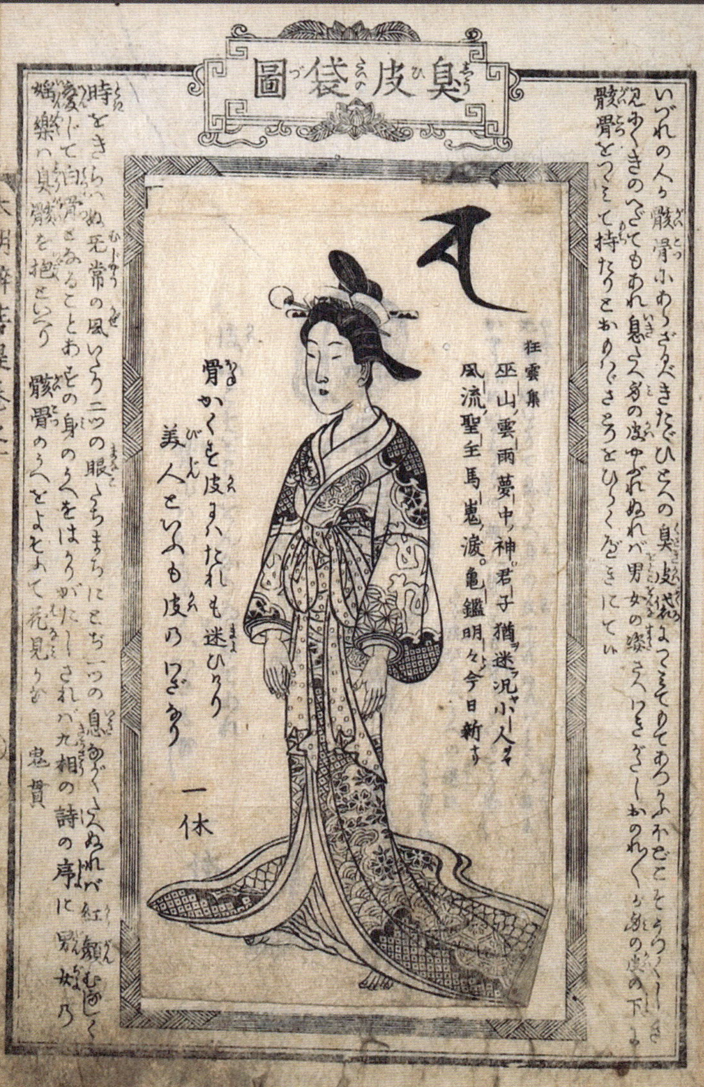

『本朝酔菩提全伝』巻之一 /
山東京伝著、歌川豊国画

文化 6 年（1809）刊 /
立命館大学 ARC 蔵

「臭皮袋図」と題する口絵は、美人もただ臭い皮袋に包まれた骸骨にすぎないという教えをあらわすもので、美人図を骸骨図の上に重ねて貼り、美人をめくると骸骨になる仕掛け。

The Complete Legend of Drunken Enlightenment in Japan

The illustrated preaching book "Ikkyū's Skeletons" introduces Buddhist teachings through the life story of a skeleton behaving like a human. Its author might be Ikkyū Sōjun, a freewheeling priest who is said to have been very eccentric during the Muromachi period. Later, Santō Kyōden referred to the book and wrote his original novel "The Complete Legend of Drunken Enlightenment in Japan." The main character of the story is a courtesan named Jigoku, meaning Hell, who exchanged Buddhist riddles with Priest Ikkyū and achieved enlightenment. Courtesan Jigoku, Priest Ikkyū, Nozarashi Gosuke and other characters in this book later became popular motives in kabuki theater plays and ukiyoe prints.

『本朝酔菩提全伝』

自由奔放な言動や奇行をなしたという室町時代の僧・一休宗純の著作とされた絵入りの説教本『一休骸骨』── 骸骨が人の営みを送るさまを描き仏教の教えを説く ── を下敷きに、地獄という名の遊女（地獄太夫）が一休と問答し、悟りを開くという内容の小説。地獄太夫や一休、野晒悟助といった登場人物は歌舞伎や錦絵で人気の題材に。

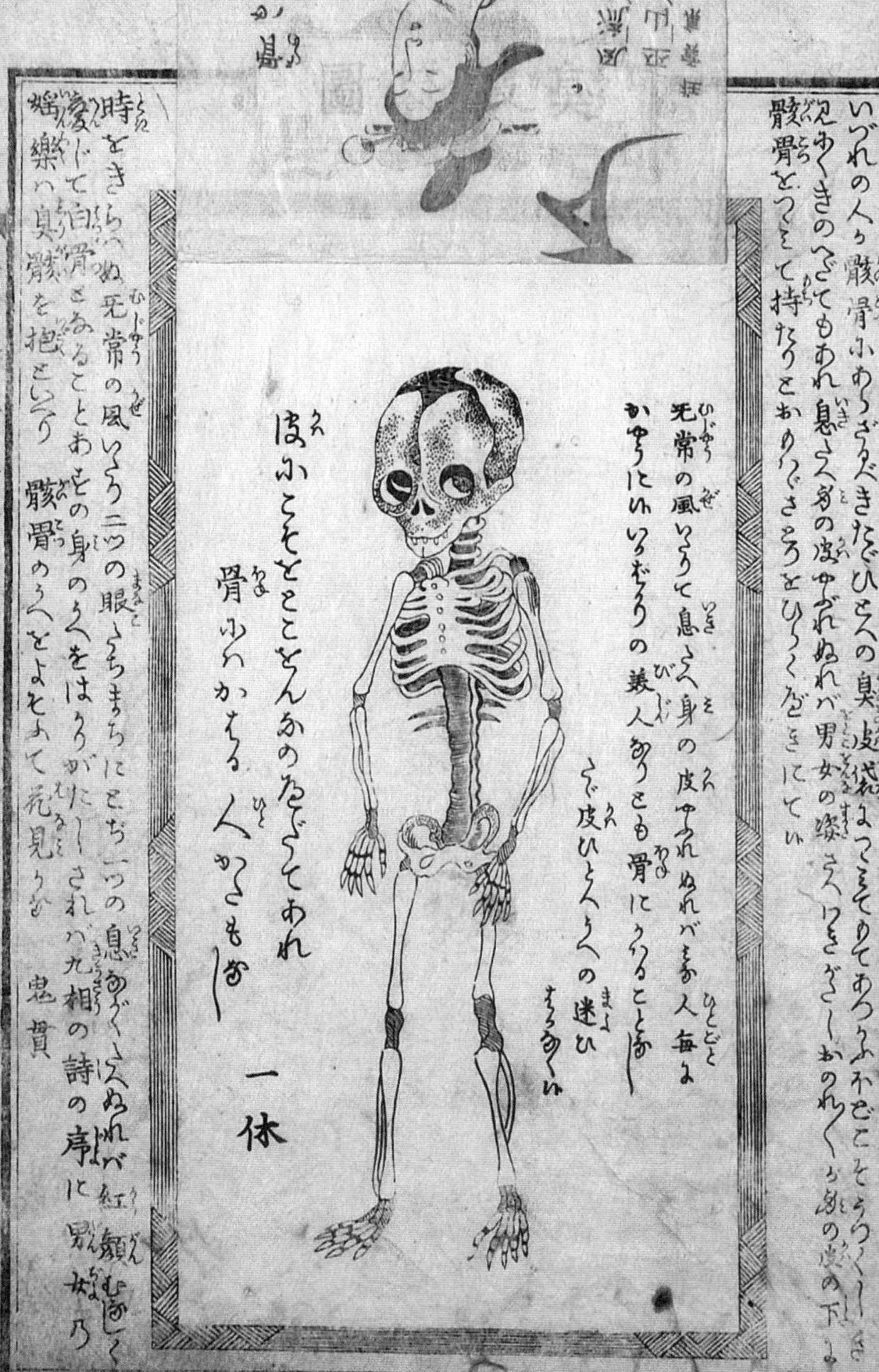

いづれの人も骸骨ふわ
ゆくさるべきたぞひとつの臭骸
にづくろべてもあれ息せぬ身の皮ぬれば男女の娑ことぞ
ゆくしおのれくら死の臭の下る

死常の風いろりて息せぬ身の皮ぬれが多人毎も
かやうにいろぞうりの義人もとも骨にうることは
を皮ひとりの迷ひ

ほふそととんかのねぞそあれ
骨ふりかする人かそも浴

一休

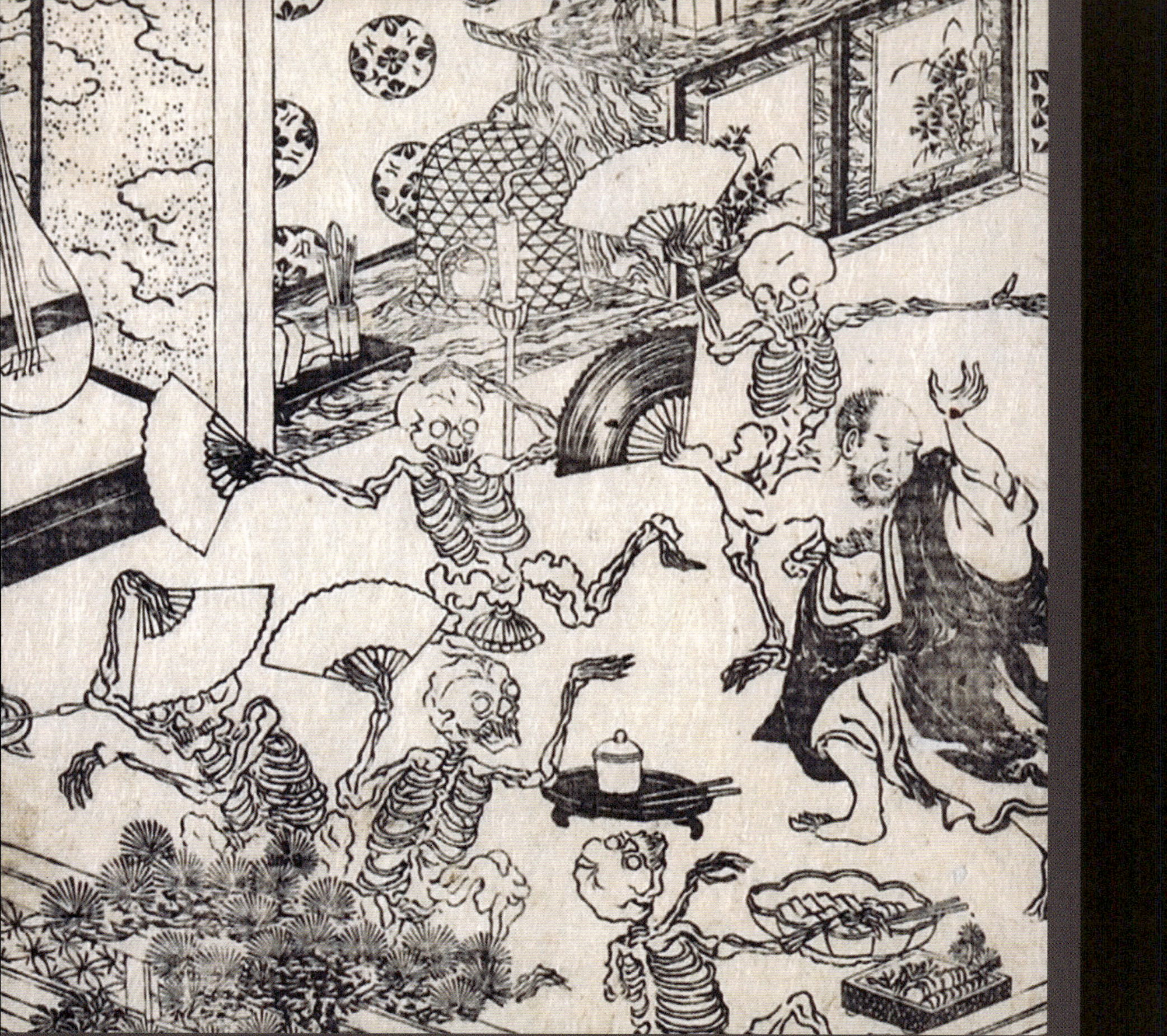

The Complete Legend of Drunken Enlightenment in Japan, The fourth volume /
Texts by Santō Kyōden, Print illustrations by Utagawa Toyokuni
Published in 1809 / Art Research Center, Ritsumeikan University

The picture depicts the following legend of Courtesan Jigoku. When she peeked into the room where Priest Ikkyū received hospitalities from geisha girls, she found that everyone except Ikkyū had become a skeleton. Courtesan Jigoku then realized that the human body was just a skeleton wrapped in a stinky skin bag, and decided to learn Buddhism teachings from Ikkyū.

『本朝酔菩提全伝』巻之四 ／
山東京伝著、歌川豊国画

文化 6 年（1809）刊 ／
立命館大学 ARC 蔵

地獄太夫が、舞妓や芸妓のもてなしを受ける一休の様子を覗いたところ、一休を除く舞妓や芸妓はみな骸骨の姿になっていた。人間の身体が「臭骸」に過ぎないことを悟った地獄太夫は、一休の教えを受けることを決意する。

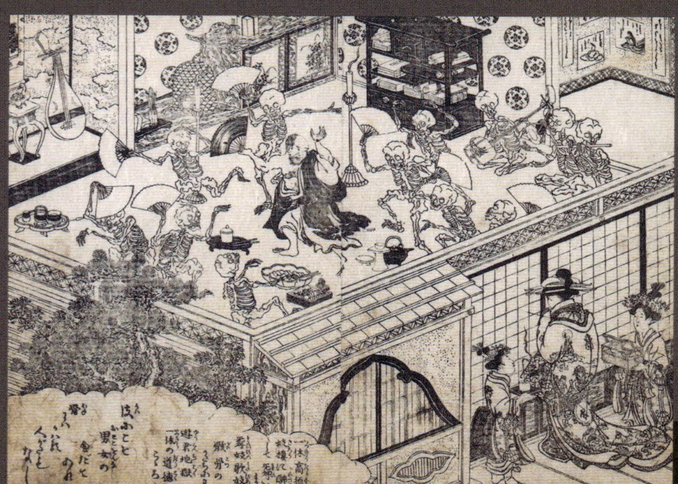

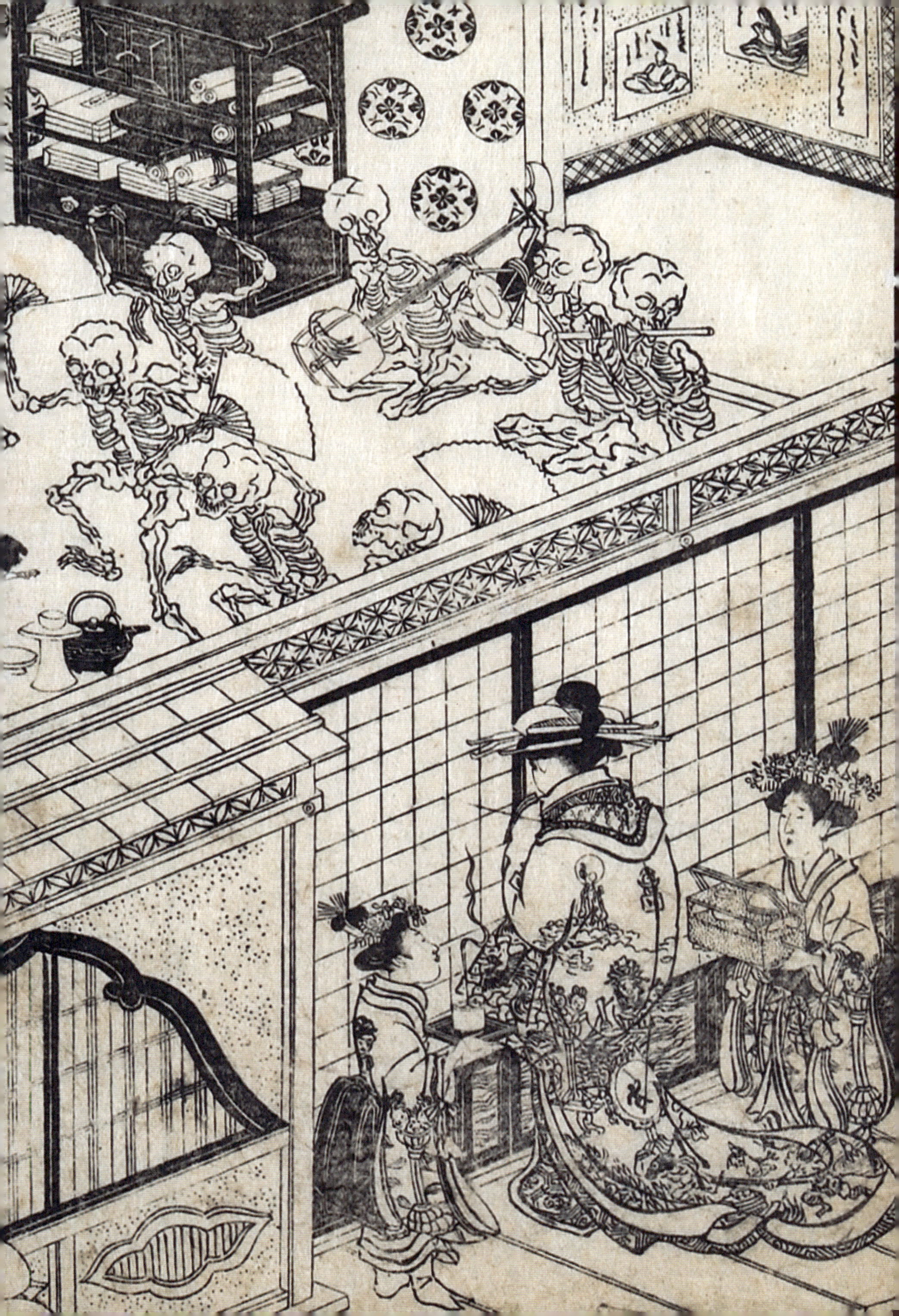

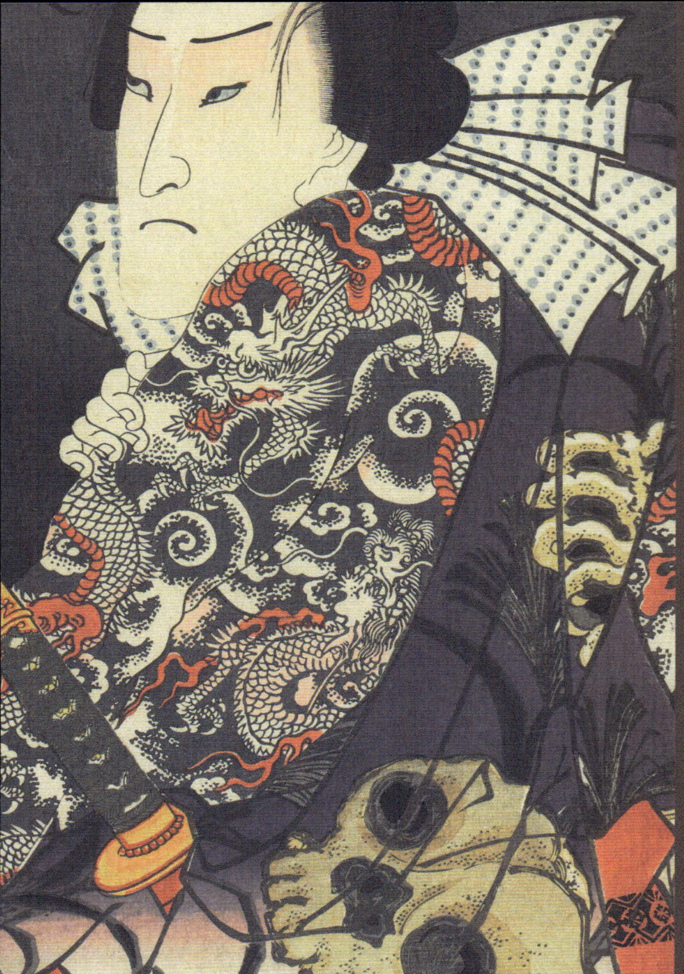

当世好男子伝
久紋竜支進に比すのざらし語助 ／
歌川豊国（３代）（初代国貞）

安政 5 年（1858） ／ 東京都立中央図書館蔵

当世の人気者を『水滸伝』の登場人物になぞらえて描いたシリーズ。本図は、野晒悟助を、水滸伝の豪傑・九紋龍史進になぞらえて描いたもの。悟助のトレードマークの髑髏が大きく描かれた衣服と、史進を象徴する龍の刺青を組み合わせた、大胆奇抜な出で立ち。髑髏の目の穴から生えた薄が象徴するように、悟助も史進も、弱きを助け強きをくじく侠客の代表だ。

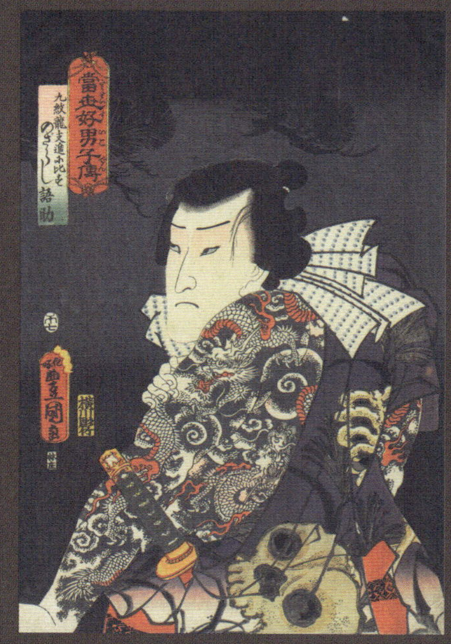

Nozarashi Gosuke as Kumonryū Shishin, from the series A Collection of Modern Handsome Men ／ Utagawa Toyokuni III, also known as Utagawa Kunisada I

1858 ／ Tokyo Metropolitan Library

This series of ukiyoe prints is based on the old Chinese novel "Suikoden," but the characters were changed into popular people from that time in Japan. Here, Nozarashi Gosuke is likened to Kumonryū Shishin, one of the heroes in Suikoden. His appearance is bold and outrageous, with his kimono's large skull pattern, which is Gosuke's trademark, while his dragon tattoos symbolize Shishin. As the pampas grass growing from the skull's eye socket metaphorically represents, both Gosuke and Kumonryū were famous chivalrous outlaws, who fought for the oppressed against the oppressor.

Nozarashi Gosuke

The novel "The Complete Legend of Drunken Enlightenment in Japan" writes of a character named Nozarashi Gosuke, who is a chivalrous but violent outlaw from Osaka. He leaves Ikkyū because of his roughness, but reflects on himself and starts helping others. There is a legend about Ono-no Komachi, a famous female poet in the 9th century, which tells that her dead body was left out in the open and became a skeleton. Then, pampas grass grew out of its eye sockets and rustled in the wind, which sounded like "Oh, my eyes hurt." Based on the legend, this picture depicts Gosuke's kimono with skull patterns, but without pampas grass. It represents that Gosuke was a chivalrous man who worked for others to eliminate their misfortunes. In addition, skulls symbolize chivalrous outlaws.

野晒悟助

『本朝酔菩提全伝』に登場する浪花の侠客・野晒悟助。乱暴な性格のせいで一休のもとを去るが、やがて行いを反省し人助けをしていく。悟助の衣服に描かれる髑髏は、小野小町の髑髏伝説 ── 野晒しの小町の髑髏の目の穴から薄が生えて、風に吹かれて「あなめあなめ（ああ目が痛い）」と音を立てる ── を踏まえ、「目の中の薄を取り去る＝人の災いを除く」という意味を込めたもの。髑髏は侠客を象徴する記号となる。

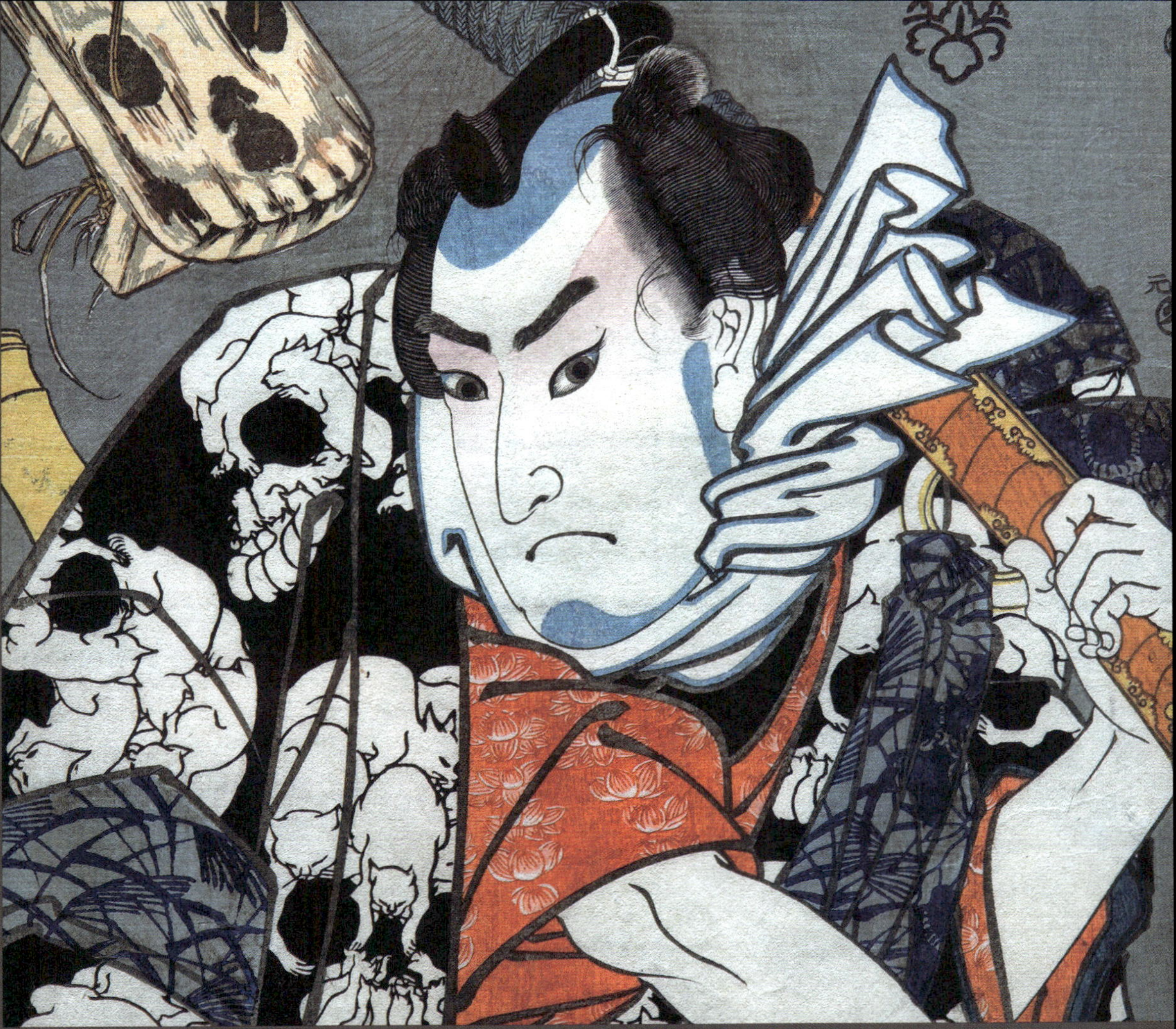

Nozarashi Gosuke, from the series Men of Ready Money
with Shōfuda Labels Attached, Kuniyoshi Fashion / Utagawa Kuniyoshi

1845 / Photo : amana

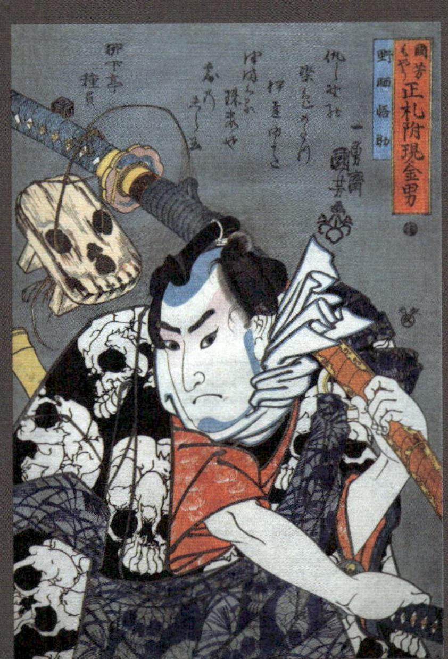

"Shōfuda" in the title means "a product label showing its honest price."
So, "an attached Shōfuda" means "something well-established and
without pretense nor exaggeration." This picture is from a series of
ukiyoe prints which depict reputable chivalrous outlaws. Here, Gosuke's
kimono has his trademark, skull patterns. Each of the skull patterns
consists of several cats. Another part of his kimono has a different
pattern of skulls, which looks like lotus flowers blooming in a pampas
grass field. The snagged clog on his sword also looks like a skull, with
pampas grass in one of the eye sockets.

国芳もやう 正札附現金男 野晒悟助 ／ 歌川国芳

弘化 2 年（1845） ／ 提供：アマナ

「正札」とは、掛け値なしの値段を書いて商品につけた札のことで、「正札
附」とはいつわりや誇張なく、世に定評のあることを指す。本図は評判
の侠客を描いたシリーズで、悟助にはトレードマークの髑髏の模様が散
りばめられている。複数の猫を組み合わせた髑髏、薄野原に浮かび上が
る蓮と見紛う髑髏、刀に引っ掛けた下駄のダブルイメージとなる髑髏。
下駄の髑髏の目からは薄が生えている。

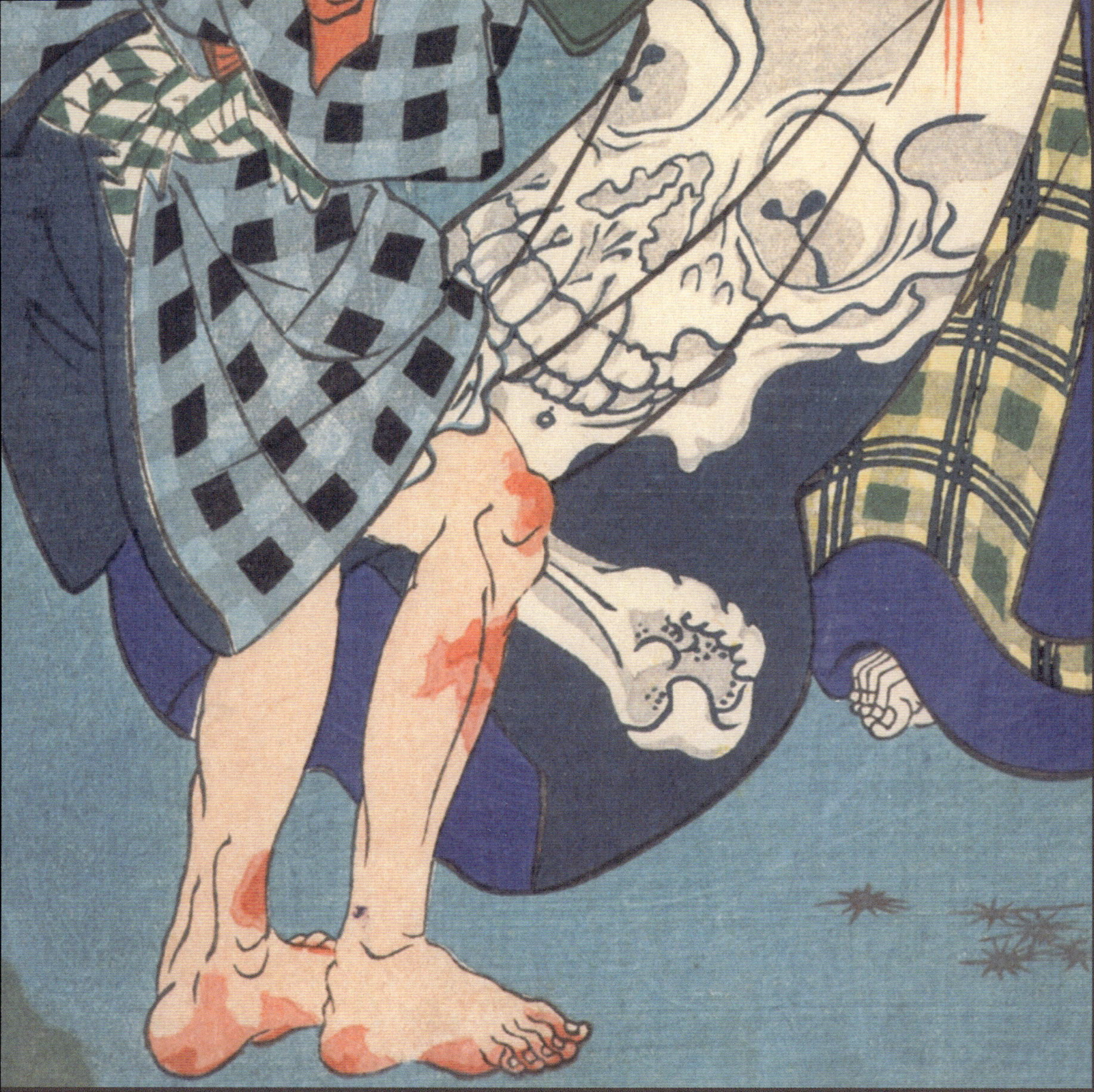

Kunisawa Shūji, from the series Twenty-Eight Famous Murders / Ochiai Yoshiiku

1867 / Keio University

The picture depicts Kunisada Chūji, a master of gambling, wearing a padded winter kimono with skull patterns. He was a legendary chivalrous outlaw in the late Edo period. This is a scene from "Kaei Suikoden," which is a novel featuring Chūji. He is identifying the decapitated head of his enemy Narukami Otoemon with his vassal. The kimono has a giant skull pattern, which seems to be glaring down at the decapitated head. The expression represents the demanding and oppressive character of Chūji.

英名二十八衆句 国沢周治 ／ 落合芳幾

慶応 3 年（1867）／ 慶應義塾大学蔵

髑髏があしらわれた褞袍を羽織るのは、博徒の親分・国定忠治。江戸時代後期の、やはり伝説化された侠客だ。描かれるのは忠治を主役とした『嘉永水滸伝』の一場面。敵である鳴神音右衛門の首実検。首を睨みつけるような巨大な髑髏が、威圧するような親分を演出している。

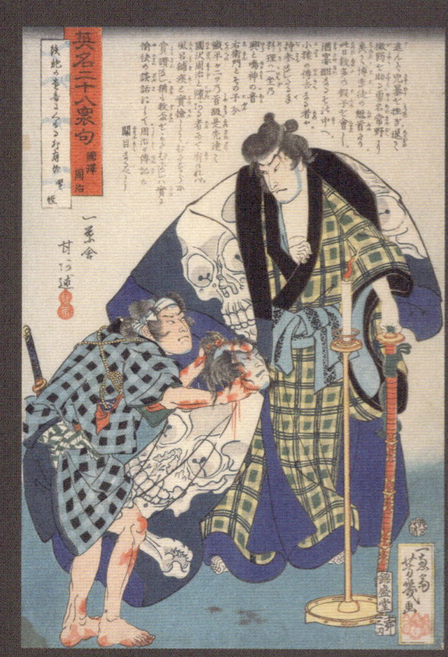

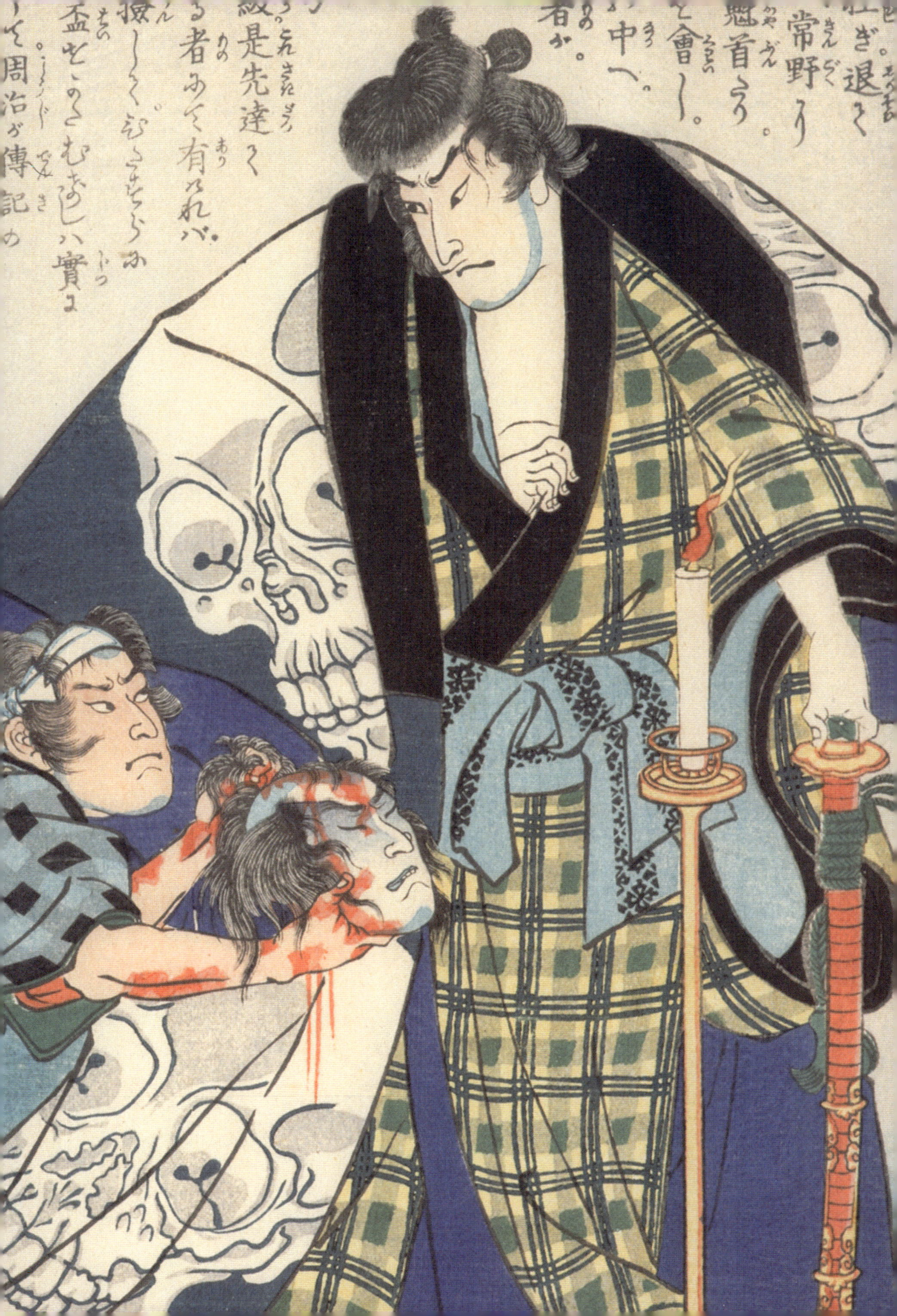
者か。
中へ。
と會し。
魁首うり
常野り
ぎ退く
緻是先達く
る者ゆく有れば
掘しくむさぶらか
盃をのさむおしハ實は
を周治が傳記の

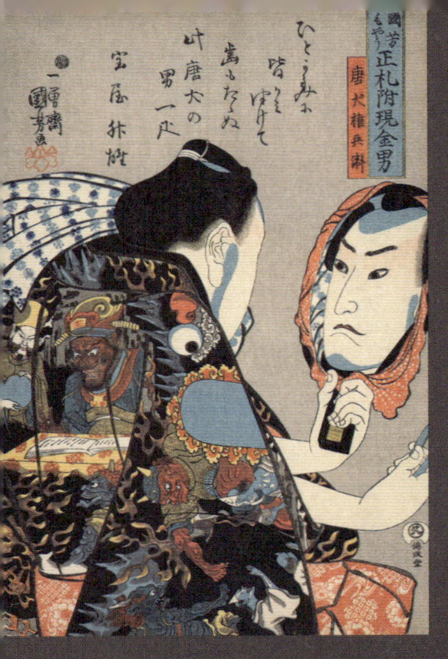

Tōken Gonbē, from the series Men of Ready Money with Shōfuda Labels Attached, Kuniyoshi Fashion / Utagawa Kuniyoshi

1845 / British Museum

Tōken Gonbē was a chivalrous outlaw at the beginning of the Edo period. His name "Tōken" means "Foreign dog," which is derived from an episode where he beat two foreign dogs to death. Later, he was beheaded, and his head was displayed at the prison gate in Suzugamori. This legend was adapted into theatrical performances and Kōdan storytellings. Actors in the role of Tōken plucked the hairs at the edge of their foreheads to broaden their sizes. The hairstyle was called "Tōken Forehead," and became in vogue. The picture depicts a kabuki actor fixing his Tōken hairstyle. Just like Courtesan Jigoku's kimono, his kimono also has a pattern depicting hell, which includes Enma Daiō, the King of Hell. He is holding up Jōhari-no Kagami, a mirror used by the King of Hell for judging if the dead were right-minded or not, before their death. But this mirror shows nothing. It might mean that Tōken Gonbē has a clear and serene life.

国芳もやう 正札附現金男 唐犬権兵衛 / 歌川国芳

弘化 2 年（1845） / 大英博物館蔵

江戸初期の侠客・唐犬権兵衛。その名は凶暴な唐犬二匹を撲殺したことに由来する。鈴ケ森で獄門に処され、芝居や講談で伝説化された。額の毛を広く大きく抜き上げる「唐犬額」を流行らせたという。本図でもその唐犬額を整えている様子だ。地獄太夫と同様に、閻魔大王のいる地獄を描いた衣服をまとう。生前の行いを映す地獄の浄玻璃の鏡には、何も映っていない。権兵衛の曇りなき人生をあらわす意図だろうか。

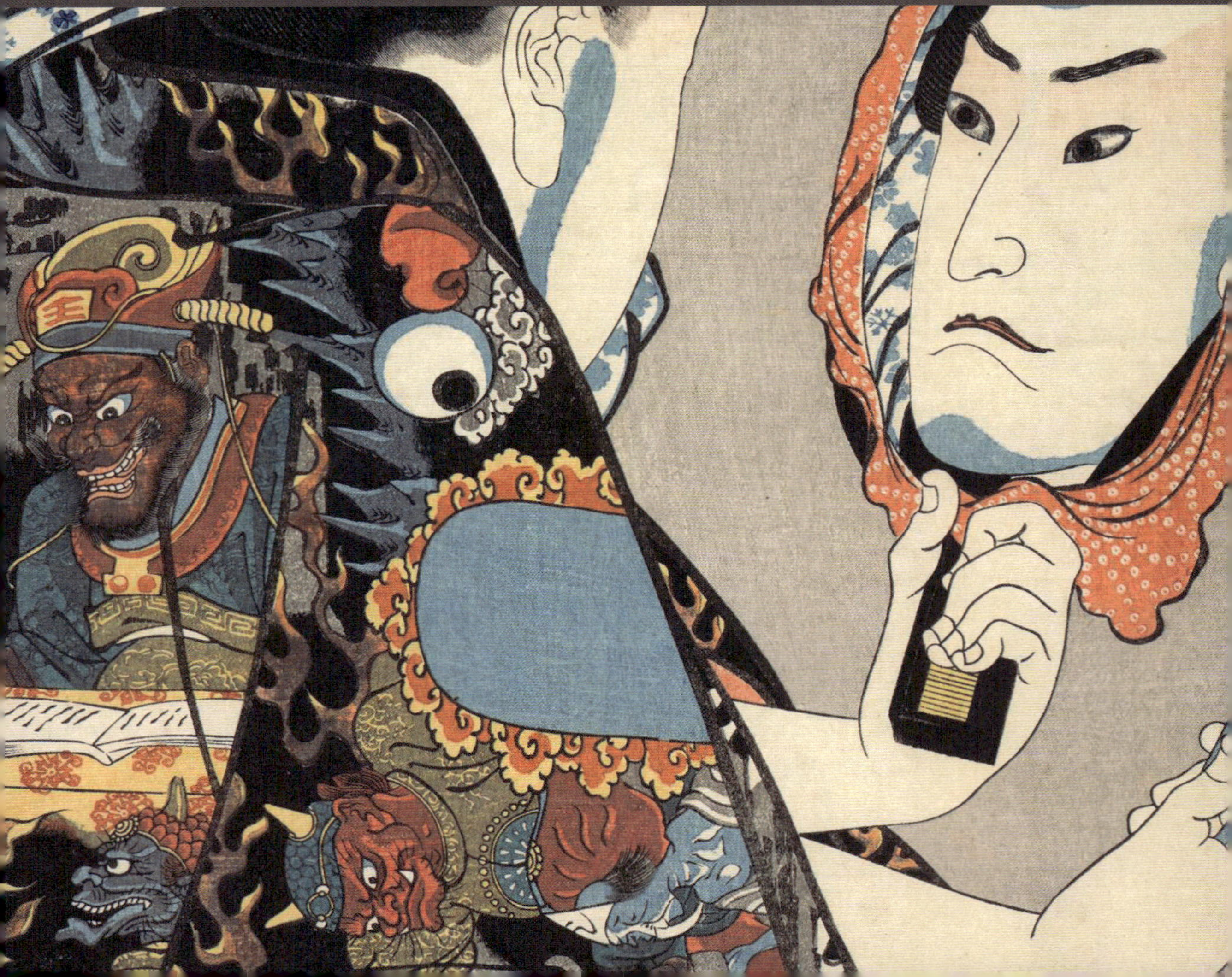

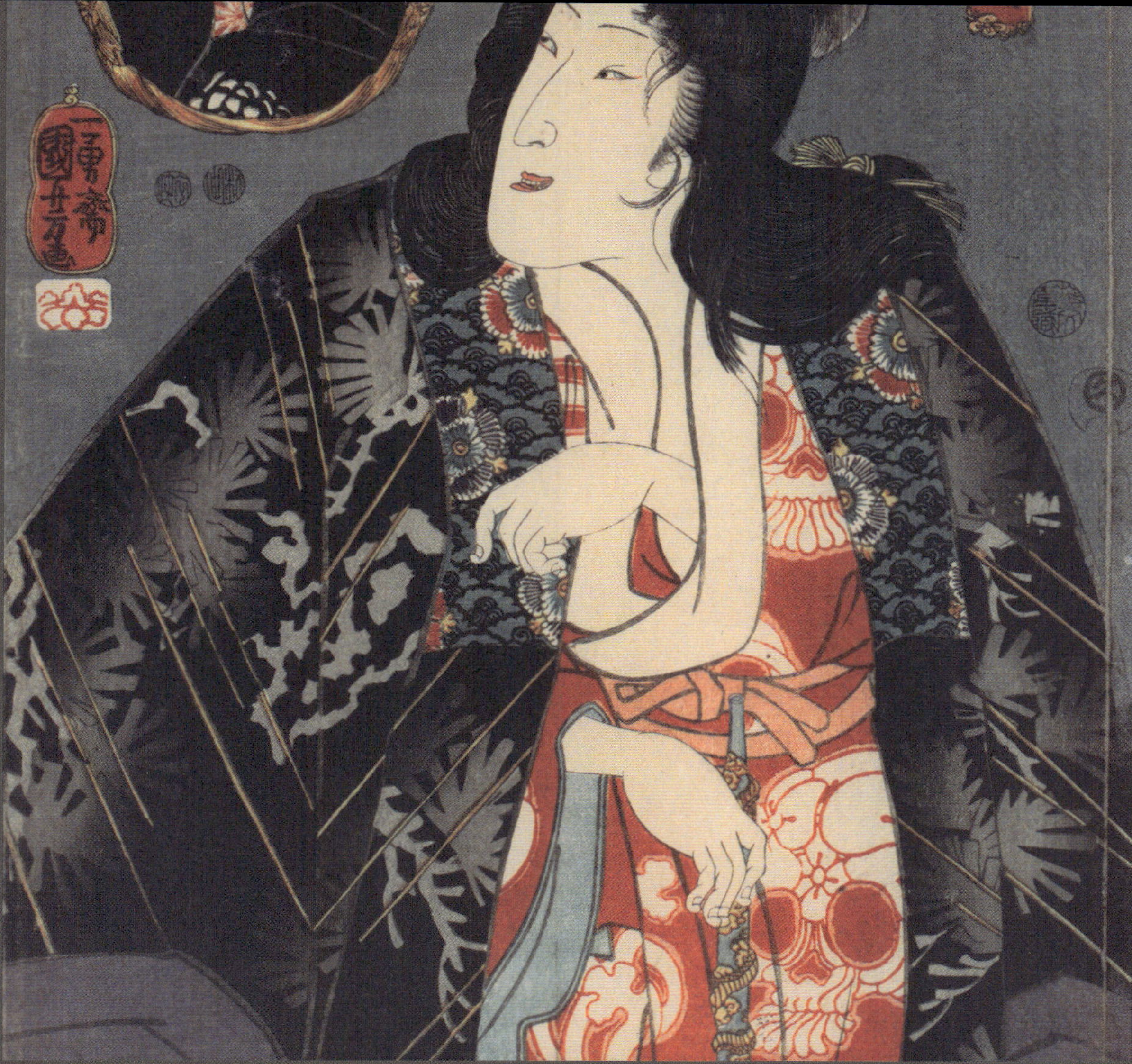

Kijin Omatsu and Natsume Shirōsaburō / Utagawa Kuniyoshi

1851 / Shizuoka Prefectural Central Library

Kijin Omatsu was a legendary female robber who repeatedly committed murders
and robberies in the mid-Edo period. Later, her stories were adapted into novels and
theatrical performances, leading to wide popularity. Omatsu, a young female robber,
repeatedly deceived travelers by using her beauty, and then robbed them of their
money and valuables. When the warrior Natsume Shirōsaburō was on a journey, he
was deceived by Omatsu and carried her on his back to cross over a river. Once over
the river, she stabbed him in the back to death. Later, Shirōsaburō's son, Sentarō,
killed Omtatsu to avenge his father. In this picture, the female robber wears a
skeleton-patterned kimono and shows a sinister smile towards the father and son.

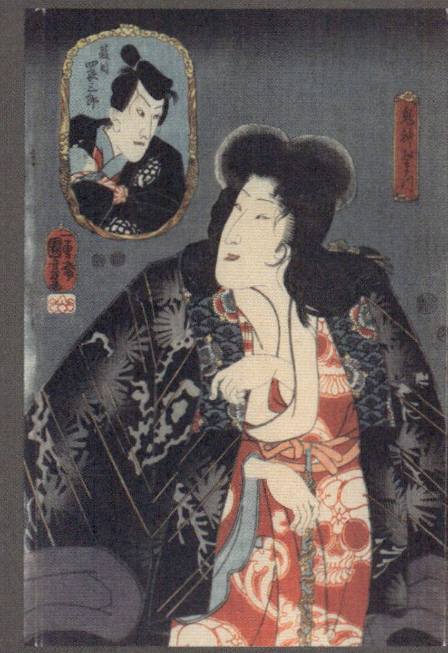

鬼神おまつ 夏目四郎三郎 ／ 歌川国芳

嘉永 4 年（1851）／ 静岡県立中央図書館

江戸後期、殺人や強盗を繰り返したという伝説の女盗賊・鬼神お松。後世、小説や
芝居などで盛んに取り上げられた。若き女盗賊お松は、美貌をもって旅人を欺き殺
しては金品を奪っていた。道中の武士夏目四郎三郎は、お松に騙されて彼女を背負
って川を渡るうち、背後から刺し殺される。四郎三郎の息子千太郎は、後にお松を
討って父の敵討を果たす。本図では、骸骨柄の着物をまとう残虐な女盗賊が、親子
に向かって不敵な笑みを浮かべている。

Minamoto-no Yoshihira, from the series Valor in China and Japan / Tsukioka Yoshitoshi

1866 / Photo : Morimiya

Legends tell that, in the Heian period, numerous skulls appeared in the mansion of Taira-no Kiyomori, who defeated the Genji clan, reaching his height of glory. The skulls merged into one giant skull. The unnatural phenomenon was said to be caused by the vengeful spirits of the Genji clan. There are other ukiyoe prints depicting not only Kiyomori's mansion, but also the Genji clan's spirits riding on a giant skull. The most popular vengeful spirit which attacked Kiyomori would be Minamoto-no Yoshihira (P.100-109). The picture only depicts the spirit of Yoshihira and the giant skull against a jet-black background, without any other motives relating to the story.

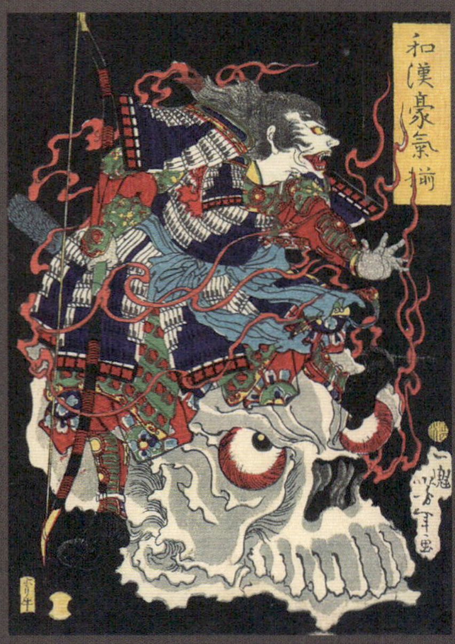

和漢豪気揃 源義平 ／ 月岡芳年

慶応 2 年（1866）／ 提供：古美術もりみや

平安時代、源氏に勝利し栄華を極めた平清盛の屋敷に無数の髑髏があらわれ、やがて巨大なひとつの髑髏になったという。この怪異は源氏の怨霊によるものとも伝えられ、清盛の屋敷とともに巨大な髑髏に乗る源氏武将の怨霊を描く錦絵も伝わる。清盛を襲う怨霊といえば、P.100-109 で見た源義平であろう。ストーリーを伝える情報を排し、漆黒を背景とした、義平と髑髏の肖像画。

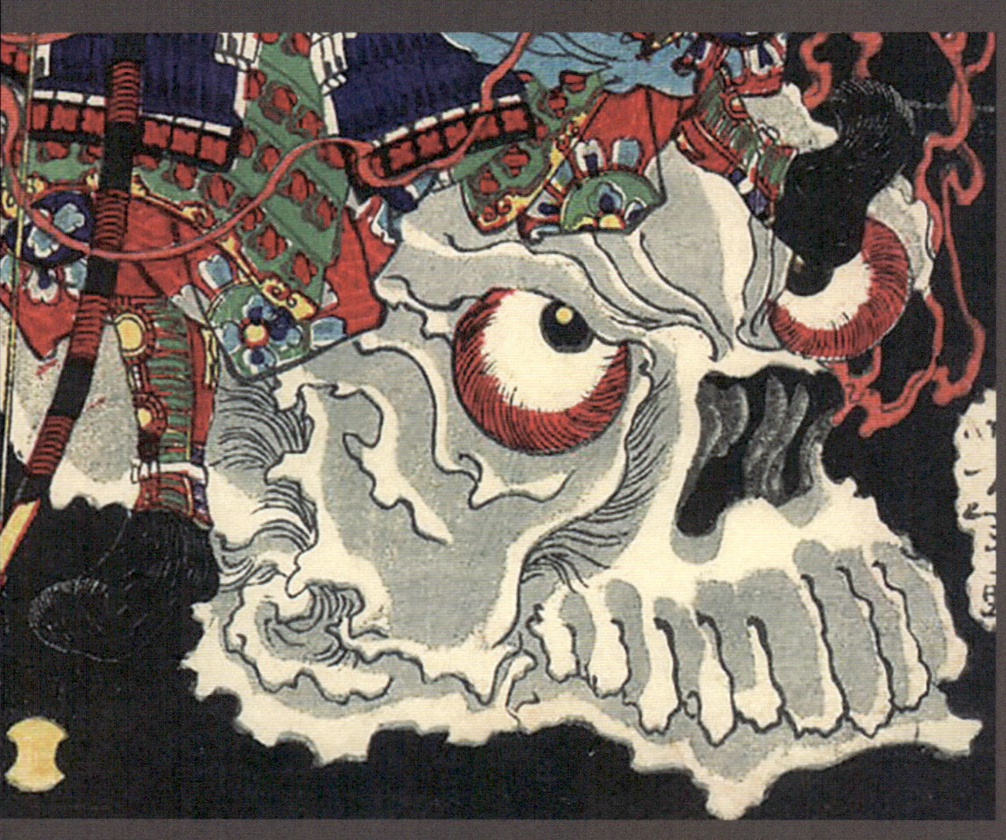

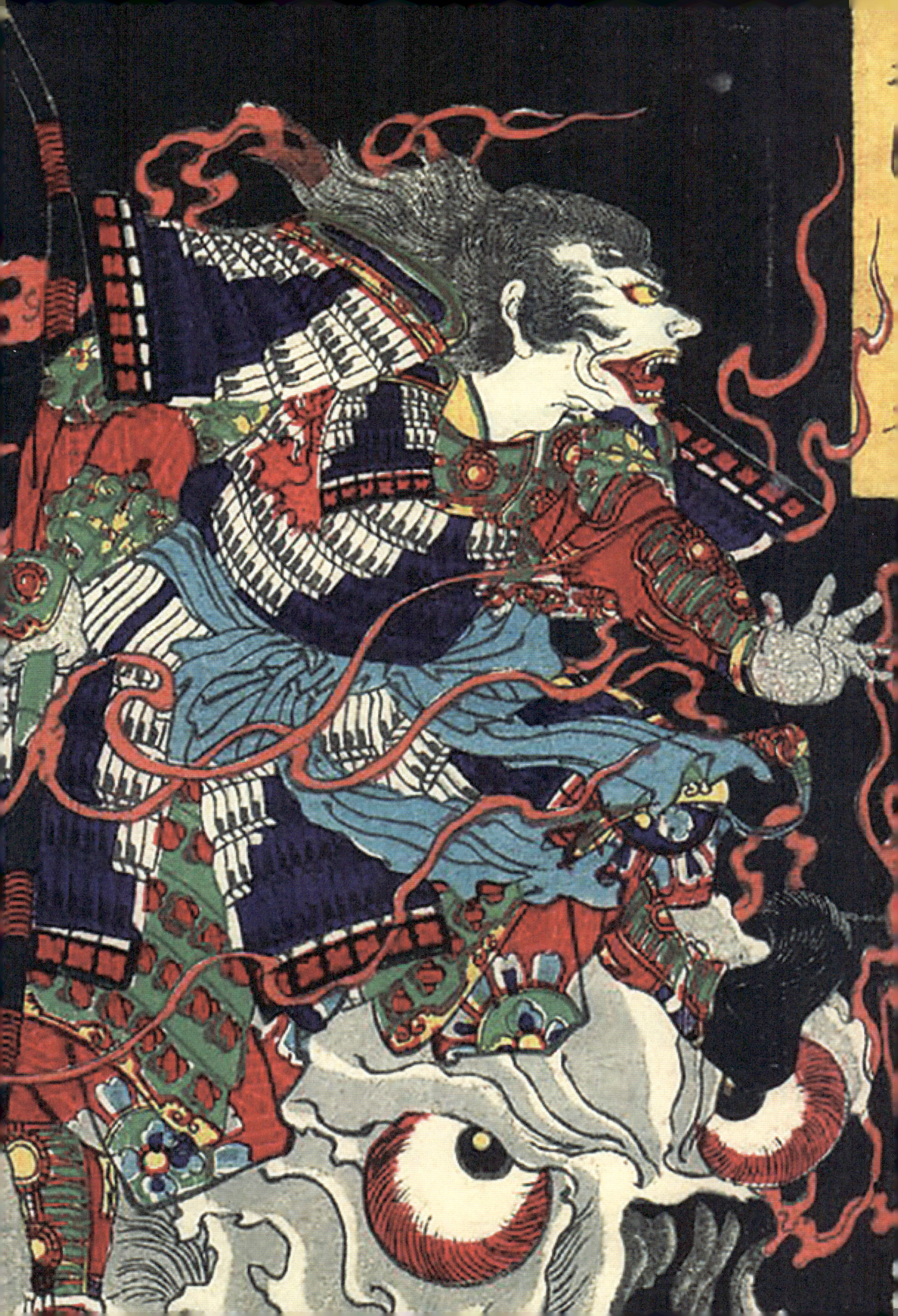

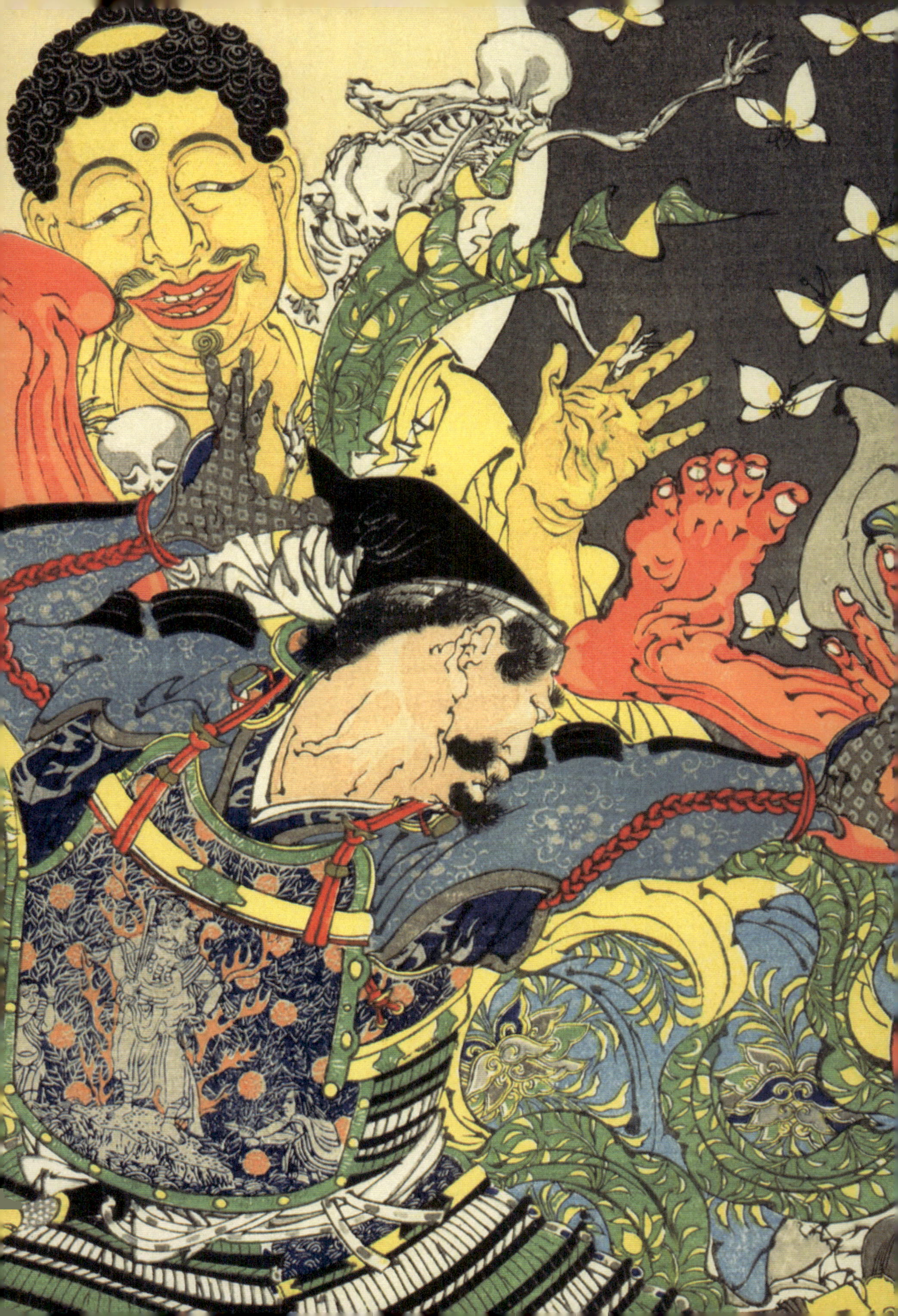

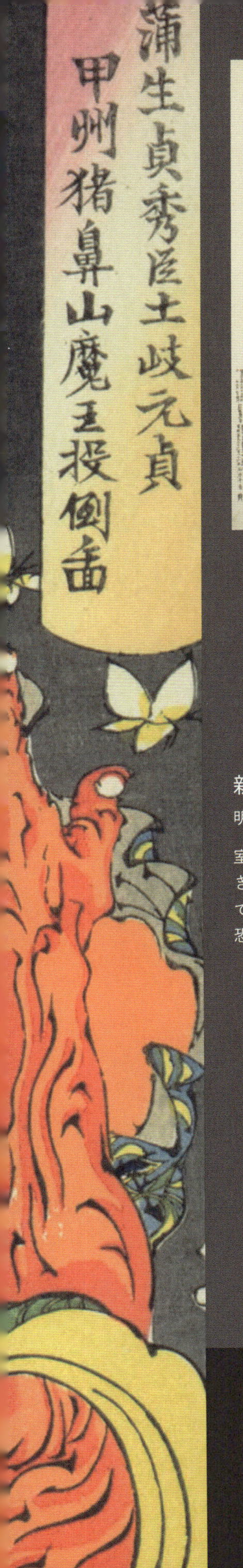

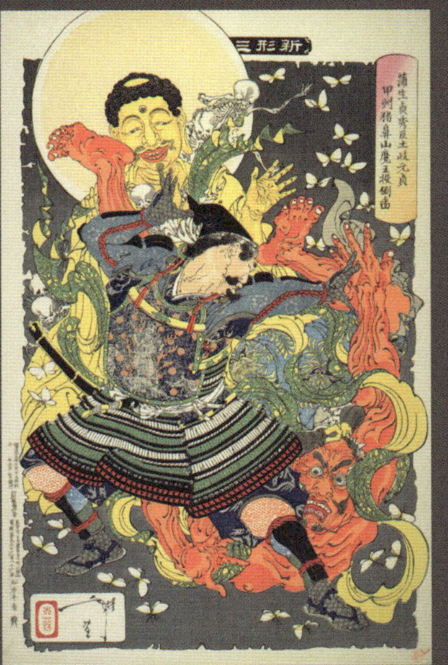

Gamō Sadahide and His Vassal Toki Motosada Wrestled a Monster to the Ground at Mount Inohana in Kōshū Province, from the series New Forms of Thirty-six Ghosts / Tsukioka Yoshitoshi

1890 / National Diet Library, Japan

Toki Daishirō Motosada was a brawny vassal of the warrior Gamō Sadahide in the Muromachi period. Legends tell that he visited the Maō Hall at Mount Inohana in Kōshū Province. There, monsters who disguised themselves as Buddhist deities of Amitabha and the Deva King offered a sumo wrestling match to Motosada. Motosada wrestled the Deva King to the ground, and crushed Amitabha with the haft of a long-handled sword. Then, a skeleton jumped out from Amitabha's belly and transformed into millions of butterflies, which then swarmed over Motosada. The flashy depiction of this picture represents a scary but fantastical spectacle.

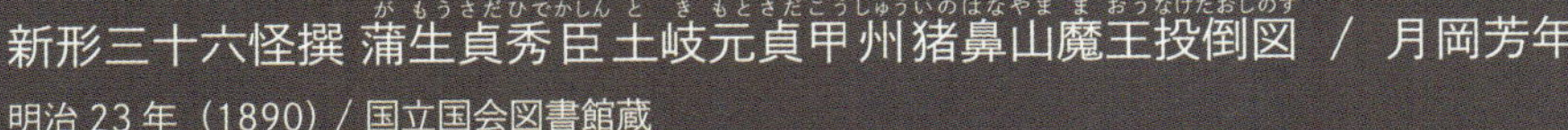

新形三十六怪撰 蒲生貞秀臣土岐元貞甲州猪鼻山魔王投倒図 ／ 月岡芳年

明治 23 年（1890）／ 国立国会図書館蔵

室町時代の武将・蒲生貞秀の家臣で力自慢の土岐大四郎元貞は、甲州猪鼻山の魔王堂を訪れたとき、阿弥陀如来と仁王に化けた妖怪に相撲を挑まれた。仁王を投げ倒し、阿弥陀如来を長刀の柄で打ち砕くと、腹から骸骨が飛び出し、さらにはそれが数百万の蝶となって元貞に群がったという。恐ろしくも幻想的な光景が華々しくあらわされた一枚。

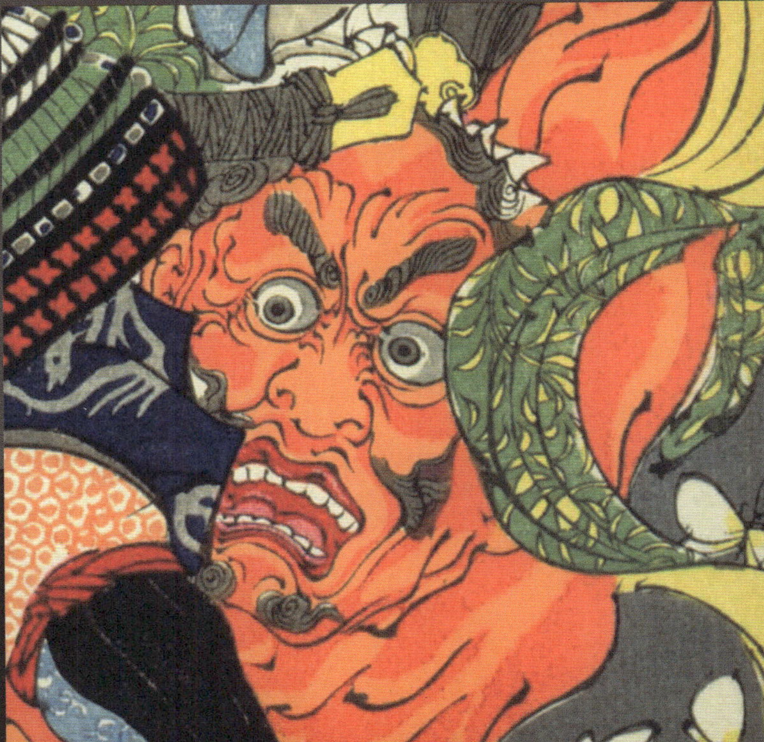

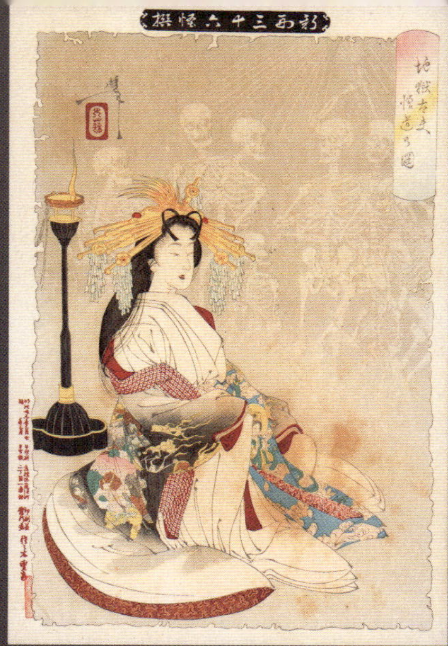

Courtesan Jigoku Attaining Enlightenment, from the series New Forms of Thirty-six Ghosts / Tsukioka Yoshitoshi

1890 / Tokyo Metropolitan Library

This picture depicts Courtesan Jigoku calmly gazing at a skeleton. She seems to have reached enlightenment. Legends tell that she was kidnapped by bandits and later became a courtesan in Sakai. She thought that her hard-luck might have been caused by bad acts in her previous life, or Buddhist incarnation. She wished to suffer tortures in this world, instead of suffering in hell after death, and named herself Jigoku, meaning Hell. She loved wearing hell-patterned kimonos. This character trait originates from the novel "The Complete Legend of Drunken Enlightenment in Japan" written by Santō Kyōden. Since the novel was first published, many painters depicted Jigoku's kimono with motives relating to hell, including images of the King of Hell.

新形三十六怪撰 地獄太夫悟道の図 ／ 月岡芳年

明治 23 年（1890）／ 東京都立中央図書館蔵

静かに骸骨を見つめ、悟りを得た様子の地獄太夫。室町時代に存在したと伝えられる地獄太夫は、幼いころ山賊にさらわれ、堺の遊女となったという。不幸な身の上を前世の報いだと考え、将来堕ちゆく地獄を先取りし、その呵責を受けようと、自ら地獄と名乗った。彼女が地獄変相図の衣を愛用するという設定は、山東京伝が『本朝酔菩提全伝』で考案したものだ。地獄太夫の衣装には決まって、閻魔大王をはじめとする地獄のモチーフが描かるようになった。

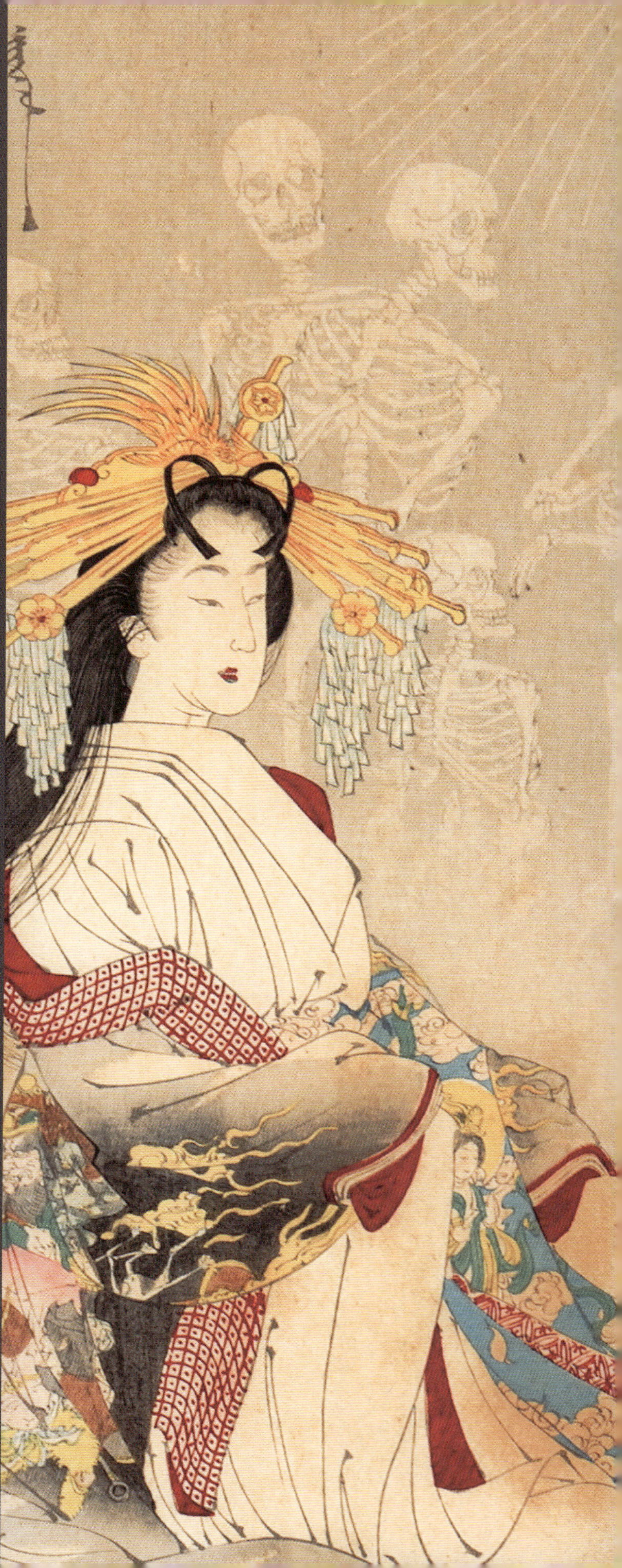

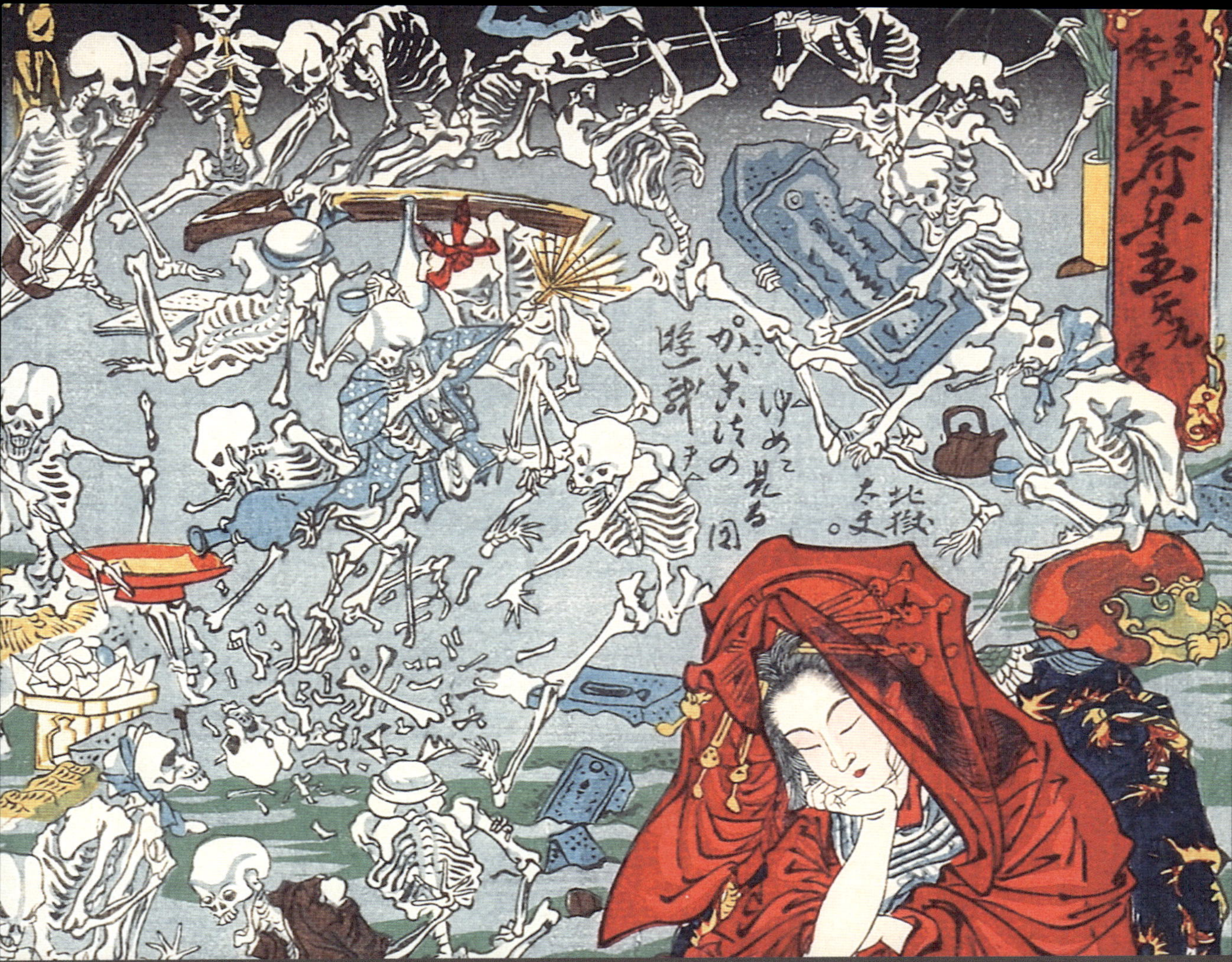

Courtesan Jigoku Saw Skeletons Making Merry
in Her Dream from "Ōju Kyōsai Rakuga No.9" /
Kawanabe Kyōsai

1874 / National Diet Library, Japan

Kawanabe Kyōsai created many pictures featuring Courtesan Jigoku.
Usually he depicted Jigoku, Priest Ikkyū, and skulls altogether in one
picture. But here, he did not depict Ikkyū, and instead, created an unusual
story setting with Jigoku seeing skulls in her dream. Probably because it is
a dream scene, these skeletons are depicted as more playful, compared
to Kyōsai's other pictures. They smash gravestones and enjoy their party
with music, games of Go and performances. The picture shows a sharp
contrast between the white skeleton and the red kimono of Jigoku.

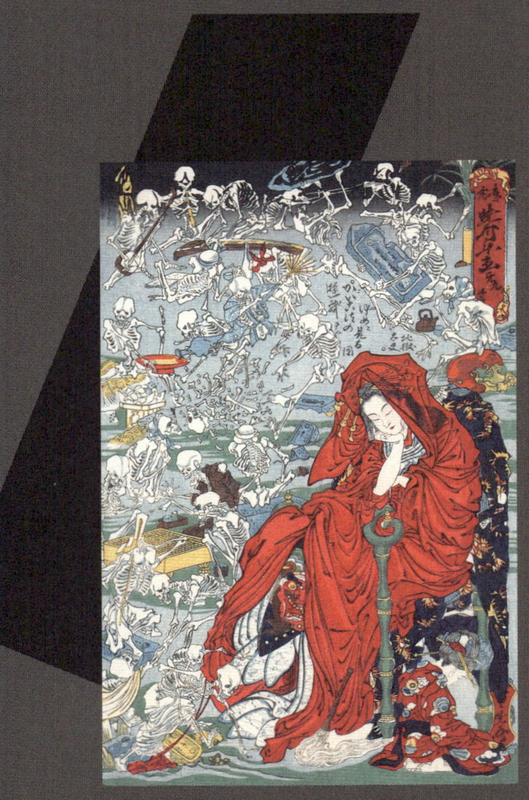

応需暁斎楽画 第九号 地獄太夫かいこつの遊戯をゆめ に見る図 / 河鍋暁斎

明治 7 年（1874）/ 国立国会図書館蔵

河鍋暁斎は、地獄太夫を描いた作品をいくつものこしている。地獄太夫
と一休、骸骨の組み合わせが定番である。本図は一休を描かずに、地獄
太夫が骸骨を夢見るという独自の設定となっている。夢であるためか、
骸骨たちは他図よりも一層ふざけた様子で、墓石を破壊しながら、音曲
や囲碁、宴会芸に興じている。白骨と地獄太夫が羽織る赤い衣とのコン
トラストが際立つ一枚。

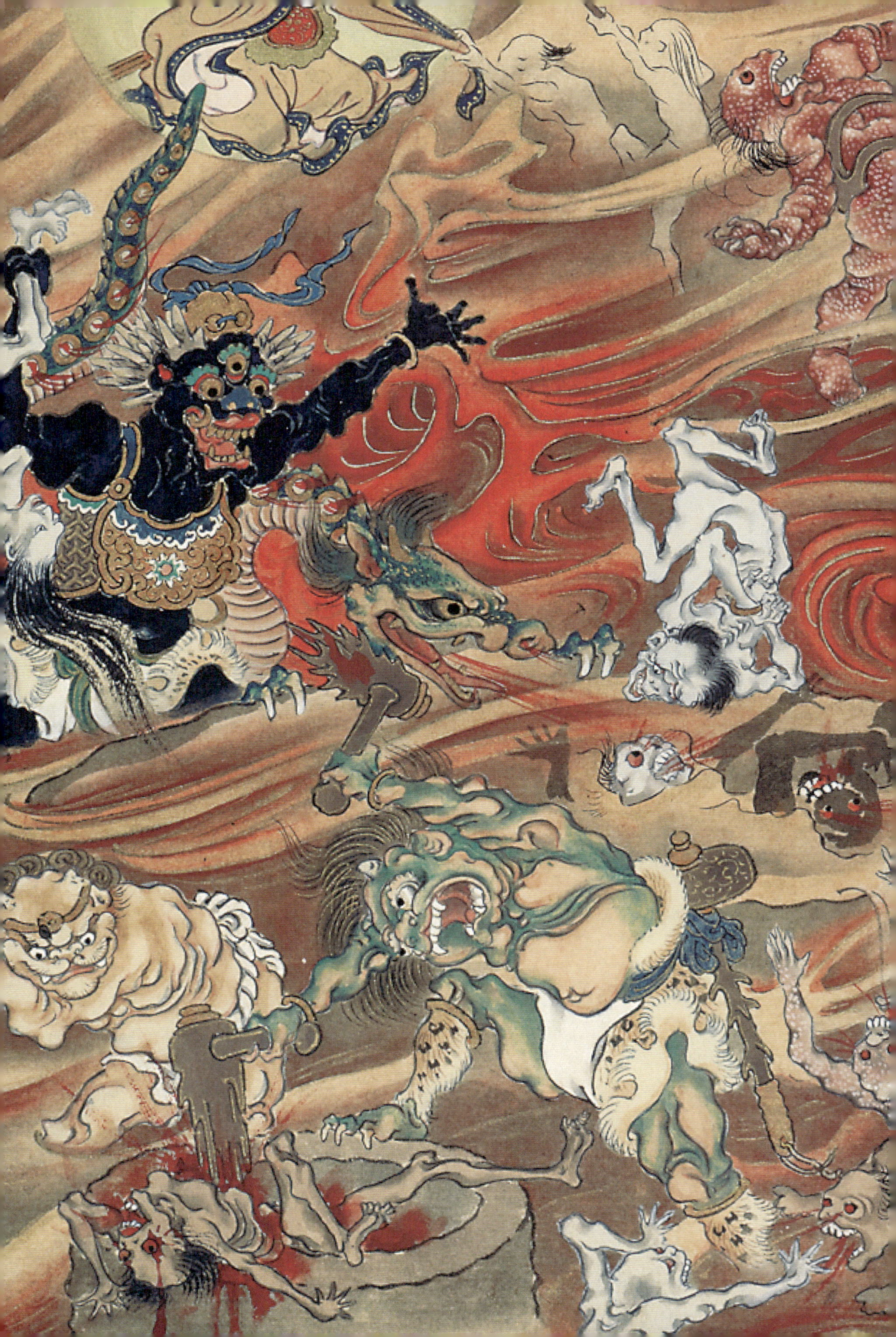

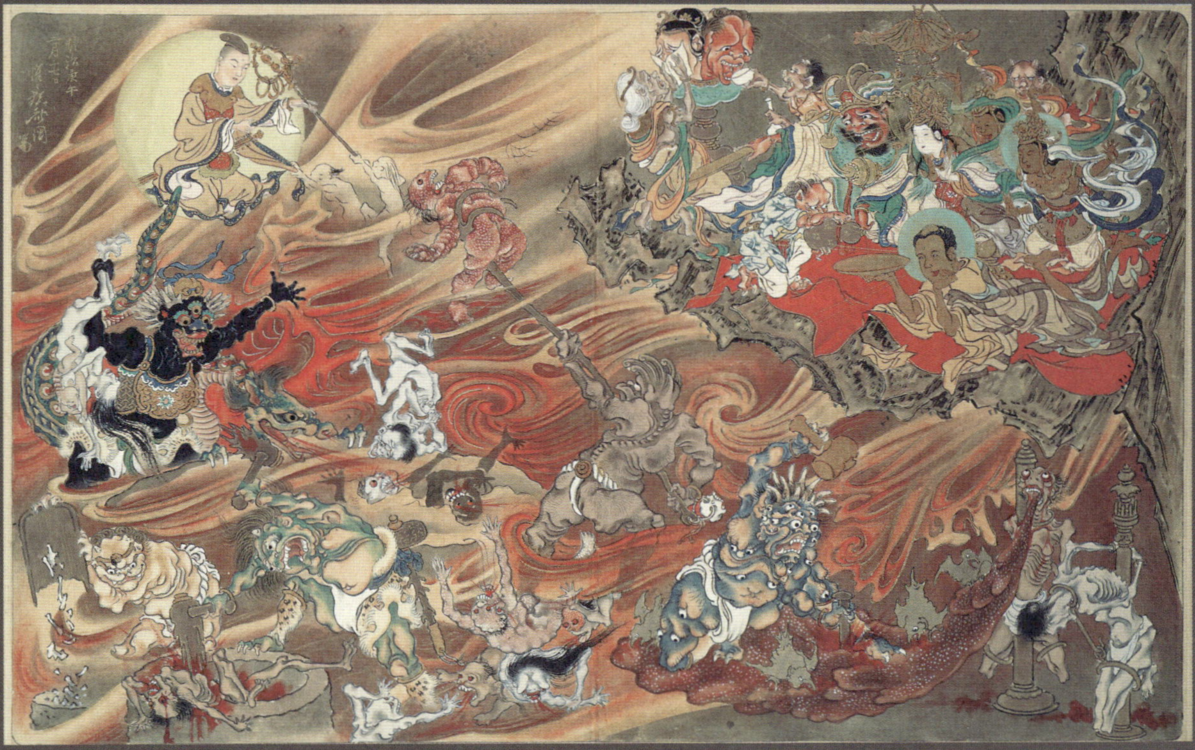

Pilgrimage to Hell and Heaven / Kawanabe Kyōsai

1869-1872 / Seikado Bunko Art Museum

Kyōsai painted this picture to offer a prayer for the departed soul of Tatsu, who was Katsuta Gohei's daughter and died at the age of 14. Gohei was a patron of Kyōsai. It is from a series of paintings which depict Tatsu's journey from this world to Buddhist heaven. This scene depicts Tatsu taking a look around hell, under the King of Hell's guidance. People are tortured by ogres in blazing fires. Tatsu and her party are watching them screaming and crying from a high and safe area. They spread a red blanket and Amitabha Buddha is starting to enjoy a glass of sake. This series consists of 40 paintings, including scenes of both hell and heaven, all of which are depicted vibrantly, vividly and humorously.

地獄極楽めぐり図 ／ 河鍋暁斎

明治 2-5 年（1869-72）／ 静嘉堂文庫美術館

暁斎の後援者・勝田五兵衛の娘、14 歳で夭折した田鶴の追善供養のために、田鶴の極楽への道中を描いたシリーズのうちの一枚。閻魔大王の案内で地獄を見物する場面だ。火炎が燃え盛り、獄卒から責め苦を受ける人々。田鶴一行はそんな阿鼻叫喚を高見の見物。レジャーシートのように赤い毛氈を広げ、阿弥陀は一杯やろうというところ。全 40 図からなる本作では、地獄も極楽も、賑やかに華々しくユーモアたっぷりに描かれている。

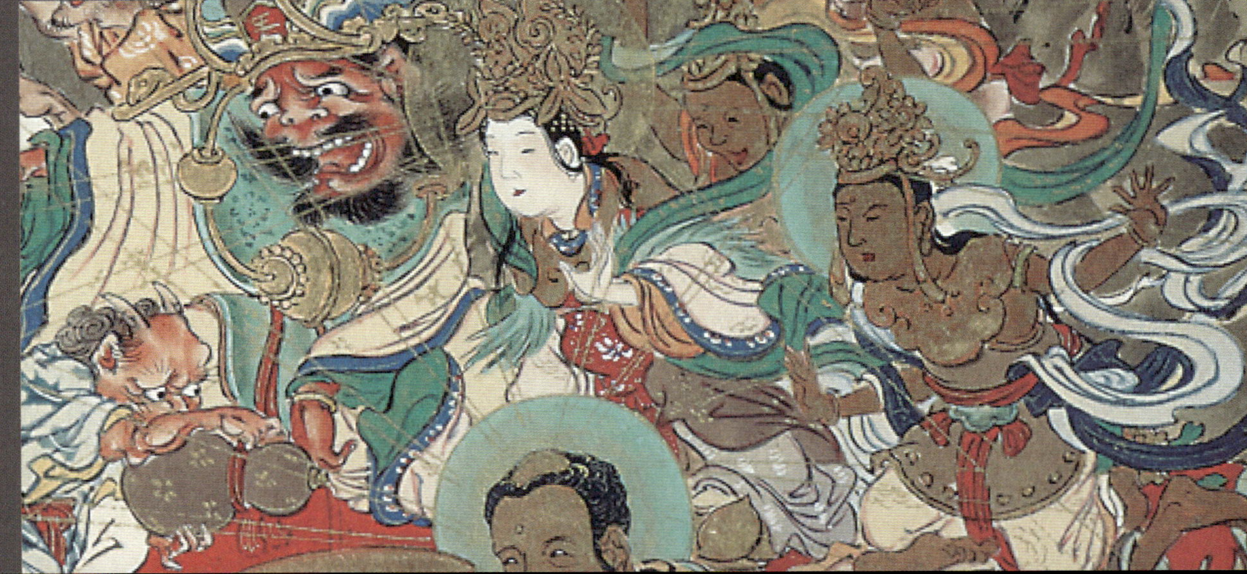

無惨の

Sparkle of
Savage Killings

煌めき

七章
Chapter 7.

From the end of the Edo period to the Meiji period, many painters depicted cruel bloody deaths. The representative painter was Tsukioka Yoshitoshi, who was famous for his Zankoku-e (Cruel Pictures) and earned the nickname Chimidoro Yoshitoshi, or Bloody Yoshitoshi. Many novels and theater plays featured such depictions during their climactic scenes, which gained popularity. Scenes of people facing their deaths stimulate viewers' emotions even today. The tremendous energies they spend resisting death and clinging to life arouse us. Such dreadful last moments also impress us with the sparkling sunset of people's lives.

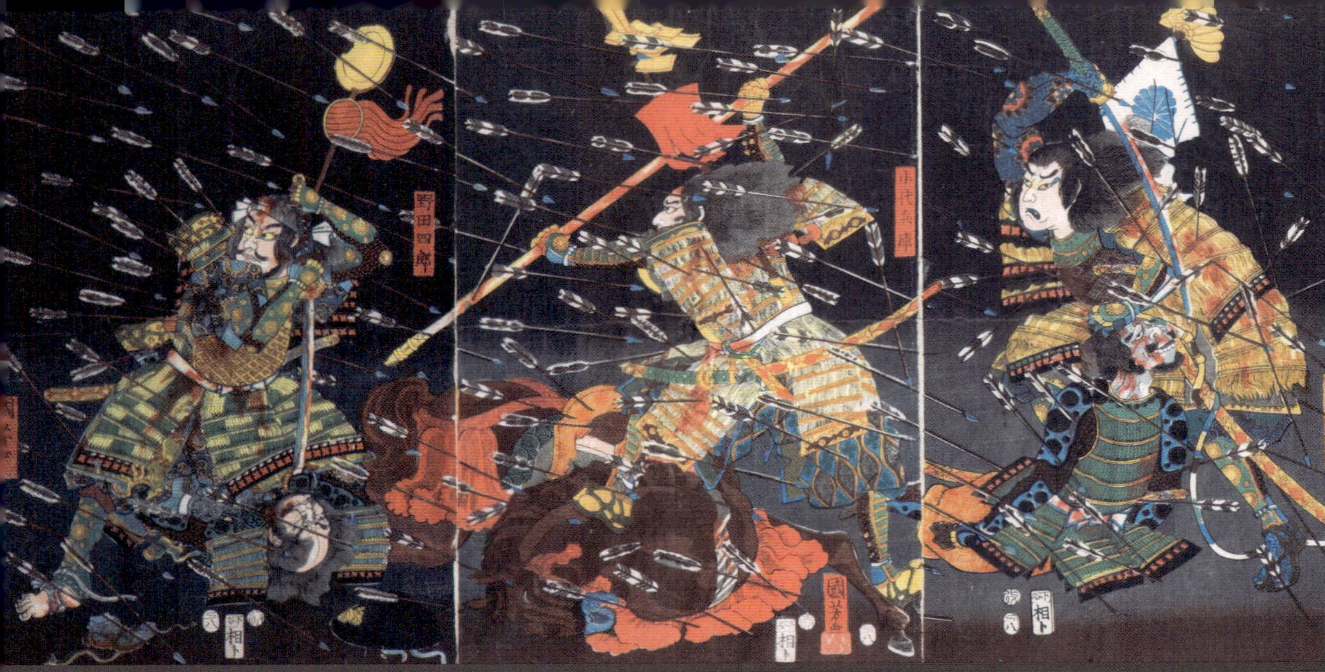

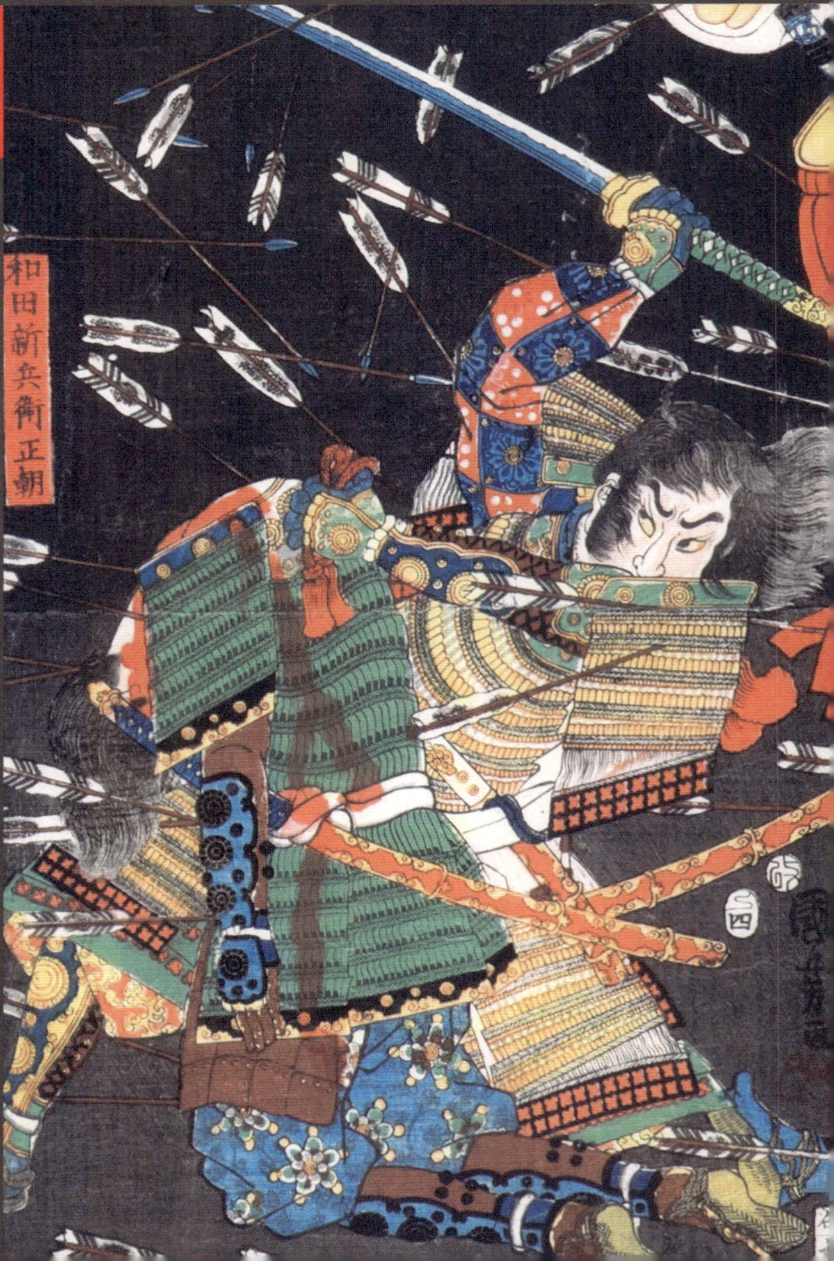

The Battle of Shijō-nawate / Utagawa Kuniyoshi

1857 / Tokyo Fuji Art Museum

The picture depicts a scene from the Battle of Shijō-nawate in the Nanbokuchō period. We see Kusunoki Masatsura, a son of Masashige, is dying in the middle of the fierce fight. Legends tell that Masatsura dived into the enemy and was shot by numerous arrows. He was only one step away from catching Kōno Moronao, an enemy commander, but failed. He eventually killed himself with his sword.

四条畷手の戦い / 歌川国芳

安政4年（1857）／ 東京富士美術館蔵

南北朝内乱期、楠木正成の息子・正行が壮絶な死を遂げたことで知られる、四條畷の戦い。『太平記』によれば南朝軍を率いた正行は、決死の覚悟で敵陣に突っ込み、無数の弓矢を射かけられるなか、敵の大将高師直まであと一歩とせまるが取り逃がし、最後は自刃して果てたという。

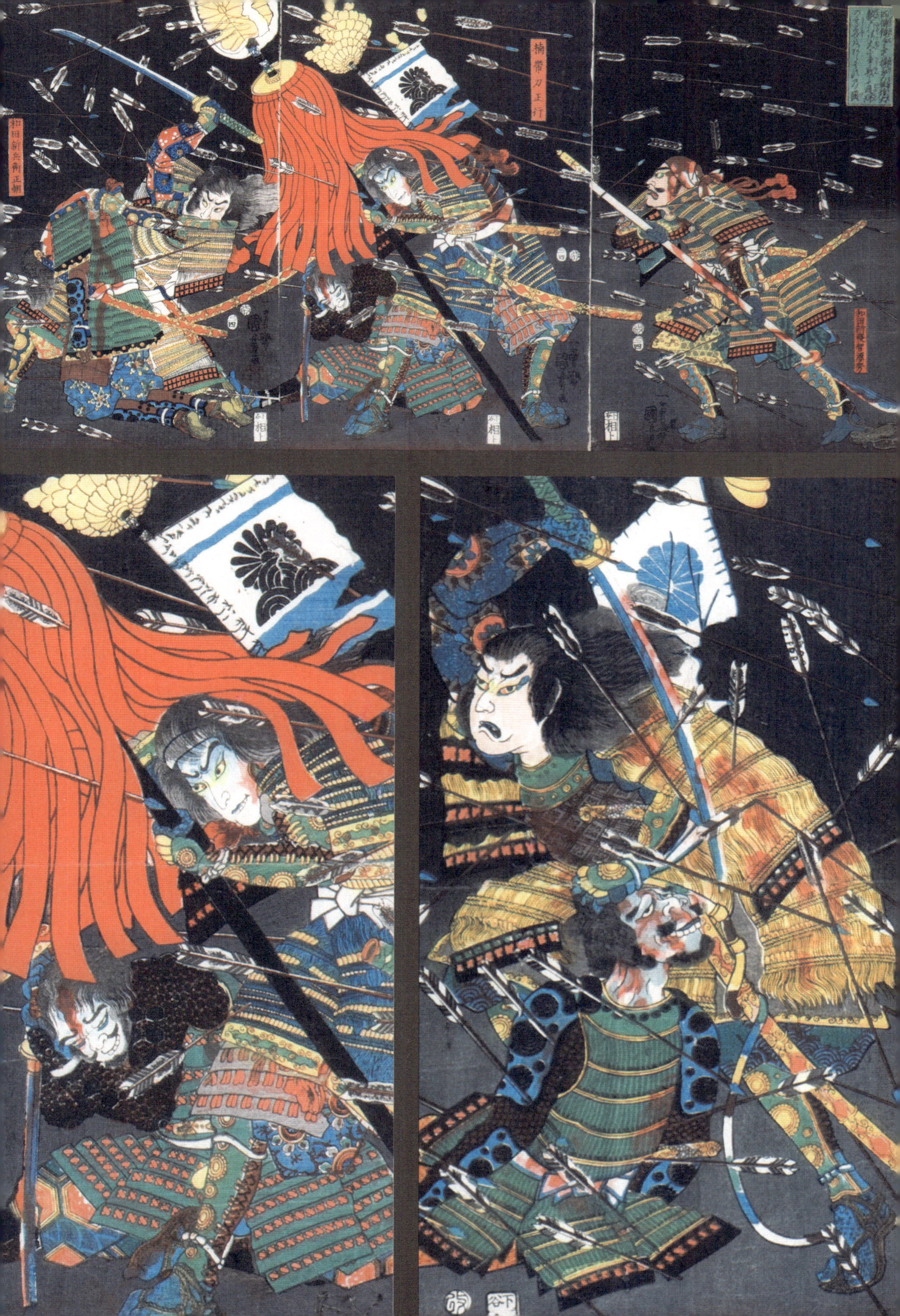
楠常刀正行
相田新兵衛正鋼

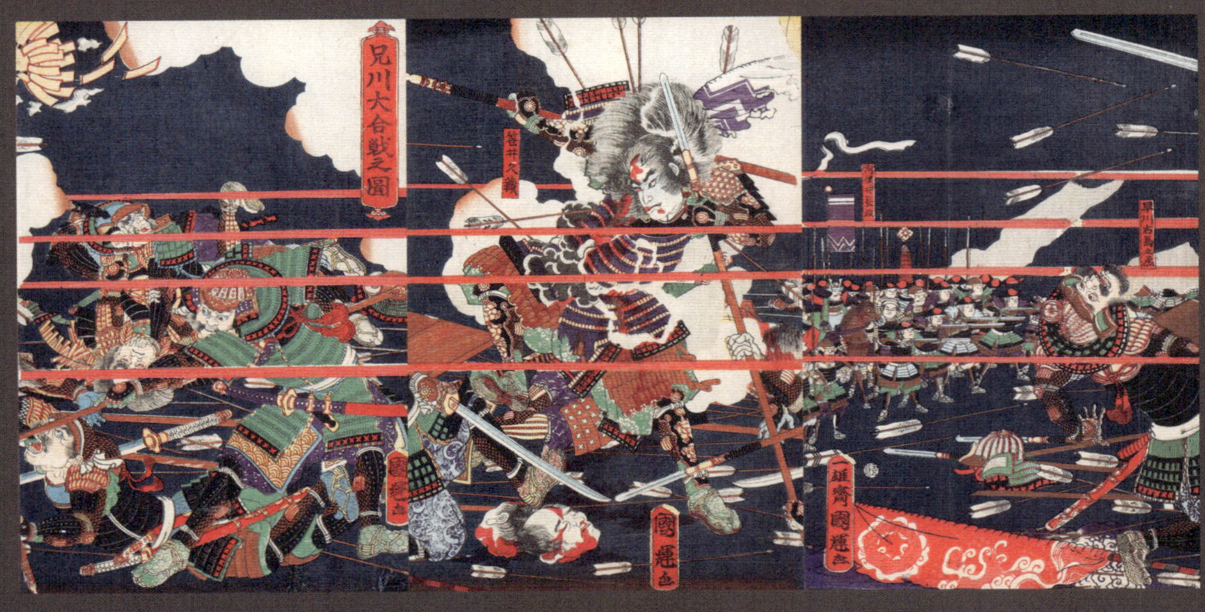

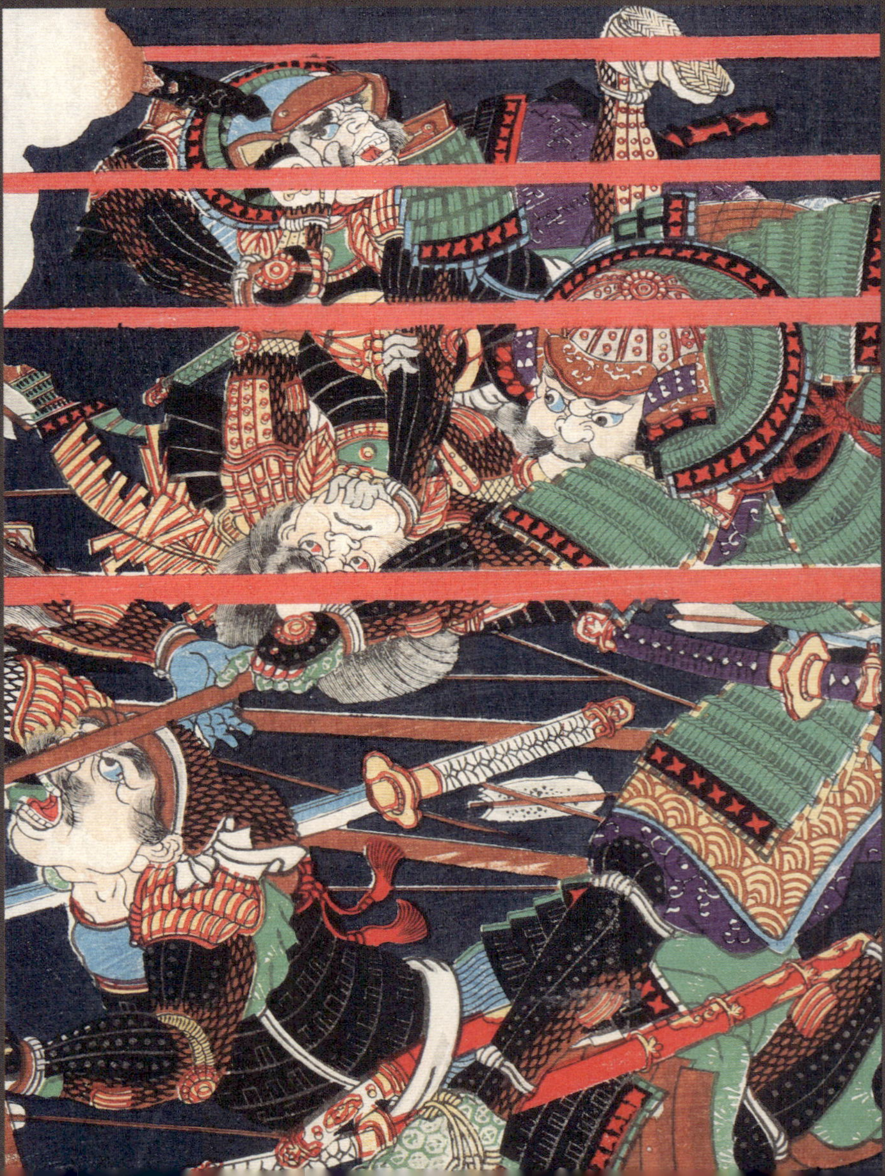

兄川大合戦之図 /
歌川国輝

慶応元年（1865）/
刀剣ワールド財団
（東建コーポレーション）蔵

織田信長軍が浅井・朝倉連合
軍に大勝した「姉川の戦い」
の一場面。開戦当初苦戦を強
いられた信長軍で先陣を切っ
た信長の小姓・坂井久蔵は、
16歳の若さで討ち死にする。
弓を受け血を流す久蔵の目
の前には生首が転がっている。
画面を水平に走る赤い線は火
縄銃の弾道を描くものだろう。
背後には鉄砲隊が並ぶ。坂井
久蔵は「笹井」、姉川合戦は「兄
川」と誤魔化して出版された。

The Great Battle of the Anigawa / Utagawa Kuniteru

1865 / Touken World Foundation

The picture depicts a scene from the Battle of the Ani River, where Oda Nobunaga's army gained a crushing victory over the Asai and Asakura allied forces. At the beginning of the battle, Nobunaga's army actually went through a tough fight. Sakai Kyūzō, a young page of Nobunaga, led the vanguard, but died at the age of 16. The picture depicts Kyūzō being shot by arrows and bleeding. In front of him, there is someone's decapitated head on the ground. The red horizontal lines might represent bullets' trajectories of matchlock guns. Troops bearing guns are standing in the background. The names of the warriors and the ukiyoe print's title are written within the frame. In its production process, to represent it as not being rebellious and to get its publication approval from Edo Bakufu, their names were slightly changed, such as Sakai to Sasai, and Anegawa to Anigawa.

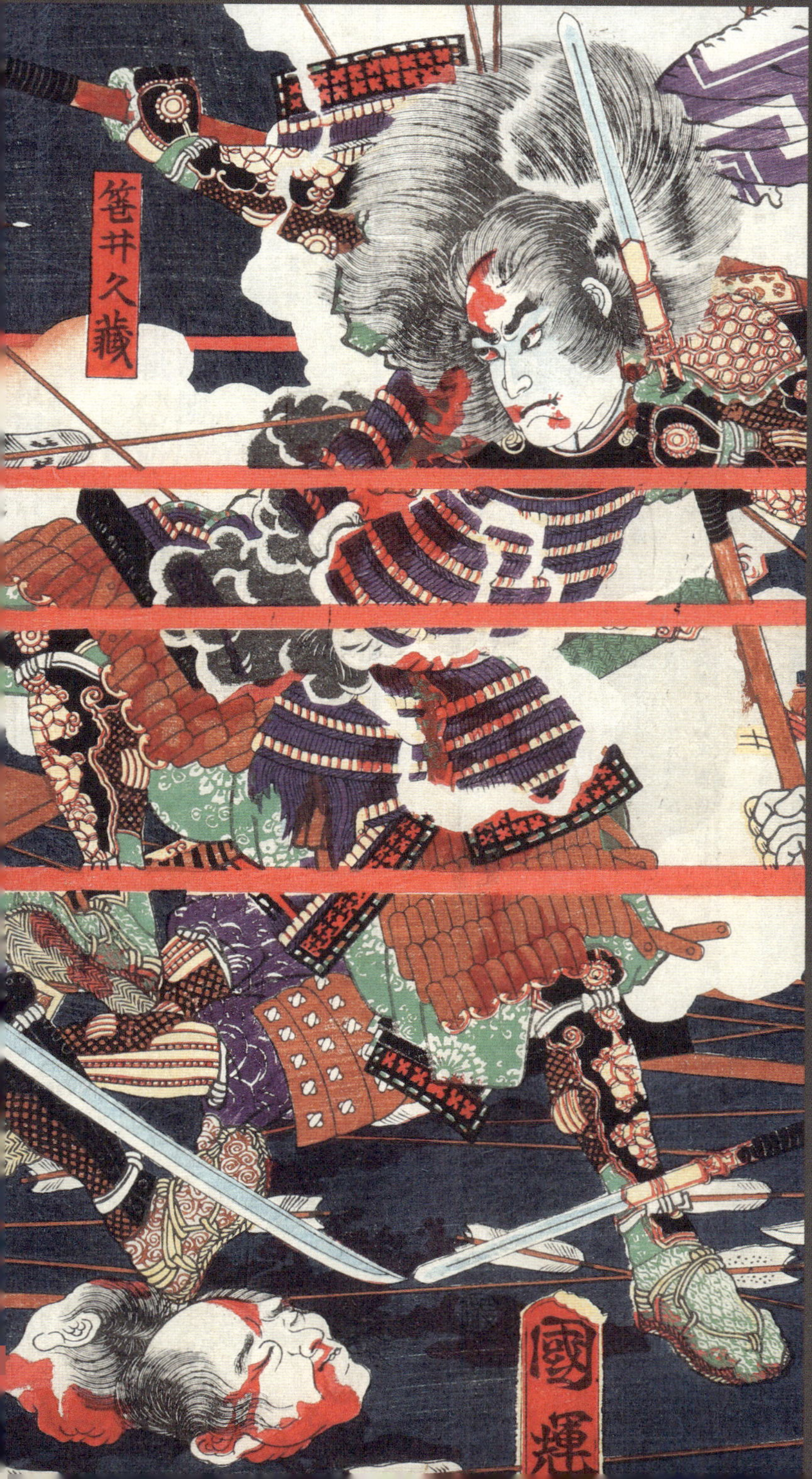

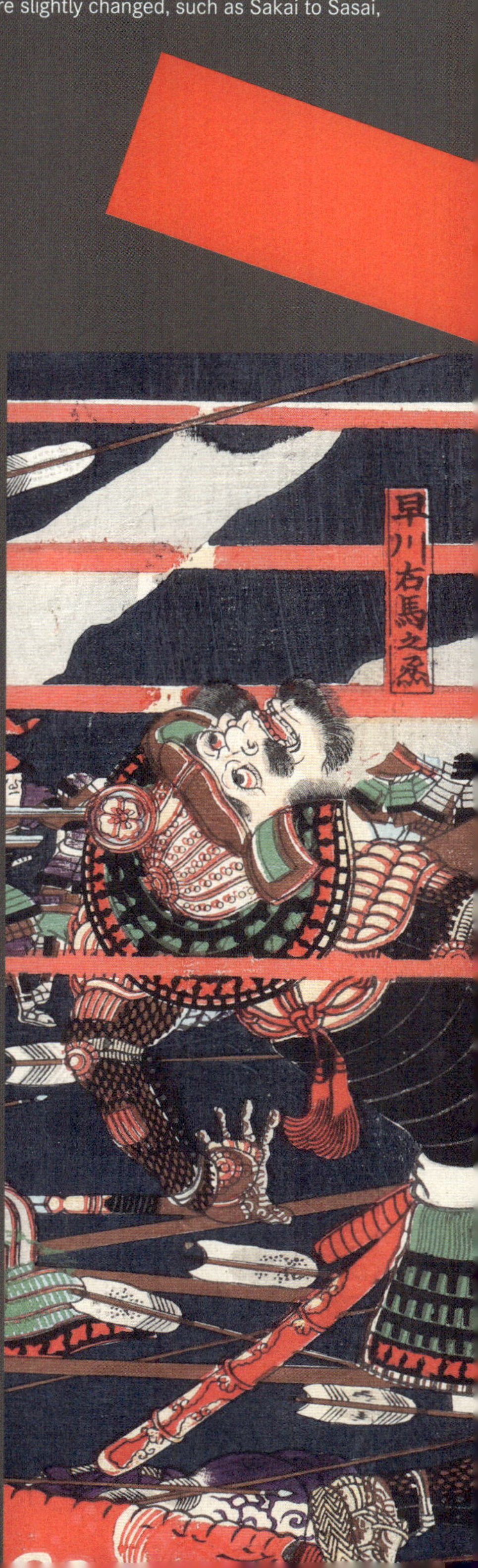

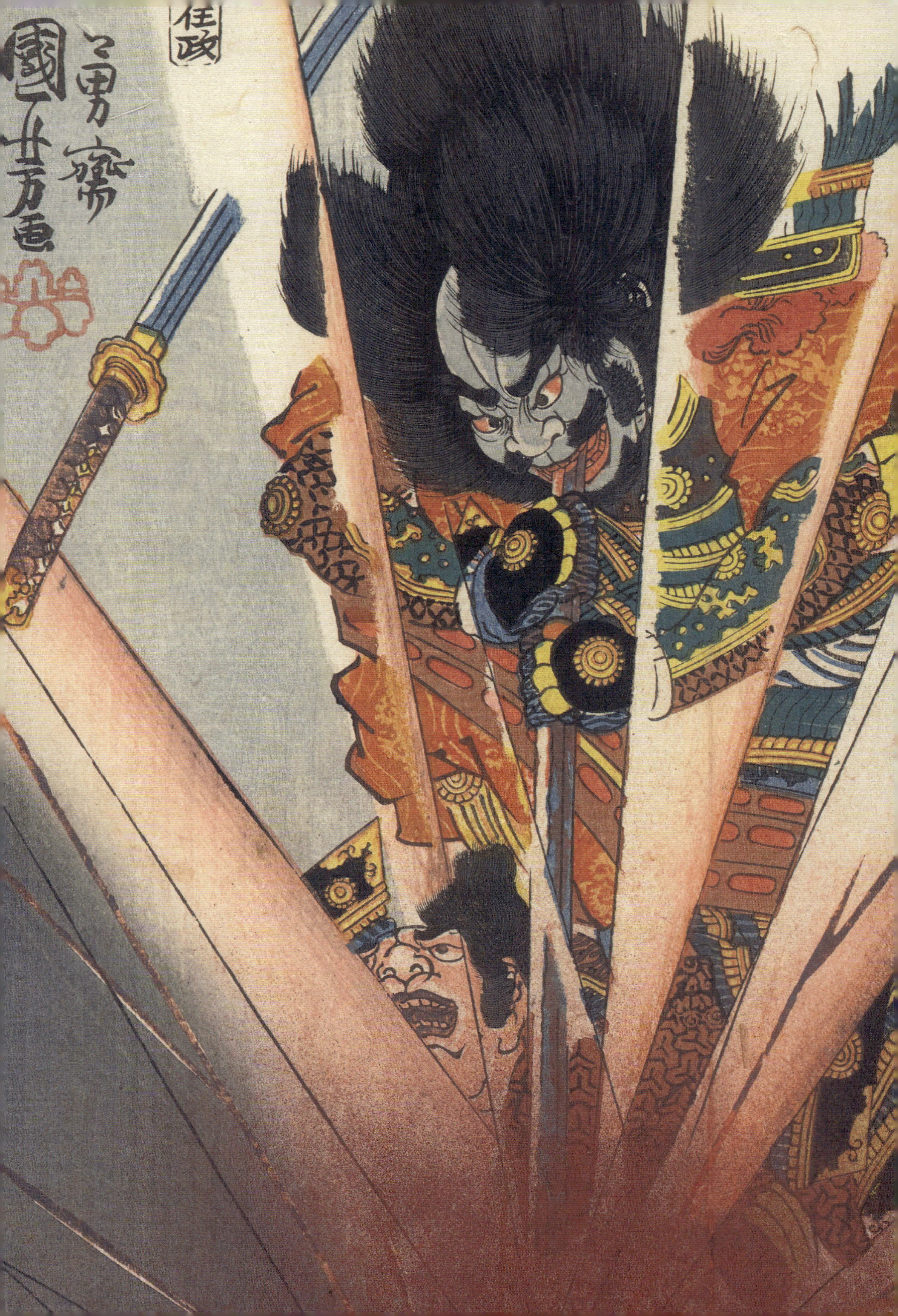
任政
一勇齋
國芳画

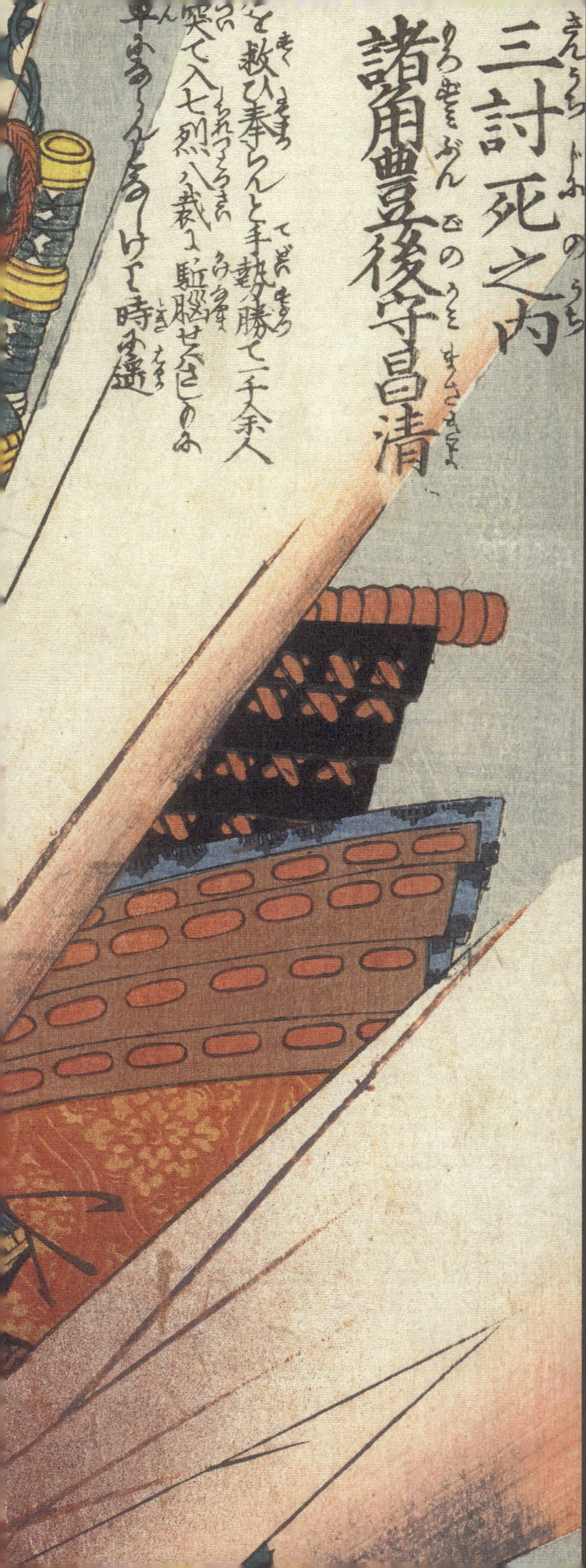

Death of Masakiyo, the Governor of Bungo Province, and One of the Twenty-four Great Warriors of Takeda Clan, from the series Legends of Bravery in Kōetsu Province / Utagawa Kuniyoshi

1847 / Tokyo Metropolitan Library

"Kōyō Gunkan" is a record of the military exploits and mental attitudes of the feudal warlord Takeda Shingen and his vassals. It is said to be the oldest existing book which has the word "Bushidō," or the spirit of samurai, and was widely read among warriors in the Edo period. Legends of Shingen and his vassals were adapted into Kōdan storytellings and military chronicles, leading to their popularity. The picture depicts the death of Morozumi Masakiyo, also known as Toramitsu, at the Battle of Kawanakajima. Legends tell that Masakiyo was burned by a landmine which was set off by his enemy, later he held a sword in his mouth and jumped into a fire to his death.

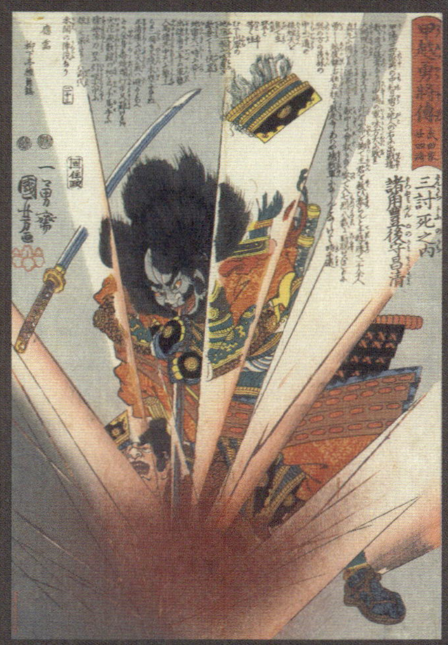

甲越勇将伝 武田家廿四将
三討死之内 諸角豊後守昌清 ／ 歌川国芳

弘化4年（1847） ／ 東京都立中央図書館蔵

「武士道」の初出とされる『甲陽軍鑑』は、戦国大名・武田信玄とその家臣たちの事跡や心構えを説いた書物で、江戸時代の武士の間で広く読まれ、信玄と家臣たちは講談や軍記などで人気を集めた。本図は、川中島の合戦での諸角昌清（室住虎光）の討ち死にを描く。敵の仕掛けた地雷で焼けただれた昌清は、陣刀を口に咥えて火の中に飛び込んで果てたという。

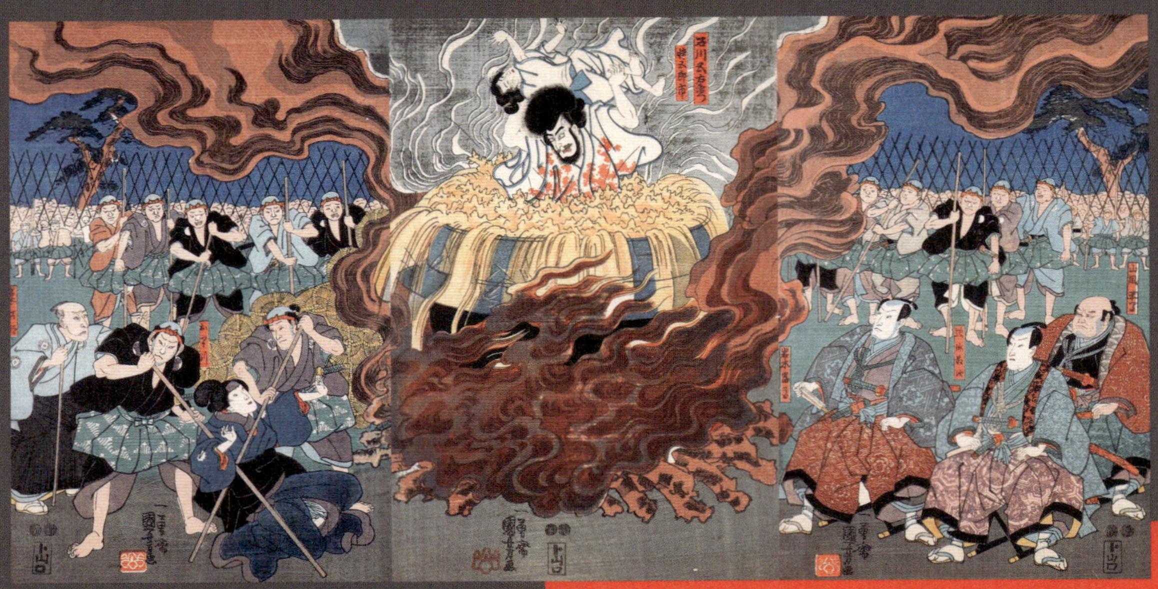

Ishikawa Goemon / Utagawa Kuniyoshi

1851 / Maizuru City

Ishikawa Goemon, a legendary thief in the Azuchi-Momoyama period, was sentenced to be roasted in a cauldron at Sanjō-gawara Riverside, Kyoto. The episode of his cruel death was adapted into many theatrical plays and novels, leading to his popularity as a tragic hero. The picture depicts a scene from the kabuki play "Kamagafuchi Futatsudomoe," played at the Edo Nakamuraza Theater in January 1851. Goemon is standing in a cauldron filled with boiling oil, and lifting his son Goroichi over his head to protect him. The blazing fire, the burning boiling oil, and the billowing smoke represent his immeasurable suffering from the heat.

石川五右衛門 ／ 歌川国芳

嘉永 4 年（1851） ／ 舞鶴市糸井文庫蔵

安土桃山時代の伝説的な盗賊・石川五右衛門は、京都三条河原で釜煎りの刑に処せられた。残酷な最期は、芝居や小説で盛んに描かれ、五右衛門を悲劇のヒーローとした。本図は嘉永 4 年（1851）正月に江戸中村座で上演された「釜淵双級巴」を描いたもの。五右衛門は煮えたぎる油の中で息子の五郎市を守ろうと頭上に持ち上げている。釜を燃やす炎と煮え立つ油、沸き起こる煙が、灼熱の苦しみを演出する。

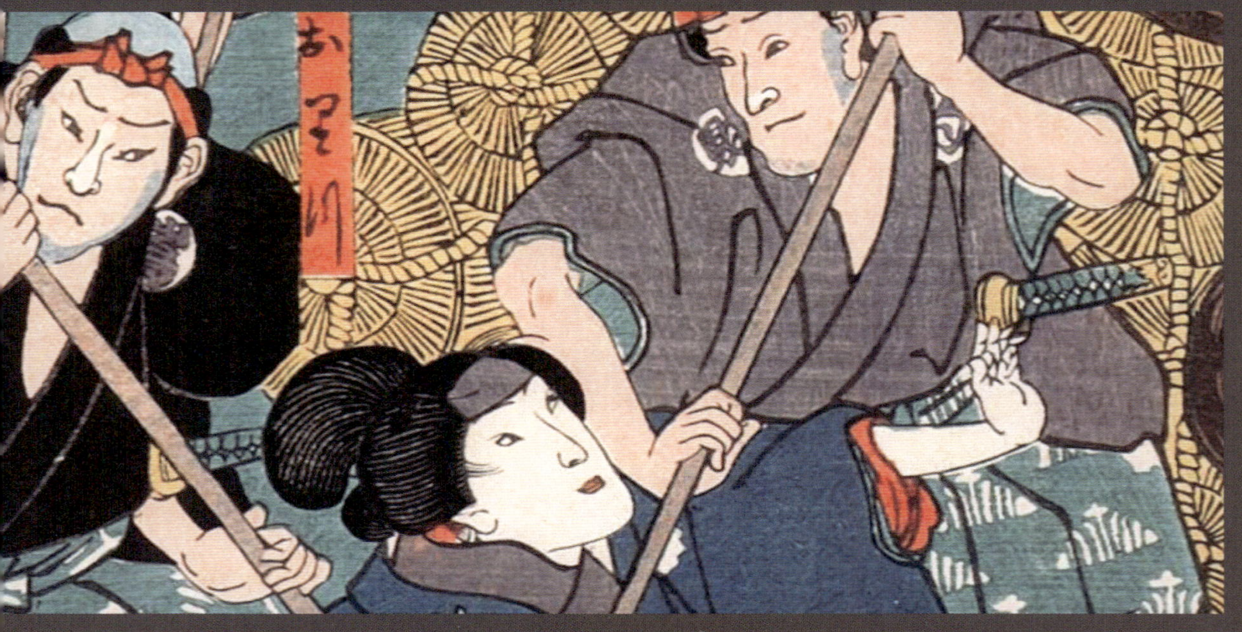

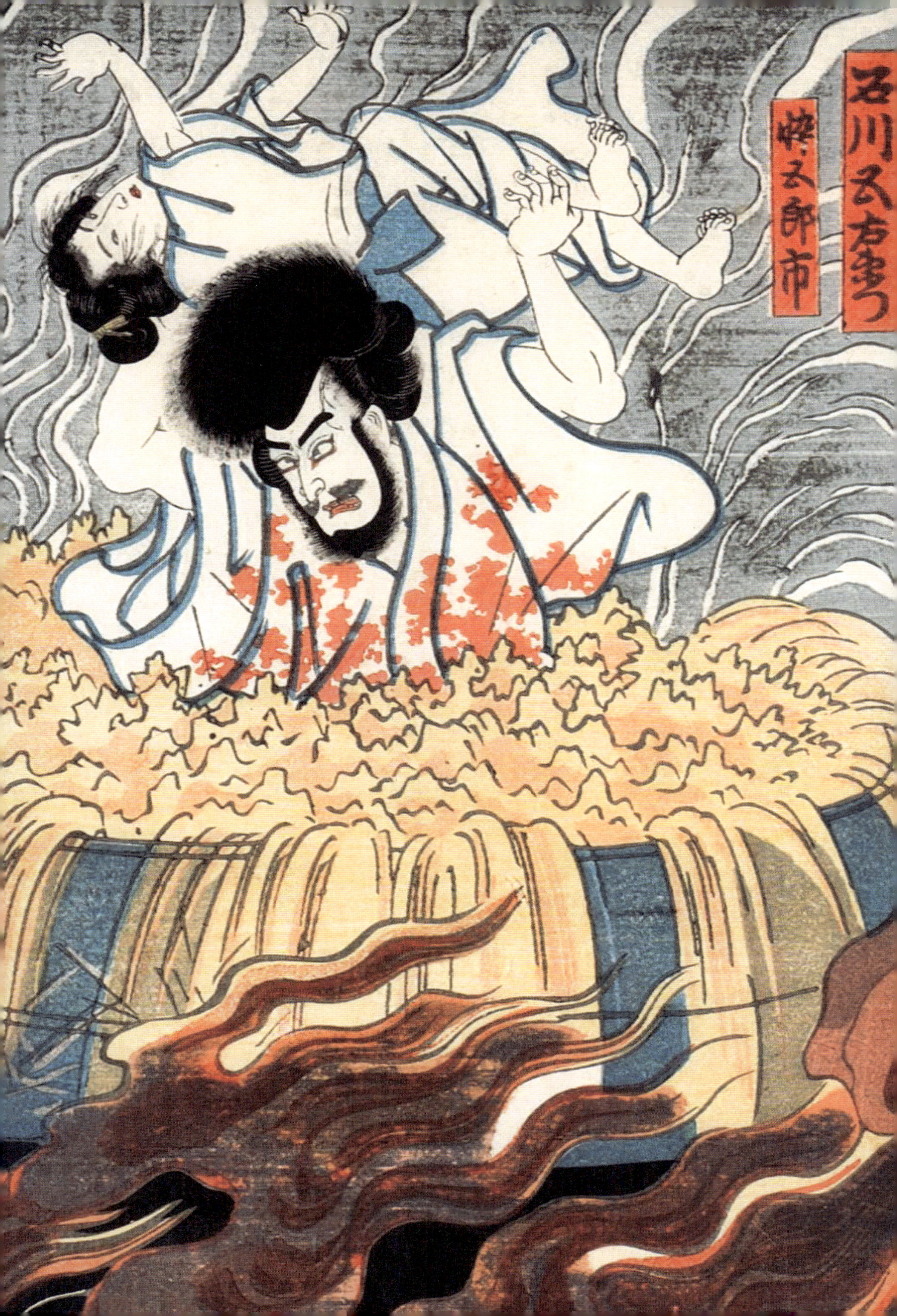

石川五右衛門
嵯モ五郎市

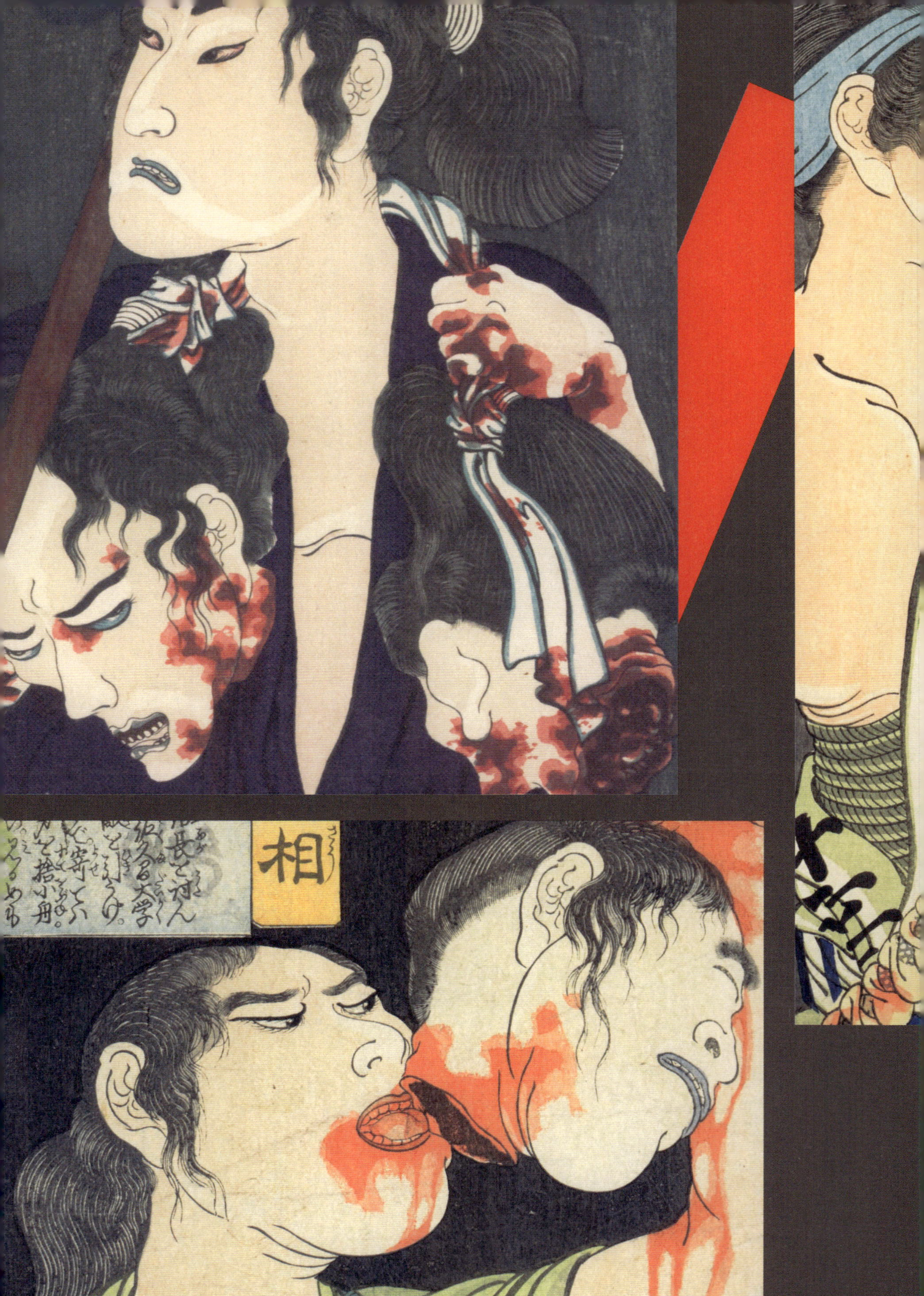
相

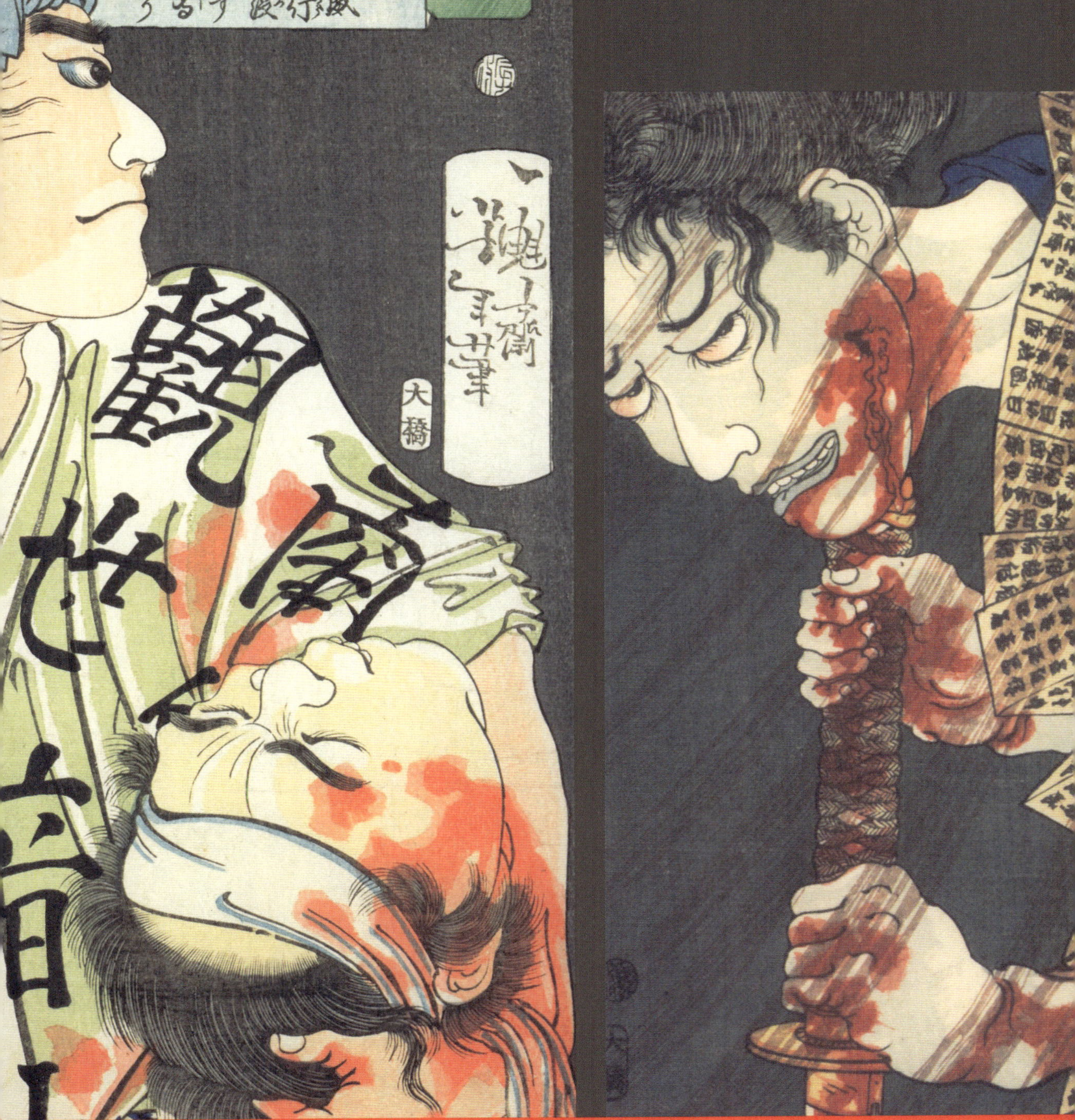

Yoshitoshi's Selection of One Hundred Warriors

Each ukiyoe print of this series depicts a bleeding warrior in a famous historical battle, in order to implicitly represent the Shōgitai troops who were defeated by the new Meiji government at the Battle of Ueno. 65 pictures among them are still preserved to this day. In almost every picture, bright red blood of the troop stands out against a dark plain background. In the Battle of Ueno, the Shōgitai mainly consisted of young people in their teens and twenties. The painter Yoshitoshi is said to have gone to see the battlefield for his creation. By depicting them in disguise as heroes from olden times, Yoshitoshi expressed the sparkles of the last moments of the young men who died without fulfilling their ambitions.

《魁題百撰相》

明治新政府に抗して上野戦争で敗れた彰義隊の武士たちを、歴史上の人物という名目で、一枚に一人ずつ「血みどろ」で描いたシリーズ。65点が確認される。背景は暗色でほぼ無背景であり、潤う鮮血がよく映える。彰義隊士は、10代から20代の若者が中心だったといい、作者の芳年は戦争の現場を取材したと伝えられる。時代に翻弄され、志なかばで散った若者たちの最期の輝きを、英雄たちの討ち死にと重ねて、讃えている。

Mori Rikimaru, from the series of Yoshitoshi's Selection of One Hundred Warriors /
Tsukioka Yoshitoshi

1868 / Tokyo Metropolitan Library

Mori Rikimaru was Mori Ranmaru's little brother and Ranmaru was a famous young page of the warlord Oda Nobunaga. It is said that, at the Honnō-ji Temple Incident, Rikimaru succeeded in decapitating two enemy troops but was defeated at the age of 17. Featuring this legend, this picture shows a young boy hanging two decapitated heads from his shoulders. Yoshitoshi used Nikawa traditional animal glue to express the shine of the red blood.

魁題百撰相 森力丸 ／ 月岡芳年

明治元年（1868） ／ 東京都立中央図書館蔵

戦国武将・織田信長の小姓として名高い森蘭丸の弟・森力丸は、本能寺の変で敵の首を二級打ち取って 17 歳で戦死したという。本図の若者も二つの首を両肩にぶら下げている。接着剤などに使用された「膠」を工夫して、照り輝く血を表現している。

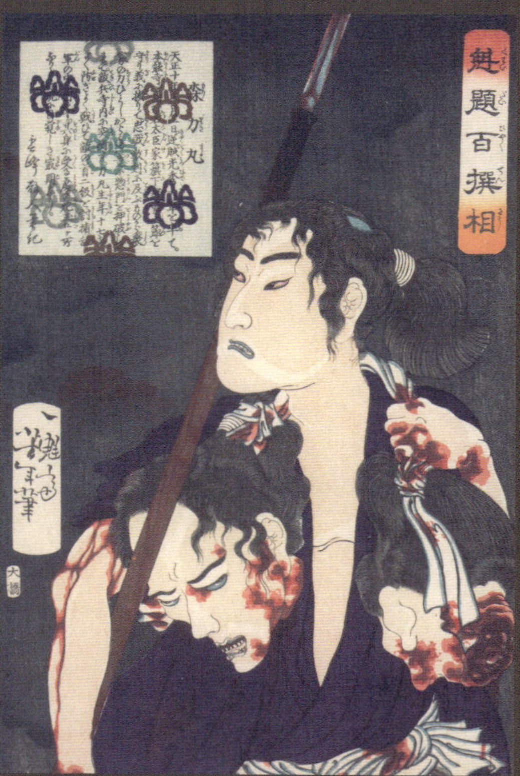

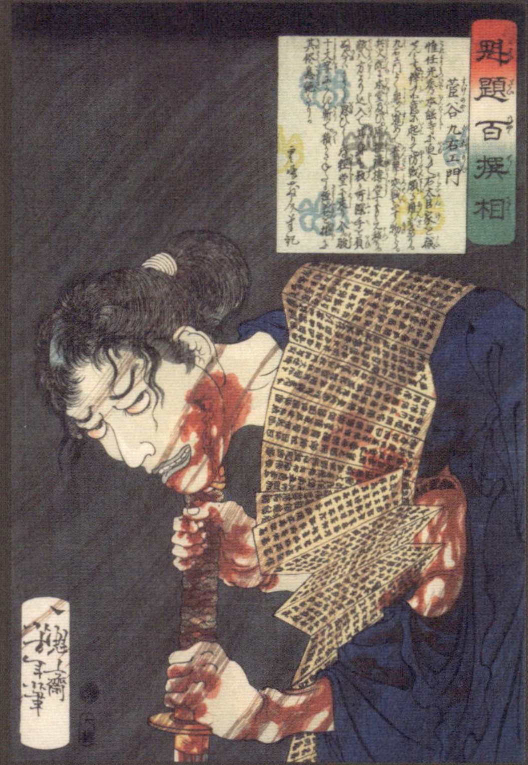

Sugenoya Kuemon, from the series of Yoshitoshi's Selection of One Hundred Warriors / Tsukioka Yoshitoshi

1868 / Tokyo Metropolitan Library

The text in this picture says that Sugenoya Kuemon, a vassal of Oda Nobunaga, rushed to Honnō-ji Temple, soon after his lord was attacked there. But in spite of his intense fighting, he eventually saw the temple hall being caught on fire, and killed himself with his sword, surrounded by piles of Buddhist sutras. Because the Battle of Ueno took place in Kanei-ji Temple, painters often created ukiyoe prints featuring the battle disguised as historical battles which took place in temples, such as the Honnō-ji Temple Incident or the Attack and Burning of Enryaku-ji Temple. This picture is one example of them.

魁題百撰相 菅谷九右エ門 ／ 月岡芳年

明治元年（1868） ／ 東京都立中央図書館蔵

織田信長の家臣・菅谷九右エ門は、文中の説明によれば本能寺の変に駆けつけて奮戦するも本堂に火が回るのを見て自刃、積み重なる経文のなかで果てたという。上野戦争は、その舞台が寛永寺であったことから、「本能寺合戦」や「延暦寺焼討」など、歴史上の寺院での戦争の名を借りて出版される場合が多かった。

Sakuma Daigaku, from the series of Yoshitoshi's Selection of One Hundred Warriors /
Tsukioka Yoshitoshi

1868 / Tokyo Metropolitan Library

In the Battle of Okehazama, Sakuma Daigaku, a vassal of Oda Nobunaga, was appointed to the defense of the Marune Fortress. He resisted against the fierce attack of Imagawa Yoshimoto's great army, but was eventually killed. The overwhelming difference of military power between these two forces resembles that of the Battle of Ueno, where the Shōgitai troops were holed up in Kanei-ji Temple, while the new Meiji government troops powerfully attacked them.

魁題百撰相 佐久間大学 ／ 月岡芳年

明治元年（1868） ／ 東京都立中央図書館蔵

織田信長の家臣・佐久間大学は、今川義元が大軍で攻めて来た桶狭間の戦いで丸根砦の守備を任され、猛攻を受けて討ち死にした。上野戦争でも、寛永寺に立て篭もった彰義隊と、攻め込んできた明治新政府との間には、圧倒的な兵力の差があった。

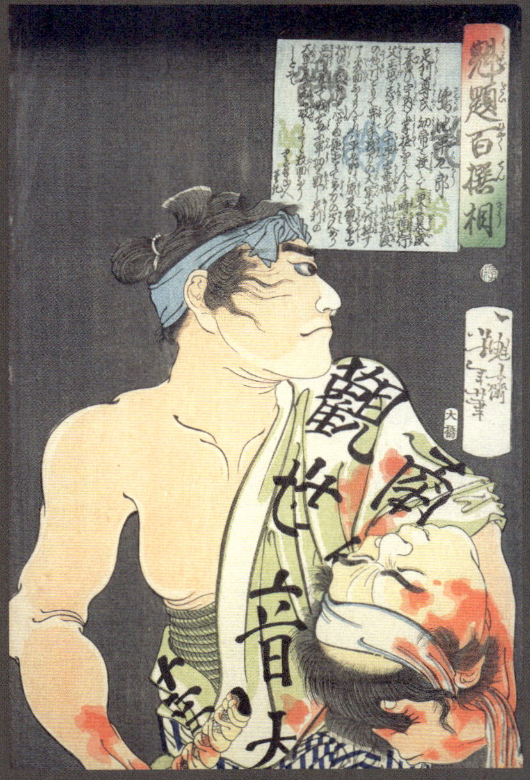

Saginoike Heikurō, from the series of Yoshitoshi's Selection of One Hundred Warriors /
Tsukioka Yoshitoshi

1868 / Tokyo Metropolitan Library

Saginoike Heikurō was a vassal of Kusunoki Masatsura in the Nanbokuchō period. While also being a farmer, he distinguished himself in battles. The picture depicts the tragic hero Masatsura who died in a fierce fight, in order to implicitly represent a coeval theme, the Battle of Ueno.

魁題百撰相 鷺池平九郎 ／ 月岡芳年

明治元年（1868） ／ 東京都立中央図書館蔵

鷺池平九郎は、南北朝期の楠木正行に仕えた武将。農夫でありながら武功を積んだ。上野戦争を、壮絶な討ち死にを遂げた悲劇のヒーロー楠木正行と結びつける一枚。

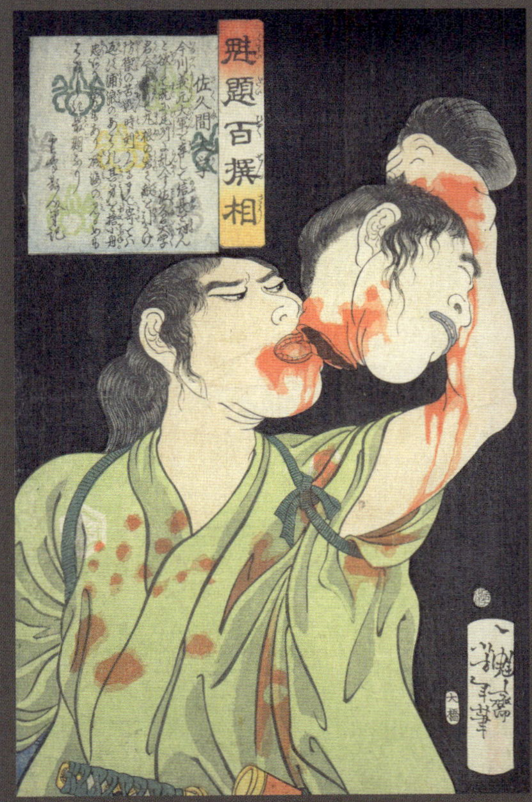

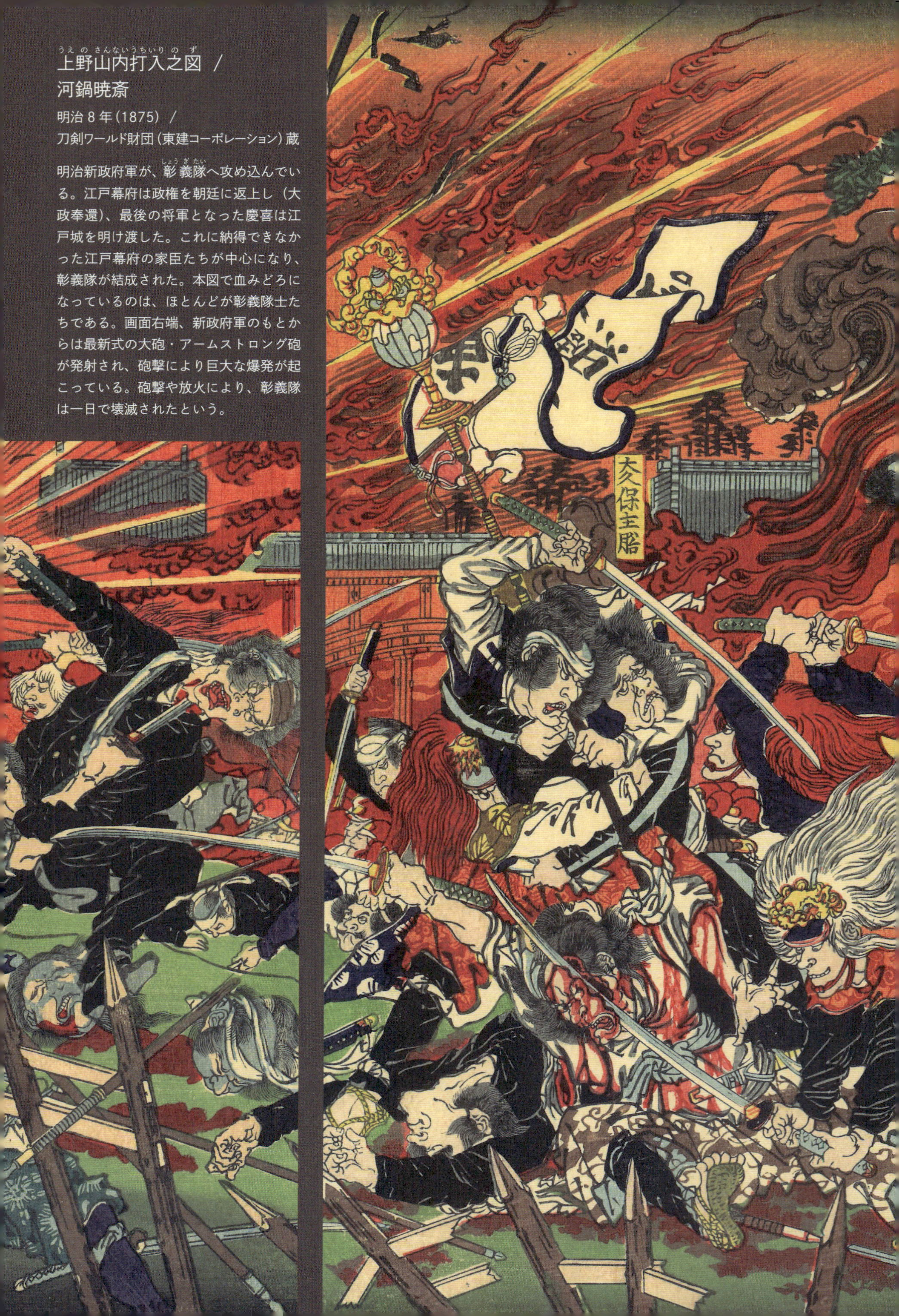

上野山内打入之図 ／
河鍋暁斎

明治 8 年（1875）／
刀剣ワールド財団（東建コーポレーション）蔵

明治新政府軍が、彰義隊へ攻め込んでい
る。江戸幕府は政権を朝廷に返上し（大
政奉還）、最後の将軍となった慶喜は江
戸城を明け渡した。これに納得できなか
った江戸幕府の家臣たちが中心になり、
彰義隊が結成された。本図で血みどろに
なっているのは、ほとんどが彰義隊士た
ちである。画面右端、新政府軍のもとか
らは最新式の大砲・アームストロング砲
が発射され、砲撃により巨大な爆発が起
こっている。砲撃や放火により、彰義隊
は一日で壊滅されたという。

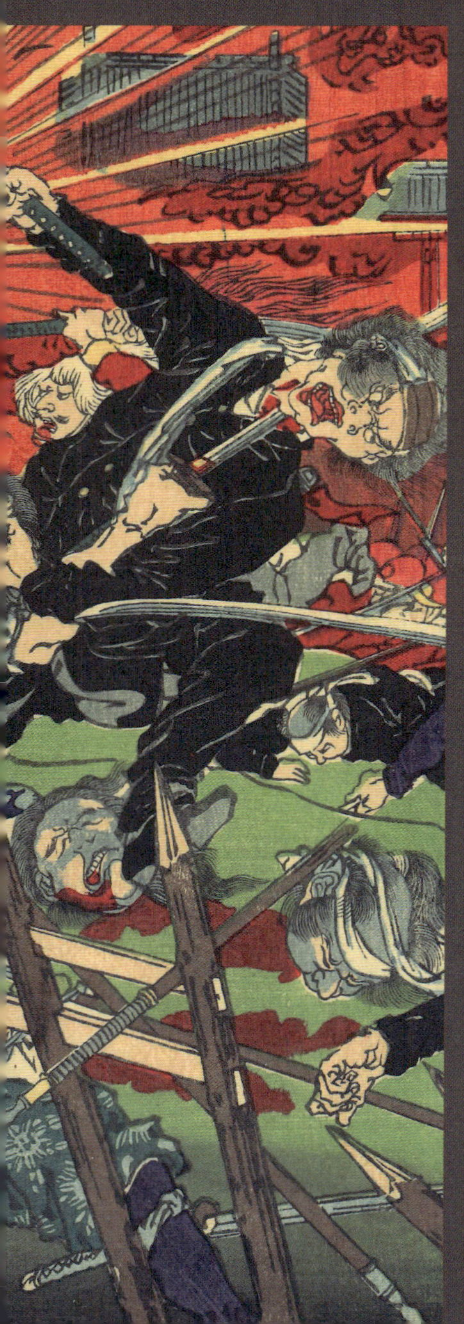

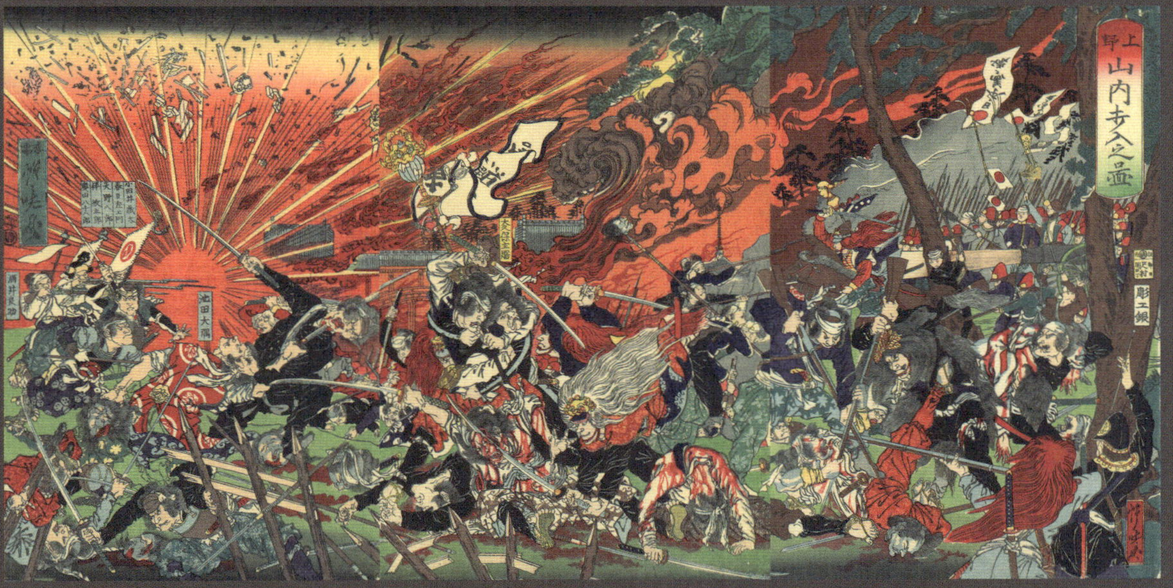

The Raid on Ueno Hill / Kawanabe Kyōsai

1875 / Touken World Foundation

In 1867, Tokugawa Yoshinobu, the last shogun of Edo Bakufu, returned political power to the emperor. This historical event is called Taisei Hōkan. In the following year, Yoshinobu abandoned Edo Castle to the new Meiji government army. Then, many vassals of Edo Bakufu, who could not accept the change, formed Shōgitai and were holed up in Ueno. Most of the bleeding people are Shōgitai troops in this picture. On the right side of the picture, the new government army fires an Armstrong Cannon, the newest style cannon at that time, which leads to a massive explosion. It is said that their artillery fire and arsons wiped out the Shōgitai within a day.

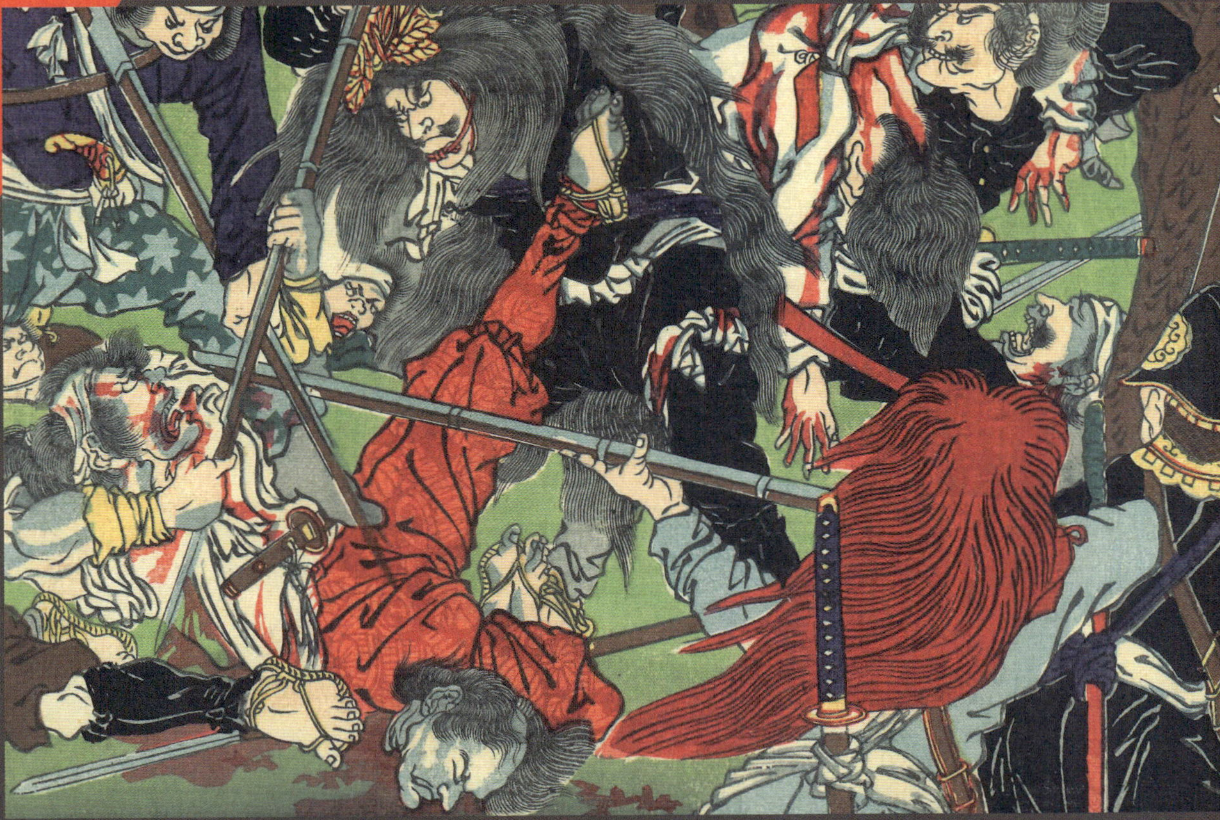

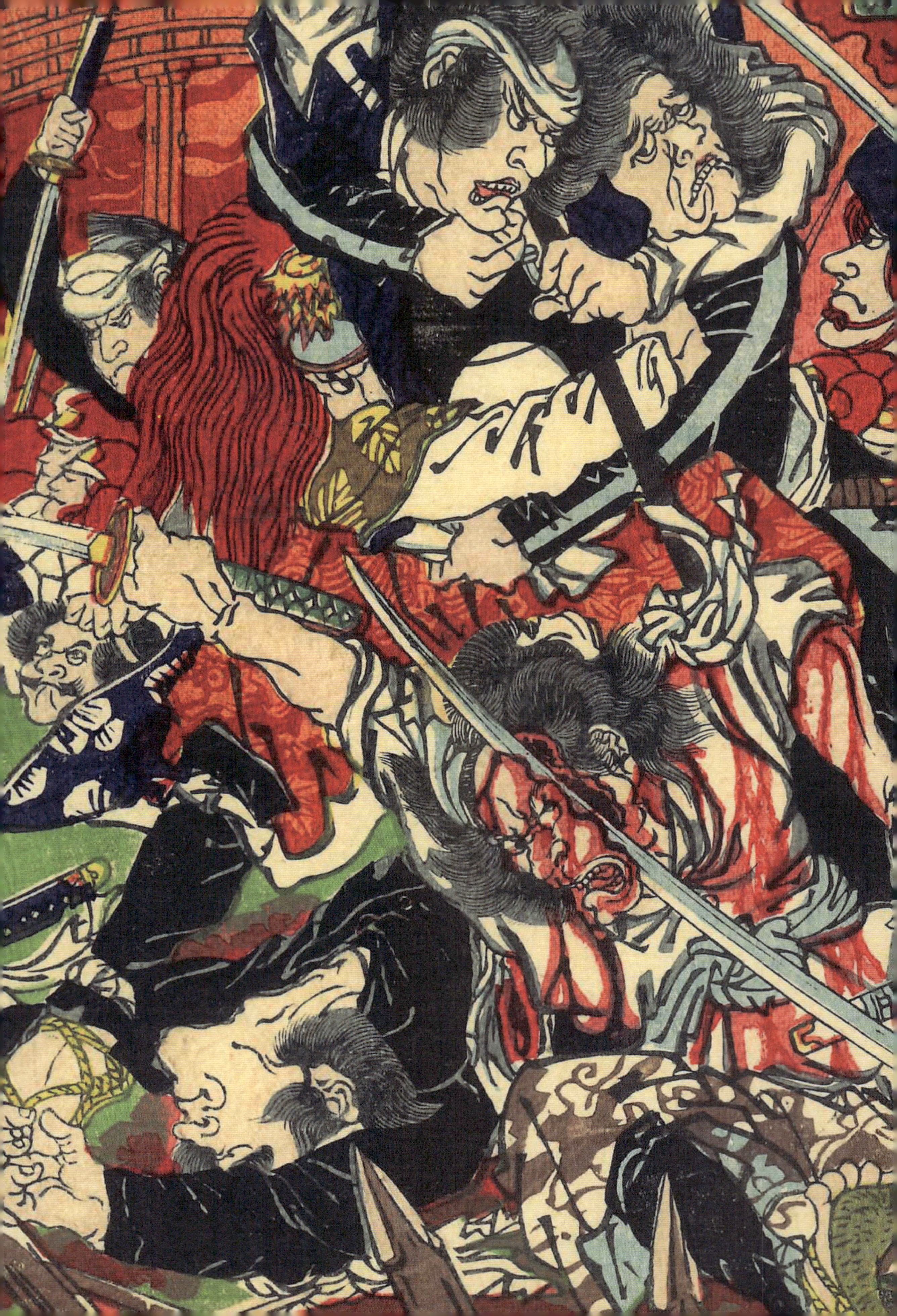

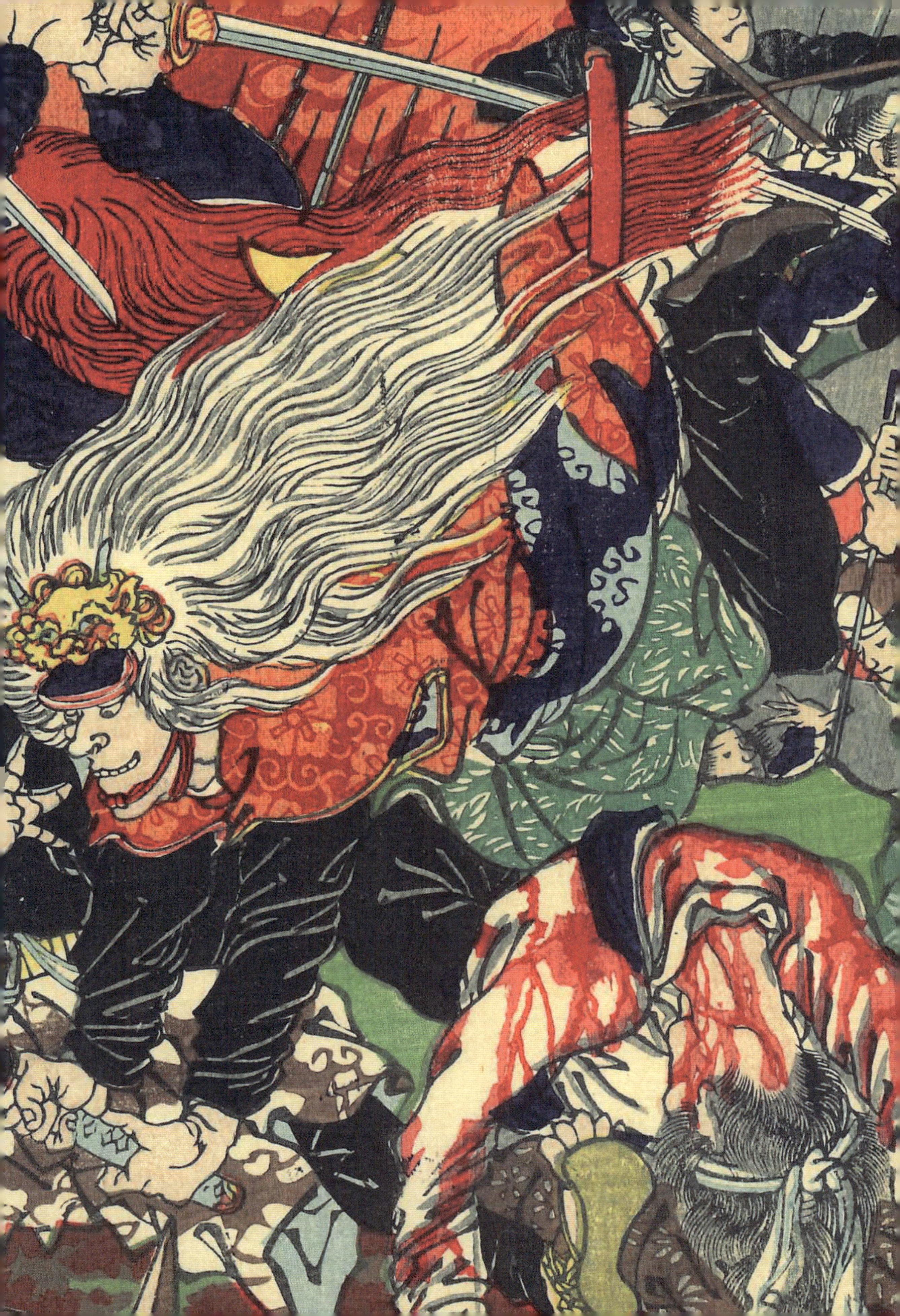

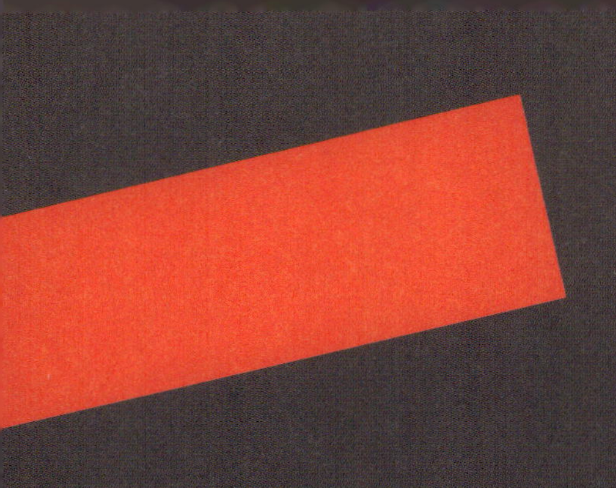

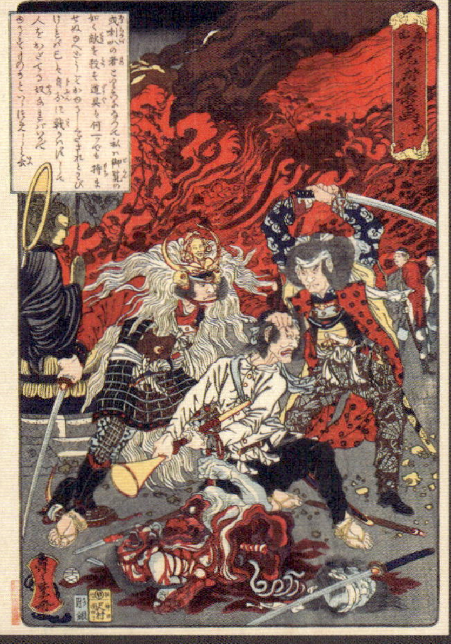

Ōju Kyōsai Rakuga No.11 / Kawanabe Kyōsai

1874 / Tokyo Metropolitan Library

This picture represents one of the moral lessons from Aesop's Fables, in a depiction which is reminiscent of the Battle of Ueno.
Kyōsai was in charge of making print illustrations for Aesop's Fables' Japanese translation, published in 1873. It shows the tale of a captive bugler who asks for quarter, by appealing that he does not have any weapons. But the enemy curses at him saying "You are the coward who should be killed first, since you do not have a direct hand in killing, but egg others on to do so." Against a background of blazing fire, there is a dead body with its internal organs spilling out. The picture tells the seriousness of the bugler's guilt, which results in this dreadful sight.

応需暁斎楽画 十一号 ／ 河鍋暁斎

明治 7 年 (1874) ／ 東京都立中央図書館蔵

上野戦争を彷彿とさせながら、「イソップ物語」の教訓を描く。暁斎は『イソップ寓話』の翻訳書『通俗伊蘇普物語』（1873 年刊）の挿絵を手がけている。捕虜になったラッパ手が武器を持っていないから助けてほしいと命乞いすると、自分は殺さないのに人に殺すように焚き付ける、お前のような卑怯者こそ一番に殺さなければならないと罵られる。燃え盛る炎に内臓が飛び出た死体。焚き付けた結果の凄惨さが、ラッパ手の罪を際立たせる。

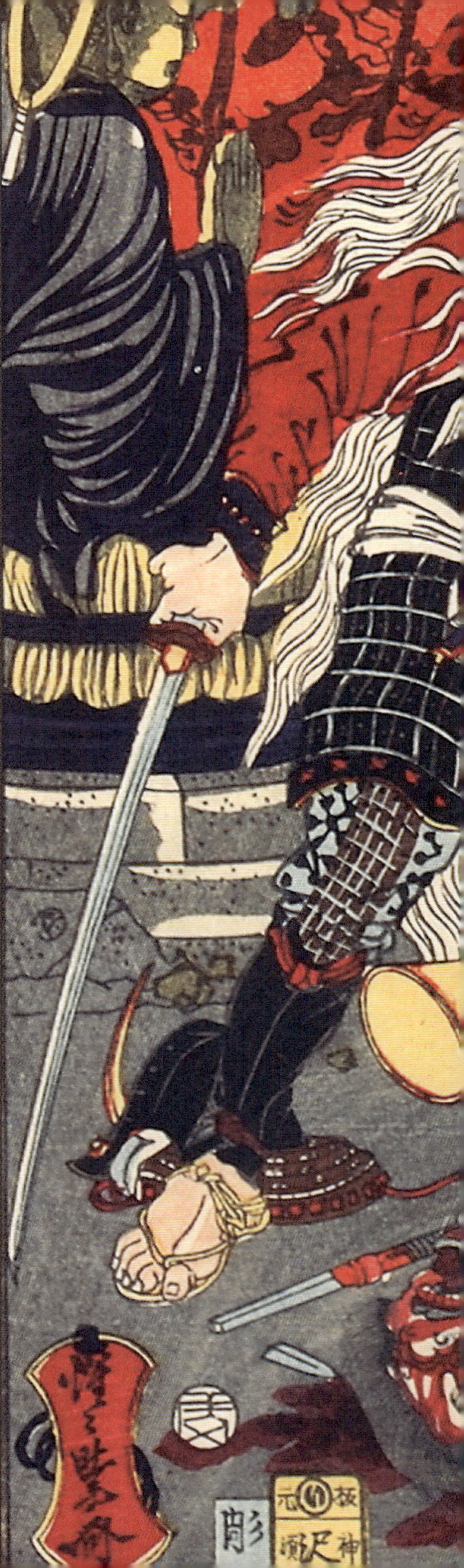

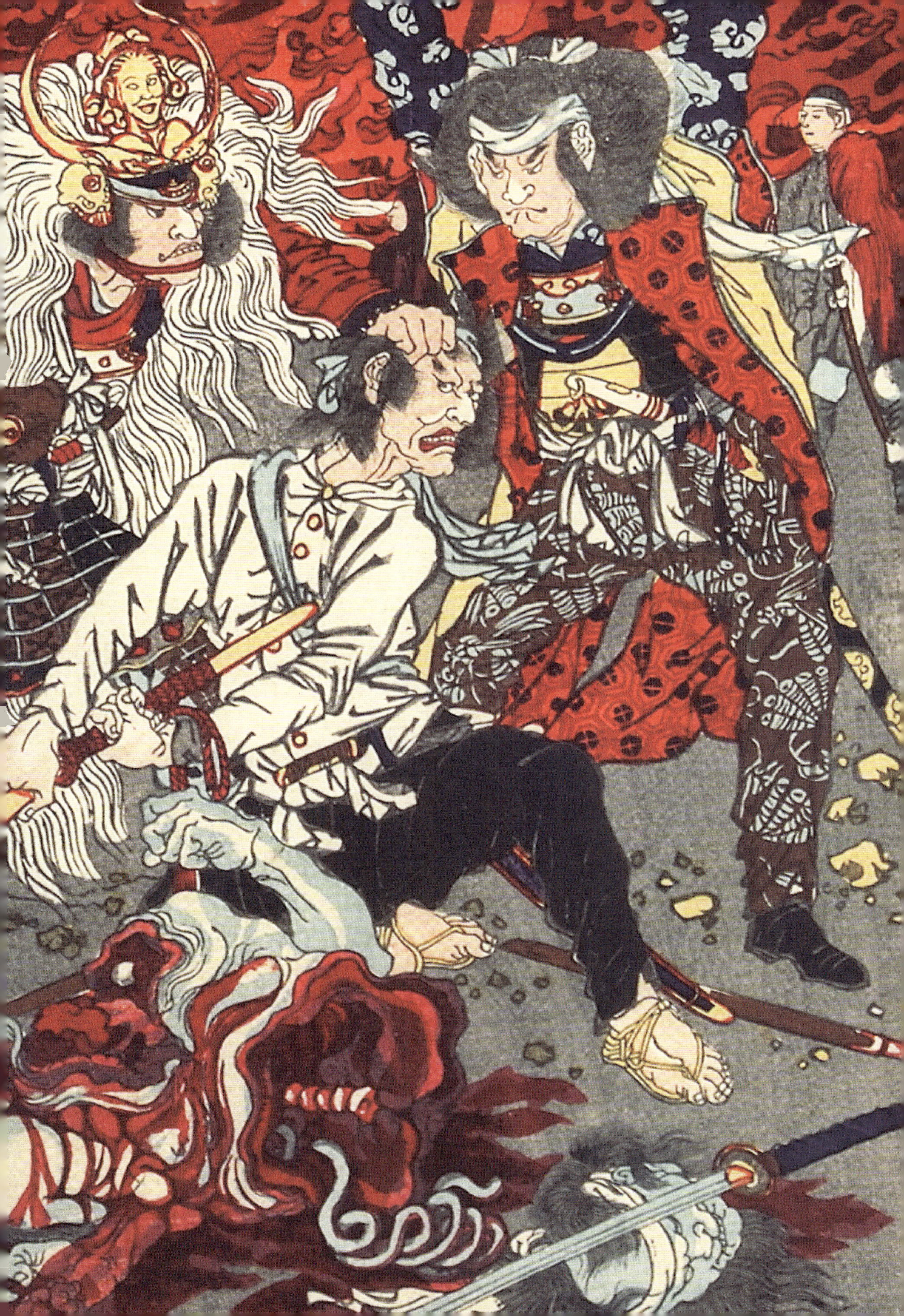

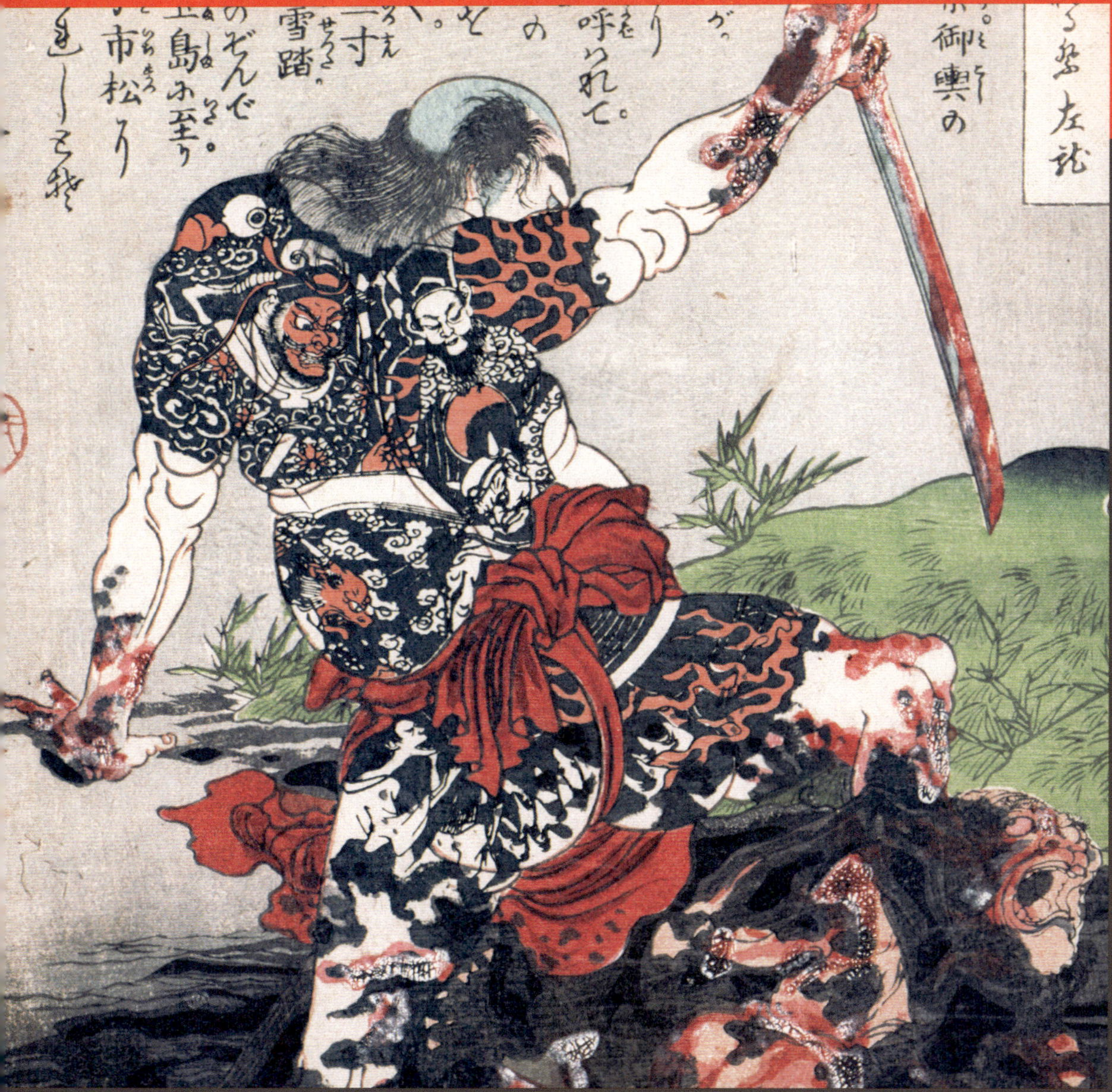

Danshichi Kurobē, from the series of Twenty-Eight Famous Murders / Tsukioka Yoshitoshi

1866 / Photo : Aflo

It is a climactic scene of the kabuki and Jōruri puppet play, "A Mirror of the Summer Festival in Naniwa." Against his will, Danshichi is brutally murdering his father-in-law, Giheiji. He has hell-patterned tattoos all over his back. The dark blue tattoos create a vivid contrast against the bright red blood and kimono obi belt. Yoshitoshi depicted the front part of the kabuki stage covered with mud. Giheiji is jumping into it and having a sword fight, and would eventually disappear into the mud.

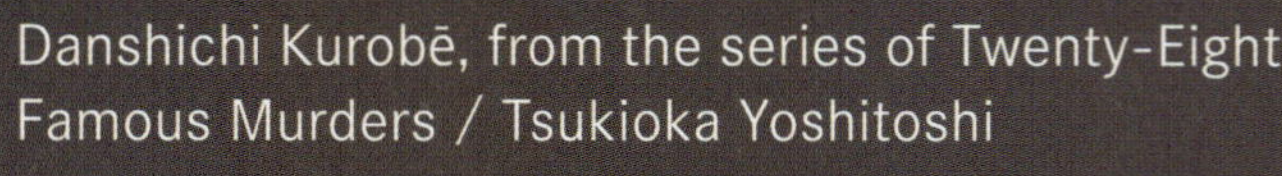

英名二十八衆句 団七九郎兵衛 ／ 月岡芳年

慶応 2 年（1866） ／ 提供：アフロ

浄瑠璃・歌舞伎の「夏祭浪花鑑」の見せ場。舅である義平次を、不本意ながら惨殺する団七。背中には一面に、地獄の模様の刺青が施されている。刺青の濃い青、下帯と鮮血の真紅が、鮮烈なコントラストをつくる。舞台の前に泥を張り、そこに飛び込んで殺陣が行われる舞台の演出を再現し、泥に消えゆく義平次を描いている。

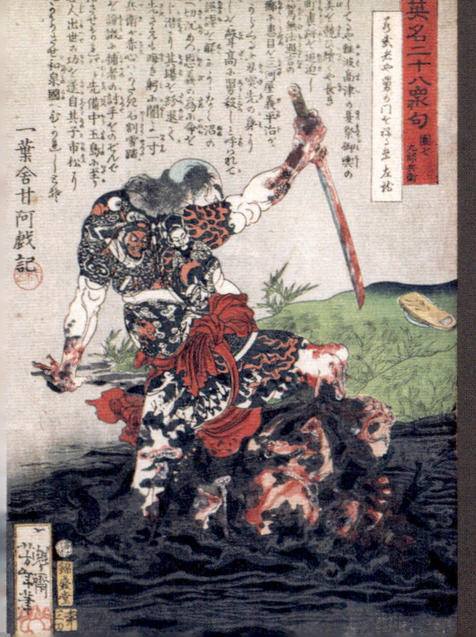

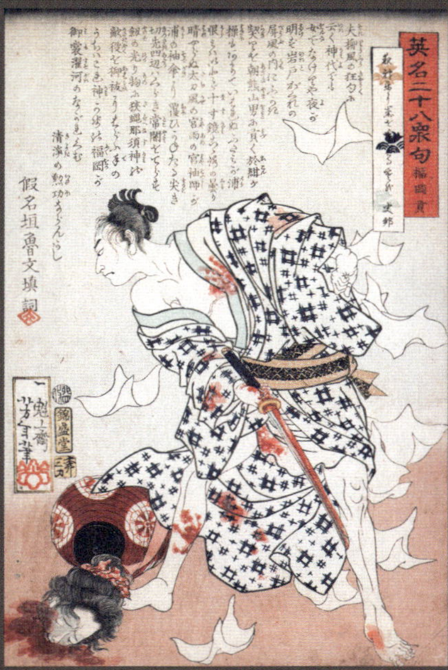

Fukuoka Mitsugi, from the series of Twenty-Eight Famous Murders / Tsukioka Yoshitoshi

1867 / Photo : Aflo

The picture depicts the climactic scene of the kabuki kyōgen play, "Iseondo Koi no Netaba," which was created based on an actual murder case called "Furuichi Jūnin-giri," which happened in Aburaya licensed quarter in Ise Province. Here, Fukuoka Mitsugi is going to slash ten people in a row, using a noted sword called Aoe-shimosaka. His white kimono stands out against the bright red blood. This expression is a reflection of kabuki stages of the same theme which emphasize the color contrast, in order to effectively represent the dramatic story.

英名二十八衆句 福岡貢 ／ 月岡芳年

慶応 3 年（1867）／ 提供：アフロ

伊勢の遊郭油屋で起きた「古市十人斬り」といわれる事件を題材にした歌舞伎狂言「伊勢音頭恋寝刃」の山場、名刀青江下坂で十人斬りに及ぶ福岡貢を描く。さわやかな白い着物に、赤い血糊が映える。色彩の対比でストーリーの明暗を強調する舞台の工夫が、錦絵にも継承されている。

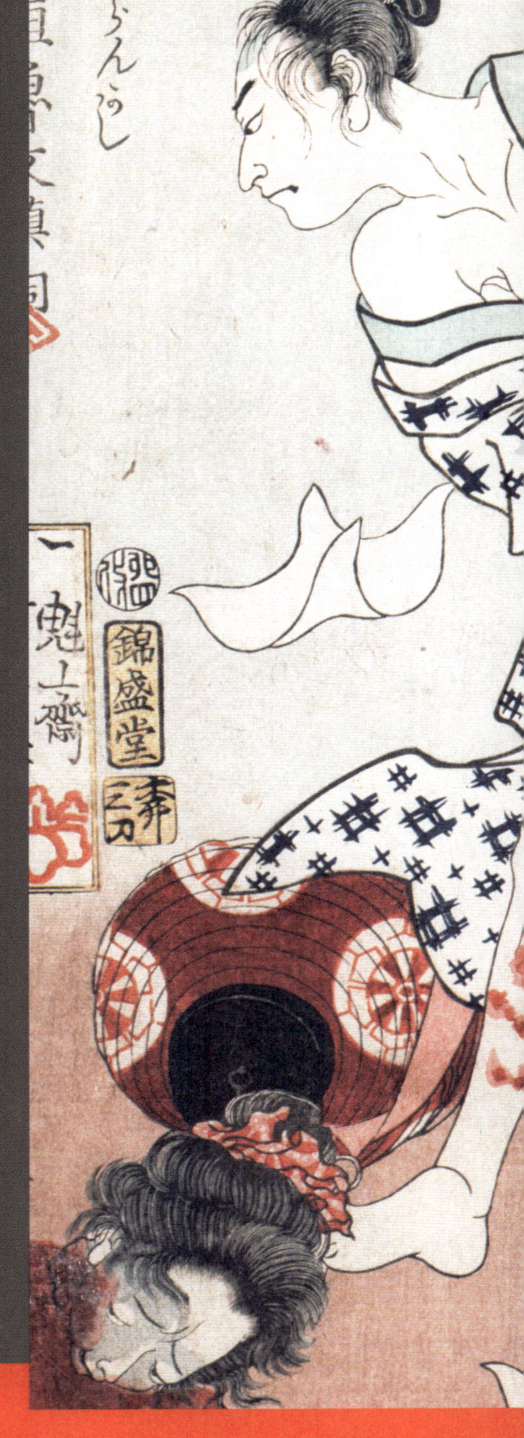

Twenty-Eight Famous Murders

It is a series of ukiyoe prints which ominously depicts bloody scenes from kabuki theater plays and Kōdan storytellings. People have called this series by several different names, such as Chimidoro-e, or Bloody Pictures, Zankoku-e, or Cruel Pictures, as well as Muzan-e, or Atrocity Pictures. The fellow painters, Ochiai Yoshiiku and Tsukioka Yoshitoshi, depicted 14 pictures each for the series. The series' title is "Eimei Nijūha'shūku" in Japanese, which was named after the following two words as they have similar sounds, "Nijūhachi-shūku," or "the 28 constellations of Chinese astrology," and "Shuku," or "various sufferings of the public."

《英名二十八衆句》

歌舞伎や講談の殺戮場面を、血がしたたるようにおどろおどろしく描く、「血みどろ絵」「残酷絵」「無惨絵」などの異名で名高いシリーズ。兄弟弟子である落合芳幾と月岡芳年が 14 図ずつ描いた。題名の「衆句」は、星座の「二十八宿」と「衆苦」にちなんだもの。

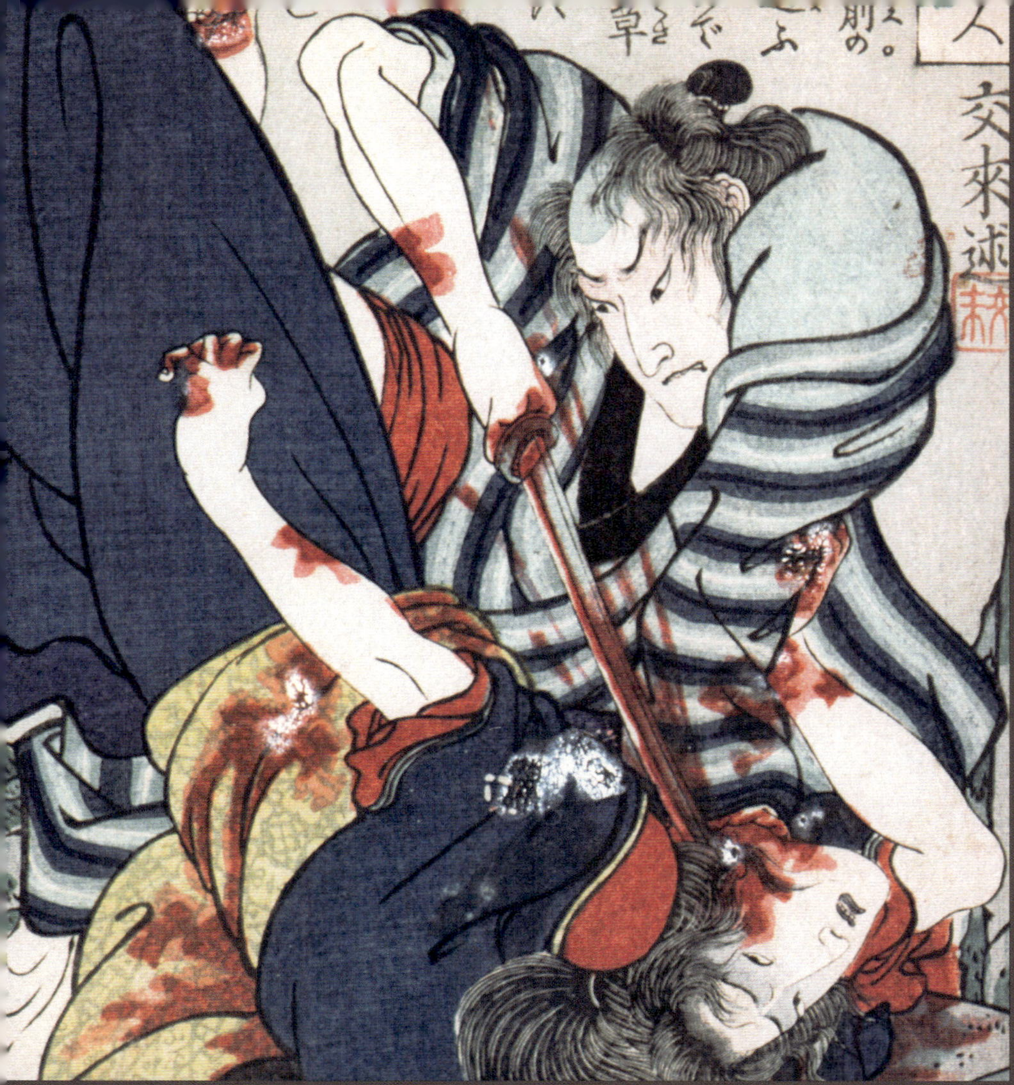

Furuteya Hachirobē, from the series of Twenty-Eight Famous Murders / Tsukioka Yoshitoshi

1867 / Photo : Aflo

It is a scene from the kabuki and Jōruri puppet play, "Sakuratsuba Uramino Samezaya." In this story, Otsuma, Furuteya Hachirobē's wife, tries to come up with money by prostituting herself, in order to secretly help her husband who has been bothering over how to raise money to save his lord in hardship. In spite of her devotion, Otsuma pretends as if she is running out of patience with Hachirobē. It causes him to misunderstand her and to eventually kill her, as depicted in this picture. Here, the miserable last moment of Otsuma is dynamically represented, with Hachirobē grabbing her upside down and cutting her head off.

英名二十八衆句 古手屋八郎兵衛 ／ 月岡芳年

慶応 3 年（1867） ／ 提供：アフロ

浄瑠璃・歌舞伎の「桜鍔恨鮫鞘」の一場面。主君の難儀を救うための金策に苦しんでいる夫・古手屋八郎兵衛のために、別の男に身をまかせて金を工面しようとする女房のお妻。愛想づかしを演じる妻を、誤解したまま斬り殺す場面。逆さまになって首を斬られる、お妻の悲痛な最期がダイナミックに表現されている。

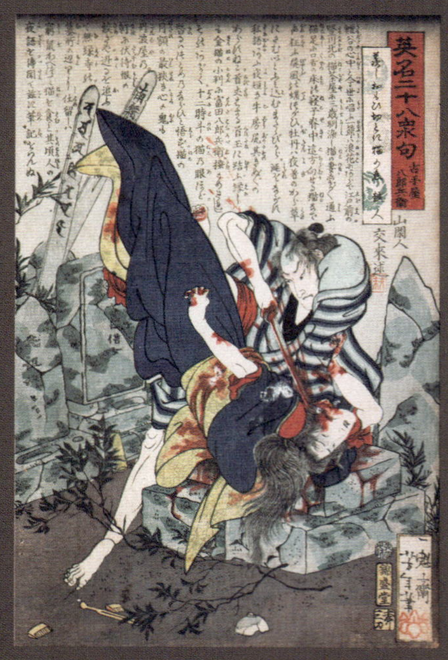

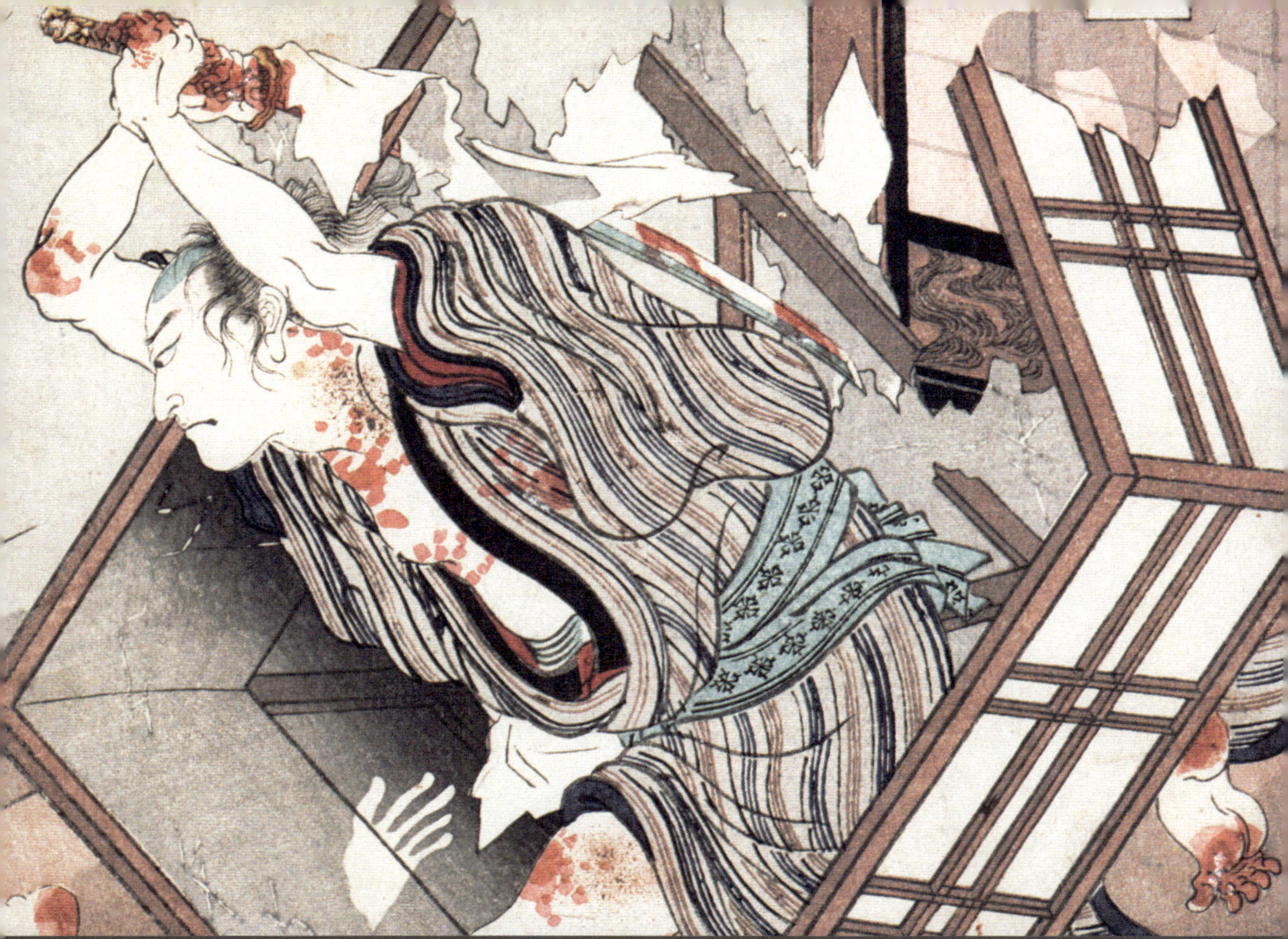

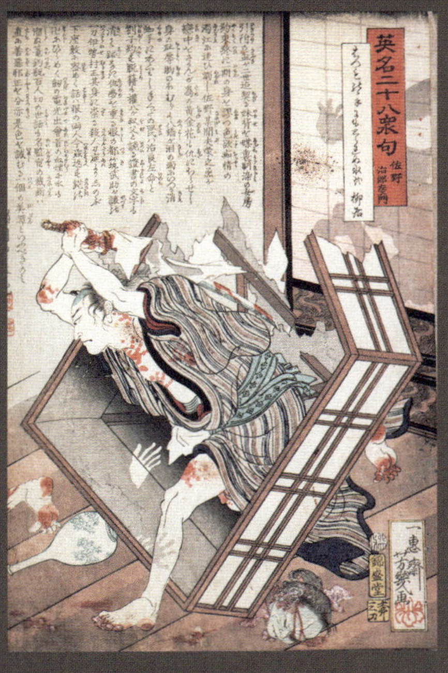

Sano Jirōzaemon, from the series of Twenty-Eight Famous Murders / Ochiai Yoshiiku

1867 / Photo : Aflo

The picture features an actual murder case called "One hundred Slashes in Yoshiwara," which was widely dramatized. Sano Jirōzaemon held a grudge against the courtesan Yatsuhashi over her faithlessness. He killed her with his sword and also slashed or killed many others in the Yoshiwara geisha district in Edo. Here, Jirōzaemon goes on a rampage with a magical sword and bursts through a large lantern which is hung from the ceiling. The many handprints on his skin and the lantern represent the despair of the departed souls.

英名二十八衆句 佐野治郎左エ門 ／ 落合芳幾

慶応 3 年（1867） ／ 提供：アフロ

吉原百人斬 ── 佐野次郎左衛門が江戸吉原の遊女八ッ橋の不実を恨んで斬り殺し、その他大勢を殺傷した事件 ── は、さまざまに戯曲化された。妖刀を手に、八間（天井に吊るす行灯）を突き破って荒れ狂う次郎左衛門。その肌や八間につけられたいくつもの手形が、死者の無念を物語る。

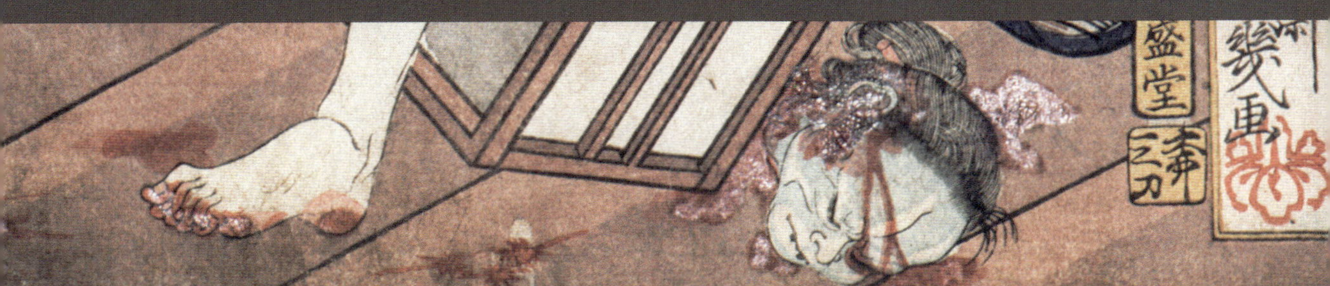

Shundō Jirōzaemon, from the series of Twenty-Eight Famous Murders / Ochiai Yoshiiku

1867 / Photo : Aflo

The picture features the kabuki and Jōruri puppet play, "Katakiuchi Tsuzureno Nishiki." The story is about Shundō Jirōemon, whose father was killed by an enemy. He sought the enemy for a long time, and eventually lost use of his leg. In the end, he succeeded in avenging his father with the help of his younger brother, Shinshichi. Here, Jirōemon is seriously bruised and his pale skin is bleeding.

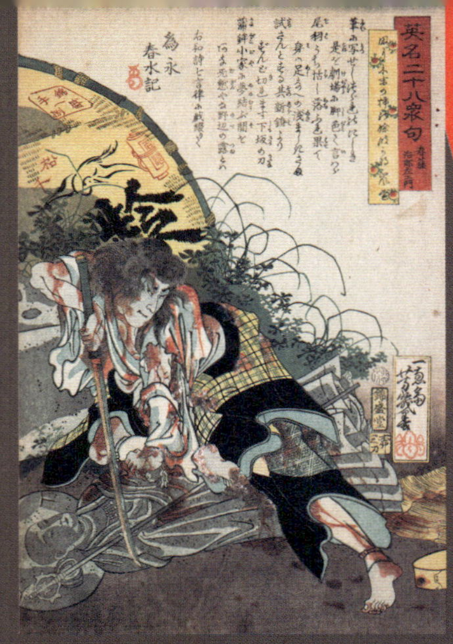

英名二十八衆句 春藤治郎左ヱ門 / 落合芳幾

慶応 3 年（1867） / 提供：アフロ

浄瑠璃・歌舞伎の「敵討襤褸錦」は、父の敵のために流浪するうち足が立たなくなった春藤次郎右衛門が、弟の新七とともに本懐を遂げる物語。深手を負い青白くなった肌に、血がしたたっている。

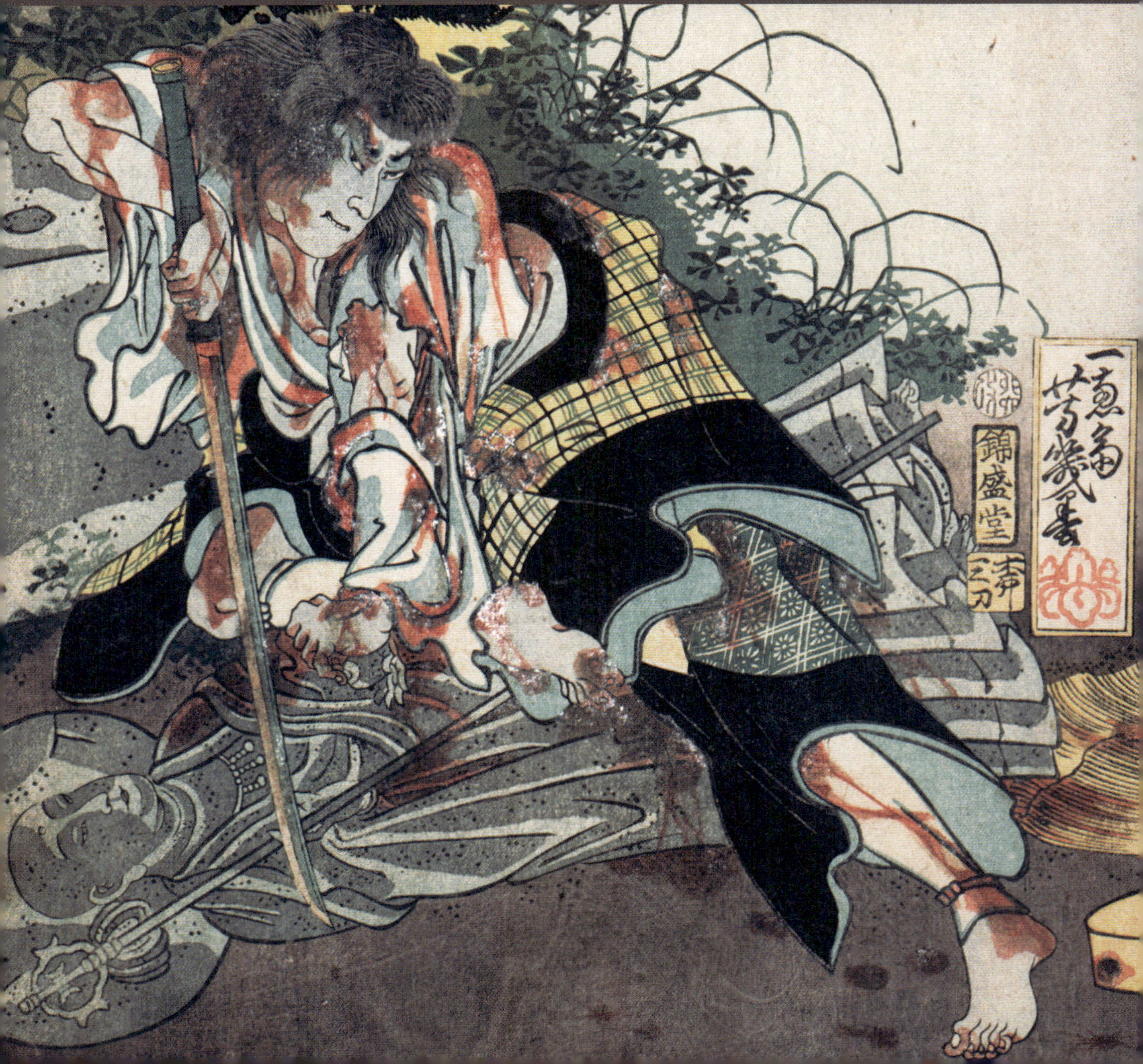

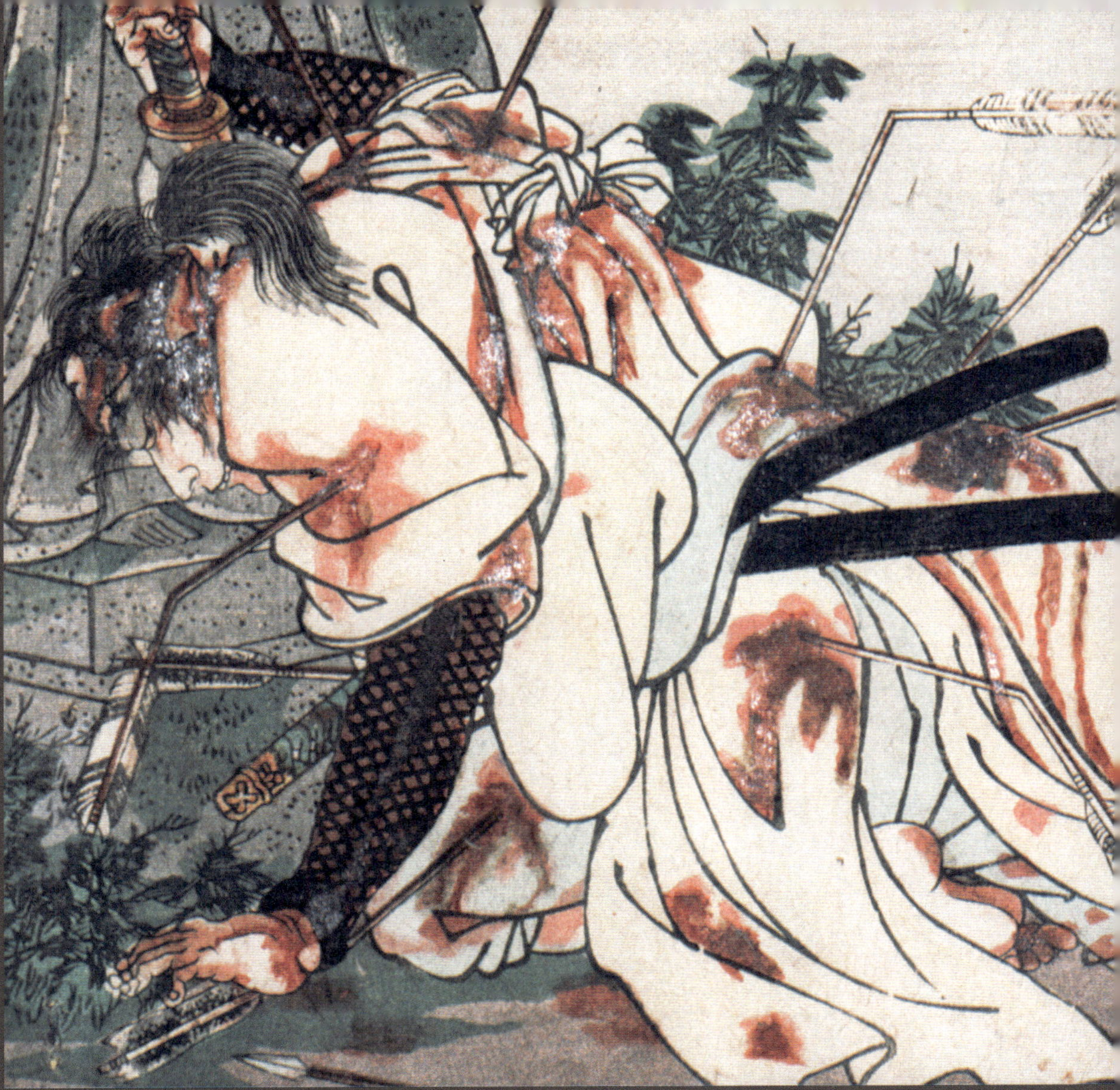

Enjō Kihachirō, from the series of Twenty-Eight Famous Murders / Ochiai Yoshiiku

1867 / Photo : Aflo

The picture features an actual incident of two elder brothers, Enjō Jizaemon and Andō Kihachirō, who tried to avenge their younger brother Sōzaemon, but they were fought back against and killed. The episode was adapted into kabuki and Jōruri puppet plays and called "Revenge at Sōzen-ji Temple." Here, Kihachirō is shot by numerous arrows and his exhausted body falls to the ground, in front of a stone statue of Jizō, the Buddhist deity. The depiction which only shows Kihachirō's back but not his facial expressions effectively represents his despair.

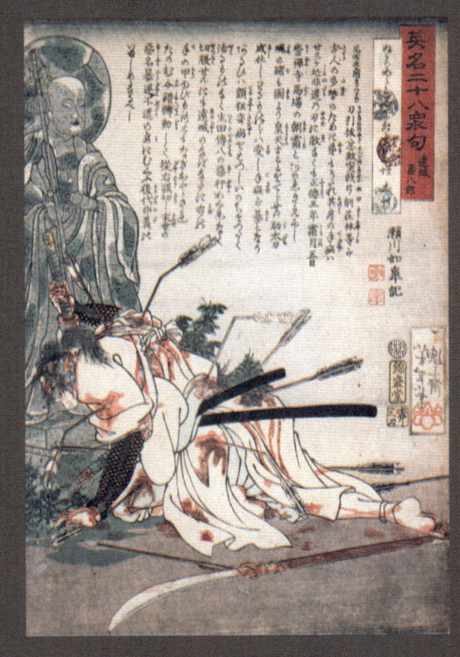

英名二十八衆句 遠城喜八郎 ／ 月岡芳年

慶応 3 年（1867） ／ 提供：アフロ

遠城治左衛門と安藤喜八郎の兄弟が、末弟宗左衛門の仇を討とうとして返り討ちにあう「崇善寺馬場の仇討ち」が、浄瑠璃や歌舞伎の題材になった。喜八郎は敵に矢をあびせられ、地蔵の足下に力尽きて倒れる。後ろ姿によって、その無念が強調されている。

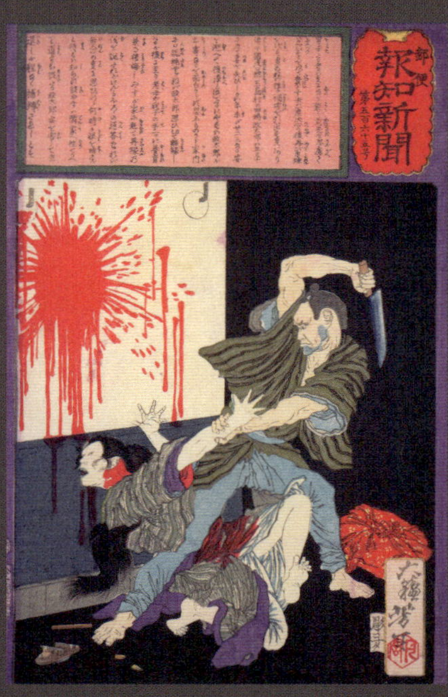

Yūbin Hōchi Newspaper, No. 565 / Tsukioka Yoshitoshi

1875 / National Diet Library, Japan

In Japan, newspapers began to be published in earnest in the Meiji period and got a lot of attention, even become souvenirs of Tokyo. However, their texts were difficult to read for the general public. Then, Nishiki-e Shinbun, or newspapers with simple texts and illustrated prints, emerged. Yoshitoshi who was already a popular painter at that time started working on print illustrations for the Yūbin Hōchi Newspaper. This picture depicts a murder of passion. The smeared blood on the wall theatrically represents the gruesome incident.

『郵便報知新聞』第五百六十五号 ／ 月岡芳年

明治 8 年（1875） ／ 国立国会図書館蔵

明治になって本格的につくられるようになった「新聞」は、東京土産になるほど話題を呼んだが、大衆には読みづらいものだった。そこで、絵と平易な詞でニュースを伝える錦絵新聞が登場。売れっ子絵師となっていた芳年は、「郵便報知新聞」の挿絵を手がけた。本図は、痴情のもつれによる殺人を報じたもの。壁にべっとりとついた血痕が、舞台美術のごとく、陰惨な事件を演出する。

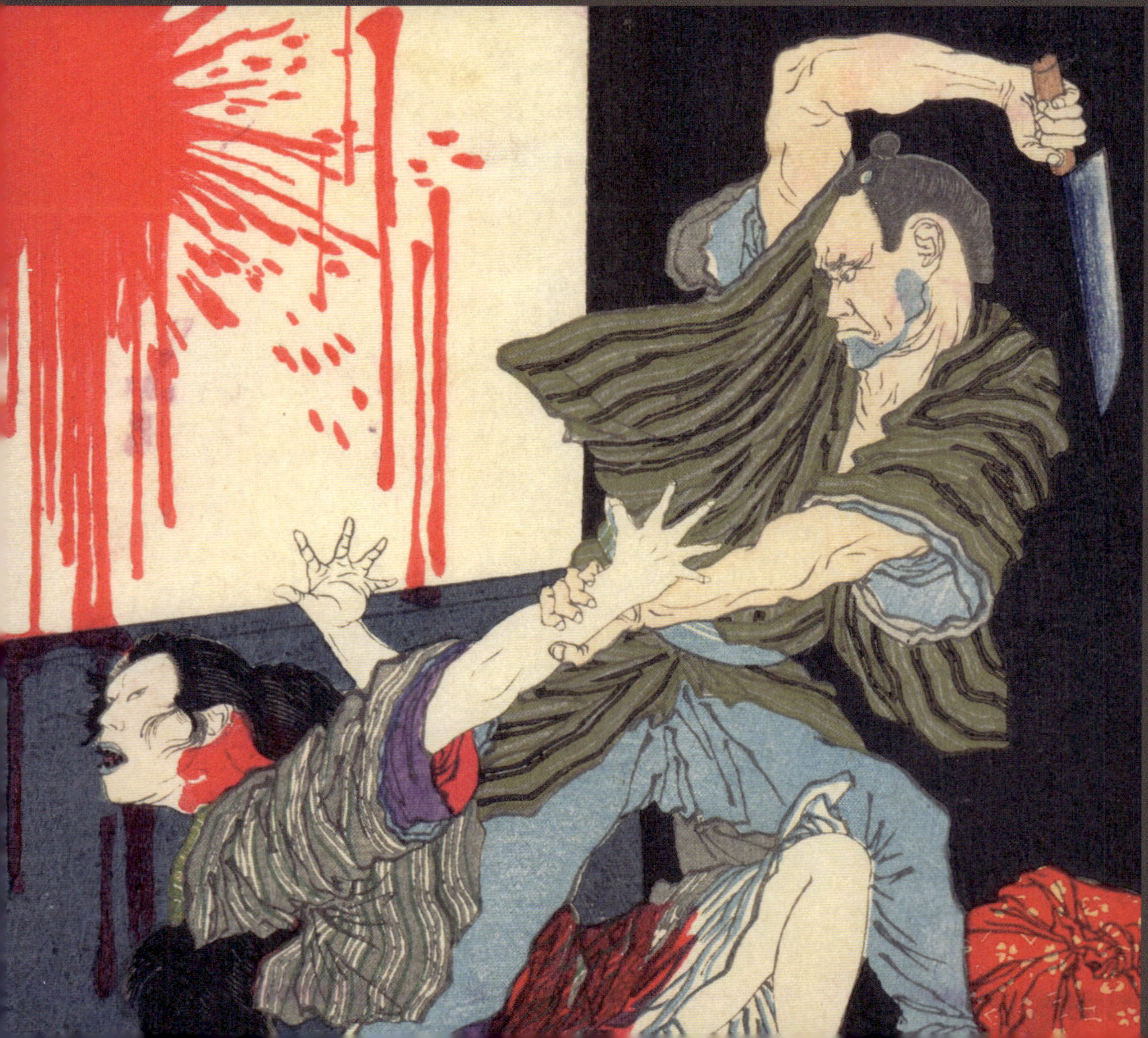

Yūbin Hōchi Newspaper, No. 623 / Tsukioka Yoshitoshi

1875 / National Diet Library, Japan

Nishiki-e Shinbun, or newspapers with simple texts and illustrated prints, often reported bizarre and sensational incidents, in order to gain popularity. This picture depicts two women who were attacked by robbers and later eaten by wolves. Their dead bodies are vividly represented with bright red blood, white skin, and limply bent necks. For many people, the main purpose of buying Nishiki-e Shinbun was to enjoy spectacular illustrations like this, rather than reading the news content.

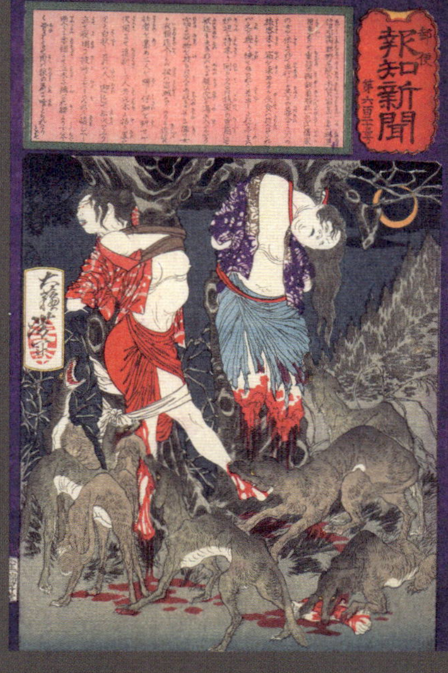

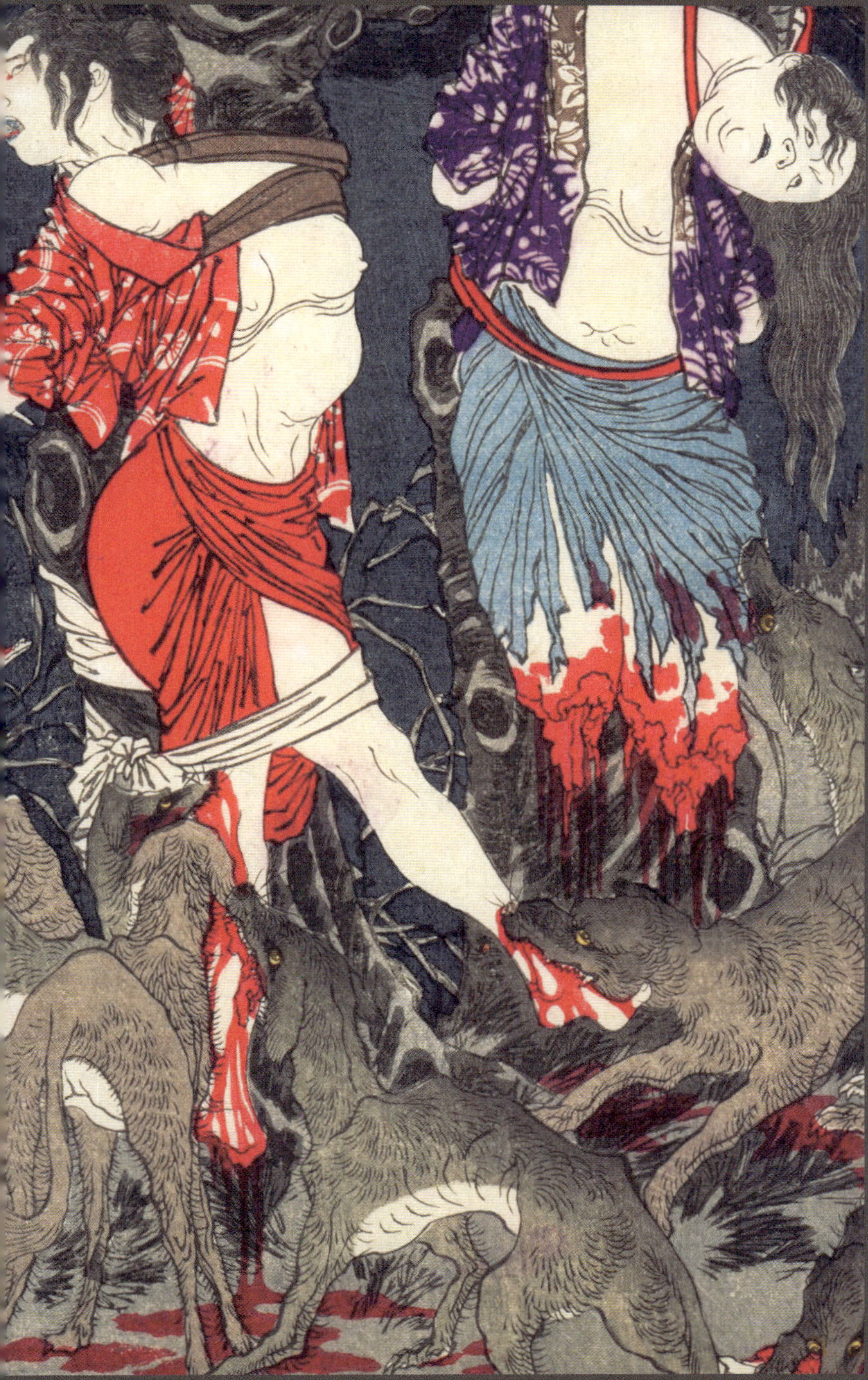

『郵便報知新聞』 第六百二十三号 / 月岡芳年

明治 8 年（1875）/ 国立国会図書館蔵

錦絵新聞は、大衆の人気を得るために、猟奇的・煽情的な内容を取り上げるものが多かった。本図は追い剥ぎに遭った女二人が放置されたうえ、狼に食われるという事件を描いたもの。白い肌に赤い血、ぐにゃりと首の伸びた死体。ニュースの内容よりも、見応えのある絵の方が、買い手の目的となっていた。

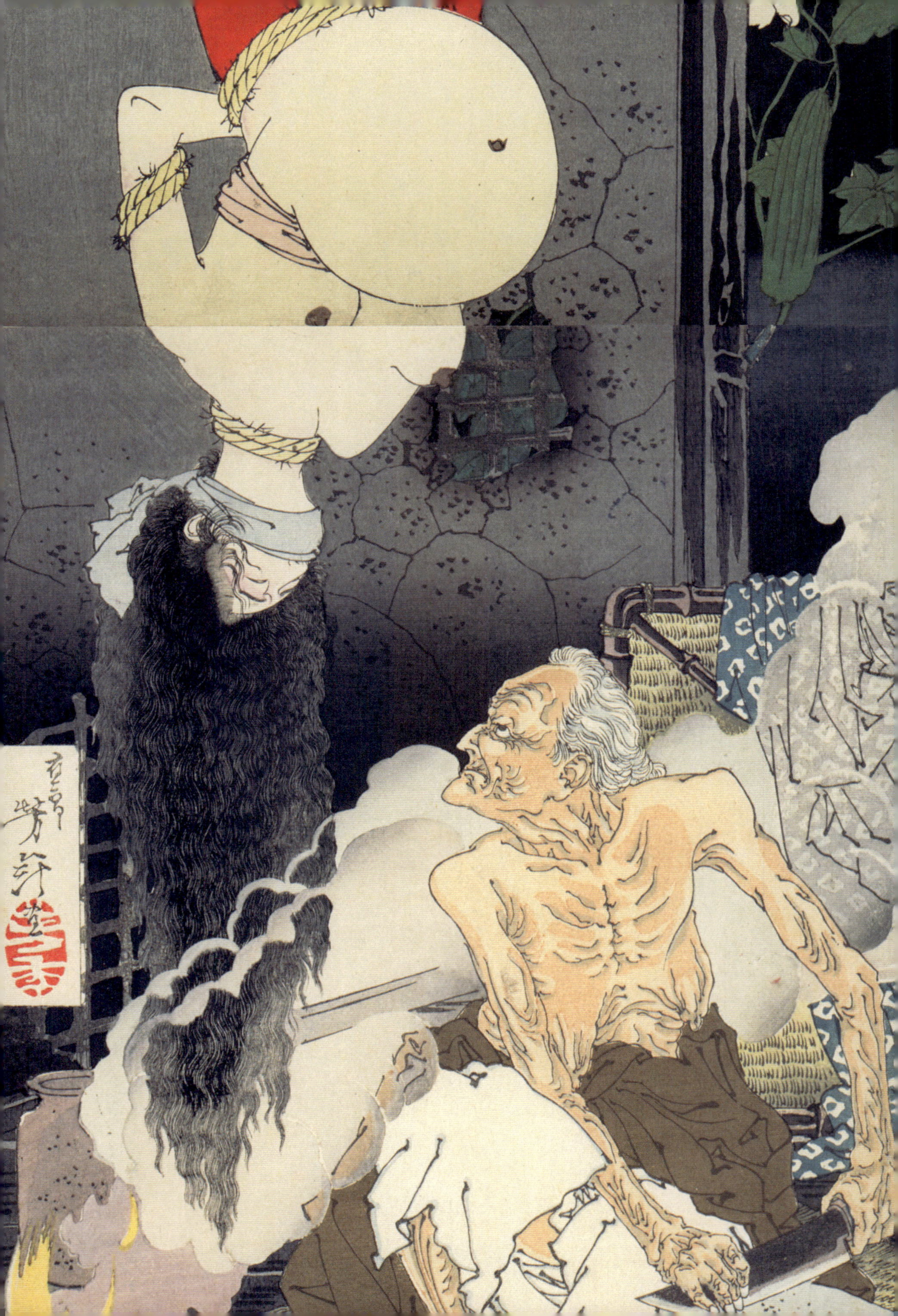

The Lonely House on the Adachi Moor in Ōshū Province / Tsukioka Yoshitoshi

1885 / National Diet Library, Japan

The picture depicts an old woman sharpening a kitchen knife in order to rip a pregnant woman's body apart, after hanging her upside down from the ceiling. According to legend, she used to be a nanny of a princess in the old capital Kyoto. Since the princess had a fatal disease, the nanny set out on a journey to look for an unborn baby's fresh liver, which was believed to be a cure. She reached the Adachi Moor in Ōshū Province and remained there for many years. One day, a pregnant stranger visited her. The old woman killed her and took out her unborn baby's fresh liver, as it is depicted here. After achieving her aim, she realized that the pregnant woman was her own daughter, whom she left in Kyoto ages ago. The dreadful murder was widely represented in kabuki and Jōruri puppet plays, and many ukiyoe prints featured the theatrical scenes. It is one of Yoshitoshi's Chimidoro-e (Bloody Pictures) or Zankoku-e (Cruel Pictures) compilations, which express brutal scenes without depicting blood.

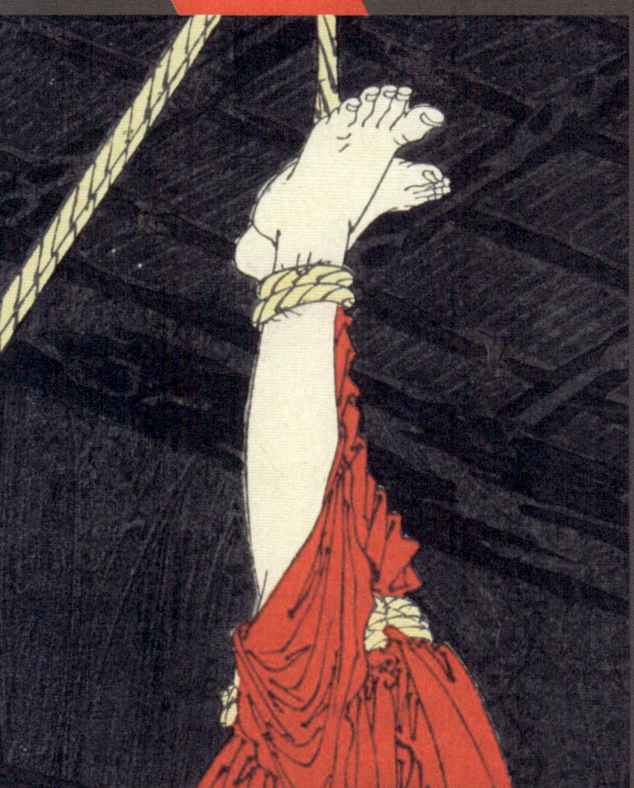

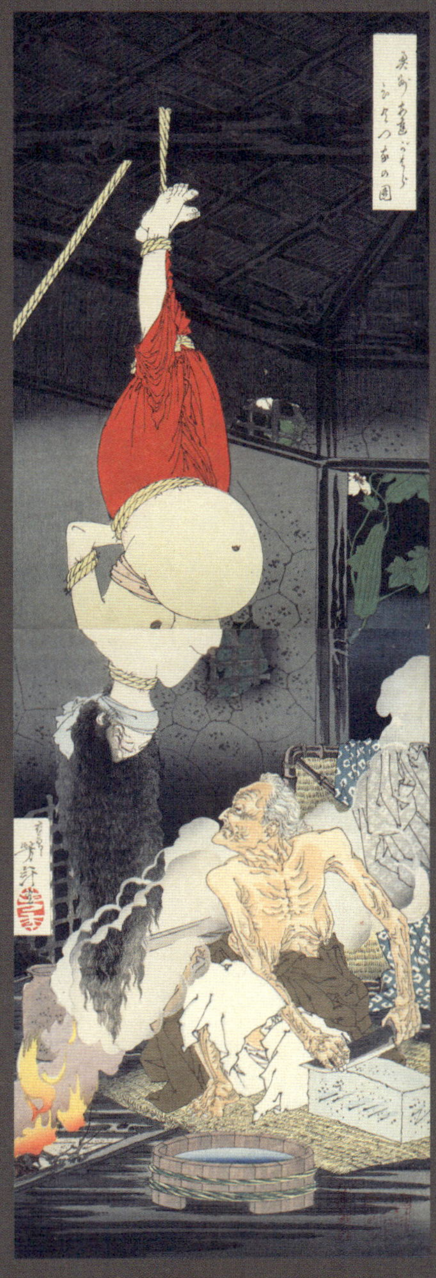

奥州安達がはらひとつ家の図 / 月岡芳年

明治 18 年（1885）/ 国立国会図書館蔵

さかさ吊りにした妊婦を、ごしごしと出刃を研ぐ老婆が、今まさに解体しようとしている場面である。この老婆、もとはある姫の乳母で、姫の不治の病に胎児の生き肝が効くといわれ、それを求めて旅に出て、奥州安達ヶ原で時を経て老婆となった。遂に身重の女が訪ねてきたので、赤子の肝を取り出そうというところ。目的を果たした後に、妊婦が都に置いてきた我が子であったことを知る。凄惨な殺しの場面は浄瑠璃や歌舞伎、それに基づく錦絵で繰り返し取り上げられた。「血みどろ芳年」の「残酷絵」の集大成は、血を描くことなく成し遂げられた。

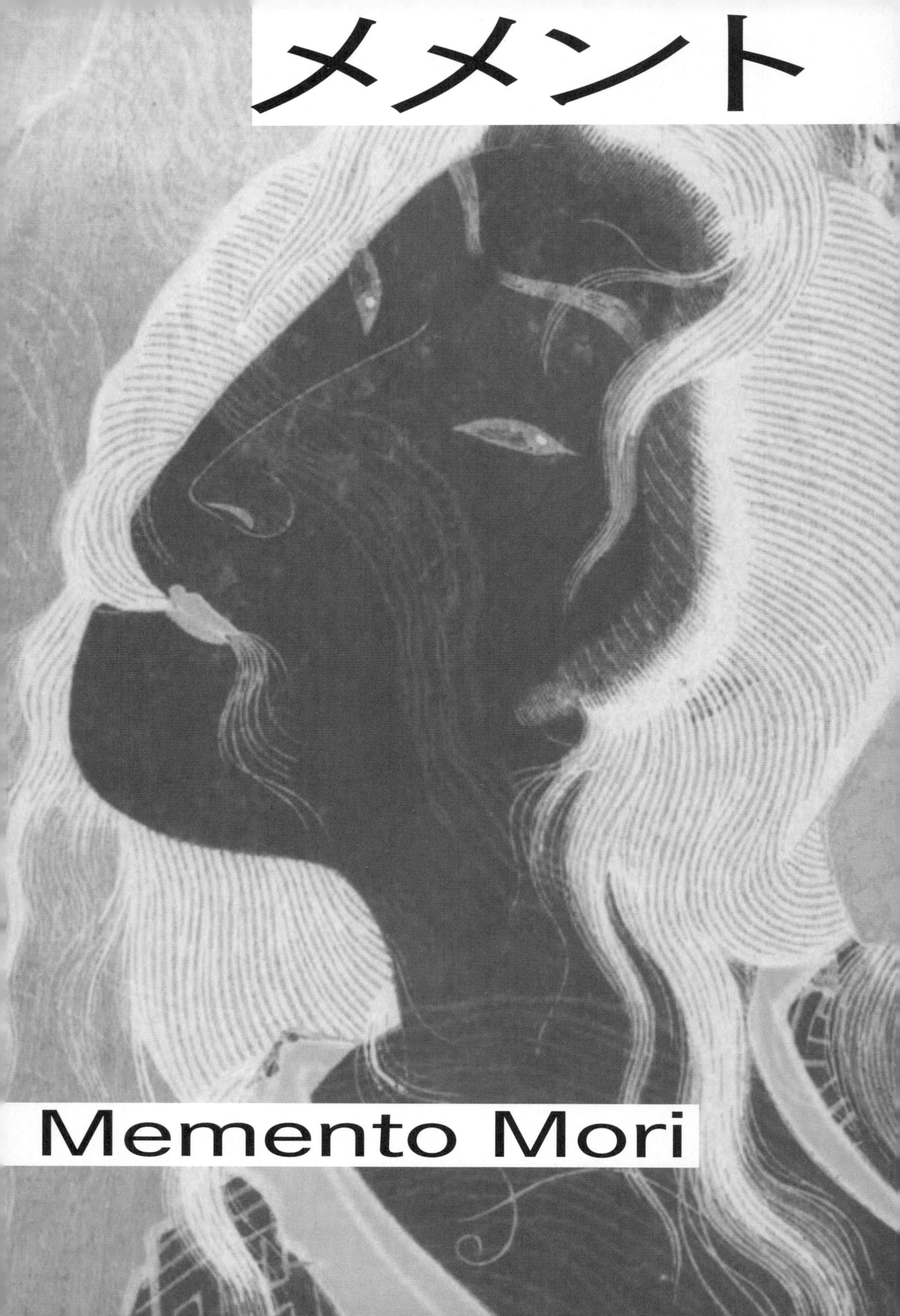
メメント
Memento Mori

・モリ ー死を想えー

八章
Chapter 8.

死者への思いや自らの死への思いは、激しさを内に秘めた、静かだからこそ力を放つ作品を生み出してきた。とりわけ「血みどろ」の過剰な演出から脱した芳年は、大げさな身振りや効果によるわかりやすい表現ではなく、控えめな動作と広い余白で、見る者の想像に委ねる余地を拡張した。登場人物の心情に仮託して、わたしたちは死を思い、生を見つめる。

Thoughts about the dead and their own deaths led painters to create motionless but powerful artworks, expressing the innermost sense of intensity. Especially, after Tsukioka Yoshitoshi broke away from his series of Chimidoro-e (Bloody Pictures) with exaggerated gestures and straightforward expressions, he began to depict similar themes with discreet gestures and large blank spaces, giving viewers room to use their own imaginations. Having compassion for the depicted figures, we would think about death and reflect on life.

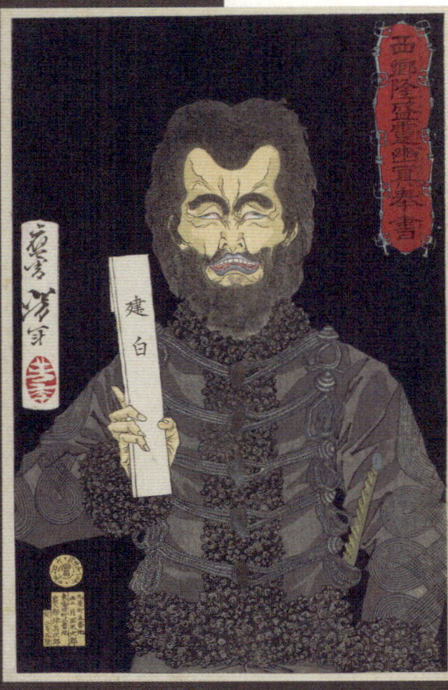

The Ghost of Saigō Takamori Holding a Petition / Tsukioka Yoshitoshi

1878 / Ōta Memorial Museum of Art

This picture depicts Saigō Takamori, a soldier and politician in the late Edo and the early Meiji periods. He looms out of the pitch-black background and looks somewhat peculiar. He has bony cheeks and pale lips, while rolling his eyes up into his head. It is in fact the ghost of Takamori. After resigning from the Meiji government, Takamori fought as the supreme commander of the former Satsuma Domain's army, which launched the Seinan War against the government, but was eventually defeated. During the battle, he died in Mount Shiroyama, Kagoshima Province in 1877. The picture was released the following year. It represents the departed soul of Takamori appearing from the next world. It tells us of his despair that his opinions were not granted in the Meiji government.

<ruby>西郷隆盛霊幽冥奉書<rt>さいごうたかもりのれいゆうめいにほうしょす</rt></ruby> ／ 月岡芳年

明治 11 年（1878）／　太田記念美術館蔵

真っ暗な画面に浮かび上がるのは西郷隆盛であるが、様子がおかしい。痩せこけた頬で白目をむき、唇は青白い。これは隆盛の幽霊だ。明治政府から退いた隆盛は、旧薩摩藩士軍が起こした西南戦争で総大将となって闘うが敗北。明治 10 年（1877 年）に、鹿児島の城山で最期を迎える。翌年に出版された本図は、死んだはずの隆盛が、建白書を捧げて冥土からあらわれたという趣向。政府に意見を聞き入れられなかった隆盛の無念が偲ばれる。

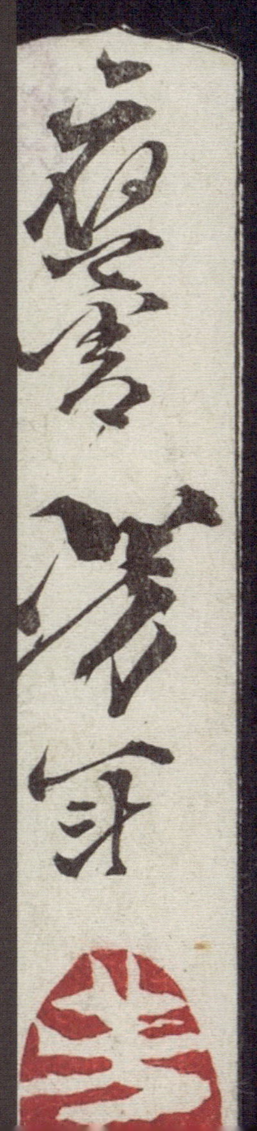

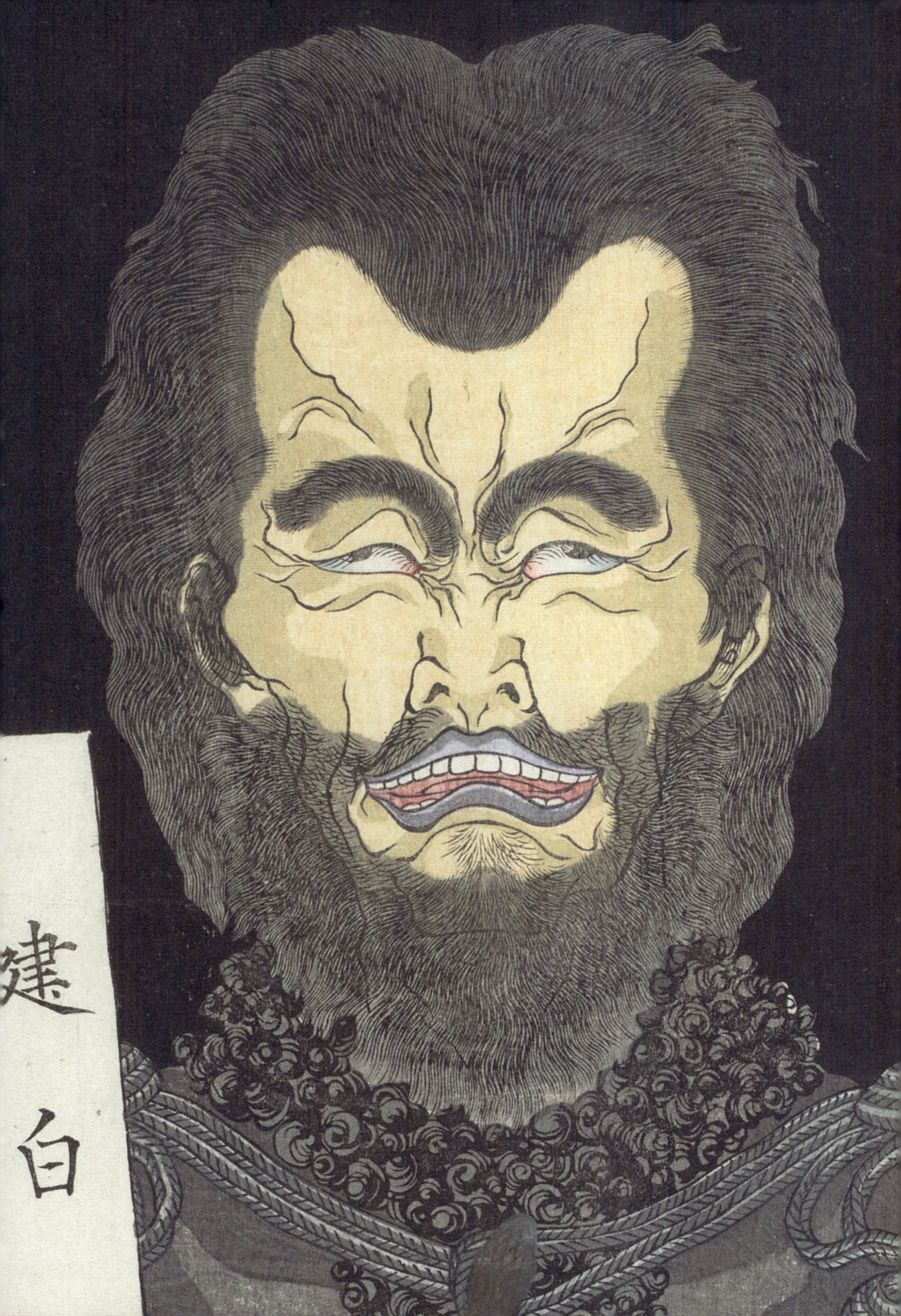

建白

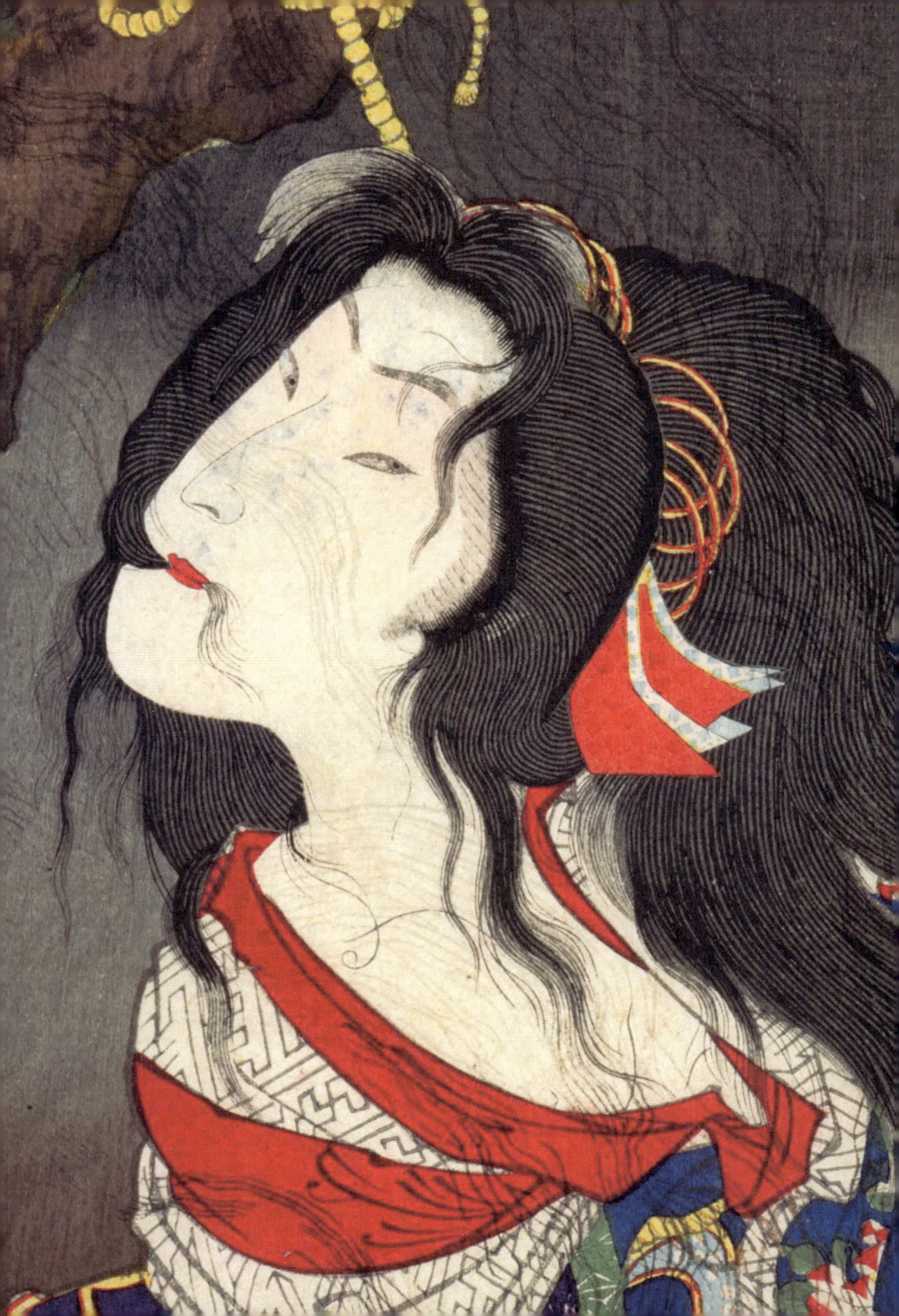

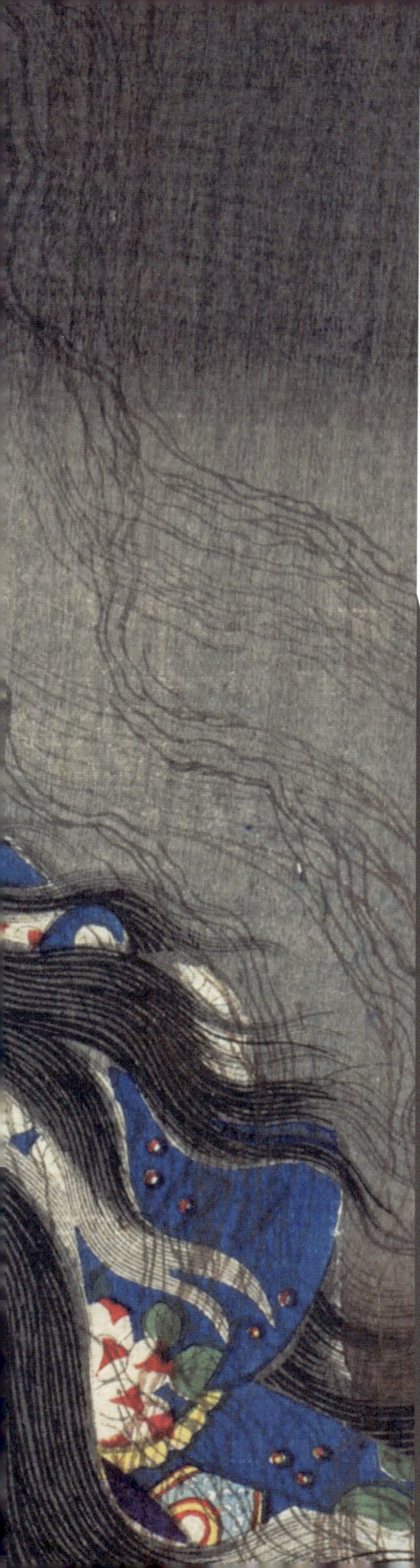

Teru-hime, Thirty-six Beauties of Right and Wrong /
Toyohara Kunichika

1878 / National Diet Library, Japan

The picture depicts Terute-hime, Oguri Hangan's wife, who appears in the legends of Oguri, which were handed down through the generations since the medieval period. Here, her name Terute-hime is slightly changed as Teru-hime. The brave warrior Oguri was once killed, but later came back to life at the discretion of Enma Daiō, the King of Hell. He reunited with his wife and got revenge against his enemy. Here is the scene of their long-awaited reunion, after Terute-hime kept yearning for Oguri, while also having been overwhelmed by his death. Her appearance wearing a glamorous kimono and chewing her untidy hair represents her voluptuous beauty, which was naturally created from her broken-heart.

善悪三拾六美人 照姫 /
豊原国周

明治 11 年（1878） / 国立国会図書館蔵

中世以降伝承されてきた小栗判官にまつわる物語に登場する、小栗の妻・照手姫（本図では照姫）。武勇に優れた小栗は殺されるものの、閻魔大王の計らいで蘇り、姫と再会し、敵への復讐を果たす。小栗の死に打ちひしがれながらも、気丈に慕い続け、遂に再会を果たす姫。艶やかな着物に身を包み、乱れた髪を咥える様は、失意に暮れるからこその妖艶な魅力を発する。

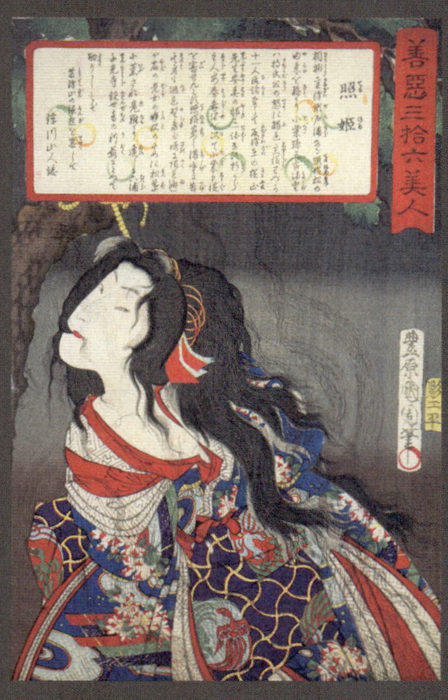

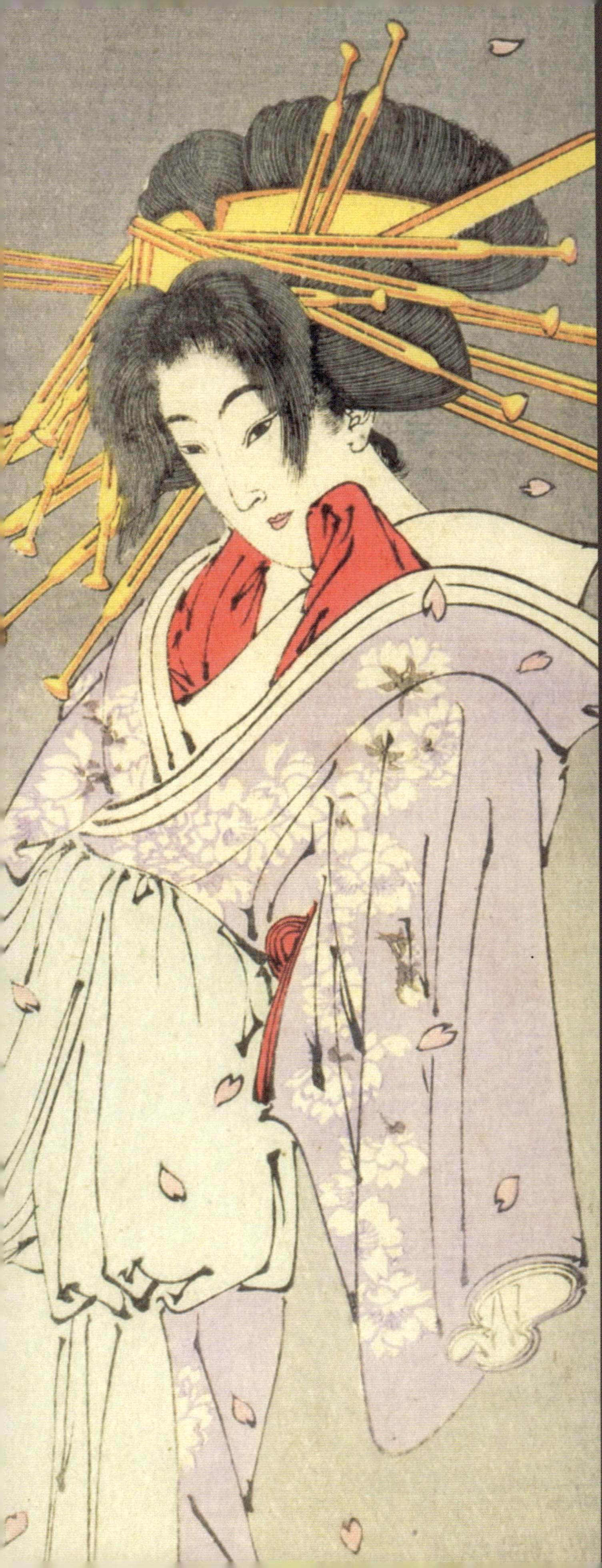

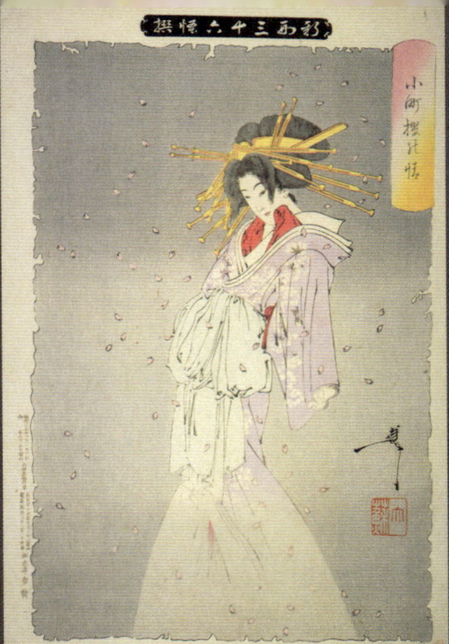

The Spirit of the Komachi Cherry Tree, from the series New Forms of Thirty-six Ghosts / Tsukioka Yoshitoshi

1890 / National Diet Library, Japan

It is a scene from the kabuki play, "Tsumoru Koi Yukino Sekinoto." The woman is a spirit of a cherry tree. She emerges from the dark night, with fluttering cherry blossoms in the air. The tree is over 300 years old and is called the Komachi Cherry Tree. The spirit transforms into a courtesan and takes a lover, but later he is killed during political upheaval. She aspires to avenge him and transform into a courtesan again. This story metaphorically represents a famous legend of Ono-no Komachi, a well-known female poet in the 9th century. She peeps a bright red undergarment from underneath her light-colored outer kimono. Her calm standing posture seems to represent how vengeful she is.

新形三十六怪撰
小町桜の情 ／ 月岡芳年

明治 23 年（1890） ／ 国立国会図書館蔵

歌舞伎の演目『積恋雪関扉』の一場面。桜が
舞い散る夜の闇に浮かびあがる桜の精。樹齢
300年のこの桜は、小町桜と呼ばれている。
この精がかつて遊女に身を変えて愛の契りを
結んだ恋人は、政変に巻き込まれて殺された。
小町に重ねられた桜の精が遊女の姿となって、
仇討ちを果たそうとする物語。淡い着物の下
から真紅の襦袢を覗かせる。静かな立ち姿の
裏で、復讐に身を焼くさまをあらわすかのよ
うだ。

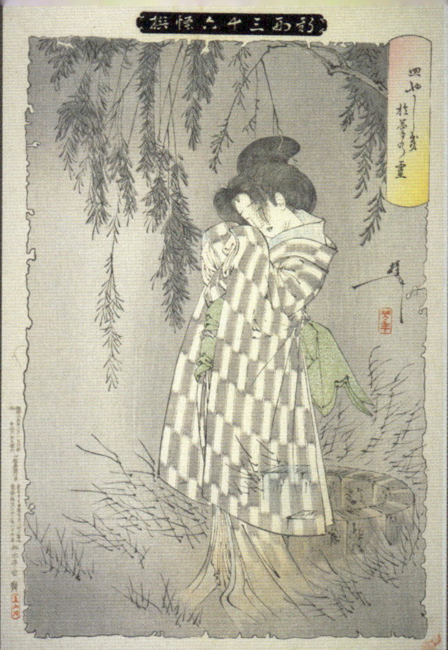

The Ghost of Okiku at the Plate Mansion, from the series New Forms of Thirty-six Ghosts / Tsukioka Yoshitoshi

1890 / National Diet Library, Japan

The picture features a famous fictional tale of Okiku, who was a maidservant but accidentally broke her lord's treasured plate. Getting so furious, the lord brutally murdered her and threw her into a water well. After that, she started to appear night after night as a ghost and continuously counted out plates. The story became widely known as "Okiku of the Plate Mansion," and various versions were created. Generally, she was depicted as a horrible ghost in the Edo period. But here, Yoshitoshi depicted her as an innocent young girl, to emphasize her unhappy background and hard-luck, rather than the horrible story.

新形三十六怪撰
皿やしき於菊の霊 ／ 月岡芳年

明治 23 年（1890） ／ 国立国会図書館蔵

秘蔵の皿を一枚割ったため、主人に惨殺され、井戸へ投げこまれたのち、その怨霊が皿を数えるようになった。「皿屋敷」のお菊は、さまざまに脚色され、江戸時代には恐ろしげな幽霊の姿で描かれるのが定番であった。いたいけな少女の姿でお菊を描く本図は、怪談の恐ろしさよりも、お菊の不幸な身の上を照らし出す。

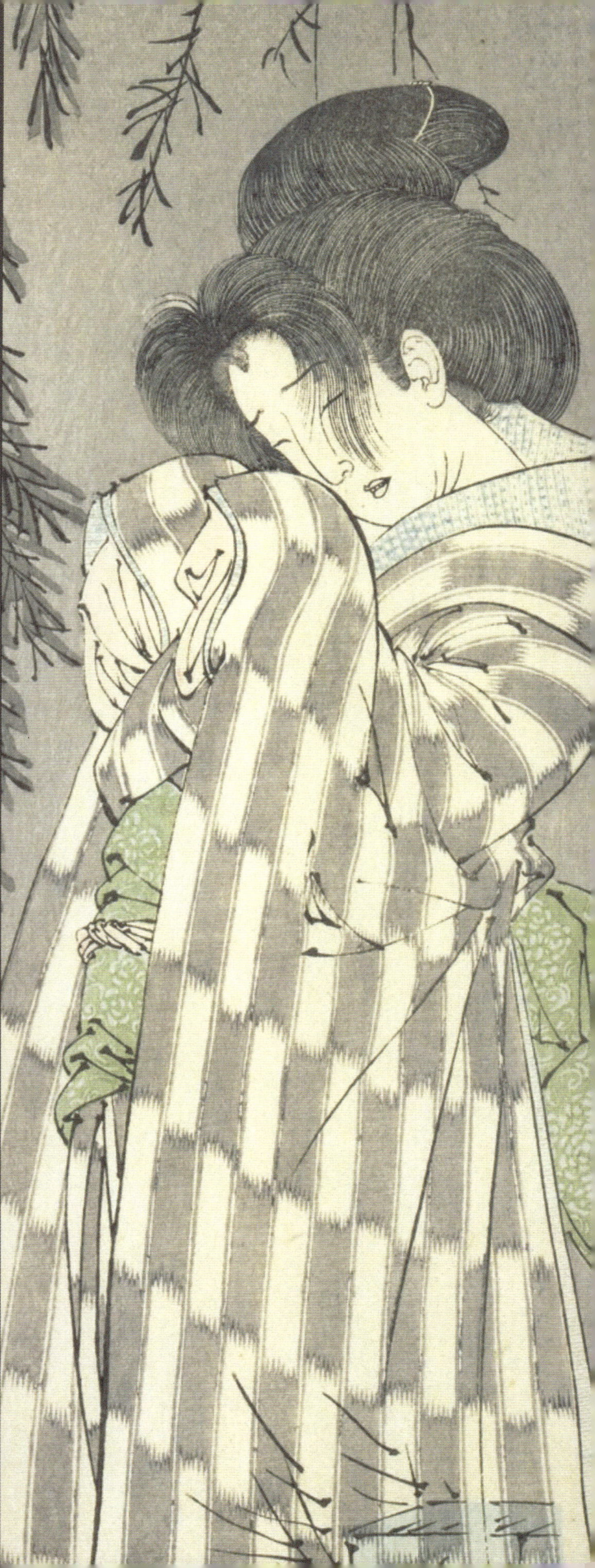

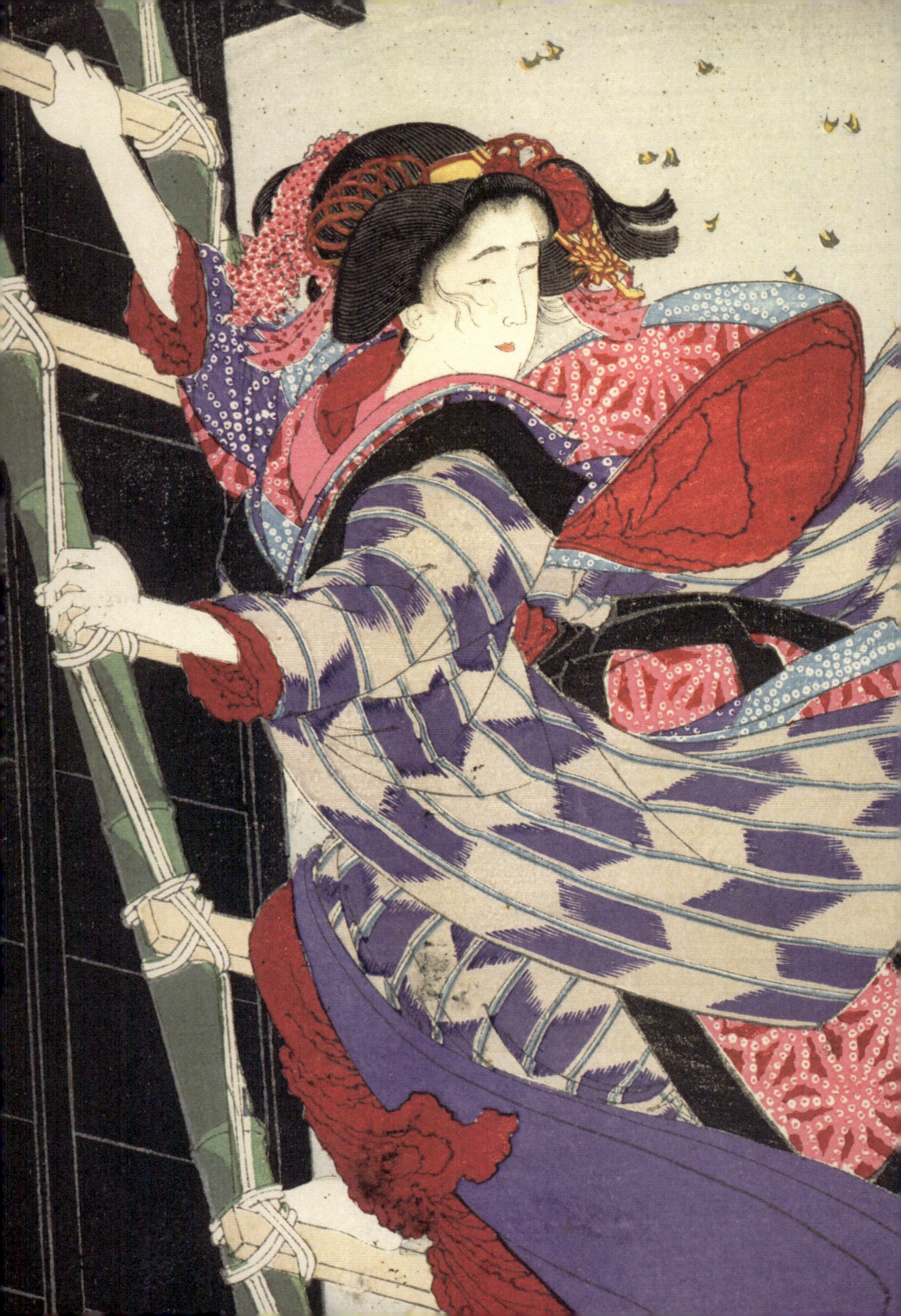

Shōchikubai Yushimano Kakegaku / Tsukioka Yoshitoshi

1885 / National Diet Library, Japan

The picture depicts a greengrocer's daughter Oshichi climbing up a ladder, which crosses from top to bottom of the vertically long frame. She turns towards the back, with her kimono fluttering in the wind. According to legend, Oshichi fled from a big fire and met a young page Sahē at their evacuation site. They fell in love with each other, and later she missed him so much that she set fire to her house, hoping to meet him again. She was accused of arson and was burned to death in Suzugamori. She was only 16 years old. The story of the girl literally burning with love was dramatized into various versions, and Oshichi became a popular tragic heroine. In this picture, she is not looking at the blazing fire, but somewhere in the air. What she is gazing at could be her lover, the rest of her short life, or her own death in the near future.

<ruby>松<rt>しょう</rt>竹<rt>ちく</rt>梅<rt>ばい</rt>湯<rt>ゆ</rt>嶋<rt>しま</rt>掛<rt>の</rt>額<rt>かけがく</rt></ruby> ／ 月岡芳年

明治 18 年（1885）／ 国立国会図書館蔵

縦長の画面いっぱいに渡された梯子をのぼり、風に衣をなびかせ振り返るのは、八百屋お七。火災によって避難した先で小姓の左兵衛と恋に落ちたお七は、再び恋人に会うために放火。その咎により鈴ケ森で火刑となった。16歳だった。文字通り恋に身を焼いた女の悲劇は、さまざまに脚色され、お七はよく知られる悲劇のヒロインとなった。燃え盛る炎を見向きもしないお七の視線の先にあるのは、恋人か、この先の短い生か、間も無く訪れる死か。

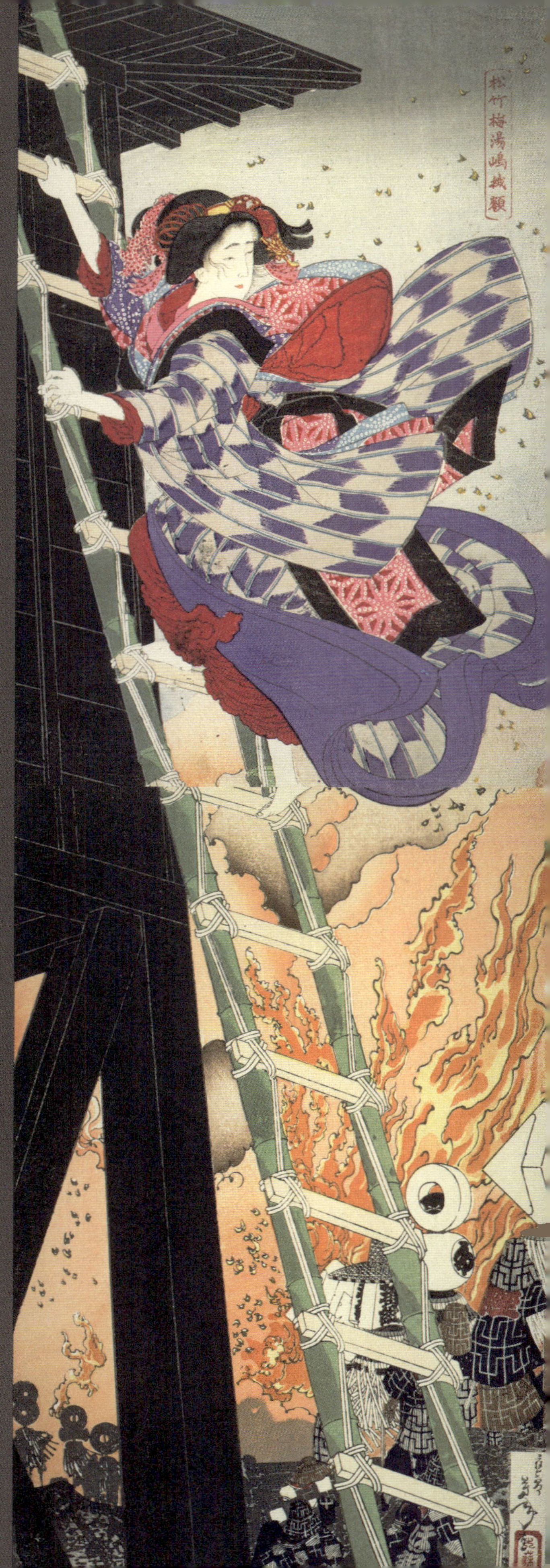

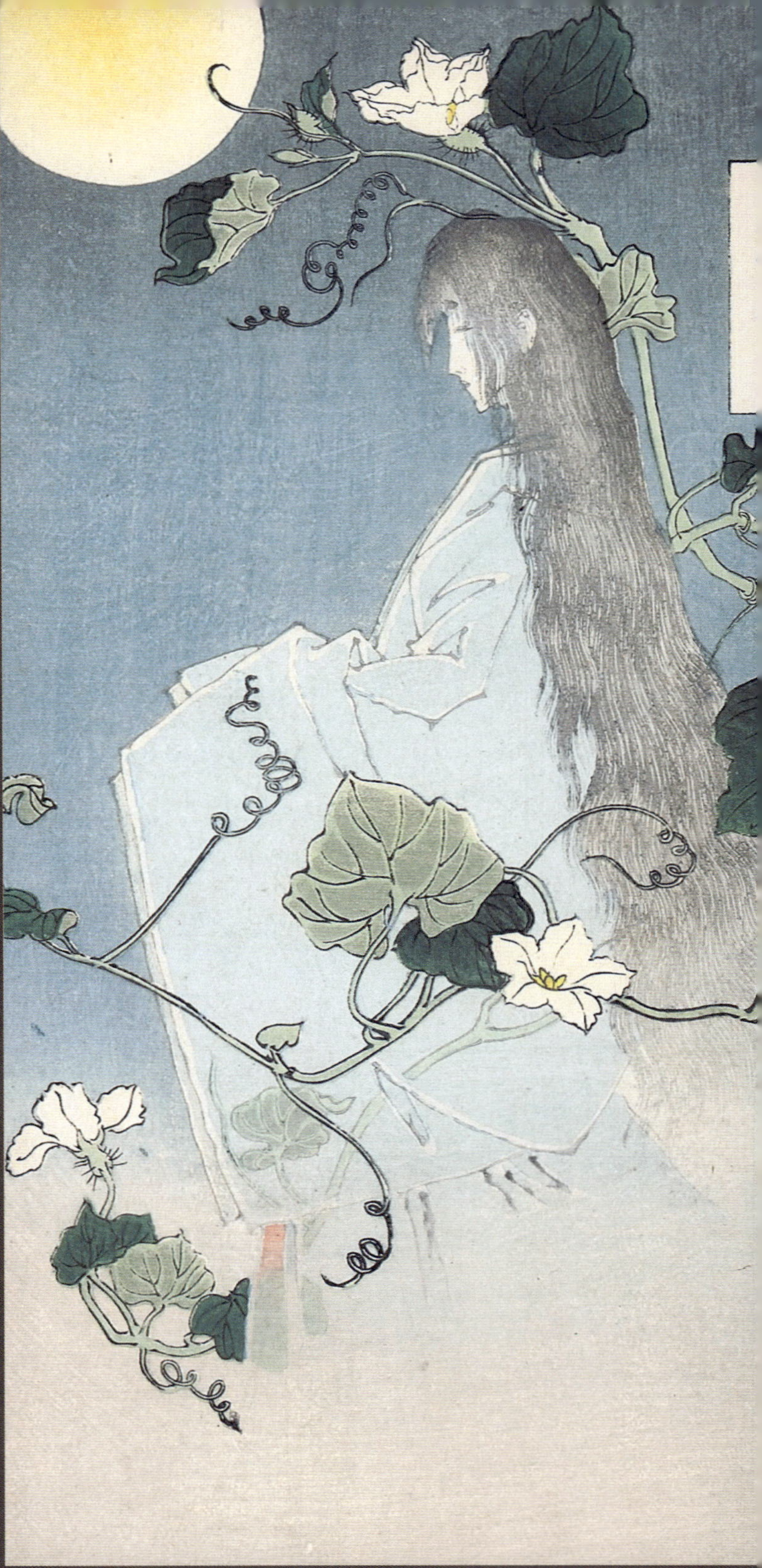

The Yūgao Chapter from The Tale of Genji, from the series One Hundred Aspects of the Moon / Tsukioka Yoshitoshi

1886 / National Diet Library, Japan

In Japanese, white bottle gourd flowers are called Yūgao, meaning "early evening face," which was derived from the habit of the flowers blooming in the early evenings of summer and wilting the following mornings. The Tale of Genji, a lengthy romance novel completed in the early 11th century, has a female character Yūgao. The main male character Hikaru Genji caught a passing glimpse of her, over a hedge of bottle gourd flowers. Genji was deeply infatuated with her, but later she was possessed by an evil spirit and was eventually killed. For a long time since then, Genji kept cherishing her memory as if she was still alive. Yūgao became a symbol of affection and the preciousness of fleeting things.

月百姿 源氏夕顔巻 ／ 月岡芳年

明治 19 年（1886）／ 国立国会図書館蔵

夏の夕方に開いた白い花が翌日の午前中にしぼんでしまうことから、夕顔と呼ばれる花がある。『源氏物語』にその名で登場する人物は、垣根に咲く夕顔の花の縁で、通りすがりの光源氏に見いだされる。源氏は夢中になるが、やがて夕顔はもののけにとり殺される。死後も長く光源氏の記憶の中に生き続け、追慕の対象となる夕顔は、儚いものの尊さや愛おしさの象徴となる。

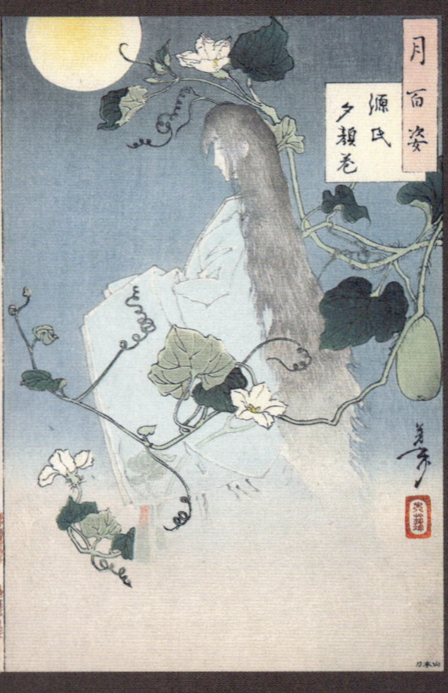

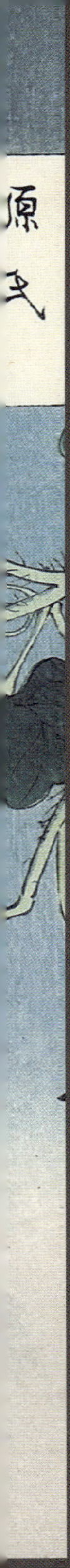

How Hopeless It is / It Would be Better for Me to Sink Beneath the Waves / Perhaps Then I Could See My Man from the Moon Capital-Ariko, from the series One Hundred Aspects of the Moon / Tsukioka Yoshitoshi

1886 / National Diet Library, Japan

According to legend, when Tokudaiji Sanesada, a court noble in the Heian period, confined himself to the Itsukushima Shrine for praying, he met Ariko, a master of biwa (Japanese lute), and loved her tenderly. After he left for the capital Kyoto, Ariko followed him, but their social class differences blocked her from seeing him again, which led her to kill herself. The picture depicts Ariko missing him in the beautiful moon-like capital, and going to sink herself into the sea whose surface reflects the moon.

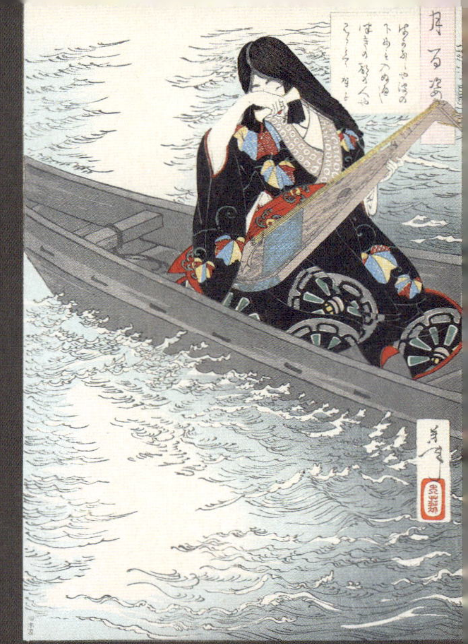

月百姿 はかなしや波の下にも入ぬへし つきの都の人や見る とて 有子 ／ 月岡芳年

明治 19 年（1886）／ 国立国会図書館蔵

平安時代の公家・徳大寺実定が厳島に詣でた折、見出されて寵愛を受けた琵琶の名手・有子。都に戻る実定を追って都に上った有子であったが、身分違いゆえに会うことができず、命を絶つことを決意する。「月の都」にいる人を思いながら、都ではなく月を映す水の底へと沈もうとしている。

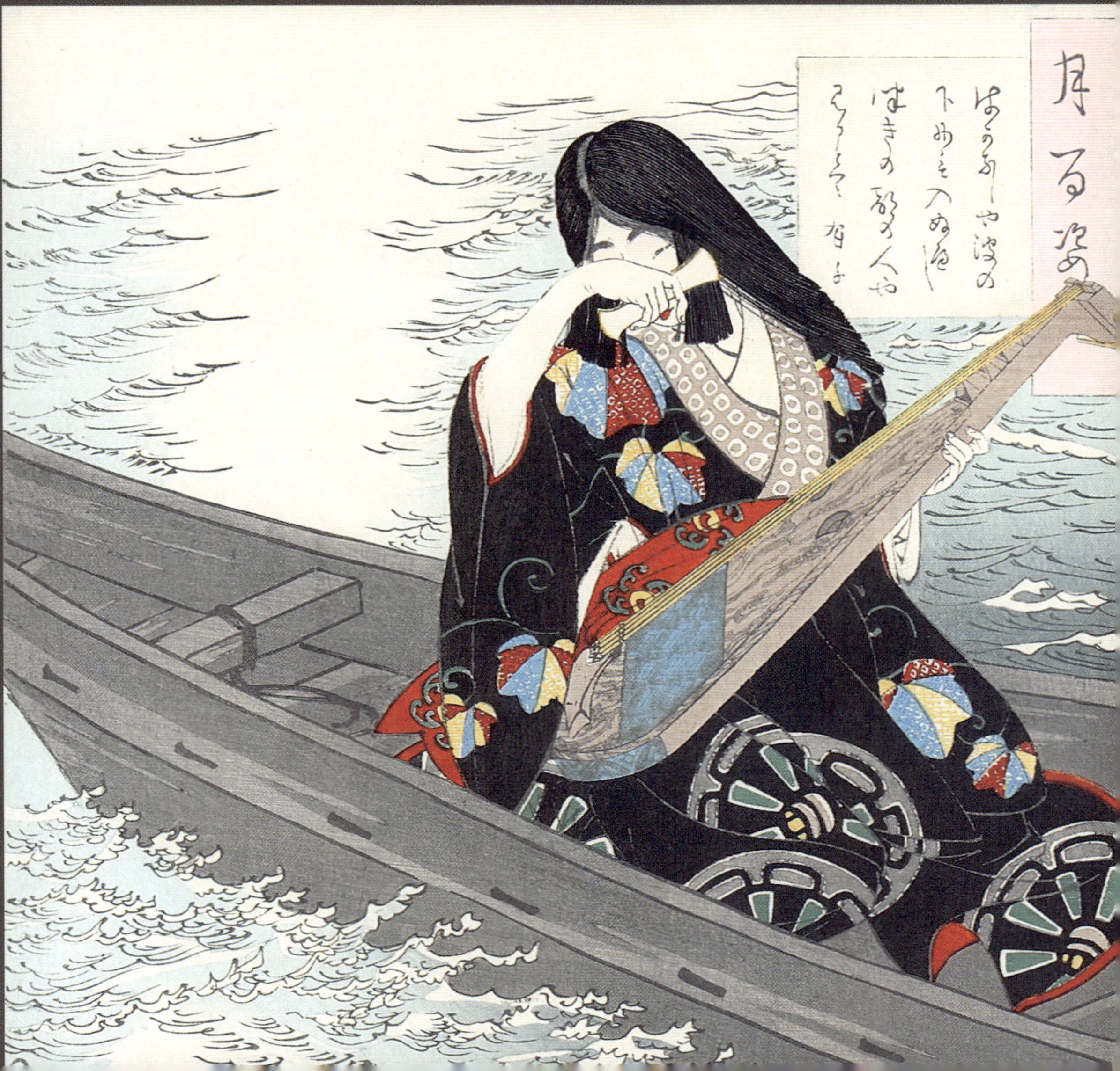

Glossary 用語解説

Ukiyoe

The word "ukiyo" has several meanings, such as "this world," an antonym for the afterlife, "present," but not past nor future, and "the real world with lustfulness." When the word "ukiyoe" was newly coined and took root in the late 17th century, it meant "pictures depicting coeval trendy customs or customs in red-light districts and theater towns." Ukiyoe can be paintings but mainly wood-block prints, which could be provided for reasonable prices, but with high quality, to the general public. Publishers were called "Hanmoto," who planned projects and directed the whole production process, working with Eshi (painters), Horishi (engravers) and Surishi (printers). With the advancement of printing techniques, ukiyoe expanded its pictorial subjects to include warriors, fictional stories, historical episodes, landscapes and more.

浮世絵

「浮世」という言葉には、彼岸ならぬ現世、過去でも未来でもない現在、そして好色の気味の濃い俗世間という多重の語義が込められている。「浮世絵」という新造語が定着した 17 世紀後半には、当世流行の最先端の社会風俗、遊里や芝居町などの風俗を描くものを指した。安価で良質な絵画を大衆に提供するために、木版画を主とした。現代の出版社にあたる「版元」の企画の下、絵師、彫師、摺師の手を経て世に出された。印刷技術の進展とともに、武者絵や物語絵、歴史画や風景画など、扱う主題も多岐に渡っていった。

Nishikie

In 1765, a new printing technique to make multicolored ukiyoe emerged, which made it possible to depict each motif in its ideal color, over the whole picture. It was named " 錦絵 (Nishikie)," using an analogy from the word " 錦繍 (Kin-shū)," or prestigious and splendid kimonos. Nishikie's standard size was initially 29 × 22 cm, but in the Tenmei era (1781 - 1789) of the late Edo period, it became larger to be 39 × 27 cm. For Nishikie production, people used Hōshoshi, a kind of traditional paper, which was thick enough to resist pressure during repeated printings of multicolored ukiyoe. Printers sometimes used a tintless engraved woodblock to create bumpy surfaces as a pictorial effect.

錦絵

個々の図様に応じた色面を画面の全面に充填する多色摺の版画が、明和 2 年（1765）に登場する。錦繍の華麗になぞらえて「錦絵」と命名された。当初は中判（約 29 × 22cm）を標準サイズとしたが、天明年間（1781 ～ 1789）以降は大判（約 39 × 27 cm）が一般となった。繰り返される摺の圧に耐えられるように、厚手の奉書紙が用いられ、色をつけずに紙に凹凸をつける技法も活用された。

Lists of Ukiyoe Painters 浮世絵師解説

Katsushika Hokusai　1760 - 1849

Hokusai became a disciple of Katsukawa Shunshō at the age of 19, and later started to release Yakusha-e (ukiyoe of kabuki actors) under his initial artist's name Shunrō. Thereafter, he left the Katsukawa school and called himself Tawaraya Sōri. Surprisingly, he had over 30 artist's names in his life, including Hokusai, Taito and I'itsu. He learned not only traditional techniques but also western copper engravings to create various Nishikie, or polychrome ukiyoe prints. He also worked on many print illustrations for Kyōka-ehon (picture books of comical and satirical poems), Yomihon (lengthy novels), and Etehon (books of painting examples). During his 70s, he released landscape prints including his representative work, "Thirty-six views of Mount Fuji." In his last years, he named himself Gakyō Rōjin 卍 (Manji), meaning "old man with the sign 卍 (svastika) who is crazy about painting," and kept pursuing his creations. According to legend, on the brink of death at the age of 90, he said, "I could be a genuine painter if I am able to live 10, or even 5 years more." Many legends of his eccentricities are known, including his frequent house - movings which he did 93 times.

葛飾北斎　　1760 - 1849

19 歳で勝川春章に入門し、春朗と号して役者絵を発表。のち勝川派を離れて俵屋宗理を襲名。以降、北斎、戴斗、為一などの改名を 30 回以上繰り返した。西洋の銅版画を模すなどした多様な錦絵とともに、狂歌絵本や読本挿絵、絵手本などの版本も手がける。70 歳代で、《冨嶽三十六景》に代表される風景版画を発表。晩年には画狂老人卍と名乗り、90 歳で亡くなる直前まで制作を続けた。あと 10 年、いや 5 年の命があれば、真正の絵描きになることができるのに、と言い残して死んでいったという。奇行で知られ、生涯に 93 回も引っ越しをした。

Katsushika Hokui　　Year of birth and death unknown

Hokui was a disciple of Katsushika Hokusai. He worked as a painter from the Tenpō era (1830 - 1844) of the late Edo period to the Meiji period (1868 - 1912). His works range from Nishikie (polychrome ukiyoe prints) to print illustrations for books, as well as original paintings.

葛飾北為　　生没年不詳

葛飾北斎の門人。作画期は天保年間（1830-1844）から明治（1868-1912）の間で、錦絵の他に版本の挿絵、肉筆画も手がけた。

Utagawa Toyokuni　　1769 - 1825

Toyokuni was a high-caliber disciple of Utagawa Toyoharu. He started to release a series of Yakusha-e (ukiyoe of kabuki actors) titled "Portraits of Actors on the Stage" in 1794. The series catapulted him into the limelight and took the Yakusha-e industry by storm. It was as if he traded places with another painter called Tōshūsai Sharaku, who disappeared from the industry around that time. He had many disciples and led the Utagawa school which was the largest ukiyoe school at the end of the Edo period.

歌川豊国　1769 - 1825

歌川豊春の高弟。寛政 6 年（1794）から発表し始めた役者絵のシリーズ《役者舞台之姿絵》により一躍脚光を浴び、東洲斎写楽が姿を消すのと交替するように役者絵界を席巻した。多くの門人を擁し、幕末最大の浮世絵の画派となる歌川派を率いた。

Utagawa Kunisada　　1786 - 1864

Kunisada was a disciple of Utagawa Toyokuni. He led the largest ukiyoe painters' group in the industry at the end of the Edo period. The number of works he made during his lifetime is thought to be the largest among all the ukiyoe painters. At one point, he officially succeeded Toyokuni the 3rd, and called himself Toyokuni the 2nd.

歌川国貞　1786 - 1864

歌川豊国の門人。幕末の浮世絵界で最大の勢力を形成し、生涯に描いた作品数も全浮世絵師中、最大数量であったといわれる。三世豊国を襲名するが、自らは二世と自称した。

Utagawa Kuniteru　Year of birth and death unknown

Kuniteru was a disciple of Utagawa Kunisada. He worked as a painter from the Bunsei era to the Ansei era (1818 - 60). His Nishikie (polychrome ukiyoe prints) include Kodomo-e depicting children at play and Kyōkun-e depicting moral teachings. He also actively worked on print illustrations for Gōkan (bound-together volumes of lengthy novels).

歌川国輝　　生没年不詳

歌川国貞の門人。作画期は文政年間から安政年間（1818-60）のころ。子供絵、教訓絵などの錦絵を制作。合巻の挿絵も多数手がけた。

Utagawa Kuniteru the 2nd　　1830 - 1874

Kuniteru was a disciple of Utagawa Kunisada. He was famous for his Kaika-e (ukiyoe prints of westernized cultures during the Meiji Restoration).

歌川国輝（2 代）　1830 - 1874

歌川国貞の門人。開化絵で知られた。

Toyohara Kunichika   1835 - 1900

Kunichika was a disciple of Utagawa Kunisada. He was excellent at Yakusha-e (ukiyoe of kabuki actors), especially Ōkubi-e which depicts their faces close-up. Legends tell of his eccentricities, including changing addresses 83 times, and remarrying over 40 times.

豊原国周   1835 - 1900

歌川国貞の門人。役者絵とくに大首絵を得意とした。83回引っ越し、妻も40回以上かえたという奇行の持ち主。

Utagawa Kuniyoshi   1797 - 1861

Kuniyoshi was a disciple of Utagawa Toyokuni. He became his disciple at the age of 15, but mired in mediocrity during the initial years after his debut as a painter. His ukiyoe series "The 108 Heroes of the Popular Suikoden" won him popularity, and he became widely known as Kuniyoshi of Musha-e (ukiyoe of warriors). His subjects range from beauties to caricatures and landscapes. Many of his works reflect his studies of western paintings. An existing portrait of him shows him wearing a hell-patterned kimono and being surrounded by several cats. Kuniyoshi trained many disciples and his painting style continued to be passed down until the modern age.

歌川国芳 1797 - 1861

歌川豊国の門人。15歳で豊国門下となり、デビュー初期は振るわず。《通俗水滸伝豪傑一百八人之一個》で一躍人気を博し、「武者絵の国芳」と評判をとって以来、美人画、戯画、風景画など幅広い作域で活躍した。西洋絵画の学習成果を反映した作品も少なくない。地獄模様の着物をまとい、何匹もの猫に囲まれる肖像画が伝わる。多くの弟子を育てた国芳の画系は近代にまで続いた。

Utagawa Yoshifusa   1837 - 1860

Yoshifusa was a disciple of Utagawa Kuniyoshi. He worked on print illustrations for Ninjō-bon (books of romantic fiction) and Gōkan (bound-together volumes of lengthy novels), but died at the early age of 24.

歌川芳房   1837 - 1860

歌川国芳の門人。人情本、合巻などの挿絵を描いたが24歳の若さで没した。

Utagawa Yoshitsuya   1822 - 1866

Yoshitsuya was a disciple of Utagawa Kuniyoshi. He was excellent at Musha-e (ukiyoe of warriors), and also known for his tattoo designs as well as the signboard design for a shop at Asakusa Okuyama, Edo, which sold realistic dolls.

歌川芳艶   1822 - 1866

歌川国芳の門人。武者絵を得意とし、刺青の下絵、江戸浅草奥山の生き人形の看板絵で知られた。

Utagawa Yoshikazu   Year of birth and death unknown

Yoshikazu was a disciple of Utagawa Kuniyoshi. He worked as a painter from the Kaei era (1848-54) to around the third year of the Meiji period (1869). He painted many Yokohama-e (ukiyoe of the modernized Yokohama town's view).

歌川芳員   生没年不詳

歌川国芳の門人。作画期は嘉永年間（1848-54）から明治3年（1869）ごろまで。横浜絵を多く描いた。

Ochiai Yoshiiku   1833 - 1904

Yoshiiku was a disciple of Utagawa Kuniyoshi and won popularity, together with his fellow painter Tsukioka Yoshitoshi. He was involved in the launches of both the Tokyo Nichinichi Newspaper and the Tokyo Eiri Newspaper, working on print illustrations for both of them. He was excellent at ukiyoe of beauties, as well as facial caricatures of kabuki actors.

落合芳幾   1833 - 1904

歌川国芳の門人で、月岡芳年とならび評判を得た。明治初期に「東京日日新聞」や「東京絵入新聞」の創刊に参加し、新聞紙上に挿絵をとりいれた。美人風俗画や役者似顔絵などを得意とした。

Tsukioka Yoshitoshi   1839 - 1892

Yoshitoshi became a disciple of Utagawa Kuniyoshi at the age of 12, and only three years later, released his first ukiyoe work. In 1866, he released "Twenty-Eight Famous Murders," which was a Zankoku-e (Cruel Pictures) series which he created with his elder fellow painter Ochiai Yoshiiku. The series gained popularity and catapulted him into the limelight. From the end of the Edo period and into the Meiji period, he concentrated his energy on pictures of historical tales. After the Meiji Restoration, he worked on print illustrations for newspapers. He had many disciples, but at the same time he seemed to have suffered from a mental disease and died heavily depressed. Yoshitoshi's Chimidoro-e (Bloody Pictures) were described as an expression of decadence by Mishima Yukio, a famous novelist in the 20th century, and continued to have a great reputation in later years.

月岡芳年   1839 - 1892

12 歳で歌川国芳の門に入り、3 年後に早くも処女作を発表。慶応 2 年（1866）に兄弟子の落合芳幾とともに描いた《英名二十八衆句》の残酷絵シリーズで一躍人気絵師となった。幕末から明治初年にかけては歴史画に傾注し、維新後は新聞挿絵で活躍した。多くの門人に恵まれたが、「精神病」に悩まされ、「鬱憂狂」で亡くなったという。その「血みどろ絵」は、三島由紀夫によって「デカダンス美術」と称され、後世なお高く評価された。

Yamazaki Toshinobu   1857 - 1886

Toshinobu, who studied ukiyoe under Tsukioka Yoshitoshi, was later thought of as one of the big four disciples of his master. He worked on Nishikie (polychrome ukiyoe prints), as well as print illustrations for newspapers.

山崎年信   1857 - 1886

月岡芳年に浮世絵をまなび、芳年門下の四天王といわれ、新聞の挿絵や錦絵などを手がけた。

Kawanabe Kyōsai   1831 - 1889

Kyōsai became a disciple of Utagawa Kuniyoshi at the age of 6. Only two years later, he quit and began studying under Maemura Tōwa, a painter of the Kano school. It is said that Tōwa appreciated Kyōsai's talent and called him "Gaki," or "Painting Demon." Later, he obtained a teaching license from the Kano school, and went through the turbulence of the Meiji Restoration, while releasing various pictures under his several artist's names including " 狂斎 (Kyōsai)." He made satirical pictures criticizing the Meiji government, which led him to be thrown into jail for a while. Later, he changed the kanji character of his artist name to " 暁斎 (Kyōsai)." He was known for having a large circle of international friends, including a journalist Charles Wirgman, and his painting disciple the architect Josiah Conder. It is said that Kyōsai once picked up a stranger's decapitated head floating in a river to sketch it and when a fire occurred, he rushed to the place to sketch the view. " 狂 (Kyō)," the first kanji character of his artist's name, means "going insane and mad," which resonates with these legends.

河鍋暁斎   1831 - 1889

6 歳で歌川国芳に入門。そのわずか 2 年後、今度は狩野派の絵師前村洞和に再入門した。洞和は暁斎の才能を評価し、「画鬼」と呼んだという。狩野派の免状を与えられ、明治維新期の動乱を「狂斎」などの画号で、多彩な絵を手がけて乗り越えた。明治政府を非難する風刺画により投獄され、釈放後に画号を「暁斎」に改めた。ジャーナリストのC・ワーグマンと親しく、建築家 J・コンドルを弟子とするなど、国際的な交遊が知られる。絵の修行のため、川を流れる生首を拾ったり、火事があれば駆けつけて写生するなど、「狂」の名にふさわしい逸話が伝わる。

Bibliography 参考文献

『国史大辞典』吉川弘文館 1979-1997年 /『新版 歌舞伎事典』平凡社 2011年 /『新版 日本架空伝承人名事典』平凡社 2012年 / 大貫菜穂「歌川国芳《通俗水滸伝豪傑百八人之一個》におけるほりものの分析と考察」『Core Ethics』vol.6 立命館大学大学院先端総合学術研究科 2010年 / 岡島奈音「衣裳文様から見る河鍋暁斎筆「地獄太夫図」」『文化学園大学・文化学園大学短期大学部紀要』第 50 集 2018年 / 菅原真弓『月岡芳年伝 幕末明治のはざまに』中央公論新書 2018年 / 菅原真弓「武者絵の研究―「歴史画」としての視点による一考察―」『哲学会誌』23号　学習院大学哲学会 1999年 / 立道恵子「「名鏡倭魂　新板」について」『河鍋暁斎研究誌』70号 河鍋暁斎記念館 2000年 / 永田生慈監修 岩切友里子・根岸美佳ほか編『新・北斎展　HOKUSAI UPDATED』展覧会図録 日本経済新聞社 2019年 / 日野原健司『月岡芳年 月百姿』青幻舎 2017年

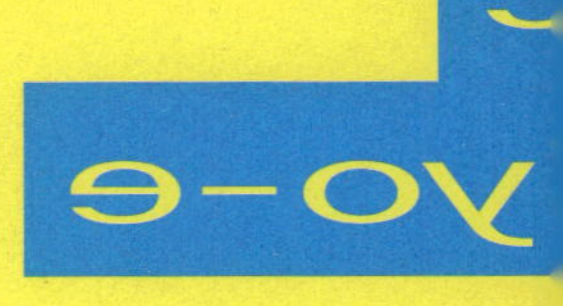

Edo-Punk!
The Dynamic World of Ukiyo-e by Kuniyoshi, Yoshitoshi & Others

Authored by Shoko Haruki
Art-directed and Designed by Toshimasa Goto
Translated by Tamayo Samejima
Proofreading by Ouraido
Edited by Suzuka Miyagi

PIE International Inc.
2-32-4 Minami-Otsuka, Toshima-ku, Tokyo 170-0005 JAPAN
international@pie.co.jp   www.pie.co.jp/english

ISBN978-4-7562-5428-3 (Outside Japan)
Printed in Japan

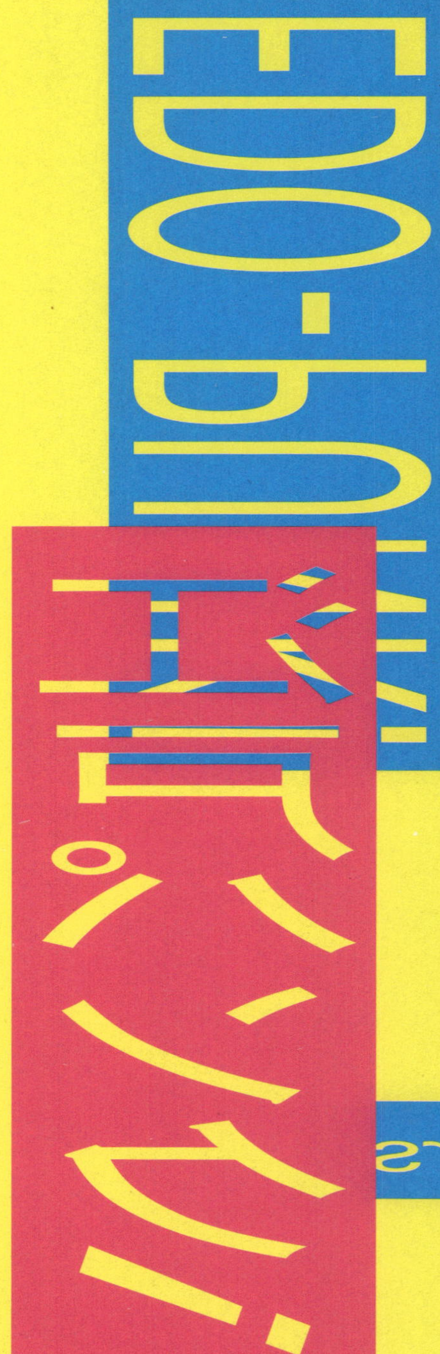

江戸パンク！　国芳・芳年の幻想劇画
Edo-Punk!　The Dynamic World of Ukiyo-e by Kuniyoshi, Yoshitoshi & Others

2022 年 11 月 24 日　初版第 1 刷発行

著者　春木晶子
アートディレクション・デザイン　後藤寿方（DK）
翻訳　鮫島圭代
校閲　株式会社鷗来堂
協力　DNP アートコミュニケーションズ / 株式会社アマナ / 株式会社アフロ
編集　宮城鈴香

発行人　三芳寛要
発行元　株式会社 パイ インターナショナル
〒 170-0005　東京都豊島区南大塚 2-32-4
TEL 03-3944-3981　FAX 03-5395-4830
sales@pie.co.jp

印刷・製本　広済堂ネクスト

©2022 Shoko Haruki / PIE International
ISBN978-4-7562-5414-6 C0071
Printed in Japan